30359714

D1539412

ɔITY
ᴖᴖᴖᴖᴖᴖ STREET
STORM LAKE, IA 50588-1798

THIS LAND IS OUR LAND

Advisory Board

LORRAINE BOOMER. Teacher, Window Rock Elementary School, Window Rock, Arizona. Consultant in Native-American Indian children's literature.

NAOMI CALDWELL-WOOD. President, American Indian Library Association. Consultant in Native-American Indian children's literature.

ORALIA GARZA DE CORTES. Youth Services Librarian, Austin Public Library, Austin, Texas. Consultant in Hispanic-American children's literature.

OPAL MOORE. Assistant Professor, English Department, Radford University, Radford, Virginia. Consultant in African-American children's literature.

JACQUELINE K. SASAKI. Youth Librarian, Ann Arbor Public Library, Ann Arbor, Michigan. Consultant in Asian-American children's literature.

KAREN PATRICIA SMITH. Assistant Professor, Graduate School of Library and Information Services, Queens College, Flushing, New York. Consultant in African-American children's literature.

THIS LAND IS OUR LAND

A Guide to Multicultural Literature for Children and Young Adults

ALETHEA K. HELBIG
and AGNES REGAN PERKINS

GREENWOOD PRESS
WESTPORT, CONNECTICUT • LONDON

Library of Congress Cataloging-in-Publication Data

Helbig, Alethea.
  This land is our land : a guide to multicultural literature for
children and young adults / by Alethea K. Helbig and Agnes Regan
Perkins.
    p. cm.
  Includes bibliographical references and index.
  ISBN 0–313–28742–2 (alk. paper)
    1. Children—United States—Books and reading. 2. Minorities—
United States—Juvenile fiction—Bibliography. 3. Minorities—
United States—Juvenile poetry—Bibliography. 4. Folk literature—
Bibliography. 5. Children's stories, American—Bibliography.
6. Children's poetry, American—Bibliography. I. Perkins, Agnes.
II. Title.
Z1037.H48   1994
[PS509.M5]
016.8108'09282—dc20   94–16124

British Library Cataloguing in Publication Data is available.

Copyright © 1994 by Alethea K. Helbig and Agnes Regan Perkins

All rights reserved. No portion of this book may be
reproduced, by any process or technique, without the
express written consent of the publisher.

Library of Congress Catalog Card Number: 94–16124
ISBN: 0–313–28742–2

First published in 1994

Greenwood Press, 88 Post Road West, Westport, CT 06881
An imprint of Greenwood Publishing Group, Inc.

Printed in the United States of America

The paper used in this book complies with the
Permanent Paper Standard issued by the National
Information Standards Organization (Z39.48–1984).

10 9 8 7 6 5 4 3 2 1

Contents

Preface

This Land Is Our Land: A Guide to Multicultural Literature for Children and Young Adults involves books of fiction, oral tradition, and poetry published from 1985 through the end of 1993 suitable for young people from preschool through high school. It deals with four major ethnic groups within the United States: African Americans, Asian Americans, Hispanic Americans, and Native-American Indians. It contains 570 entries on 559 books (a few are considered in more than one category, e.g., anthologies of both fiction and poetry). Also included in these entries is information about 188 other books by these writers published during this period. In addition, 90 related earlier books are cited to help identify the writer and amplify the information about the book. (We use the term "writer" throughout because retellers and editors are represented as well as authors.)

As teachers for more than twenty-five years of children's literature to college students, most of whom are prospective teachers, we have long been concerned with the issue of quality in multi-ethnic books of imaginative literature. We ourselves have read and considered all the books included here and have judged them primarily on such literary values as plotting, style, and characterization. An example of how important evaluating such literary features can be appears with stereotypes. However sympathetically portrayed, stereotyped characters may engage the reader's emotions but do not promote real understanding.

Our work has been aided by a board of advisors representing the four ethnic groups, all of whom examined lists of books we had compiled, pointed out those they found unsuitable, explained why, and added works they thought we should consider that were not on our lists. We found their advice invaluable, as we have found the suggestions of many other people who work with children, including our students. The final selections, however, have been our own.

Our biggest challenge arose in delineating the scope of inclusions in order to fit the allotted space. When we considered the number of books that have been published in the past few decades about each of the groups, we realized that a large bibliography could be filled with just the best of these. The result, we soon saw, would be a list consisting mostly of already well-known books which appear in previous selection guides easily available in libraries. Since most of these references were published before 1985, we set that year as a beginning date for the books we include here. A reference book with more recent titles fills an obvious gap.

Other considerations influenced our choices as well. Since this bibliography focuses on the American ethnic experience (including Puerto Rico), works set in other countries are excluded, except for the oral tradition of Asian and Hispanic peoples, because these latter groups within the United States have not developed extensive oral literature based in this country. This is not true of African Americans, however; a large body of folk material set mainly in the American South has grown up. It derives its roots from Africa, but the versions are distinctively American. Therefore, we have not included retellings directly from African oral tradition, even though many extremely attractive and valuable books of that sort exist. Native-American Indian oral tradition, of course, has its origins in what is now the United States. We have also included originally oral material from such groups as the Aztecs and Maya because these relate to the Native-American Indian experience and to the Hispanic experience as well. We have placed them under Native-American Indians.

Deciding on what constitutes the ethnic experience is not easy. Distinctions are not clear cut. Certainly, in each of the groups are people whose lives are like those of anyone in mainstream America, and this very fact is a part of their ethnic experience. In recent years, many books reflect this situation, especially picture-story books about African-American children.

Books about an ethnic group have not been included unless the book, in story or at least in illustration, is mainly about minority characters. A number of the books we considered for inclusion have one or more characters from a particular ethnic group, but the story's protagonist is Anglo. Our effort has been to choose those in which the predominant problem or action of the story concerns the minority figures but not those in which they are merely incidental friends of the Anglo or in which the primary development in understanding has been for the white protagonist.

Since the scope of this bibliography includes high school students, much of the poetry and a number of the novels and short stories were originally published for adults. Where the material requires more than usual maturity or contains elements that might be objectionable, we have so indicated in the annotations.

While we made every effort to include all the appropriate books from this period, we could not secure a few in time to meet our deadline. We would like to have a better balance in the number of books from the four groups, but this was not possible. Not surprisingly, many more books for young people about African Americans have come out in recent years than for any of the other groups. Increasingly these reflect a broad spectrum of middle-class American life, unlike books in earlier years where the emphasis was more specifically on the inner-city experience or on discrimination from the dominant society.

In the Hispanic section, bilingual stories and retellings of folktales for younger children provide a special experience. Poetry is notably sparse in the Asian section, but among Native-American Indians it is unusually extensive and rhythmically informed by tradition. In fiction, many Asian-American and Hispanic-American novels and short stories for adults are of high literary quality, and among the Native-American Indians short stories in particular excel, many of which, like the poetry, are accessible to later middle school, although intended for adults. Fantasy fiction is little represented throughout, and picture books and illustrated books of oral tradition, in all groups, tend to be of extraordinary beauty, even though the pictures sometimes overshadow or are forced to bolster pedestrian texts.

Entries appear in alphabetical order by writer within each ethnic group, with subsections within each group for fiction (including picture books of fiction), oral tradition, and poetry. Each entry includes standard bibliographical information; age and grade levels; a brief plot summary incorporating themes; critical comments with a judgment of the book's value as an example of its genre; and, where pertinent, other books by the writer, if not given in separate entries, and related books of importance. Cross-references direct the reader's attention to books with similar themes or works by the writer in other genres.

The length of an entry does not necessarily indicate the book's importance or quality, since some plots can be summarized more briefly and critical judgments stated more succinctly for some books than for others. In a few instances, entries have been repeated as a time-saver for the user. For example, *Nothing but Net* by Dean Hughes appears in both the African-American and Hispanic-American fiction sections because the protagonists are a black boy and a Chicano boy of equal importance in the story. When books contain more than one genre, they have sometimes been included under both, depending on the book's emphasis, of course; an example here would be Sherman Alexie's *The Business of Fancydancing: Stories and Poems*.

All these books have been written by Americans or by residents of the United States. Sometimes several entries appear by the same writer. Various reasons governed our choices in such cases. Some writers have been more prolific in this period than others, like Walter Dean Myers and Gary Soto. In instances in which the works by a writer are similar, they have been included in a single entry, like those of Tony Hillerman. The book featured is usually the most recent or the most highly regarded from this period. Sometimes, however, the works of an author fit into more than one genre or subgenre, and these have been given separate entries. For instance, Laurence Yep has written novels of family life, fantasy, and historical fiction, has edited anthologies of oral tradition, fiction, and poems, and has retold folktales for picture book format.

A word should be said about age and grade level indications. In most instances, we have followed the suggestions of the publishers, except where our experience with children leads us to judge differently. Particularly in oral tradition, suggested levels should not be followed rigidly. Since folktales, myths, hero tales, and fables were intended for all ages, the retellings can usually be treated with flexibility, and, depending upon the proposed use, may have no age limits. Even with the other genres, age and grade level designations should not be adhered to slavishly. Children differ greatly, and their receptivity to books depends on the skill and enthusiasm of the adults working with them.

Most users will be familiar with the terms we employ, but a few may need explanation. By realistic fiction we mean books in which events could have happened some time in the world as we know it, as opposed to an imaginary or fantastic world, and not necessarily that the action is convincing or plausible. Historical fiction includes those books in which actual historical events or figures function in the plot or in which the specific past period is essential to the action and in which the story could not have occurred at any other time. By picture-story books we mean those highly illustrated books of a single original short story. Although books from oral tradition are often single stories highly illustrated, these are included under oral tradition rather than fiction. Books of rhymes and songs are included with poetry, as are picture-story books of verse.

Several indexes are included. In all of these, items are keyed to entry numbers: a title index (with writers' names in parentheses), an index of writers, an illustrator index, a grade-level index, and a subject index. The subject index includes genres by ethnic group; subgroups within the larger ethnic group, for example, Koreans, Sioux Indians; settings, for example, New York City, farms; and such general subjects as intergenerational conflict, women's concerns, baseball, pride in heritage, prejudice against Asian Americans, and so on.

We ourselves have done all the selecting, reading, research, and writing for *This Land Is Our Land*. We have had valuable assistance from many sources, especially our advisory board members: Lorraine Boomer, Naomi Caldwell-Wood, Oralia Garza de Cortes, Opal Moore, Jacqueline K. Sasaki, and Karen Patricia Smith.

In addition, we express our appreciation to the Eastern Michigan University Library and the Ann Arbor, Michigan, Public Library for the use of their extensive collections and their ongoing encouragement and support. Specifically we thank Brian Steimel and Thomas Staicar of the Interlibrary Loan Department of Eastern Michigan University for their help in obtaining books not available locally and Margaret Best and Rosina Tammany for their help in establishing the working lists.

The assistance of the Ann Arbor Public Library staff has been of immense value to us. We thank the reference librarians and the clerical and library staff, especially the following: Sherry Roberts, Paula Schaffner, Cynthia Chelius, Shutta Crum, Betsy Baier, and Yvette Shane (Director), all of the Youth Department at the Main Library, and Ieva Bates and Timothy Grimes at the Loving Branch. Our appreciation also goes to Kathy Wasil of the Ypsilanti, Michigan, Public Library for helping in a variety of ways. Last, but not least, we thank Kim Pietrack of Ann Arbor, Michigan, Huron High School for generously sharing her book lists with us.

1

African Americans: Books of Fiction

1 Adoff, Arnold, *Hard to Be Six*, illus. Cheryl Hanna, Lothrop, 1991 (hardcover), ISBN 0-688-09579-8, $12.95, unp. Ages 4–8, grades PS–3.

Realistic picture-story book of contemporary family life, spoken by a six-year-old boy who wishes he had the stature and capabilities of his ten-year-old sister. He longs to stay up later, ride a big bike as Sis does, and not hear "baby brother" talk from her friends. In his very private moments, he pretends to be the biggest and best. Through the week, various family members try to soothe the hurt. Sis says to think big about the things he can do, Momma plays trains with him, Daddy takes him to the park, and Grandma takes him to visit his Grandpa's grave and inspires him to try always to do his best, as his Grandpa did. The full-page, close-up pictures establish the family as middle-class African Americans (the text is silent about race), possibly biracial with a white father; characterize the cast; depict situations; convey the boy's emotions; and reveal the family as close and loving. While the narrative is sensitive to the feelings and yearnings of the age, the tone is occasionally not quite right for a child, and the diction betrays the writer, who seems to be trying to talk like a child but does not quite achieve it. Word inversions, puns, and rhymes, for example, come through as affectations.

2 Albert, Burton, *Where Does the Trail Lead?*, illus. Brian Pinkney, Simon & Schuster, 1991 (hardcover), ISBN 0-671-73409-1, $13.95; (paper), ISBN 0-671-79617-8, $5.95, unp. Ages 4–8, grades PS–3.

Evocative picture-story book of a young African-American boy exploring alone on a summertime seacoast, through flowers, along sandy beaches and over-grown railroad tracks, over crests of sand dunes, past abandoned shanties, and back to his family's picnic campfire. With a minimum of text and an abundance of illustration, done with scratchboard renderings colored with oil pastels, the book gives a feeling for the salty air, expanse of space, and mystery of a solitary exploration along a shoreline.

3 Ansa, Tina McElroy, *Baby of the Family*, Harcourt, 1989 (hardcover), ISBN 0-15-110431-X, $18.95, 265 pp. Ages 14 up, grades 9 up.

Growing-up novel of Lena McPherson, who is babied and doted upon and considered special not only because she is much younger than her two brothers but also because she was born with a caul covering her face, which the old-time people think gives her psychic powers. Life in the small Georgia town of the 1950s is seen mostly through her eyes as the center of attention in a prosperous African-American family and among the varied clientele of her father's bar and grill. That she actually does see spirits, including that of a slave who drowned herself, is a secret she tries to hide until she is sixteen, when her paternal grandmother, Miss Lizzie, who has always lived with the family, dies, visits Lena after death, and urges her to use her powers and not to be afraid. Most of the book is a rather slow-moving slice of life in the home and community; Lena's extraordinary abilities are not always woven in well. The novel was published for adults, but despite much coarse language in the dialogue, there is nothing unsuitable or too difficult for high school readers.

4 Armstrong, Jennifer, *Steal Away*, Orchard, 1992 (hardcover), ISBN 0-531-05983-9, $15.95, 207 pp. Ages 9–13, grades 4–8.

Slave-escape historical novel, set a few years before the Civil War. At the death of her parents in 1855, Susannah Emmons is taken from her Vermont home to Virginia, to live in the family of her minister uncle. Having been raised to think of slavery as a sin, she is horrified to be given her own slave, Bethlehem, about her own age of thirteen. Desperately unhappy, she decides to run away and enlists the aid of Bethlehem, not appreciating the terrible risk to the black girl. When the sexual attention of Susannah's cousin, Byron, seventeen, become an unbearable threat, Bethlehem steals off with Susannah, and they make their way, with many adventures and great difficulty, until they come, with Susannah ill, to a farm of Quakers where Bethlehem seeks help, knowing that she may be captured and returned. The good people care for Susannah and, when she is well, set the girls on their way through the Underground Railway. Susannah is determined to get back to Vermont where the family of a friend, Nat Emmons, whom she eventually marries, will take her in, and she expects Bethlehem to go there, too. The black girl more clear-sightedly sees that she must get to Canada to be safe and, despite what has become a close and interdependent friendship, realizes that Susannah will not go with her. The story is set in a complicated three- or four-level framework, involving Susannah's granddaughter and others who learn the story later, which may add to the feeling of authenticity, but the adventure can stand on its own as a better than average escape story, in which the relationship between the dual protagonists lends depth and insight into the slave experience.

5 Banks, Jacqueline Turner, *Project Wheels*, Houghton, 1993 (hardcover), ISBN 0-395-64378-3, $13.95, 107 pp. Ages 8–12, grades 3–7.

Realistic school and growing-up novel set in a middle-class, mixed-ethnic community of Plank in western Kentucky. Present-day African-American Angela Collins, twelve, enjoys life with her mother, who directs a community center, her professor father, and her dearest friends, Judge and Jury Jenkins, who are twins, and Faye Benneck, who is white. But she notices disturbing changes: The boys are behaving differently around girls, and, when Faye gets a crush on Jury, tension builds between Angela and Faye. Complicating matters is Faye's idea to have the class Christmas project be a fund-raiser for a new wheelchair for Wayne DeVoe. The project succeeds beautifully (and predictably), and the children realize that the boy-girl tension is just part of growing up. Style is breezy, diction contemporary, narrative structure undemanding, plot fast moving, and plot problems the kind that appeal to the intended audience. The humor is often strained and obvious. The few occasions of racism seem intrusive; for example, the principal looks only Faye in the eyes, never Angela or Tommy, who is Asian. Tommy, being Asian, is regarded as a math-sci whiz. In this pleasant story with an upbeat tone, everything works out as it should.

6 Barrett, Joyce Durham, *Willie's Not the Hugging Kind*, illus. Pat Cummings, Harper, 1989 (hardcover), ISBN 0-06-020416-8, $14.00; Trophy, 1991 (paper), ISBN 0-06-443264-5, $4.95, 32 pp. Ages 4–8, grades PS–3.

Realistic picture-story book set in a present-day city or town, which stresses the importance of family love and of developing independence of thought. Since Jo-Jo, his best friend, makes fun of hugging, Willie, perhaps eight or nine, rejects the affectionate overtures of his family, until, longing to give and receive loving, he hugs his mother before breakfast one day and then happily gives hugs to everyone when he leaves for school. The realistic, full-color illustrations, which have the tone of easy-reader pictures, show the family as middle-class African Americans, Jo-Jo as Asian, and some classmates as white, but the text does not specify race. The diction is undistinguished and within the capacity of most early readers, the end is predictable, and Willie's feelings seem typical of his age.

7   Belton, Sandra, *From Miss Ida's Porch*, illus. Floyd Cooper, Four Winds, 1993 (hardcover), ISBN 0-02-708915-0, $14.95, 40 pp. Ages 7–11, grades 2–6.

Picture-story book whose text is longer than most of its kind. The young narrator tells how she and her best friend, Freda, love to go to sweet, dignified, old Miss Ida's house on Church Street. There, when the sky gets "kind of rosy around the edges," neighbors gather and swap stories about the old days. Tonight Mr. Fisher relates how, back in the late 1930s, Duke Ellington came to Virginia. Refused a room at the local hotel, he stayed at the rooming house where Mr. Fisher lived. Mrs. Fisher, called Shoo Kate, tells about hearing Marian Anderson at the Lincoln Memorial, because Constitution Hall was closed to her, and Daddy describes how he heard her in 1965, twenty-five years later, at Constitution Hall. The stories present slices of African-American history pleasingly told and encourage pride in heritage and self without overt instruction. The full-color paintings show the story's cast at different stages of the narrative and distinctively characterize them. The pictures have a certain fuzziness that adds to the nostalgia. Author's notes and a list of books and sound and video recordings about Ellington and Anderson are included.

8   Berleth, Richard, *Samuel's Choice*, illus. James Watling, Whitman, 1990 (hardcover), ISBN 0-8075-7218-7, $14.95, unp. Ages 8–12, grades 3–7.

Historical fiction in picture-story book form about a slave boy who aids Washington's troops during the retreat from Brooklyn to Manhattan after the Battle of Long Island in 1776. Samuel Abraham, fourteen, a slave in the flour mill belonging to Isaac Van Ditmas, has been taught to sail so he can take Isaac's wife and daughters to Manhattan and Staten Island. When the American forces are penned at the Brooklyn end of Long Island and Isaac has fled, Samuel takes the boat and rescues load after load of soldiers from the marshes along Gowanus Creek. His last passenger is Major Mordecai Gist, commander of the Maryland soldiers, whom he delivers to Brooklyn Heights. Later, he is pressed into service to aid in the retreat of Washington's men to Manhattan, volunteering to carry across a rope so that other boats can follow in the stormy night. With Van Ditmas's property turned over to the Army of the Continental Congress, Samuel becomes orderly to Major Gist. A map at the front and a historical note at the end make it possible to follow the action and to know that, although Samuel and the other African-American characters are fictional, slaves did help Washington's men in the retreat. Although highly illustrated with evocative pictures in colored ink and colored pencil, the book has more text than most picture stories and will appeal to children through middle-school years.

9 Bogart, Jo Ellen, *Daniel's Dog*, illus. Janet Wilson, Scholastic, 1990 (hardcover), ISBN 0-590-43402-0, $11.95; (paper), ISBN 0-590-43401-2, $3.95, 32 pp. Ages 5–8, grades K–3.

Picture-story book of a young African-American boy who solves his sibling problem by adopting an imaginary dog for comfort and companionship. When Daniel's little sister is born and his mother seems always to be busy with her, he feels left out until he remembers his grandfather, now dead, telling him about the "ghost dog" that came to him whenever he needed her, and he decides that he has been sent Lucy, a spaniel, to keep him company. He explains all this to his Asian-American friend, Norman, and offers Norman Lucy's friend, Max, to comfort him while his father is away. Lucy is shown in ghostly, transparent image in a number of the illustrations. In this very simple, appealing story, Daniel, his baby sister, and his mother are shown as realistic and attractive blacks in a middle-class environment, but nothing in the text indicates the ethnic background of the characters.

10 Boyd, Candy Dawson, *Charlie Pippin*, Macmillan, 1987 (hardcover), ISBN 0-02-726350-9, $12.95, 182 pp.; Puffin, 1988 (paper), ISBN 0-14-032587-5, $3.99, 192 pp. Ages 8–12, grades 3–7.

Realistic novel of school and family life set in a mixed-ethnic, middle-class neighborhood in Berkeley, California, in 1985 and focusing on the effects of the Vietnam War on the next generation. African-American Charlie Pippin, eleven, class entrepreneur and independent thinker, is assigned by her sixth-grade teacher to a group working on war and peace and chooses to explore the Vietnam conflict because her father is a veteran of that war. The war changed her father, Oscar, once a "dreamer" and now a "man of rules and responsibilities" inclined to fly into rages and tyrannize the household. Charlie's discovery that her father was decorated for valor, her participation in an oratory contest, and her unauthorized trip to the memorial in Washington, D.C., predictably lead to a greater understanding between father and daughter. The placating mother; snippy, boy-crazy elder sister; rock-solid, sensible, mediating grandparents; and beloved, understanding uncle, also a veteran but with a view of the war opposite that of her embittered father, complement and foil the characters of Charlie and Oscar but like them are conveniently typecast. The dialogue about war in specific and in general terms seems instructive and trite, and the dilemma of black soldiers in Vietnam overintellectualized and pat. Charlie is the typically strongly assertive girl and the rebellious, rash adolescent. Good features are the middle-class unity, the grandparents as ballast, the strength of the family unit in spite of extreme tension, and the sense of the continuing trauma of the war. Another girl's story is *Circle of Gold* (1984) about a Chicago family struggling after the death of the father. Its companion is *Breadsticks and Blessing Places* (1985), also published as *Forever Friends* (1986), which tells how twelve-year-old Toni Douglas's problems with entering King Academy accelerate when her best friend, Susan, is killed in an accident and Mattie Mae Benson of *Circle of Gold* helps her come to terms with her grief and gain new perspectives on life.

11 Boyd, Candy Dawson, *Chevrolet Saturdays*, Macmillan, 1993 (hardcover), ISBN 0-02-711765-0, $14.95, 176 pp. Ages 8–12, grades 3–7.

Realistic contemporary novel of family and school life set in Berkeley, California. African-American Joey Davis, ten, misses his father, especially after his mother, a beautician, marries Mr. Johnson, to whom Joey has trouble relating. He is pestered by the class bully and feels put down by the new teacher. Doc, the elderly pharmacist, advises him to work hard, saying that that is how one wins out. Three circumstances turn life around: Mr. Johnson speaks up for him against the teacher when she wants him tested for attention deficit and Mama urges that he be tested for giftedness; Mr. Johnson needs his help with the sideline construction business he runs out of his '53 Chevrolet truck on Saturdays, work the boy increasingly enjoys; and, most of all, Joey is careless, leaves the gate open, and Josie, Mr. Johnson's beloved dog, gets out. Joey takes responsibility for finding the dog that has been hit by a car, and gets a job with Doc to help pay the vet bills. By Thanksgiving he realizes he wants to spend time with Daddy when he flies west from Chicago, but he also enjoys being with and much respects "Mr. J.," a term he adopts for his stepfather that symbolizes his more mature attitude. Joey has too many problems for credibility, and the dialogue is lame, but the sorts of concerns he has as a middle-class child are typical. The plot is not ethnic specific, but the bully happens to be white, Mr. Davis has his new job in Chicago because he complained about being discriminated against, and Mr. J.'s race makes it difficult for him to get contracts for big jobs.

12 Brown, Kay, *Willy's Summer Dream*, Harcourt, 1989 (hardcover), ISBN 0-15-200645-1, $13.95, 132 pp. Ages 9–14, grades 4–9.

Realistic sociological problem and boy's growing-up novel set in a lower middle-class Brooklyn, New York, neighborhood in recent years. Willy Palmer, fourteen, big for his age and slow in school, chafes at the ridicule he receives from his classmates and the unwanted attention he gets from his teachers. He yearns to shoot hoops with the guys, who scorn his advances, and to get in touch with his long-absent father. Several events during summer vacation raise his self-esteem, among them being tutored by the girl who is visiting next door, to whom he eventually even composes a letter, and teaching a younger boy to swim. At the end of the summer, he is about to start vocational school and has shown the boys he is as good as they are at shooting hoops. He now realizes that life holds tests and failures but also opportunities and successes and that he "just gotta make the best of it" from where he is. Although Willy and most of the people he associates with are African-American, Willy's single-parent life and problems are not tied to the black experience, and Willy, though individualized, is convincingly representative of mentally slow children. In spite of its "leapin' and lingerin'" style, the book moves fast and seems true to Willy's point of view although events are not related by him. A good scene is the one in which the boys are impressed by Willy's courage when he once again asks to shoot hoops with them even after he had been so painfully rejected previously.

13 Bunting, Eve, *Summer Wheels*, illus. Thomas B. Allen, Harcourt, 1992 (hardcover), ISBN 0-15-207000-1, $14.95, 46 pp. Ages 5–8, grades K–3.

Highly illustrated chaptered book for early readers about the Bicycle Man, the old man who fixes bicycles in Mrs. Pirelli's garage, then lends them to the neighborhood kids with only a few rules: Sign the bike out and back in, return it by four o'clock, and repair (with the Bicycle Man's direction and help) anything that happens to the bike while you have it. Lawrence, the narrator, and Brady, both eleven, have favorite bikes they claim regularly by being the first at the garage each morning. After a slightly older boy takes Lawrence's favorite, signing out as "Abrehem Lincoln," and fails to return it, they hunt him down and force him to bring it back. When he does not return a second bike he takes, they discover him showing off for a group of older boys, riding down stone steps with both tires flat. This time he comes willingly, grumbles at the idea of repairing it, but offers the Bicycle Man a jelly doughnut he has saved and announces that his real name is Leon. Nothing in the text indicates the race of the main characters, but illustrations show that Lawrence and Abrehem/Leon are African Americans; Brady and the Bicycle Man are white. The simple story is pleasant but didactic, continuing about two pages too long in order to nail home the lesson about the possibility for good even in the seeming wicked. The mostly full-page illustrations are done in charcoal, pastel, and colored pencil.

14 Burgess, Barbara Hood, *Oren Bell*, Delacorte, 1991 (hardcover), ISBN 0-385-30325-4, $15.00, 182 pp. Ages 10–14, grades 5–9.

Humorous novel of African-American family and school life set in Detroit's inner city in the early 1980s. Because he opened his eyes during the reverse-curse ceremony engineered on the first day of school by his bossy twin sister, Latonya, to allay the evil spirit of the empty house that stands next door to the condemned one under the Lodge Freeway which the Bell family rents from the city of Detroit, Oren, twelve, is convinced that he has caused the disasters that befall him and the neighborhood all year. The new teacher initiates a buddy system that pairs him with a bright *girl*; he is assigned third trumpet in the band; the class embarks on a historic house project that involves the haunted house; his best friend, an American Indian orphan named Fred, is found murdered in the evil house; Granddaddy Bill's alcoholism lands him in the VA hospital; Mama loses her job when the J. L. Hudson store closes; distemper takes most of the new puppies; and Mama gets close with the veterinarian, handsome Jack Daniels, among other sometimes poignant, often hilarious matters. The climax of action results in Oren's improved self-esteem when he rescues his "weird" little sister, Brenda, from her perch on the icy roof. Unlike most inner-city stories, this lively, contemporary in diction mystery shows a warm, loving family, who are happy and optimistic in spite of such problems as urban decay, deteriorating commercial districts, single parenting, drugs, and theft rings. If there seem to be too many problems and if Jack Daniels is too much of a Prince Charming even as a deus ex machina, the accent is on fun, and the conditions that influence the lives of these people are left to speak for themselves.

15 Caines, Jeannette, *I Need a Lunch Box*, illus. Pat Cummings, Harper, 1988 (hardcover), ISBN 0-06-020984-4, $14.00, unp. Ages 3–7, grades PS–2.

Realistic picture-story book about a common early childhood experience. A little boy, the preschooler who tells the story and is shown as African-American in the pictures, yearns for a lunch box like that of his big sister who is school age. He even dreams of having a different colored one for each day of the school week and of the wonderful foods he would put in them. To his joy, on the day Doris starts school, Daddy surprises him with one of his own. The back cover shows him racing happily away with the box clutched tightly in his hand. The full-color, realistic pictures depict family members in home scenes and the objects the little boy yearns for in much the style of primers or books for the very young. The short narrative is simply told with easy diction and syntax and is uncomplicated enough for early readers. Pat Cummings's realistic illustrations for Caines's *Chilly Stomach* (1986), about child molesting, show the prepubescent protagonist/narrator as white. Sandy tells how she is so uncomfortable by his unwanted attentions every time Uncle Jim visits that she asks to sleep over with African-American Jill and her family, whose Uncle Fred is fun in what Sandy knows is a wholesome way. In simple, brief text, the book addresses Sandy's fears and her uncertainty about how to deal with the situation.

16 Cameron, Ann, *More Stories Julian Tells*, illus. Ann Strugnell, Knopf, 1986 (hardcover), ISBN 0-394-96969-3, $13.95, 82 pp.; Random House, 1989 (paper), ISBN 0-394-82454-7, $2.99, 96 pp. Ages 6–9, grades 1–4.

Five amusing realistic episodes of African-American family life and domestic adventures set in a contemporary middle-class residential neighborhood. The stories are told by earnest, active Julian Bates, first met in *The Stories Julian Tells* (1981), and involve Julian's spunky little brother, Huey, and his best friend, clever, fun-loving Gloria. Typical is the episode in which Julian derides Huey as "bean sprout" and Dad seems angry. Dad brings home a cardboard box he tells them to open; inside, they find two baby pet rabbits. The book is aimed at children Julian's age just past primers to read for themselves. Dialogue is extensive, vocabulary is easy, and sentences are short and uncomplicated but often employ pithy and unusual but not difficult expressions. The humor is gentle and often ironic, and the view of life is upbeat, arising out of warm, respectful interpersonal relationships. The children are loved, well brought up, and typically active for their age. Though the text does not specify race, the pictures show the characters as African American. Further adventures of Julian and his friends appear in the more cohesively constructed *Julian's Glorious Summer* (1987), where Julian gets in trouble because he does not tell the truth; *Julian, Secret Agent* (1988), in which Julian, Gloria, and Huey become detectives; and *Julian, Dream Doctor* (1990), a much shorter book in which Julian and Huey set out to make their father's birthday special.

17 Cartier, Xam Wilson, *Be-Bop, Re-Bop*, Ballantine, 1987 (paper), ISBN 0-345-34883-8, $4.95, 147 pp. Ages 15 up, grades 10 up.

Contemporary realistic novel with flashbacks to historical events set among African-Americans in Saint Louis and San Francisco. The female narrator begins her story in Saint Louis at the funeral of her father, Double, a forty-three-year-old postal employee, who came to Saint Louis to enroll in teachers' college, married a level-headed but often acid-tongued social worker, and tried to instill black pride in his daughter. She describes her failed marriage to

Charlie (Hawk), a medical student, her alcoholism, and her move to San Francisco with her four-year-old daughter where she goes on welfare. Historical incidents, of which she has been told, appear here and there in her sometimes free-association narrative, including racism surrounding the Louis-Schmelling fight and against blacks in World War II, the *Brown vs. Board of Education* decision, and the unease of their moving into a white neighborhood. Social comment is plentiful on broader matters as well as, among others, on the black issues of how to deal with white institutions without which they cannot get ahead but within which they are not given the support to succeed and of "ricochet racism." Particularly examined is the problem facing black women of how to maintain personal integrity while at the same time giving sufficient emotional support to the faltering egos of their men. The book is especially notable for its melodious, vigorous style which makes full use of blues, jive, jazz, rap, and swing rhythms, rhyming and chiming, clever plays on words, varieties of wit, spicy alliteration, and pungent colloquialisms. Focusing on a black woman piano player is *Muse-Echo Blues* (1991), which confronts similar issues but is more openly erotic, more complicated in structure, and more demanding in style and diction.

18   Chlad, Dorothy, *Playing Outdoors in the Winter*, illus. Clovis Martin, Children's, 1991 (hardcover), ISBN 0-516-01972-4, $15.00, 32 pp. Ages 4–7, grades PS–2.

Realistic picture-story book stressing safety, one in the Safety-Town series. Young Darryl, who tells the story, describes how he, his parents, and friends enjoy the out-of-doors in wintertime, building snowmen, making angels, clearing the snow, sledding, skiing, and skating. He emphasizes obeying the rules, like never throwing snowballs, lest a window break or someone be hurt, and always testing the ice before going out on it. Diction is easy, sentences uncomplicated, and tone didactic in keeping with the book's intent, and the five main rules are listed for repetition at the end. The paintings are bold and colorful and show Darryl and his parents as good-looking middle-class African Americans. The facial expressions and bodies of all the characters (which are mixed race) are stiff and unnatural.

19   Corey, Dorothy, *Will There Be a Lap for Me?*, illus. Nancy Poydar, Whitman, 1992 (hardcover), ISBN 0-8075-9109-2, $11.95, unp. Ages 3–7, grades PS–2.

Picture-story book of a young African-American boy who feels increasingly left out because his mother's pregnancy seems to push him aside as her stomach grows larger and larger. After his baby brother is born, his mother seems so busy that there is no special place for him until, understandingly, she makes time to hold him on her lap just as she used to do. Illustrations are slightly cartoonish but not distorted. Text pages are framed with colored lines and decorated with birds, fruit, and toys. Kyle's family members are all black, but the story applies to a child of any race.

20 Cote, Nancy, *Palm Trees*, illus. Nancy Cote, Four Winds, 1993 (hardcover), ISBN 0-02-724760-0, $14.95, unp. Ages 4–7, grades PS–2.

Picture-story book set in a contemporary, unnamed urban area. Since the hot, muggy August atmosphere makes her hair unmanageable, young African-American Millie twists it into two almost vertical ponytails and secures them with rubber bands. When her friend Renee calls them palm trees, Millie feels silly. Just as she is about to snip them off, she answers the doorbell to find Renee standing outside with three palm trees of her own. Shades of yellow and red suffuse the off-the-page pictures that catch the spirit of friendship in this story which inventively makes the most of a common problem for girls— what to do with uncooperative hair.

21 Crews, Donald, *Bigmama's*, illus. Donald Crews, Greenwillow, 1991 (hardcover), ISBN 0-688-09950-5, $13.95, unp. Ages 3–8, grades PS–3.

Autobiographical picture-story book set on a Southern farm in the 1940s. The author/illustrator, his siblings, and their Mama take the train one summer to Bigmama's (his Mama's Mama's) house on her farm in Cottondale, Florida, where they savor water from the well, hunt for eggs, dig worms in the cane pulp, check on the horses, go fishing, and enjoy getting caught up on news with relatives from down the road at a joyful family dinner. Small, important touches lend credibility to the impressionistic watercolors and gouaches, like the children's too-big heads and hands and their homely features, the Sears catalogs, and the "COLORED" sign in their Southern Railway passenger car. The simple, unadorned, declarative sentences reveal the same sense of authenticity and down-home atmosphere, with, for example, the children's immediate need "to see that nothing has changed" since last year, which is true to the way children think, and their spending hours checking to make sure. The text does not specify, but the pictures show the family to be African American. This comfortable, real-seeming book in both story and pictures has a sequel, *Shortcut* (1992), an intensely dramatic account of how the same children have a nearly fatal encounter with a train on the track near Bigmama's house. The atmospheric pictures are less impressionistic than those in *Big-*

mama's and more reminiscent of Crews's *Freight Train* (1978). *Bicycle Race* (1985) and *Flying* (1986) are almost textless storybooks with Crews's characteristic posterlike pictures. There are no protagonists, but background figures are multiracial.

22   Curtis, Gavin, *Grandma's Baseball*, illus. Gavin Curtis, Crown, 1990 (hardcover), ISBN 0-517-57389-X, $13.95, unp. Ages 4–8, grades PS–3.

Realistic picture-story book set in the present day. Because she takes over his room, is a stickler about homework, and insists on decorum, the young boy narrator is not sure he likes having Grandma, the widow of a ballplayer, living with his family, until he discovers she has Grandpa's old, autographed baseball and she teaches him how to throw sinkers. Accompanying this pleasing but not always logically motivated story about a grandmother and grandson learning to get along are soft-toned watercolors. They show the family as middle-class, urban African Americans. The diction and syntax are easy enough for early readers, although the book is not intended as an easy-to-read.

23   Davis, Ossie, *Just Like Martin*, Simon & Schuster, 1992 (hardcover), ISBN 0-671-73202-1, $14.00, 215 pp. Ages 10 up, grades 4 up.

Historical novel of events among African Americans in an unidentified Alabama city from mid-August to mid-December of 1963. Stone, fourteen, is junior assistant pastor of Holy Oak Baptist Church and hopes to attend Morehouse University as his idol, Martin Luther King, Jr., did and, like him, become a preacher and civil rights activist. He plans to join the Freedom March in Washington, D.C., soon to take place, along with Reverend Cable and his church and school friends, but his father, Ike Stone, traumatized by the Korean War and opposed philosophically to nonviolence, refuses to let the boy participate. Reverend Cable starts nonviolence workshops at Holy Oak, two girls are killed when the church basement is bombed, the commemorative march the youths organize turns ugly, and Ike is severely beaten by racist police and decides to move to California. During a sermon given by Dr. King, however, Ike has a change of heart, and Stone is relieved at his father's improved personality and at being able to remain at Holy Oak. Though slow at first, the pace picks up well, and the book is meaty, if heavy on instruction, and rises to an exciting and dramatic climax. Characters are types but fulfill their roles well, and the different African-American attitudes toward the treatment they receive from whites and the gaining of rights are the book's strongest aspects. For comparison, see *Freedom Songs* (no. 92).

24 De Veaux, Alexis, *An Enchanted Hair Tale*, illus. Cheryl Hanna, HarperCollins, 1987 (hardcover), ISBN 0-06-021623-9, $15.00, 42 pp.; Trophy, 1991 (paper), ISBN 0-06-443271-8, $4.95, 48 pp. Ages 4–8, grades PS–3.

Lighthearted, poetically told, realistic picture-story book about self-esteem. Teased by adults and children because his hair is different, being "wild mysterious," like his mother's, a "fan daggle of locks and lions and lagoons," Sudan, a little African-American boy in an unspecified urban area, gets "just plain evil" and leaves home. On a back street he encounters a troupe of circus trampoline tumblers with hair like his, bounces for a while, and is escorted home by an old friend of his mother's, whose admonition to "just be your pretty self" he takes to heart. The bouncy be-boppy rhythms and distinctive turns of phrase keep the book's message from sounding instructive. Sculptured realistic, black-and-white drawings fill the pages with clever, almost surrealistic details.

25 Dove, Rita, *Fifth Sunday*, University of Kentucky Press, 1985 (paper), ISBN 0-912759-06-0, $8.95, 68 pp. Ages 14 up, grades 9 up.

Six short stories of African Americans from different walks of life, some reflecting the color issue, most simply about life matters. A couple of them appear with minor changes as episodes in the novel *Through the Ivory Gate* (no. 26), improvising on Dove's own family history. In others, an eccentric genius-musician fixatedly performs on a vibraphone that dominates his existence; a fourteen-year-old girl faints in church on a hot Sunday, giving rise to the rumor that she is pregnant; the Zulu motorcycle crew attends a brother's wedding apparently uninvited; a talented, young, part-black German artist spray-paints public buildings in Cologne and is interviewed by a psychiatrist in a home for disturbed juveniles; and a deranged bag lady expresses herself in a shopping arcade. While plot drives a few stories, most are character oriented, and it is the details of character revelation and of background texture that give the stories resonance.

26 Dove, Rita, *Through the Ivory Gate*, Pantheon, 1992 (hardcover), ISBN 0-679-41604-8, $21.00; Vintage, 1993 (paper), ISBN 0-679-74240-9, $11.00, 278 pp. Ages 14 up, grades 9 up.

Realistic novel set one fall in the 1980s telling of a young African-American woman's search for self. The plot is quickly summarized: Virginia King, bright, beautiful, college-educated in dramatic arts, accomplished cellist, mime, and puppeteer, returns to her native Akron, Ohio, from which her parents moved when she was nine, to serve as artist (puppeteer) in residence in an elementary school. She helps the students put on a play, becomes reacquainted with her grandmother and aunt, and has a brief romantic fling with the handsome divorced father of one of her pupils. Realizing they have nothing but sexual attraction in common, she moves on to try a career in New York. Giving body to the novel are Virginia's numerous flashbacks to and ruminations on family situations and school days, eloquently expressed in scenes graphic with telling detail, like that when in her childhood her best friend, a white girl, in anger at Virginia's all A report card, knocks her down, destroys the card, and calls her nigger; when she and her class go to a gamelon concert; when she discovers her music colleague lover is bisexual; and when she visits Aunt Carrie and learns dismaying family history. Although occasionally the author overwrites and some scenes, like that in which a pupil suffers a self-inflicted injury, seem superfluous, the total effect is quietly gripping. Some material sounds autobiographical, and some derives from the family history that forms the substance of her poems in *Thomas and Beulah* (no. 199). The Homeric title suggests the ironic nature of Virginia's search, perhaps to be taken as symbolic of the illusory, self-deluding quest of the educated, intelligent black woman for happiness outside herself, in the "perfect" man and the "perfect position."

27 Dragonwagon, Crescent, *Home Place*, illus. Jerry Pinkney, Macmillan, 1990 (hardcover), ISBN 0-02-733190-3, $14.95; (paper), ISBN 0-689-71758-X, $4.95, unp. Ages 5–8, grades K–3.

Picture-story book made up of speculation about who lived in an old house, now just a part of a chimney and a foundation almost disappeared into the woods and marked only by still-blooming daffodils. In poetic prose, the voice of a modern child, who imagines or intuits the past, tells of a family from the nineteenth or early twentieth century—Mama, Papa, Uncle Ferd, Anne, and Timmy, going through a typical evening. Lavish oversized, full-page and double-page illustrations done in pencil and watercolor, with many decorative embellishments, picture the narrator as white but the family of the home place as African-American. A beautiful, quiet book for thoughtful readers.

28 Duffy, James, *Uncle Shamus*, Scribner's, 1992 (hardcover), ISBN 0-684-19434-1, $13.95, 132 pp. Ages 9–11, grades 4–6.

Realistic contemporary mystery novel set mostly in a mixed-racial shantytown on the outskirts of a small Oklahoma community. Ten-year-old African-American Akers Johnson and his white schoolmate, Marleena Radford, both from poor families, are glad of the money they earn doing errands for old, blind, black Uncle Shamus, who has returned to town after a thirty-year prison sentence. They unwittingly become involved in helping him recover the loot from the armored car robbery that sent him to jail. Although the plot emphasis is on the question of Uncle Shamus's identity and the reason for his return, the hardships of the working poor in a waning mill town and the "invisibility" of the African Americans are worthy elements. The three main characters are distinctive, and the conclusion, which resolves sticky moral issues, is pat but appropriate to the events and characters as presented.

29 Engel, Diana, *Fishing*, illus. Diana Engel, Macmillan, 1993 (hardcover), ISBN 0-02-733463-5, $14.95, unp. Ages 5–8, grades K–3.

Picture-story book about Loretta, a young African-American girl who loves to fish with her grandfather. After her mother gets a new job and they move up north, Loretta is very lonely. One day she rigs up a line and a paper-clip hook and sits in her garden with her eyes closed, pretending she is on Grandpa's boat. A tug on her line proves to be a girl just her age who wants to play fishing with her. The ink and watercolor illustrations are slightly cartoonish, but not distorted. Both the loving relationship between child and grandfather and Loretta's unhappiness in her new home are simply but convincingly told.

30 Flournoy, Valerie, *The Patchwork Quilt*, illus. Jerry Pinkney, Dial, 1985 (hardcover), ISBN 0-8037-0097-0, $10.95, unp. Ages 4–8, grades PS–3.

Realistic picture-story book of family life. Little Tanya, whom the illustrations show as African American, realizes that making a quilt out of scraps of material that commemorate events and people is very important to her Grandma as a symbol of family continuity and pride in heritage. While Grandma lies ill, Tanya continues Grandma's "masterpiece," so that when the old woman is able to sew again, the quilt is soon finished, and all the family members can find the pieces that are special to them. Jerry Pinkney's typically impressionistic, colorful paintings invest the family members with distinctive personalities, create convincing scenes of extended family life at different times of the year, and exude family warmth and unity. They give the story strength and keep it from becoming sentimental. The "quilt" depicted, however, is not, strictly speaking, a quilt, but rather a "comforter," since the layers of material are tied together and not stretched and then quilt-stitched. Best is the strong sense of love, respect, and pride in self and ancestry.

31 Gilchrist, Jan Spivey, *Indigo and Moonlight Gold*, illus. Jan Spivey Gilchrist, Black Butterfly, 1992 (hardcover), ISBN 0-86316-210-X, $13.95, unp. Ages 5–11, grades K–6.

Realistic picture-story book of a young African-American girl, Autrie, who stays up later than her siblings and is allowed to go out onto the porch in the dark, while her mother watches through the window. She experiences the exhilaration of night beauty and wants to freeze time, then realizes that the perfect moment, like all things in life, must pass. The illustrations are stunning oils on canvas, with Autrie in her white nightgown on the shadowy porch and, in more impressionistic pictures, dancing in delight. While the illustrations may please younger children, the understanding that comes to Autrie requires more maturity to grasp. A special book, not likely to be a favorite for all children.

32 Golden, Marita, *A Woman's Place*, Doubleday, 1986 (hardcover), ISBN 0-385-19454-4, $19.00; Ballantine (paper), ISBN 0-345-34650-5, $4.95, 240 pp. Ages 14 up, grades 10 up.

Feminist novel focusing on the lives of three African-American women who are roommates at a university in Boston in the 1960s, showing the difficulties of being black and female that each encounters and how each copes in a different way. Faith, who becomes pregnant, drops out, loses her baby, converts to Islam, and changes her name to Aisha, marries an older man, has several children, and suffers through his repressive jealousy, finding her true strength only after he is disabled by a stroke. Crystal, daughter of a teacher, becomes a poet, takes a white lover, marries him, is unfaithful, and finally accepts his love for her, without great hope for ultimate happiness. Serena, a vibrant activist from Detroit, goes to Africa, tackles women's problems, has a baby by the Alhaji, the local leader, and eventually is made chief of a village. Each chapter is told in first person by a different character, usually one of the three women but occasionally one of their lovers or parents, and at the end by Tameka, Aisha's sixteen-year-old daughter, who is now struggling with questions about her own self-identity. The continually shifting point of view is well handled, with the voices varied enough to be convincing, and the three diverse plots are held together by the women's continued friendship and mutual support. Golden's later novel, *Long Distance Life* (1989), which tells the story of a woman who makes her way to Washington, D.C., from North Carolina in the 1920s and follows her life through the 1980s, uses many of the same stylistic elements but employs more stereotyped situations. Stylistically different, her *And Do Remember Me* (1992) is the story of a Mississippi girl scarred for life by incest. When Jessie runs away from home she is drawn into the Civil Rights protests of the 1960s by a good and loving man, Lincoln

Sturgis, a playwright, who gets her started on a very successful acting career, but the fear of men induced by her father never leaves her and eventually drives Lincoln away. Not until her father's death is she able to return home and begin to forgive her mother for not protecting her. Though the early part of the book, about the dangerous and idealistic Civil Rights movement, is interesting, the concentration on Jessie's psychological damage makes the story predictable and perhaps less suitable for a high school audience.

33 Gray, Libba Moore, *Miss Tizzy*, illus. Jada Rowland, Simon & Schuster, 1993 (hardcover), ISBN 0-671-77590-1, unp. Ages 5–9, grades K–4.

Picture-story book about an old African-American woman, Miss Tizzy, who seems peculiar to adults but delights the neighborhood children by letting them pick her flowers, bake cookies with her, make puppets and put on shows, play in a band led by her bagpipes, draw pictures and deliver them to shut-ins, play dress up, and roller skate in a train holding on to her long skirt. Every activity is first described, and then concluded by the phrase, "The children loved it." When Miss Tizzy becomes ill, the children follow the pattern she has set, cheering her up with cookies, puppet shows at her window, pictures in her mailbox, and a gift of a new pair of roller skates. The children in the full-page illustrations, done in watercolor and pen and ink, are an ethnically mixed band, individualized in appearance and in age. Miss Tizzy has a convincingly wrinkled face and dumpy figure. A warm and appealing book, despite the self-conscious integration of the children.

34 Greenfield, Eloise, *Grandpa's Face*, illus. Floyd Cooper, Philomel, 1988 (hardcover), ISBN 0-399-21525-5, $14.95; Sandcastle, 1991 (paper), ISBN 0-399-22106-9, unp. Ages 4–8, grades PS–3.

Realistic picture-story book about an African-American family (so identified in the pictures). Little Tamika and her Grandpa, an actor, have always been very close, but when one day she observes him make a "hard face . . . [with] cold, cold eyes" in the mirror, she worries because "she couldn't be sure that he might not some day look at her with that face that could not love." When she confides her fears to Grandpa on a "talk-walk," he explains that it is "just pretending," reassures her of his love, and makes everything all right again. Although the problem is patly and unconvincingly if heartwarmingly resolved, the diction is melodious, flowing, uncondescending, and distinctive. Tamika's fears, typical of the age, are aptly caught with phrases like "scared places in her stomach." The deep, tawny-toned pastels boost the text by adding details of setting and story and are especially good at characterizing Grandpa and Tamika in their exquisite portraits.

35 Greenfield, Eloise, *Koya Delaney and the Good Girl Blues*, Scholastic, 1992 (hardcover), ISBN 0-590-43300-8, $13.95, 124 pp. Ages 9–12, grades 4–7.

Novel of family life featuring African-American Koya Delaney, a sixth grader known for her congenial disposition and her ability to make everyone laugh, who discovers that sometimes anger is an appropriate response. Two big events loom in Koya's life, the double-ditch jumprope contest, in which her sister, Loritha, and her best friend, Dawn, will both perform, and the visit from her cousin, Delbert, Junior, now a popular musician with a hit record, who is coming to give a benefit performance for the homeless and is planning to stay with Koya's family, where he lived for a while after his parents died in a fire. Koya knows that Dawn resents the celebrity stature she and Loritha gain at school as cousins to Del, but she is astonished at the all-city double-dutch contest to discover that Dawn has maneuvered to change the routine and pretended that she could not reach them to tell of the special practice, so that a substitute has taken Loritha's place. Although Koya is shocked, she does not want to "get mad" at Dawn, and her efforts to stay friendly alienate Loritha, who starts snidely to call her "Good Girl." It is not until Del's boorish fans shout and stamp at his concert, drowning out much of his music, that Koya lets her anger out and realizes that sometimes taking a stand is important. She forces Dawn to admit what she did and to apologize to Loritha, thereby restoring their happy three-way friendship. The girls are recognizable eleven-year-olds, with normal middle-class sixth-grade concerns, but their parents are more than ordinarily understanding and events are contrived to make a point. Koya's ability to keep not only her classmates but also an audience of adults at the school talent show roaring with laughter is not very believable from the samples of her humor in the book. The characters are evidently all black, but the dialogue gives no hint of ethnic origin.

36 Greenfield, Eloise, *William and the Good Old Days*, illus. Jan Spivey Gilchrist, HarperCollins, 1993 (hardcover), ISBN 0-06-021093-1, $15.00, unp. Ages 4–8, grades PS–3.

Realistic picture-story book of family life told by a little African-American boy. William recalls how he loved going to Grandma's restaurant because of the good food and pleasant company there. But Grandma falls ill and loses her sight, maybe because of a fly she killed there, he thinks. He dreams of the good old days and looks forward to more good times when she feels better again. William's naive perceptions and his focus on certain people and incidents, his yearning for his Grandma's love and once active way of life seem accurate to the age and give the book an air of poignancy. The people in the full-color, off-the-page realistic paintings seem molded like sculptures, those of William showing him as an especially handsome, big-eyed child in various moods and poses. The technique of superimposing one or more remembered scenes in different tones on the real ones is remarkably evocative.

37 Grifalconi, Ann, *Kinda Blue*, illus. Ann Grifalconi, Little, Brown, 1993 (hardcover), ISBN 0-316-32869-3, $13.95, unp. Ages 4–8, grades PS–3.

Realistic picture-story book set on a Georgia farm in recent years. When little African-American Sissy, seven, feels down because her daddy is dead and her mother, grandmother, and siblings are busy, Uncle Dan cheers her up by carrying her on his shoulders over to the cornfield. There he shows her how every corn plant is different and has special needs and assures her that her loving family will always care for her special needs, too. Extending the simple story told by Sissy in colloquial language are sweeping double-page, watercolor, pastel, and pencil impressionistic illustrations, sometimes farm scenes, sometimes closeups of the characters. They show Uncle Dan as a young, powerfully muscled, good-looking farmer with a straw hat, overalls that almost hide a belly bulge, and kind, laughing eyes, and the child as sweet faced, chubby cheeked, wistful eyed, and ponytailed, somewhat younger than the seven the text specifies. Although a little sentimental, this is a heartwarming book most effective for its stunning illustrations.

38 Guy, Rosa, *And I Heard a Bird Sing*, Dell, 1987 (paper), ISBN 0-440-20152-7, $3.25, 232 pp. Ages 12–18, grades 7–12.

Contemporary mystery-detective novel featuring African-American Imamu Jones, eighteen, who appeared previously in *The Disappearance* (1980), and *New Guys around the Block* (1983). Once a troublesome Harlem street kid, half-orphaned Imamu now lives with his recovering alcoholic mother in a Brooklyn apartment not far from their friends and benefactors, the solidly middle-class African-American Aimsleys. Imamu's determination to keep his mother from regressing takes second place to his own well-being when, while delivering gourmet food to a wealthy white family, he discovers the paralyzed daughter of the house floating dead in the swimming pool and is soon accused of murder. In his efforts to help Detective Otis Brown uncover the truth, Imamu encounters racism from his previously kind white employer, the dead girl's family, and the police, and he is suspected of rape. The dead girl's beautiful aunt even tries to seduce him. The mystery is adequate, and a low-keyed romance between Imamu and Gail Aimsley adds dimension. Best are the portrayal of Imamu as a conscientious, warm, life-loving young man, normal in his emotions and aspirations for respect and a better life.

39 Guy, Rosa, *The Music of Summer*, Delacorte, 1992 (hardcover), ISBN 0-385-30599-0, $15.00; Doubleday, 1992 (paper), ISBN 0-385-30599-0, $5.00, 180 pp. Ages 12 up, grades 7 up.

Contemporary realistic girl's growing-up novel set mostly in a beautiful old mansion on Cape Cod. African-American, New Yorker Sarah Richardson, seventeen, poor but talented pianist, only child of a single-parent, hardworking mother, savors the chance for a vacation away from the hot city on Cape Cod with her childhood friend, Cathy Johnson. When ruthless, self-centered Cathy and her shallow, upper middle-class, light-skinned friends scorn dark-skinned Sarah, Sarah's misery is lessened by a romance with a handsome young man from Martinique. Through Jean Pierre, Sarah grows in self-esteem, sees new options in life, and sorts out her values. The predictable plot, one-sided characters, flimsy motivations, and fortuitousness are relieved by good tension, careful pacing, skillful exploitation of emotion, and convincing views of economic and color barriers among African Americans. There is some explicit sex. Also by Guy for older readers is the more stylistically demanding *My Love, My Love; or the Peasant Girl* (Holt, 1985), a retelling of Hans Christian Andersen's "The Little Mermaid." Concerning the ill-fated love of a black peasant girl for a wealthy mulatto boy on a lush, tropical Caribbean island, it was made into the Broadway musical, *Once on This Island.*

40 Guy, Rosa, *The Ups and Downs of Carl Davis III*, Delacorte, 1989 (hardcover), ISBN 0-385-29724-6, $13.95, 113 pp. Ages 10–14, grades 5–9.

Contemporary, epistolary, realistic novel about African Americans set in the southern town of Spoonsboro, South Carolina. Intelligent, grandiloquent, conceited only child Carl Davis III, son of a New York City doctor and nurse, protests in a series of letters home about being sent to live with his grandmother Davis. Enrolled there in a school for bright youth of all races, he sets out to amplify the history curriculum with facts of black history and encounters hostility not only from the white teacher but also from fellow black students who fear backlash. Over the next four months, Carl gains new perspectives. He becomes less arrogant and even recognizes his own sexist and intellectual bigotry. Situations involve overt racism against blacks seeking their rights and the dilemma that blacks face because of fearful or apathetic blacks and that sympathetic whites encounter because of racist whites. Not all dialogue and events are believable, and Carl's letters are too garrulous and detailed to be completely convincing. The book's message is obvious but is toned down by abundant humor. For the picture book set is *Billy the Great* (1992; originally published in Britain in 1991) about a spunky black boy and his parents and their relationship with a next-door white family. The realistic, strongly composed, full-color paintings by Caroline Binch compensate for a text that goes awry at the end.

41   Hamilton, Virginia, *The Bells of Christmas*, illus. Lambert Davis, Harcourt, 1989 (hardcover), ISBN 0-15-206450-8, $17.95, 59 pp. Ages 8–11, grades 3–6.

Highly illustrated Christmas story set in 1890 in rural Ohio near Springfield along the National Road. Twelve-year-old Jason Bell tells of the anticipation he and his sister, Melissy, seven, feel for the great day itself when his uncle's family, including his favorite cousin Tisha, come in their sleigh, and of the gifts and dinner shared by his friend, Matthew Lawson, who lives down the road. Although the text is much longer than most picture books, the lack of conflict or any plot keeps it from being more than a slice-of-life illustrating the period. In their actions and in the gifts they receive, the children seem much younger than their given ages, but strangely in the pictures they look older. Except for the rather wooden illustrations, there is nothing to indicate that the Bell family is African American.

42   Hamilton, Virginia, *Cousins*, Philomel, 1990 (hardcover), ISBN 0-399-22164-6, $14.95, 125 pp. Ages 8–12, grades 3–7.

Novel of an extended family in a small town or semirural area, where eleven-year-old Cammy frequently sneaks into the nursing home to see her Gran Tut, ninety-four, to whom she is very close, a habit tolerated by most of the Care Home help and known to her brother Andrew, sixteen, who is supposed to watch her while her mother works. She attends day camp along with her cousin, Patricia Ann, the epitome of the perfect child, whom she despises, and a more distant cousin, L.O.D. (Elodie), a neglected adopted child of a migrant worker. When Patty Ann is drowned saving L.O.D., who has fallen in the swollen river at camp, Cammy suffers from guilt and starts having screaming nightmares, dreaming that Patty Ann is sitting in her room. Her condition worsens until she is frequently hallucinating. It brings her divorced father back into her life and is eventually cured by Gran Tut, who helps her get her tangled feelings and her horror of death into perspective.

The love and understanding between Cammy and her bedridden grandmother is the strongest element in the book. Relationships between the girls and between Richie, Patty Ann's no-good older brother, and Andrew, who is continually supportive to him, are believable but not as interesting. Dialect is rural southern, but very little else indicates that the characters are African American. The setting and tone of the novel are similar to those in Hamilton's first novel, *Zeely* (1967) and in *M. C. Higgins, the Great* (1974), both of which take place in southern Ohio.

43   Hamilton, Virginia, *Drylongso*, illus. Jerry Pinkney, Harcourt, 1992 (hardcover), ISBN 0-15-224241-4, $18.95, 54 pp. Ages 7–11, grades 2–6.

Brief novel with fantasy qualities set in farming country west of the Mississippi in the drought of 1975. Lindy and her parents hopefully continue to plant, although the soil is dry as powder, until a dust storm sweeps toward them like a brown wall, with a tall boy running ahead of it. After they pull him into the house and he stops choking, he tells them his name is Drylongso and that he became separated from his family in the storm. After it passes, he dowses for water and directs them to plant in an old stream bed, predicting that it will not rain until the end of the decade. Although Lindy adopts him for her brother, he soon departs to find his family, leaving his divining rod for her. Illustrations are frequent, but the text is much longer than that of picture books. The character of the boy is hard to believe on a realistic level, yet if he is a "part-mythic" embodiment, as suggested in an author's note, the story is not strong enough to be convincing.

44   Hamilton, Virginia, *The Mystery of Drear House*, Greenwillow, 1987 (hardcover), ISBN 0-688-04026-8, $13.95, 224 pp. Ages 10–13, grades 5–8.

Mystery sequel to *The House of Dies Drear* (1968), a novel containing many Gothic elements about a large house in southern Ohio once owned by an abolitionist and used as a station on the Underground Railway and about the treasure he left in a cave on the property. Like the first book, the sequel stars Thomas Small, thirteen, and little Pesty, the orphan adopted by the rough Darrow family, and again involves elaborate secret passages and sinister threats. It diminishes the possible impact by including such unbelievable items as silken bedcovers and taffeta table skirts, surviving in beautiful condition more than one hundred years in underground rooms. The best element is the picture of Mrs. Darrow, Pesty's mentally ill foster mother, partly because of whom the two families finally reach a sort of understanding and peace. A slightly more plausible mystery is *Junius Over Far* (1985), set partly on a Caribbean island, involving munitions smugglers but notable for its use of island dialect and its recognition of the prejudice against islanders felt by many other African Americans.

45 Hamilton, Virginia, *A White Romance*, Philomel, 1987 (hardcover), ISBN 0-399-21213-2, $14.95, 191 pp. Ages 13 up, grades 8 up.

Romance set in an unnamed city where the mostly African-American high school has been made a target school and is therefore integrated with a flood of white students. Although most students stay tensely with their own kind, Talley Barbour, an African American, and Didi Adair, a tall, beautiful blond, become friends through their love of running. Talley, whose widower father is very strict with her, is at first disturbed that Didi makes love with Roady Lewis, who is often spaced out on drugs, but then becomes herself involved with David Emory, a handsome white drug pusher who is obviously Roady's supplier. Eventually, stable, moral black Victor helps her rescue herself. Told mostly through Talley's black-dialect stream of consciousness, the novel is extremely slow paced, with the reader knowing long before Talley that David is a dealer and that he is manipulative and, after establishing control, will drop her. An earlier romance, *A Little Love* (1984), is similarly slow and also has an extremely forbearing, decent boy rescue a wayward girl.

46 Hansen, Joyce, *Which Way Freedom?*, Walker, 1986 (hardcover), ISBN 0-8027-6623-4, $12.95; (paper), ISBN 0-380-71408-6, $2.99, 120 pp. Ages 11–14, grades 6–9.

Slave-escape story set during the Civil War in South Carolina and Tennessee. With the help of old Buka, black Obi, sixteen or seventeen, leaves secretly by night from the Jennings farm with Easter, thirteen, and they make their way to the coast, where Obi gets to an island and eventually joins the Union Army, fights and is wounded in Tennessee. The dramatic escape through woods and swamps takes up much of the book, while the more original material about African-American soldiers in the northern army is not highly developed. The sequel, *Out from This Place* (1988), follows the fortunes of Easter through the war and early years of Reconstruction and ends before she and Obi are reunited but with the hope that they may find each other. Both novels are strong in revealing the inconsistencies and unfairness of the Union Army and later the federal government policies toward escaped and freed slaves. Despite flaws in structure, they provide insight into aspects of the period not often fictionalized.

47   Hansen, Joyce, *Yellow Bird and Me*, Clarion, 1986 (hardcover), ISBN 0-89919-355-8, $12.95; (paper), ISBN 0-395-55388-1, $3.95, 155 pp. Ages 9–11, grades 4–6.

Realistic novel for middle-schoolers set in the Bronx in the modern period about an African-American girl who helps her dyslexic classmate to do his homework and eventually to become the lead in their school play. After her friend Amir moves to Syracuse, the narrator, Doris Williams, is frequently annoyed at the sixth-grade class cutup, Yellow Bird, and at first helps him only because Amir has asked her to do so. Gradually, she comes to see another side to Bird and, after he explains that words and figures seem to move on the page and sometimes looks backwards so that he has great difficulty in reading, she becomes his staunch defender. Although predictable, the story has warmth and many small details of sixth-grade and black family life that ring true.

48   Hartmann, Wendy, *All the Magic in the World*, illus. Niki Daly, Dutton, 1993 (hardcover), ISBN 0-525-45092-6, $12.99, unp. Ages 5–8, grades K–3.

Picture-story book of Lena, a little African-American girl who is awkward and feels left out until Joseph, the old odd-jobs man, shows her the magic in ordinary things. He teaches her to make cat's-cradle figures with string and to listen for the sea in a shell, and he makes her a chain necklace of pop-bottle caps, all things that are magic to her and turn her into a princess in her own esteem. The colorful illustrations capture her excitement and fascination as each new wonder is revealed to her.

49   Haskins, Francine, *Things I Like About Grandma*, illus. Francine Haskins, Children's Book, 1992 (hardcover), ISBN 0-89239-107-3, $13.95, unp. Ages 5–9, grades K–3.

Picture-story book of the close relationship between a young African-American girl and her grandmother, who "always hugs me good," is "always glad to see me," and "makes every day special!" The two sew together, make cookies, shop, and go to church. The narrator listens to the stories Grandma tells, the memories of her card-playing friends, the gossip at the hairdresser's. The deliberately childlike illustrations are bright and include many interesting details, but the faces of the characters may seem grotesque to some readers, with their exaggerated features and open, toothless mouths. An earlier picture-story book by Haskins, with similar illustrations, is *I Remember "121"* (1991), about the family home in Washington, D.C.

50 Havill, Juanita, *Jamaica Tag-Along*, illus. Anne Sibley O'Brien, Houghton, 1989 (hardcover), ISBN 0-395-49602-0, $12.95; 1990 (paper), ISBN 0-395-54949-3, $4.80, unp. Ages 4–8, grades PS–3.

Realistic picture-story book of a little, present-day girl depicted as African American in the illustrations. When her older brother, Ossie, refuses to let her join him and his friends in shooting baskets at the school playground, Jamaica builds a tower in the sandbox. At first she rejects the overtures of a toddler named Berto (perhaps Hispanic, to judge from the pictures), but when she hears his mother warn him away in almost the same words Ossie had used to her, she relents, and they make a giant castle happily together. This story of a younger child's coping with hurt feelings and of sharing is mildly didactic in dealing with a common childhood situation. The illustrations are realistic paintings and show a racial mix on the playground. An earlier book, *Jamaica's Find* (1986), seems similarly instructive in telling of Jamaica's discovery of a tattered stuffed dog on the playground, which she fails to turn in at the lost-and-found site until her conscience pricks.

51 Heath, Amy, *Sofie's Role*, illus. Sheila Hamanaka, Four Winds, 1992 (hardcover), ISBN 0-02-7443505-9, $14.95, unp. Ages 4–8, grades PS–3.

Realistic picture-story book set in an unspecified present-day urban area. Young Sofie (shown as an African-American girl in the pictures although the text does not indicate race) looks forward to making her "big debut" helping her parents at the family bakery the day before Christmas. Early in the morning she helps prepare the goods and stock the cases, but when customers flock in, no one pays attention to her efforts to wait on them. She finally finds her role in answering and preparing phone orders, and just before closing, the press of customers relaxed, she waits on a girl from school, her very first direct customer. The first-person narrative exudes youthful excitement and enthusiasm, made even more intense with occasional onomatopoetic words and mention of specific baked goods. The full-color paintings capture the elation of the season, the fellowship of the family and employees, the happiness of their beaming faces, the beautifully decorated Christmas goodies, and the exuberant customers. This is a pleasing and joyful book.

52 Higgensen, Vi, with Tonya Bolden, *Mama, I Want to Sing*, Scholastic, 1992 (hardcover), ISBN 5-590-44201-5, $13.95, 182 pp. Ages 9–14, grades 4–9.

Realistic girl's growing-up, career, and autobiographical novel set in Harlem from 1946 to 1952. At eleven, her voice already considered exceptional, African-American Doris Winter is invited to join the choir of Mt. Calvary Full Gospel Church. For fifteen months after her father, the church's minister, dies of a heart attack, however, she mourns and is unable to find joy in singing until Sister Carrie, a former blues singer and church stalwart, persuades her to perform at a church jubilee. Then, inspired by the words of her friend Toni's father to broaden her horizons and remembering her father's admonition to pursue her dream and keep faith, she continues to sing in church and, behind her disapproving mother's back, also learns "worldly music," aspiring to become a pop star. Late in high school, she forms a group with three of her friends, herself the lead singer. The Halos win their first audition and hit the big time. The story is told in a frame of Doris's returning to Mt. Calvary years later, an internationally known singer and songwriter with many albums to her credit. She pays tribute to her church for her success and sets up a school for musically gifted children in her mother's name. The book starts slowly and moves unevenly, Doris's development is more told than shown, dialogue is lame, and coincidence and predictability abound. Unfortunately, her sneaking around in the last half of the book reduces her likability, since her father, mother, and church are early established in a positive light. Best are the descriptions of singing at services and the sense of continuing support, concern, and high values of the African-American church, even though some members are presented as busybodies. If the book's intention is to emphasize perseverance and hard work toward a goal, that is achieved. Sister Carrie is an especially interesting character who serves the plot well. The book is based on the Broadway musicals of the same name in the early 1980s and 1990s. Some black stars make cameo appearances.

53 Hoffman, Mary, *Amazing Grace*, illus. Caroline Binch, Dial, 1991 (hardcover), ISBN 0-8037-1040-2, $14.00, unp. Ages 4–8, grades PS–3.

Realistic picture-story book set in an unspecified urban area about a persevering little African-American girl who discovers that she can achieve her goal if she tries hard enough. Grace, who loves to act out stories, is discouraged by classmates from trying out for the part of Peter Pan because she is black and a girl. But after Nana takes her to see Nana's friend Rosalie, a black ballerina, dance Juliet, Grace practices, gives the audition her all, gets the part, and performs stunningly. Strongly composed, full-color paintings are warmly representational, individualize the characters, contribute humor, and augment the predictable text with interesting details. The pictures in which Grace playacts various storybook characters, accompanied by her ubiquitous cat, steal the book, especially the one where she hangs from a bar as a bony Anansi the spider. Another warm, lighthearted if anticipatory and less strongly illustrated story of a common childhood predicament is *Nancy No-Size* (1987), for about the same age audience. Nancy is either too big or too little for whatever she wants to do until she is five and is just the "right age and size to go to school."

54 Hopkins, Lila, *Eating Crow*, Watts, 1988 (hardcover), ISBN 0-531-10499-0, $13.95, 143 pp. Ages 8–12, grades 3–7.

Realistic novel of school and neighborhood life set at the time of publication in a mixed racial, semirural area of the United States. To repay Crazy Ole Miss Sophie, the "root woman" most of the schoolchildren fear, for healing his golden retriever wounded by a bobcat, African-American class clown Croaker Douglas, about ten, makes a solemn pact with God to save "some other living creature." His chance to make good comes when his teacher, Mrs. Daniels, asks him to befriend a new boy, white Zeke Silverstein, mute since his parents were killed in a plane crash. Although the two get off on the wrong foot, when Zeke is robbed by some bullies and then his pet crow, Piccolo, is shot, Croaker comes to the rescue. The end is predictable—Zeke's mutism is cured and the bullies get their comeuppance—but Croaker seems real in his emotions and mischievousness, the dialogue is convincing, and the school scenes are believable. Particularly entertaining are the episodes involving the dog and the crow, and the book, though not ethnic specific textually, does have a slowly developing, convincing interracial friendship and offers plenty of action. Croaker's accident- and trouble-prone life continues in *Talking Turkey* (1989), where he enters seventh grade, soon incurs the wrath of Mrs. Daniels, now assistant principal, gets involved in a turkey project for science, is wrongfully accused of theft, and uncovers disturbing instances of child abuse in clearing himself. Like its predecessor, the book, though of no great moment, is fast moving, consistently entertaining, and upbeat.

55 Hopkinson, Deborah, *Sweet Clara and the Freedom Quilt*, illus. James Ransome, Knopf, 1993 (hardcover), ISBN 0-679-82311-5, $15.00, unp. Ages 5–11, grades K–6.

Picture-story book of historical fiction set on a Southern plantation in pre–Civil War days. Sweet Clara, twelve, a seamstress in the Big House, tells how she uses information picked up from her fellow slaves to fashion a quilt that serves as a map to the Ohio River and the Underground Railroad, then runs away for freedom. She leaves the quilt behind to guide other slaves north. The story, longer than most picture book narratives, is based on true events and can stand by itself. Typical of Ransome's work, the strongly executed, full-palette paintings give the characters individuality, portray events, and lend reality to this facet of history. The pictures of Sweet Clara show the underlying courage that motivates her.

56   Hort, Lenny, *How Many Stars in the Sky?*, illus. James E. Ransome, Tambourine, 1991 (hardcover), ISBN 0-688-10103-8, $13.95, unp. Ages 5–8, grades K–3.

Very simple picture-story book. Unable to sleep when Mamma is away, the narrator and his father go in his truck first to the city, where there are too many lights to count stars, then deep into the country where there are too many stars to count. The text makes no mention of ethnic origin, but the illustrations, fully covering the large pages, portray an African-American boy of about five or six, with his clean-cut father and Dalmation dog. Their home is in a middle-class neighborhood, the unnamed boy has a pleasant room and a yard with a picnic table and tree house, and the language is standard English. Although not much happens, the illustrations are handsome and the effort to show that minority characters can be just like anyone else is pleasantly handled.

57   Howard, Elizabeth Fitzgerald, *Mac & Marie and the Train Toss Surprise*, illus. Gail Gordon Carter, Four Winds, 1993 (hardcover), ISBN 0-02-744640-9, $14.95, unp. Ages 4–9, grades PS–4.

Realistic period picture-story book set at the turn of the century at the author's family's Big House near Patapsco, Maryland. The text, longer than average for a picture book, tells of an African-American brother, Mac, nine, and his younger sister, Marie (actual people), who receive a letter from their uncle, a railroad man. He says that, when he next goes by their house, he will toss a special gift for them from the train. They wait, with growing excitement, from early evening until dark, when their patience is rewarded with a delicate pink conch shell from Florida. The watercolor portraits of the family members are impressive, and the blue-toned night scenes evoke well the sense of early evening. The author's note gives background material. Although the same writer's *Aunt Flossie's Hats (and Crab Cakes Later)* (1991) captures the spirit of childhood and James Ransome's oils depict the characters with strength and personal identity, the text is stiff and seems less spontaneous than *Mac & Marie*. In it, young African-American Sarah and Susan visit their favorite aunt, who over tea and cookies tells them stories about her large array of hats, which they model, and then takes them for crab cakes. Two earlier picture-story books, both in period settings, are *Chita's Christmas Tree* (1989; illus. Floyd Cooper), a warm, happy account of holiday family life in which Papa and Chita pick out an evergreen that Santa brings on Christmas morning, and *The Train to Lulu's* (1988; illus. Robert Casilla), a joyful but often artificial-sounding, first-person account of how two young sisters travel by train from Boston to Baltimore in the 1930s to spend the summer with their great-aunt.

58 Hudson, Cheryl Willis, *Afro-Bets ABC Book*, illus. Cheryl Willis Hudson, Just Us Books, 1987 (paper), ISBN 0-940975-00-9, $3.95, unp. Ages 2–7, grades PS–3.

Alphabet book with black characters and some of the letters illustrated with African or African-American subjects (cornrows for C, Nefertiti for N). Each letter has three words printed out and illustrated (M has mask, monkey, and magician) as well as the letter printed in both upper and lower case and acted out by black children (M has a boy and a girl standing facing each other to form the uprights and holding hands to form the slanted lines). Illustrations are in bold colors with no background and while somewhat cartoonish are not grotesque. Compared with other alphabet books, this is not inspired but may serve a need to make African-American children feel included. A companion book is *Afro-Bets 123 Book* (1987), with numbers illustrated through ten. Each number is pictured with a phrase that rhymes (one yellow sun) or employs near rhyme (seven purple feathers), and with African-American children acting out the numerals, some of which require rather awkward poses.

59 Hudson, Cheryl Willis, *Good Morning, Baby*, illus. George Ford, Cartwheel, 1992 (hardcover), ISBN 0-590-45760-8, $5.95, unp. Ages 2–5, grades PS–K.

Board book for the very young, employing only fifty words and showing an African-American toddler in a very happy morning routine. The illustrations show different activities, but the facial expressions, unvarying wide smiles, detract from the realism of the pictures. Companion book is *Good Night, Baby* (1992).

60 Hudson, Wade, *Jamal's Busy Day*, illus. George Ford, Just Us, 1991 (hardcover), ISBN 0-940975-21-1, $12.95; (paper), ISBN 0-040975-24-6, $6.95, unp. Ages 4–7, grades PS–2.

Amusing and realistic picture-story book, narrated by a middle-class African-American boy. The story follows one day in the life of Jamal, seven or eight, from dressing and eating breakfast with his father and mother through school and back by bus and into bed at day's end. Jamal also reflects on what his daddy, an architect, and his mommy, an accountant, are doing at work. Jamal uses language that early readers can handle for the most part, occasionally (and amusingly) expressing himself in grown-up terms; for example, he does "research" in the library, helps his "supervisor" (teacher), and settles "disagreements between my co-workers" (stops arguments among class-mates). The clear, representational paintings show the family as close, happy African Americans, although the text is not racially specific, and present them, and people of other races, as uniformly good-looking and well-dressed.

61   Hughes, Dean, *End of the Race*, Atheneum, 1993 (hardcover), ISBN 0-689-31779-4, $13.95, 152 pp. Ages 10–15, grades 5–10.

Sports novel set one recent summer in Wasatch, Utah, a mountain city. When track Coach Heywood assigns African-American Davin Carter, son of a well-to-do businessman, and white Jared Olsen, son of a college professor, to run the 400-meter event, the two twelve-year-olds find common cause in their disappointment but decide to train together. Several matters threaten their budding friendship: Davin's sense that Jared does not "level" with him because he is black; the realization that the judges give Davin an edge over Jared because of his color; and what is gradually revealed as a long-standing animosity between their fathers, particularly the hostility of Mr. Carter toward Mr. Olsen, both of whom had been star high school athletes. Although training and races occupy a large portion of the narrative, this is mostly a story of interpersonal relationships, how two boys sensibly come to terms with racial stress and decide that tensions of the 1960s need not divide them in the 1990s. Although some episodes seem too pat and some conversations too deliberately contrived, Davin's bitterness at being set apart because he is the only black in town, at being goaded by his father to defeat Jared to sustain his father's pride, and at never knowing who his friends are and Jared's perplexity about handling his irascible friend seem genuine.

62   Hughes, Dean, *Nothing but Net*, illus. Dennis Lyall, Knopf, 1992 (hardcover), ISBN 0-679-93373-5, $6.99; (paper), ISBN 0-679-83373-0, $2.99, 108 pp. Ages 8–11, grades 3–6.

Realistic sports novel set in a desert town in southern California. African-American Miles Harris is clearly the most competent basketball player on the Angel Park Lakers coed team in the twelve-and-under league, but mean, snide Coach Donaldson rides him and refuses to let him play in his natural way, denigrating him as a "street player" and a show-off. Miles, who is sure that the coach's hostility is racially based, considers leaving the team, and when Mexican-American Kenny Sandoval describes to his father the team's situation, losing because the coach refuses to play Miles, Mr. Sandoval encourages Kenny to stand up to the coach on behalf of Miles and the team. Kenny does, the coach puts him in charge of practice, the team gathers around Kenny and Miles, who gives them pointers he has learned, and two games later the Lakers, who have a miserable record, win their first game. This story of the importance of standing up for what one believes takes place almost entirely on the court and is filled with rapid action, descriptions of plays, and jargon. The style is not elegant but neither is it stilted or patronizing, and those who like sports stories written by someone in the know or those sports enthusiasts who read reluctantly and need enticing will find this a very enjoyable book. The book, which includes a glossary and diagrams of plays, is one of the Angel Park Hoop Stars series.

63 Johnson, Angela, *The Leaving Morning*, illus. David Soman, Orchard, 1992 (hardcover), ISBN 0-531-05992-8, $14.95, unp. Ages 4–8, grades PS–3.

Picture story of a little African-American boy and his sister that tells of their move from their city apartment to "someplace we'd love." They watch the moving-van men, say goodbye to their friends and the people in their building, have long, affectionate farewells with their relatives, sit with their parents on the floor of the empty living room, and finally wave goodbye as they get into a car. The realistic watercolor paintings, which fill all the pages with the simple text superimposed, show an attractive black family in a slightly integrated neighborhood. Other books by the same author-illustrator team include *Tell Me a Story, Mama* (1989), *When I Am Old with You* (1990), and *One of Three* (1991). All present the world through the eyes of a young child, telling with quiet wit of life with two older sisters, talking to a grandfather, and describing her mother's childhood under the guise of listening to a bedtime story. Another picture-story book by Johnson for even younger children is *Do Like Kyla* (1990), illustrated with oil paintings by James E. Ransome, in which a preschool girl imitates her older sister throughout a day. Although all these books show African Americans in the illustrations, none of the warm, rhythmic texts is ethnic specific.

64 Johnson, Angela, *Toning the Sweep*, Orchard, 1993 (hardcover), ISBN 0-531-05476-4, $13.95, 103 pp. Ages 12 up, grades 7 up.

Realistic novel of an African-American girl going to the California desert to help her grandmother, who has inoperable cancer, pack and dispose of her belongings before coming to live with her family in Cleveland. Emily, fourteen, has visited her grandmother, Ola, every summer and loves the desert, the people in the isolated homes, and her special friend, David Two Starr, a sixteen-year-old orphan taken in by Ola's friend who always has a houseful of foster children. Through video-taping, ostensibly for Ola, the house, the countryside, and the many people who love her grandmother, Emily learns much she did not know about the adventurous, unconventional woman and about her grandfather, who was shot in 1964 in Alabama for being an "uppity nigger." She also learns about her own mother, Diane, who has never forgiven Ola for yanking her from her familiar Southern surroundings and fleeing to the desert before she had time to grieve for her father. After one of Ola's friends tells her about the South Carolina custom of "toning the sweep" when a relative dies, banging on a sweep, a kind of plow, to let everyone know and to "sing" the spirit to rest, Emily takes her grandfather's picture and a hammer and drives to an old water tower, the closest thing she can find to a sweep. Diane finds her there, and together they tone the sweep, performing the long overdue ceremony for the grandfather and also, the reader realizes, for the coming death of Ola. Although Emily's discovery of how her grandfather died is important, the unusual book makes very little of the ethnic background of the characters; except for David, who presumably is a Native American, the desert people are not identified by race. Emily's exploration of her roots is confined to her immediate family but is no less meaningful for its narrow focus. The work has good characterization and an interesting first-person voice.

65 Johnson, Charles, *Middle Passage*, Atheneum, 1990 (hardcover), ISBN 0-689-11968-2, $17.95, 209 pp. Ages 14 up, grades 9 up.

Historical novel of a slave ship set in 1830, written as a ship's log recording a journey from New Orleans to Bangalang on the African coast and most of the way back. Rutherford Calhoun, about twenty, a slave freed at his master's death in Illinois who has drifted south, stealing, gambling, and generally leading a disreputable life, stows away aboard the *Republic* to escape his debtors and the threat of marriage to a very proper free black girl, Isadora Bailey. As the cook's helper, he endures the fanaticism of the half-mad dwarf captain, Ebenezer Falcon, the terrible mistreatment of the Allmuseri tribesmen loaded as cargo, the planned mutiny of the crew which is preempted by a bloody uprising of the slaves, weeks of terrible weather and drifting in the decrepit ship beset by illness, and the final explosion of the *Republic* before he is picked up along with the cook and the three surviving Allmuseri, all children, and reunited with Isadora. The novel is extremely graphic about bodily functions and the filth, suffering, and degradation, including cannibalism, of the return voyage. The scoundrelly narrator and many of the other characters are well drawn, but the journal format is not convincing, partly because of the length and detail of the entries and partly because the language belongs to the late twentieth century, not to the period of the action, as it can be judged by nineteenth-century diaries and journals.

66 Johnson, Dolores, *The Best Bug to Be*, illus. Dolores Johnson, Macmillan, 1992 (hardcover), ISBN 0-02-747842-4, $13.95, unp. Ages 5–9, grades K–4.

Picture-story book of early school life. When parts are chosen for the school play, Kelly is disappointed to be a bumblebee especially when all her friends have more interesting roles like ladybugs, toads, and butterflies, but her parents persuade her to do the best she can, and at the performance her success as a bumblebee makes all the other kids want that part next year. The text is longer than many picture-story books, and each illustration takes up a page and a third. In a somewhat too-studied ethnic mix, Kelly and her parents are pictured as African Americans; other children as white, black, and Asian; and the teacher has a Hispanic name. The strongest element is the fidelity to a child's point of view, a characteristic of such earlier books written and illustrated by Johnson as *What Kind of Baby-Sitter Is This?* (1991), in which the new woman who comes to stay with Kevin turns out to be a middle-aged baseball fan, and *What Will Mommy Do When I'm at School?* (1990), in which a little girl's worry about starting school is concentrated in her concern for her mother's loneliness while she is gone.

67 Johnson, Dolores, *Now Let Me Fly: The Story of a Slave Family*, illus. Dolores Johnson, Macmillan, 1993 (hardcover), ISBN 0-02-747699-5, $14.95, unp. Ages 5–9, grades K–4.

Picture-story book telling the history of African-American slavery as exemplified by one family, from the capture of Minna as a child in Africa in 1815 to the escape to freedom of two of her four children. Minna marries Amadi, a boy she met on the slave ship, but he is sold away when their children are young. One son, Joshua, is sold to a distant plantation and becomes a blacksmith. Sally, who has taught herself to read, leaves with a group of escaping slaves for the North. Mason joins Seminole Indians in Florida, and when they are uprooted and sent to Oklahoma, he goes with them. Only Katie, a house slave, stays with her mother. Although the text is longer than that of many picture books, the necessary oversimplification and the idealized illustrations do an injustice to the terrible experience.

68 Johnson, Dolores, *Your Dad Was Just Like You*, illus. Dolores Johnson, Macmillan, 1993 (hardcover), ISBN 0-02-747838-6, $13.95, unp. Ages 5–8, grades K–3.

Picture-story book of Peter, who wants to live with his grandfather because he has broken a stupid purple thing on his father's dresser and made him angry, as usual. Grandfather tells him about his father as a child and about the origin of the purple jar, which he made as a trophy for his son when the race the boy hoped to win was called off because of rain. Although the grandfather's understanding is commendable, and Peter's repair of the trophy is meant to indicate a new relationship between him and his father, there is another, less comfortable possible interpretation—the lack of sympathy that Peter's father shows for Peter is the echo of the way the grandfather admits acting, a perpetuation of an unfortunate pattern, not as reassuring as the book is meant to be. Peter, his father, and his grandfather are shown in the illustrations as African American.

69 Johnson, Herschel, *A Visit to the Country*, illus. Romare Bearden, HarperCollins, 1989 (hardcover), ISBN 0-06-022849-0, $13.95, unp. Ages 4–8, grades PS–3.

Realistic, contemporary, picture-story book, in which the pictures portray the characters as African American, but the text does not specify race. On a visit to his grandparents' farm, Mike helps with chores, then plays by the creek where he finds a baby cardinal on the ground, cares for it with Grandma's help, and names it Max. When Max is grown and Mike realizes he should be with his own kind, he takes his pet to the creek and releases him. The story gives a warm picture of intergenerational relationships and farm life and deals nondidactically with the common childhood predicament of what to do with a wild pet. The conclusion is predictable, but the moral dilemma is led up to convincingly, and touches of humor relieve the underlying seriousness. The remarkably expressive paintings evoke the feel more than the sights of farm life in mainly loose, deep palette, distorted watercolors. The portrait of the cardinal is magnificent.

70 Jones, Rebecca C., *Matthew and Tilly*, illus. Beth Peck, Dutton, 1991 (hardcover), ISBN 0-525-44684-2, $13.95, unp. Ages 4–8, grades PS–3.

Realistic picture-story book of a friendship between a little white boy and a little African-American girl. Dual protagonists Matthew and Tilly enjoy playing together in their urban neighborhood—walking in the rain, riding bikes, selling lemonade, playing hopscotch, getting cones, coloring—until Matthew accidentally breaks Tilly's purple crayon. Angry words and name-calling result in a temporary rift in their relationship. They reconcile when both realize they are lonely, and Matthew says he is sorry. The pictures clearly portray them of two races, although the text never specifies. The impressionism of the smudgy, dark-toned paintings emphasizes the universality of the situation and gives a sense of the inner-city setting that seems to reflect ideas about the setting current in an earlier era, though the style of art itself is contemporary. Both children are shown as typical in dress and appearance (boy wearing a T-shirt, girl with little pigtails), and the "filled-in" pictures make the setting generic of middle-class, mixed-racial, urban neighborhoods. The mostly simple sentences and concrete diction make the book suitable as an easy-reading choice.

71 Ketteman, Helen, *Not Yet, Yvette*, illus. Irene Trivas, Whitman, 1992 (hardcover), ISBN 0-8075-5771-4, $11.95, unp. Ages 3–8, grades PS–3.

Yvette, a little African-American girl, helps her father prepare a birthday party for her mother in this simple but lively picture-story book. They clean the house, make a cake and ice it, buy gifts and wrap them, and decorate the dining room with balloons and streamers, with Yvette continually asking, "Is it time yet, Dad?" and her father patiently answering, "Not yet, Yvette." The bright illustrations, in gouache and pencil, depict an appealing but not idealized little girl in pigtails in a middle-class home and on rainy city streets.

72 Kincaid, Jamaica, *Lucy*, Farrar, 1990 (hardcover), ISBN 0-374-19434-3, $16.95, 164 pp.; Plume, 1991 (paper), ISBN 0-452-26677-7, $8.95, 176 pp. Ages 14 up, grades 9 up.

Realistic novel of a woman's self-discovery, sexual and social, set in New York City in the late 1960s. African-American Lucy Josephine Potter, nineteen, emigrates in January from the West Indies to work as an au pair for a wealthy family, including beautiful Mariah and Lewis, a lawyer, and their four daughters, whom she sees as "golden." She early makes comparisons between home and New York in such obvious matters as the climate, and also between this family and the one she left behind. By the following January, the couple have divorced, Lewis having fallen for Mariah's friend, Lucy and Mariah have become friends, and Lucy sees that while she is different from the mother she wanted to get away from she has also become her mother in many ways. Lucy moves into an apartment, in charge of her life as she wished to be, but she suspects her roommate, Peggy, may have appropriated her man-friend, and at story's end she is close to despair. While at first one can admire Lucy's spunk at leaving home, her own voice reveals that her separation from family is as much from adolescent rebelliousness and arrogance as it is from her sense that it is time to be on her own and thus she loses sympathy. Lucy's story is not only one of growing up and generational conflict (Lucy resents, for example, her mother's planning careers for her sons but not for her), but can also be read as a feminist commentary on women's lives and gender conflicts, between women as well as between women and men, both in the islands and in the United States. The prose has exquisite twists and turns of expression and is mostly serious with occasional touches of wry humor. Some scenes are sexually explicit. Among Kincaid's other novels are *Annie John* (1984) and *A Small Place* (1988), both set in the Caribbean.

73   Kroll, Virginia, *Masai and I*, illus. Nancy Carpenter, Four Winds, 1992 (hardcover), ISBN 0-02-751165-0, $13.95, unp. Ages 4–8, grades PS–3.

Realistic picture-story book told in the first person by the main character. After learning about the Masai of East Africa in school, contemporary African-American middle-class schoolgirl Linda imagines herself in Masai situations comparable to those in her own life, like living accommodations, meals, owning pets, and playing outside. The strongly executed full-page oils make the contrasting situations very clear and show Linda and her Masai self as lively and attractive figures. More obviously didactic is the same author's *Africa Brothers and Sisters* (illus. Vanessa French, 1993), another realistic picture-story book in which a father and son play a question-and-answer game about African tribes.

74   Lexau, Joan M., *Don't Be My Valentine*, illus. Syd Hoff, Harper, 1985 (hardcover), ISBN 0-06-023872-0, $8.95; (paper) ISBN 0-06-444115-6, $3.50, 64 pp. Ages 5–8, grades K–3.

Picture-story book in early reader form, set in an integrated classroom and featuring two African-American children, Sam and Amy Lou, who always wants to correct and boss Sam. When they make valentines, Sam draws a monkey on his and rhymes, "Violets are blue," with "How did you ever get out of the zoo?," intending to send it to Amy Lou and adding, "DON'T BE MY VALENTINE." Through a series of mix-ups, their teacher gets the rude card, Sam blames his friend Albert, and eventually, when Amy Lou confesses to finding and sending it, they make peace. At the end, the pattern of antagonism seems about to repeat itself. The humor and cartoonlike illustrations should attract young readers, but it is possible that some adults may consider the know-it-all black female a negative stereotype.

75   Lillie, Patricia, *When This Box Is Full*, illus. Donald Crews, Greenwillow, 1993 (hardcover), ISBN 0-688-12016-4, $14.00, unp. Ages 3–7, grades PS–2.

Realistic picture-story book about the months and sharing intended for the youngest listeners and viewers. The brief text has seventy-six words, including the twelve for the months. Each month a little African-American boy puts in a box some article typical of that time of year, like a red leaf or toasted pumpkin seeds. On the last page, he confusingly says that he will share "it with you," the "you" perhaps meaning the viewer or perhaps the little African-American girl on the book's cover. The word "it" is also confusing, since "them," referring to the articles, would be more appropriate at that point in the book. Although the text has little significance, the illustrations are attractive doublespreads, bold, colorful, strong depictions of the objects, but the human figures have a smudgy, disconcerting indistinctness.

76 Lotz, Karen E., *Can't Sit Still*, illus. Colleen Browning, Dutton, 1993 (hardcover), ISBN 0-525-45066-1, $13.99, unp. Ages 4–9, grades PS–4.

Realistic picture-story book with an expressive, poetic text, in which a young African-American city girl of seven-to-ten years of age engages in activities that follow the seasons. In the autumn, she plays in the leaves and savors the spicy winds. Winter finds her dancing in the snow and snuggling into grandma's patchwork. In the spring she sketches in the park and enjoys the baby kittens, and in the summer she pirouettes through the hydrant water and skips sidewalk cracks. She also does tasks her mother suggests in little conversation inserts. While the text (which never specifies race) wavers between poetry and prose, the watercolor pictures score very high. They depict events, establish mood, and show the girl winningly in her everyday homeliness, a pony-tailed, lively, life-loving child. Except for the spring greens, which are too blue to suit the time of year, the clear, vivid colors, scenes within scenes, and bleeding pictures catch her exuberance perfectly. Of the four introductory, two-page spreads that establish each season, particularly effective are those of autumn, done in rusty reds, and of winter, executed with hundreds of little splotches in shades of cool blues that create the figure of the girl playing in a heavy snowstorm.

77 Lyons, Mary E., *Letters from a Slave Girl: The Story of Harriet Jacobs*, Scribner's, 1992 (hardcover), ISBN 0-684-19446-5, $13.95, 146 pp. Ages 12 up, grades 7 up.

Biographical novel based on the published narratives of a slave's life from the age of eleven in 1825 until she escapes from Edenton, North Carolina, to the North seventeen years later. In the form of letters mostly to her dead parents and other relatives, written to comfort herself and not meant to be sent, Harriet Ann recounts the cruelties of slavery, the closeness of her African-American family, and her struggle to free herself and her children from bondage. Especially poignant are her fears of the sexual advances of her owner, Dr. Norcom, her turning for protection to another white man, Samuel Sawyer, by whom she has two children, and her hiding for an almost unbelievable seven years in a cupboard under the roof of her Gran's little house before she is able to make her way to freedom. Included are a brief summary of her life for the next fifty-five years, photographs of some of the people and places in her narrative, drawings, maps, family trees, and a bibliography. Although her slavery is not as physically abusive as some and she has certain advantages—her mistress has taught her to read and her black family has mostly stayed together—the weight of her bondage is oppressive, and she is constantly worried about her children, whose father keeps recanting on his promise to free them.

78 Martin, Ann, *Rachel Parker, Kindergarten Show-Off*, illus. Nancy Poydar, Holiday, 1992 (hardcover), ISBN 0-8234-0935-X, $15.95, unp. Ages 4–8, grades PS–3.

Realistic picture-story book of school and family life. African-American Olivia, a five-year-old, is delighted when white Rachel Parker, also five, moves in next door but soon loses her enthusiasm for her new friend when she realizes that Rachel is an overachiever like herself. The various acts of one-upsmanship the two engage in result in an argument. The rift between them lasts until their teacher, Mrs. Bee, comes up with a clever and practical idea for reconciling them. The classroom scenes and the behavior of these two strong-minded girls seem typical. Supporting this story of friendship lost and regained are full-color illustrations that depict situations at home and in school, reveal character, establish emotion, and add to the gentle humor. They show the school as a mixed-ethnic one.

79 McKissack, Patricia C., *The Dark Thirty: Southern Tales of the Supernatural*, illus. Brian Pinkney, Knopf, 1992 (hardcover), ISBN 0-679-81863-4, $15.00, 128 pp. Ages 10–15, grades 5–10.

Ten original stories, all based on beliefs, motifs, or themes from African-American oral tradition. Each is preceded by a brief introduction telling something of the setting, the occasion, or the type of tale. One, "We Organized," is based on an actual slave narrative and is set in verse. Others include such elements as a lynching by the Ku Klux Klan, its perpetrator brought to justice by the ghost of his victim; second sight, which saves the family of its possessor; a conjure woman, whose unwelcome answer to a girl's request for a brother teaches her to appreciate the baby soon to be born; and Sasquatch or Big Foot, who saves an injured child. Few of the tales are particularly spine-chilling, and a couple fall flat, but the large-format book is beautiful and enough variety is provided to suit different tastes.

80   McKissack, Patricia C., *Flossie and the Fox*, illus. Rachel Isadora, Dial, 1986 (hardcover), ISBN 0-8037-0250-7, $14.00, unp. Ages 3–8, grades PS–3.

Picture-story book fantasy of an African-American girl's adventures with talking animals, retold from a story the author's grandfather told and making use of some of the richly colorful, colloquial speech the author recalls he used. Flossie Finley, maybe five, of rural Tennessee, encounters a sly fox while taking eggs to Miz Viola at the McCutchin Place. Unlike Red Riding Hood, whose story this one recalls, Flossie outfoxes the tricky old redcoat by pretending not to recognize that he is a fox, frustrating him to distraction and making him vulnerable to McCutchin's hound. The strongly composed, richly textured, framed watercolors are especially good at showing the nature of the different animals Flossie meets, as well as her own, and the final picture, of Flossie grinning in victory, basket of eggs intact under her arm, is a perfect way to end the book. An author's note appears at the beginning. On the other hand, *Nettie Jo's Friends* (1989), a lively, near tall tale in which three anthropomorphized animals, natural enemies, help a little girl get the needle she needs to sew her doll's dress, falls short because of the illustrations. The smudgy, indistinct, orangey paintings by Scott Cook distract, but the story is high in humor and action, and Nettie Jo is a likable protagonist.

81   McKissack, Patricia C., *A Million Fish . . . More or Less*, illus. Dena Schutzer, Knopf, 1992 (hardcover), ISBN 0-679-80692-X, $14.00, unp. Ages 4–10, grades PS–5.

Spirited tall tale, picture-story book told with some dialect and set probably in Louisiana. When early one morning young African-American Hugh Thomas is fishing in Bayou Clapateaux, Papa-Daddy and Elder Abbajon row "out of the gauzy river fog," swap outrageous bayou tales, and inform Hugh Thomas that the bayou "is a mighty peculiar place." Hugh Thomas's skepticism wanes when he catches a million fish, but on the way home he loses almost all of them to alligators, raccoons, birds, and Chantilly, the neighborhood cat. With only three left, he boasts to Papa-Daddy and Elder Abbajon of his marvelous catch, and when he is pressed about whether or not it was really a million, Hugh Thomas replies with a wink, "More or less." The heavy palette pictures overflow the pages and look as though the colors were applied with a knife. They depict scenes and perfectly catch the humor, especially those of the mounds of multicolored fish, the various wily animals, and the two old men lolling in their boat.

82 McKissack, Patricia C., *Mirandy and Brother Wind*, illus. Jerry Pinkney, Knopf, 1988 (hardcover), ISBN 0-394-88765-4, $14.00, unp. Ages 4–10, grades PS–5.

Picture-story fantasy set in a rural area of the American South, perhaps at the turn of the century. Determined to win the cake at her very first cakewalk dance, Mirandy tricks Brother Wind into her father's barn where she shuts him in, the price of his release being that he give her partner, ungainly Ezel, the grace and nimbleness they need to win the cakewalk. The detailed watercolors enhance the lightheartedness of the story, perfectly catch Mirandy's determination, and enlarge on the setting, showing such aspects as helpful neighbors and rural areas. Brother Wind is early introduced as a high-stepping strutter, a well-built, well-dressed gentleman whose misty-blue tones stand out among the other impressionistic, multicolored hues. The climax picture is appealingly apt, showing Ezel as a younger counterpart of Brother Wind, proud, agile, graceful, the winner Mirandy has been determined to make him. The illustrations depict the characters as light-skinned blacks. An author's note explains the cakewalk.

83 McKissack, Patricia, and Fredrick McKissack, *Constance Stumbles*, illus. Tom Dunnington, Children's, 1988 (hardcover), ISBN 0-516-02086-2, $11.95; (paper), ISBN 0-516-42086-0, $2.95, 32 pp. Ages 3–7, grades PS–2.

Realistic, limited-vocabulary, picture-story book, A Rookie Reader, intended for those just mastering printed language. An accident-prone, pigtailed, little African-American girl is repeatedly cautioned by a friendly owl to "Watch out" or "Take your time," among other admonitions, to no avail. She has such misadventures as falling over the dog and taking a terrific tumble when she skateboards downhill. But she heeds advice about learning to ride a bicycle and succeeds. The repetitive text serves its purpose, and the comic, full-color illustrations extend the story greatly, adding characters and showing situations and emotion. They are obviously and amusingly overdramatic for effect. The thirty-three words are listed at the end. Similarly told in thirty-three words is *Bugs!* (1988; illus. Clovis Martin), also A Rookie Reader, in which the repetitive text introduces the numbers from one to five with one red bug, two yellow ones, and so on, using individual words and phrases, but no sentences. Two children, a pigtailed African-American girl and a red-haired white boy, walk through fields and by a lily pond and climb fences, observing insects of various kinds. The story is more serious than *Constance Stumbles* and serves its purpose but is uninspired. The full-color illustrations are also overly dramatic and have an air like that in most readers. There is a word list at the end.

84 McMillan, Terry, ed., *Breaking Ice: An Anthology of Contemporary African-American Fiction*, Viking, 1990 (hardcover), ISBN 0-670-82562-X, $27.50, 690 pp.; Viking Penguin, 1990 (paper), ISBN 0-14-011697-4, $13.00, 400 pp. Ages 15 up, grades 10 up.

Fifty-seven selections by as many different African-American writers, some well established, like Ishmael Reed, Alice Walker, and Rita Dove; others less well known, like Cliff Thompson and Colleen McElroy. Some are short stories, like "Hoodoo" by Connie Porter, about an albino girl under a spell from her black grandmother that renders her colorless, and "Sarah" by Tina McElroy Ansa, in which two little girls precipitate a rift between families when they explore their bodies. Others are passages from such novels as *Mama Day* (no. 105) by Gloria Naylor and *Seduction by Light* (no. 177) by Al Young. McMillan intends to show the concerns of present-day black writers:

> Most of the literature by African-Americans appearing from the thirties through the early sixties appeared to be aimed at white audiences. We were telling them who we were and what they'd done wrong. . . . We do not feel the need to create and justify our existence anymore [sic] . . . to prove anything to white folks. If anything, we're trying to make sense of ourselves to ourselves. . . . Our backgrounds as African-Americans are not all the same. Neither are our perceptions, values, and morals. The following stories are not filled with anger [but are] warmhearted . . . zingy . . . break your heart, or cause you to laugh out loud.

This is a hefty book, meaty, often sexually explicit and earthy, demanding for the most part, addressing mature matters, including such items that are on the general consciousness as homosexuality, infidelity, abortion, lawbreaking, and abuse, in addition to traditional values. McMillan has also published novels of love and family life, for example, *Waiting to Exhale* (1992) and *Mama* (1987), which are sexually very explicit and salacious in dialogue.

85 Mendez, Phil, *The Black Snowman*, illus. Carole Byard, Scholastic, 1989 (hardcover), ISBN 0-590-40552-7, $13.95; 1991 (paper), ISBN 0-590-44873-0, $4.95, unp. Ages 4–10, grades PS–5.

Picture-story fantasy promoting African-American pride in heritage, self-worth, and personal initiative. Young Jacob, resentful of his color and the poverty he associates with it, at the suggestion of his little brother, Peewee, reluctantly helps to build a snowman in their urban complex yard using the slushy, sooty snow. When they wrap the blackish snowman in the colorful cloth Peewee finds in the trash, which happens to be a magical African *kente* (shawl), the snowman comes alive, discusses the beauty of blackness, conjures up visions from Africa's mighty past, and at the cost of his own life, enables Jacob to save Peewee from a burning building and thus to feel better about himself and acquire hope for the future. The story is patently didactic, predictable, and not always convincing, especially in dialogue. Best are the marvelously expressive full-color paintings. Mostly dark and often brooding, they have an appropriately majestic quality. The story is longer than that of most picture books.

86 Meyer, Carolyn, *Denny's Tapes*, McElderry, 1987 (hardcover), ISBN 0-689-50413-6, $14.95, 209 pp. Ages 14 up, grades 9 up.

A coming-of-age novel, told first-person as if into a tape recorder by Denny Brown, seventeen, who has been brought up by his white mother after his African-American father, a jazz musician, wandered off when Denny was a young child. He is driving across the country from Vicksburg, Pennsylvania, to San Francisco seeking his father and knowledge of his roots, having been kicked out by his stepfather, a white doctor named Grant West, who was infuriated to discover him embracing Stephanie, West's daughter by a former marriage. In the course of his odyssey, Denny visits Chicago, where his black grandmother, Eugenia Brown, considers herself and her family socially superior to his mother, and Roxanne, age twenty-four, a cousin by marriage, seduces and makes frequent love to him, and Nebraska, where his white grandmother, Grace Sunderland, is slowly dying under the scornful care of his uncle's bigoted, small-minded wife. Although he does not find his father, he finds himself, deciding that he will never fit fully into either side of his family and may never get back with Stephanie, whom he truly loves, but that his destiny is in music as his father's has been. With considerable humor, the book explores the pretensions and misconceptions of both blacks and whites. Denny, a very bright underachiever, is an attractive protagonist, and his irreverent voice does not get tiresome. The upper middle-class black community in Chicago is of particular interest.

87 Meyer, Carolyn, *White Lilacs*, Harcourt, 1993 (hardcover), ISBN 0-15-200641-9, $10.95, 242 pp.; (paper), ISBN 0-15-295876-2, $3.95, 242 pp. Ages 10–14, grades 5–9.

Historical novel set in 1921 in the fictional town of Dillon, Texas, about the removal of the African-American community of Freedomtown from the center of the city to make way for a park, based on an actual evacuation of the residents of Quakertown in Denton, Texas. At first, the family of Rose Lee Jefferson and her neighbors mostly have some hope that the removal project can be sidetracked, but the overwhelming white vote, backed by a Ku Klux Klan march, soon discourages most of them, and they sell out, at half the value of their property, and leave town or move to the undesirable tract designated by the city. The only opposition comes from Miss Emily Firth, a young art teacher at the exclusive school for young ladies, who loses her job as a result, and from Rose Lee's brother Henry, a World War I veteran and admirer of Marcus Garvey, who urges resistance or a move to Liberia and is tarred and feathered and partially crippled by masked young white men. Before she leaves, Miss Firth gives Rose Lee a sketchbook and urges her to draw Freedomtown, house by house, before it is destroyed. When Henry, now working as a gardener for the wealthy Bells, refuses to wash the car for the son of the family, Rose Lee discovers plans to flog and perhaps lynch him, and she enlists Catherine Jane Bell, fifteen, the spoiled and headstrong but decently motivated daughter who used to be her playmate, to drive Henry secretly to a farm of relatives, from which he can get a train north. Rose Lee gives him her book of Freedomtown sketches to remember them by. Although the plight of the Freedomtown community is hopeless, the rescue of Henry and Rose Lee's determination to make something of herself save the book from being totally depressing. A number of good characters are drawn: patient, loving Grandfather Williams; Aunt Susannah Jones, a smartly dressed teacher from Saint Louis; impractical, fiery Henry; and Catherine Jane, who saves Henry mostly for the lark of it but understands, a little, what the loss of Freedomtown means to its people. Rose Lee's voice as first-person narrator is convincing, and her attitudes are those of the 1920s, not the 1990s.

88 Miles, Betty, *Sink or Swim*, Knopf, 1986 (hardcover), ISBN 0-394-85515-9, $13.95, 200 pp. Ages 9–11, grades 4–6.

Realistic novel of family and community life. With the Fresh Air Project, B. J. Johnson, eleven, an African-American boy from New York City, spends two weeks with a small-town white family in New Hampshire. Despite a good deal of culture shock, the visit is wonderful; his only real problem is that he has said he can swim, but actually he has never been in a pool or lake. He learns to help with the rabbit, chickens, and the garden; adores the old dog; rides bikes; plays in the tree house; attends church; picks raspberries and wins third place for his jam at the fair; goes backpacking; and, best of all, learns to swim. By the time he must return to the city he is devoted to Jimmy Roberts, the son his age, Linda, five, and the parents, Jackie and Norm. Although a few are condescendingly overfriendly, all the local people are delighted to have him. The total picture, which is perhaps unrealistically idyllic, is saved partly by B. J.'s convincing voice and his firm sense of self-esteem. An un-demanding venture in interracial understanding.

89   Miner, Jane Claypool, *Corey*, Scholastic, 1986 (paper), ISBN 0-590-40395-8, $2.50, 170 pp. Ages 10–15, grades 5–10.

Historical romance and girl's growing-up novel set in the last months of the American Civil War telling about an African-American slave girl's flight to freedom. When Yankee soldiers burn her mistress's South Carolina plantation, Corey, fifteen, runs away with her sweetheart, Ned. Parted from him during a short battle, with luck, resource, and courage she reaches Philadelphia, where she finds safety and hospitality with Friends, in whose school she teaches the youngest pupils. Complicating her story are her desire to find her mother, who had been sold off the plantation, to decide the direction of her life, and to make up her mind about whether to marry Ned, now a Yankee soldier about to go West to fight Indians, a vocation she finds revolting, or to continue her friendship, and possible romance, with Penn Wilson, an edu-cated, well-off descendant of black freedmen, who at first has little knowledge of or emotional attachment to the newly liberated blacks with whom she iden-tifies. Corey's journey is accomplished with relatively few problems; characters are obviously illustrative; her marriage to Penn is predictable; and Corey seems often to express values more typical of the late twentieth century than of her times, especially for blacks. The book's tone is intimately engaging; events move briskly; and, best of all, there is a strong sense of servitude for even favored blacks, like Corey; of the ironic disruption in their lives brought about by the war; and of the various attitudes of the slaves toward their own-ers, the Yankees, the war, and each other. There is a cameo appearance by Abraham Lincoln. This book is one of a series for girls by Sunfire about "fas-cinating young women who lived and loved during America's most turbulent times."

90   Mitchell, Margaree King, *Uncle Jed's Barber Shop*, illus. James Ransome, Simon & Schuster, 1993 (hardcover), ISBN 0-671-76969-3, $15.00, unp. Ages 4–10, grades PS–5.

Period picture-story book set among African Americans in the rural South in the late 1920s, a portrait of a much-loved, respected man. Little Sarah Jean describes how Uncle Jed, an itinerant barber, travels on horseback to ply his trade among the farmers and sharecroppers, a jovial, happy man with a dream of some day having his own shop. When Sarah Jean falls ill of an unexplained problem and needs an operation, he gives the family $300, delaying his dream, and when the banks fail he loses the more than $3,000 he has left. Indomitable, he continues to work and save and opens his own shop years later, at age seventy-nine, when Sarah Jean joyfully sits in his chair, a grown woman, and his neighbors and friends gather to celebrate his achievement. Ransome's typically realistic oils make the book. They bring the people and especially big, burly, beneficient Uncle Jed alive and depict interiors and landscapes with convincing details that flesh out the story. Unfortunately, the narrative lapses into didacticism with an intrusive passage explaining segregation. Ransome's picture of the hospital waiting room with a "colored only/white only" sign is much more effective at making the point.

91 Moore, Emily, *Whose Side Are You On?*, Giroux, 1988 (hardcover), ISBN 0-374-38409-6, $14.00, 134 pp. Ages 9–11, grades 4–6.

Novel of a developing friendship between two African-American sixth graders, Barbara Conway, eleven, and T. J. Brodie, twelve, both of whom live in a Harlem coop. When Barbara gets an "unsatisfactory" in math, T. J., the boy she thinks of as nothing but a pest, is chosen to tutor her. As they work together, she learns more about him—how his stage-singer mother keeps promising to send for him and how he lives with and cares for his aging grandfather—and she begins to like him until, when he disappears, she is determined to find him and get him to come back. Intertwined are subplots about the painfully excluding cliques among the girls and Barbara's discouragement when she is compared to her brilliant twin brother. The first-person narrative voice is convincing, and the story is believable, but despite the stated setting, there is little to distinguish this from any novel of middle-class preteen girls in any American city or town.

92 Moore, Yvette, *Freedom Songs*, Orchard, 1991 (hardcover), ISBN 0-531-05812-4, $14.95, 168 pp.; Puffin, 1992 (paper), ISBN 0-14-036017-4, $3.99, 176 pp. Ages 12 up, grades 7 up.

Historical novel set among African Americans in Brooklyn, New York, and rural North Carolina from April to June of 1963. Pretty, bright, fourteen-year-old Sheryl Williams loves and admires her mother's brother, the often abstracted Peter James, a nineteen-year-old college student. When on an Easter weekend visit to her grandmother's in North Carolina, she discovers Peter has become a freedom worker, she fears for him but also is outraged at the way blacks are treated in the rural area where he and her mother grew up. Back again in Brooklyn, she learns of violence against the freedom workers and organizes a concert at her church among the young people of the neighborhood to raise money for the civil rights cause. Just before the performance, she learns that Uncle Peter has died from wounds received when a Freedom

School he helped organize is bombed. The book offers a good picture of life among middle-class, Northern African Americans and of life among rural blacks, the former comfortable and safe in comparison, and also voices different attitudes toward the movement, such as Martin Luther King's and Ghandi's nonviolence as opposed to the militancy of Malcolm X. Characters are types but play their roles well, and Sheryl's feelings about what is happening are all the more telling because she is an average, well-brought-up early teen with the age's usual concerns about boys, clothes, and the like, and her people also ask only the normal necessities from life. Though some episodes seem conventional because overused, if valid, like the one where the storeowner snubs blacks to wait on whites, others rely on less used vistas about the times, like the lunch counter sit-in and the voter registration scenes. The book presents an interesting contrast to Ossie Davis's *Just Like Martin* (no. 23).

93 Morrison, Toni, *Beloved*, Knopf, 1987 (hardcover), ISBN 0-394-53597-9, $24.95, 288 pp.; Plume, 1988 (paper), ISBN 0-452-26136-8, $9.95, 275 pp. Ages 15 up, grades 10 up.

Historical novel by a Nobel Prize–winning writer of postslavery days beginning in 1873 mostly just outside Cincinnati, Ohio, and in flashbacks on a slave farm in Kentucky. For eighteen years, Sethe has been living an isolated, hardscrabble existence in a big old house in rural Ohio alone with her daughter, Denver, whom she bore when she fled to freedom. Out of her past comes Paul D, an ex-slave like herself from Sweet Home, and like herself a survivor of almost unimaginable horrors while enslaved and during the war. His arrival and that of a strange, brooding young woman who calls herself Beloved provide the catalyst for memories and events both terrible and noble that plummet Denver into adulthood, bring Sethe to the brink of insanity, and give Paul D a new reason for living. A substantial and engrossing plot with touches of fantasy, fully fleshed characters, and an inventive, individual style make this Pulitzer Prize winner a uniquely haunting novel about the triumph of the human spirit over adversity. The book contains sexually explicit scenes. Less cohesive and suspenseful is *Jazz* (1992), which tells of an ill-fated love affair and is set in the City (New York?) in 1926 among working-class blacks, many of whom have migrated from the South only to find violence and lack of respect in the North, too, some of it from their own people. Ragtime and jazz rhythms distinguish the style.

94 Moss, Marissa, *Regina's Big Mistake*, illus. Marissa Moss, Houghton, 1990 (hardcover), ISBN 0-395-55330-X, $13.45, unp. Ages 5–8, grades K–3.

Questions of artistic inspiration and originality form the central problem of a very simple picture-story book with a little African-American girl protagonist.

Provided with paper and crayons and directed to draw a jungle or a rain forest, most of the children in Mrs. Li's class start confidently, but Regina is afraid of making mistakes and even crumples up her first effort. Told by her teacher not to waste paper and to draw around her mistakes, Regina improvises until she has a page full of jungle things, even converting her wobbly sun into a moon and coloring the background purple-black for a night sky. In an integrated classroom, Regina wears blue jeans and has her hair in cornrows ending in eight braids. The children's drawings are suitably childlike.

95 Moss, Thylias, *I Want to Be*, illus. Jerry Pinkney, Dial, 1993 (hardcover), ISBN 0-8037-1287-3, $14.99, unp. Ages 5–8, grades K–3.

Picture-story book narrated by an African-American girl, shown as perhaps eight to ten, in answer to the question, "What do you want to be?" She thinks about it as she runs, plays, and dreams, coming up with many ideas in extravagant prose: "I want to be beautiful but not so beautiful that a train moving in the sun like a metal peacock's glowing feather on tracks that are like stilts a thousand miles long laid down like a ladder up a flat mountain (wow!) seems dull," and "I also want to be sound, a whole orchestra with two bassoons and an army of cellos. Sometimes I want to be just the triangle, a tinkle that sounds like an itch." After a number of other ideas, she concludes, "I want to be life doing, doing everything. That's all." The illustrations, done in pencil, colored pencil, and watercolor, are highly realistic and picture the same girl, close up, on every page, sometimes with other children or grown-ups. A self-consciously poetic book, it may appeal more to adults than to an early childhood audience.

96 Mowry, Jess, *Way Past Cool*, Farrar, 1992 (hardcover), ISBN 0-374-28669-3, $17.00, 310 pp.; HarperCollins (paper), ISBN 0-06-097545-8, 320 pp. Ages 12 up, grades 7 up.

Gritty, inner-city novel set in Oakland, California, focusing on two minor street gangs of twelve- and thirteen-year olds, with a few younger hangers-on, whose lives revolve around their skateboards, guns, beer, and cigarettes, in about that order of importance. The Friends, led by Gordon but masterminded by Lyon, who started life when his prostitute mother abandoned him in a dumpster and later retrieved him, are caught in a feud with the Crew, a similar gang of half a dozen kids with adjoining territory. The conflict is stimulated by Deek, a drug-dealer of sixteen, who plans that the two gangs will either wipe each other out, leaving the area free for his young street salesmen, or will be forced to work for him themselves. The situation is complicated by decent, naive Ty, Deek's bodyguard, whose younger brother, Danny, is a schoolmate of both gangs. Full of violence and language both raw and scatological, the story has shock value and force, with its drive-by shootings, the menace of Deek's cruising black Trans-Am, corrupt police, knife wounds, and drunken twelve-year-olds, and much of the dialogue and the scenes of trash-filled alleys and hallways smelling of urine have power. Also the fierce loyalty these street-wise kids feel for each other and their insistence on "the rules" in gang dealings ring true. Less convincing are the conversations between the young kids and between Ty and Danny about love and the meaning of life for African-American city kids. There is some explicit sex. Mowry also published a book of short stories, *Rats in the Trees* (1990), and a second novel, *Six Out Seven* (1993), also set mostly in Oakland.

97   Myers, Walter Dean, *Crystal*, Viking Penguin, 1987 (hardcover), ISBN 0-670-80426-6, $14.95; Dell (paper), ISBN 0-440-20538-7, $3.95, 198 pp. Ages 10–14, grades 5–9.

Career novel of Crystal Brown, a beautiful sixteen-year-old African-American girl who seems destined to be one of the top young models in New York, rescuing her family and her future from relative poverty and substituting for her mother's disappointed hopes of being a singer. At first happy and excited at the attention she receives, she gradually comes to hate the pressure of overwork and the need to ward off the sexual demands of the sleazy photographers and promoters. When a friend, a slightly older model, commits suicide, Crystal gives up a movie contract and her modeling career to return to high school and her ordinary life in Brooklyn. Details of the hard work of a model and the psychology of a well-brought-up girl out of her depth in a cutthroat business are good; descriptions of Crystal as looking "not really black, more oriental" are perhaps questionable.

98   Myers, Walter Dean, *Fallen Angels*, Scholastic, 1988 (hardcover), ISBN 0-590-40942-5, $13.95, 336 pp. Ages 12 up, grades 7 up.

Historical novel of the Vietnam War, following the fortunes of the narrator, African-American Richard Perry, seventeen, from Harlem. Having enlisted with no real conviction, he is thrown into a war he does not understand, where it is impossible to distinguish friend from enemy, and where allegiance, in the tradition of battlefield stories, is mainly to the men of his immediate squad. The mental strain, discomfort, misery, boredom, and horrors of war are depicted graphically, as well as the racial prejudice against both black soldiers and Vietnamese by some of the army personnel. Serious passages are lightened by humorous dialogue, usually sharp and convincing, and the overall tone is ironic. This is a moving, if somewhat conventional, war novel.

99 Myers, Walter Dean, *The Mouse Rap*, Harper, 1990 (hardcover), ISBN 0-06-024343-0, $16.89, 186 pp. Ages 12–15, grades 7–10.

Amusing novel of Mouse Douglas, a fourteen-year-old Harlem boy, and his friends, Styx, Omega, Sheri, and Beverly, as they rap and jive through the last weeks of school and the summer, becoming involved in a number of basketball games, a dance competition, and a hunt for the treasure hidden by Tiger Moran, a long-dead gangster. An additional element, the return of Mouse's father and his attempt to reinvolve himself in the lives of his wife and son, is introduced but never fully developed. Although the plot does not hold together convincingly, the language of the story, narrated by Mouse, is memorable smart-talk by a clever kid; each chapter also is introduced by a rhyming rap. Despite the 1990s setting in time, life in Harlem has an almost Norman Rockwell innocence, with sex limited to one steamy kiss, violence to a threatened playground fight averted by Bev's Kung Fu demonstration, and family life generally supportive, with "the moms person" understanding and families of the other teenagers helpful and interested.

100 Myers, Walter Dean, *The Righteous Revenge of Artemis Bonner*, HarperCollins, 1992 (hardcover), ISBN 0-06-020844-9, $18.89, 140 pp. Ages 10–14, grades 5–9.

Tall tale novel which romps through the Wild West of 1880. Pure farce, it uses the overblown language of the dime novel as Artemis Bonner, fifteen, relates how he trails his uncle's murderer, Catfish Grimes, and Catfish's companion, Lucy Featherdip, from Tombstone, Arizona, to California, Mexico, and Alaska, and various points in between, trying to bring the scalawag to justice and find the treasure in gold nuggets hidden by his uncle. Artemis is joined by Frolic Brown, a twelve-year-old whose mother was a Cherokee; together they suffer unbelievable hardships, many of them brought on by their naivete and misplaced sense of honor. Although Artemis, Catfish, and Lucy are all African-Americans and they find a generous population of others wherever they travel, there is nothing in their adventures specific to the black experience. Since the happenings are highly implausible, and meant to be, the novel must be classed as good-natured though outlandish humor.

101 Myers, Walter Dean, *Scorpions*, HarperCollins, 1988 (hardcover), ISBN 0-06-024364-3, $13.00, 160 pp. Ages 10–14, grades 5–9.

Sociological problem novel dealing with a street gang, featuring Jamal Hicks, a twelve-year-old African-American Harlem boy, designated by his older brother, who is now in prison, to take over the leadership of the Scorpions, despite his youth. Reluctantly, Jamal, along with his friend, Puerto Rican–born Tito Cruz, becomes involved in fights and shootings, at the same time squabbling with his little sister, worrying about his overburdened mother, and confronting the bully who challenges him at school. Although employing mostly stock situations and characters, the story presents them convincingly and makes Jamal's choices seem inevitable. The total tone is depressing, and the ending, while not hopeless, offers no guarantee that Jamal will survive the rough city life better than his brother. For a slightly younger audience and much lighter in tone and incident are the sports novels of a Little League baseball team made up mostly of orphans and newly adopted ex-orphans, *Me, Mop, and the Moondance Kid* (1988) and its sequel, *Mop, Moondance, and the Nagasaki Knights* (1992), whose main characters are two African-American brothers and their tough-talking friend, Mop, a white girl who plays catcher on their team.

102 Myers, Walter Dean, *Somewhere in the Darkness*, Scholastic, 1992 (hardcover), ISBN 0-590-42411-4, $14.95, 168 pp. Ages 12 up, grades 7 up.

Growing-up novel of an African-American adolescent. The tall, dark-skinned stranger waiting for fourteen-year-old Jimmy Little in his New York City hallway turns out to be Crab, the father he can hardly remember, newly escaped from prison and dying of kidney problems. During an often nightmarish trip to Chicago and then to Arkansas, Crab awkwardly tries to make some emotional connection with the wary boy and to convince him that, although his life has been far from faultless, he did not commit the murders with which he was charged. Although frightened and homesick for Mama Jean, the woman who has cared for him since his mother's death years before, Jimmy gradually gains some understanding of what Crab's life has been and compassion for the suffering man. The vacillation of emotions of both main characters is set against backgrounds of African-American sections of several cities and the semirural South, with characters like the young single mother in the tenement, jazz musicians in Chicago, and the conjure man in Arkansas adding color.

103 Myers, Walter Dean, *Sweet Illusions*, Teachers and Writers, 1987 (paper), ISBN 0-915924-14-5, $13.95, 142 pp. Ages 14 up, grades 9 up.

Fourteen stories, each in first person by a different character, about teen-aged girls who are pregnant and seek help at the Piedmont Counseling Center. Five are in the voices of the young men, mostly still in their teens, who are responsible for the pregnancies, one in that of a younger brother, one in that of a mother, and one in that of the director of the center. The girls pursue different courses. Only one has an abortion. One gives her child up for adoption. One marries the father of her son. Designed as a teaching tool as much as a novel, the book provides lined pages at the end of each story on which the reader is supposed to write a continuation or some advice for the character. Despite this didactic purpose, the stories are convincing and have interest in themselves, revealing the self-delusion, longing for love, and irresponsibility of the young people, and treating them as more than case histories, as real people in difficulty, not wicked or beyond hope.

104 Naylor, Gloria, *Linden Hills*, Ticknor & Fields, 1985 (hardcover), ISBN 0-89919-357-9, $16.95, 304 pp. Ages 14 up, grades 9 up.

Glimpses into the lives of affluent, middle-class African Americans in an upscale section of an American city, as seen through the eyes of two young men, unemployed poets, who earn Christmas money doing odd jobs for the residents and discover the insecurity, greed, hypocrisy, and madness hidden beneath the complacency and elegance of Linden Hills. Almost all the people with whom they come in contact are flawed by their desperate striving for status and are manipulated by the owner of the land, satanic Luther Nedeed, whose own insane secret is uncovered at their final job on Christmas Eve. Among the prominent characters are a homosexual who marries against his true nature; an alcoholic minister; a desperately unhappy career woman whose husband has just left her; and a newly widowed man redecorating his house for a new wife even before the funeral of the first one. The stories have more cohesiveness than those in Naylor's earlier and best-known book, *The Women of Brewster Place* (1982), connected short stories, all set in the same unnamed city but at the opposite end of the social scale. The women who live on the short, deteriorated, dead-end street are all scarred but not defeated by life, more genuinely survivors than their Linden Hills counterparts. Strong in characterization, both books present well-realized individuals and evoke strong emotion. A later novel by Naylor, *Bailey's Cafe* (1992), tells the life stories of about ten down-and-outers, mostly horribly ill-used women, in a fantasy frame of a cafe that seems to be in skid-row areas of many different cities. The extremely graphic descriptions, with strong elements of violence and degradation, make the novel inappropriate for all but a few very mature students.

105 Naylor, Gloria, *Mama Day*, Ticknor & Fields, 1988 (hardcover), ISBN 0-89919-716-7, $17.95; (paper), ISBN 0-679-72181-9, $10.00, 312 pp. Ages 12 up, grades 7 up.

Bordering on fantasy, this novel alternates between the stories of an old black woman on one of the Sea Islands off the coasts of South Carolina and

Georgia and her great niece, a smart, successful, young businesswoman in New York City, dipping back into their heritage from a slave who, in 1823, was deeded the island by her master. Daughter of the seventh son of a seventh son, Mama Day is thought by her neighbors to have supernatural powers that she uses mostly to foretell events but also to save her great niece from the voodoo of a jealous islander at the cost of the young woman's unbelieving husband. A long and graphic book, the novel demands mature readers but holds the attention with its strong evocation of the semitropical island, the isolated culture, a sense of mystery, and well-realized characters, in particular Mama Day and Ophelia, her great niece.

106 Nelson, Vaunda Micheaux, *Mayfield Crossing*, illus. Leonard Jenkins, Putnam, 1993 (hardcover), ISBN 0-399-22331-2, $14.95, 88 pp. Ages 8–11, grades 3–6.

Sports novel set in 1960 in some northern area of the United States. When the school in Mayfield Crossing is closed and the children, about half of whom are African American, are sent to Parkview Elementary, they encounter prejudice for the first time and are ignored when they try to join the schoolyard baseball game. Meg, nine, shows up the classroom bully by knowing all the states in alphabetical order, and when he attacks her on the playground and her eleven-year-old brother, Billie, comes to her rescue they both get into trouble. Billie, the pitcher for Mayfield Crossing, comes up with a plan: a baseball game challenge to the Parkview team. Although they have only eight players and almost have to forfeit the game, Meg, the catcher, saves the day by enticing one of the Parkview girls to join their team, the first step in establishing understanding. Although the solution is oversimplified, the situation and the characters are well drawn and the baffled hurt of the Mayfield children is convincing. Unlike many baseball novels, this does not describe the games exhaustively.

107 Patrick, Denise Lewis, *The Car Washing Street*, illus. John Ward, Tambourine, 1993 (hardcover), ISBN 0-688-11452-0, $14.00, unp. Ages 3–10, grades PS–5.

Realistic picture-story book of life in a middle-class, mixed-residential, African-American and Hispanic-American (to judge by the illustrations), urban neighborhood. Every Saturday morning, Matthew loves watching the men on his street wash their cars in front of their brownstones. This hot Saturday as Matthew and Daddy sit on their steps and sip orange juice, they watch a good-natured waterfight break out and join in. Everyone gets wet and cool, licks Miss Emma's fruity ices, and sits on the front steps drying off and chat-

ting happily, including the Rodriguezes from down the way. The book celebrates the simple pleasures of a father's close relationship with his son and of
neighbors enjoying one another's company. Even though no one appears to
be either as hot before or as wet afterward as the text implies he or she should
be, the close-up and panoramic views in Ward's full-color, realistic paintings
bring the people and situations to life. The text moves pleasingly but does not
specify race.

108 Patrick, Denise Lewis, *Red Dancing Shoes*, illus. James E. Ransome,
Tambourine, 1993 (hardcover), ISBN 0-688-10392-8, $14.95, unp. Ages
4–9, grades PS–4.

Realistic picture-story book of middle-class, African-American family life.
Dismayed because in her exuberance she has fallen and scuffed the shiny red
shoes her Grandmama brought from a trip, the little girl who tells the story
finds she can dance happily in her shoes again after Aunt Nen cleans and
polishes them. The strongly composed, full-page, full-color, representational
paintings support the realism of the story, individualize the family members,
show something of their characters, and establish the affectionate family relationships and the middle-class, suburban neighborhood setting. Although the
narrative never so specifies, the pictures show the characters to be African
Americans. In the pictures the protagonist seems older than she appears to
be in the text.

109 Paulsen, Gary, *Nightjohn*, Delacorte, 1993 (hardcover), ISBN 0-
385-30838-8, $14.00, 92 pp. Ages 12 up, grades 7 up.

Short historical novel of slavery on a pre–Civil War Southern plantation,
location not specified. Slim and not entirely plausible, the plot is quickly summarized. Cruel owner Clel Waller buys for $1,000 Nightjohn, a slave known
to be fractious, who teaches Sarny, the twelve-year-old slave narrator, her
letters late at night. When his efforts become known, Waller maims Nightjohn
by cutting off his middle toes. As soon as he is able, Nightjohn runs but
returns, in obviously symbolic action, to organize a late-night school that includes slaves of the neighboring plantations. Sarny describes in unschooled,
unrelentingly stark, serious, understated prose inhumane, brutal conditions
that encapsulate the worst aspects of American slavery, like horrible beatings;
lack of food, clothing, and the simplest of creature needs; animal-like conditions; and gross inhumanities like forced breeding.

110   Peters, Julie Anne, *The Stinky Sneakers Contest*, illus. Cat Bowman Smith, Little, 1992 (hardcover), ISBN 0-316-70214-5, $12.95, 57 pp. Ages 8–11, grades 3–6.

Brief, humorous chaptered book for younger readers about a contest sponsored by a shoe company to find the smelliest sneakers. Earl envies his best friend, Damian, whose usually absent father gives him lavish birthday presents, and he forgives his friend's constant habit of cheating on any bet or competition until he reads about the Stinky Sneakers Contest open to all ten-year-olds, the prize being an annual pair of new Jaguar Jetstreams for ten years. Earl sees this as a way to get the much coveted shoes his family cannot afford, and he resents Damian's plan to win by buying old shoes at Goodwill and doctoring them with liverwurst and Limburger cheese. In the end, Damian realizes that their friendship is more important than winning, and Earl triumphs with new Jag-Jets and the dubious honor. The cartoonlike illustrations picture both boys and Earl's supportive family as African Americans. The fourth-grade humor is right on target for the intended audience.

111   Pinkney, Andrea Davis, *Seven Candles for Kwanzaa*, illus. Brian Pinkney, Dial, 1993 (hardcover), ISBN 0-8037-1292-8, $14.99, unp. Ages 5 up, grades K up.

Realistic picture-story book in which the pictures tell the story of how an African-American family celebrates Kwanzaa while the text supplies information about the festival. After a brief history of the celebration, emphasizing its ancient connection, the text details daily activities as they are practiced today, including the gathering of fruits and vegetables, making gifts, lighting candles, giving the significance of the candles' colors, and explaining the seven principles informing the celebration. The pictures accompanying the text emphasize the family-oriented element of Kwanzaa. The illustrations, which make the book a stunning work of art and elevate the bland, patently didactic text, are full-color, full-page scratchboards, strongly composed and boldly designed. Borders with African motifs add to the attractiveness. An author's note precedes the text, and a bibliography concludes the book.

112   Pinkney, Gloria Jean, *Back Home*, illus. Jerry Pinkney, Dial, 1992 (hardcover), ISBN 0-8037-1168-9, $15.00, unp. Ages 4–10, grades PS–5.

Realistic picture-story book about an African-American family set in North Carolina probably in the 1930s. Young Ernestine travels by herself on the train from the North to visit her mama's relatives, Great-Uncle June Avery and Aunt Beula and Cousin Jack, a little older than she, on their farm where she was born. Right away she feels welcomed and loved by the grown-ups, but Jack plays mean tricks on her. Her short visit of several days over on Sunday with a trip to her grandmother's grave, she prepares to leave for home and is surprised when Jack presents her with a bundle of hard corn kernels so that, he says, she will remember the fun they had together. The story ends abruptly and unconvincingly, without preparation for Jack's change of heart. The slightly indistinct watercolor and pencil pictures suffused with golden tones and filled with homely details like quilts, farm animals, a plow, old truck, sewing basket, and a cat on the bed project the air of nostalgia and create the setting in time and place. They are stronger than the text.

113 Polacco, Patricia, *Chicken Sunday*, illus. Patricia Polacco, Philomel, 1992 (hardcover), ISBN 0-399-22133-6, $14.95, unp. Ages 5–10, grades K–5.

Picture-story book of an interracial friendship based on the author's child-hood. The narrator, a girl of Ukrainian descent, often goes to church and has Sunday dinner with her neighbors, two African-American boys and their grandmother, Miss Eula. Because they love her and especially because they appreciate her chicken dinners, the three plan to buy the hat she particularly admires in Mr. Kodinski's shop. Through a misunderstanding, Mr. Kodinski accuses them of throwing eggs at his door, and in order to show their good will, the children make him a basket of *Pysanky* eggs, decorated in the tra-ditional Ukrainian way. At his suggestion, they make more and sell them in his shop, earning enough to buy the beautiful hat for Miss Eula. Although the narrator is white, the warm story focuses on the large, loving grandmother, whose voice "sounds like slow thunder and sweet rain." The illustrations show highly individualized faces and interior scenes of houses, church, and store with many telling details.

114 Porte, Barbara Ann, *I Only Made Up the Roses*, Greenwillow, 1987 (hardcover), ISBN 0-688-05216-9, $12.95, 114 pp. Ages 12 up, grades 7 up.

Very clever novel of life in a biracial family, told in the voice of a white girl of seventeen whose stepfather is black, dealing with their immediate and extended family, mostly on the African-American side. Cydra tells about her grandparents and aunts, her serious and precocious half brother, Perley, nine, her artist mother, her own devastating attempt to get to know her biological father, and the wonderfully understanding support she receives from her stepfather. Interspersed throughout are stories told by older people about their lives, fourth-grade type jokes by Perley, folk tales told to Perley by Cydra, and items from African history, proverbs, and biographical notes of black Americans collected and posted for them to learn by their father after his father's death. Although there are anecdotes about discrimination that ring true, the book is free from stereotypical scenes of prejudice and treats the eccentricities of the characters with fond humor. This is an entertaining book with unexpected depth.

115 Raschka, Chris, *Yo! Yes?*, illus. Chris Raschka, Orchard, 1993 (hardcover), ISBN 0-531-05469-1, $13.95, unp. Ages 3–8, grades PS–3.

Almost wordless, realistic, contemporary picture-story book of a developing friendship between an African-American boy and a white boy. Two lonely boys meet on the street. The black boy initiates the exchange with "Yo!," to which the white boy responds, "Yes?" When the second boy admits he is bored because he has no friends, the black boy offers himself, and the two walk together hand in hand. They are last seen leaping exuberantly into the air and shouting, "Yow!" The thirty-four words, entirely in dialogue, are perfectly supplemented by full-color, amusing, sparsely detailed cartoons, the black boy alone on the left with his speeches, the white one alone on the right with his, on mostly light blue or tan grounds. When they join hands on the second to the last page, they are surrounded by happy yellow tones. The faces and body language express their feelings well. Although the message is overly obvious, this exuberant book catches the emotions and holds the interest.

116 Rinaldi, Ann, *Wolf by the Ears*, Scholastic, 1991 (hardcover), ISBN 0-599-43413-6, $13.95; (paper), ISBN 0-590-43412-8, $3.50, 252 pp. Ages 12 up, grades 7 up.

Biographical novel of Harriet Hemings, born in 1801, thought to be the daughter of Thomas Jefferson by his slave, Sally Hemings. Since little is verifiable about Harriet's life beyond the dates of her birth and her leaving Monticello, most of the novel is fiction based on what historical facts are available and on records of the lives of slaves in early nineteenth-century Virginia. Fair-skinned, red-haired, and more than three-quarters white, Harriet is considered a "nigra" and is a slave, although she has always been treated far better than most and her mother has been promised that she will be given her freedom when she becomes twenty-one. Written as long entries in her journal starting in 1819, the story records her uncertainty about her future and her hesitance to leave Monticello, which she loves, and Jefferson, whom she admires and adores with a sort of awe. At the urging of Thomas Mann Randolph, son-in-law to Jefferson and governor of the state, she makes plans to accept her freedom, go to Washington, D.C., as the betrothed of a young admirer, Thad Sandridge, and pass as white, but she grieves to know that she will lose contact with her brothers and the other people of the estate, and that Jefferson will never acknowledge her as his daughter. A convincing narrative of what might have happened. The title is a quotation from Jefferson describing what slavery is to America.

117   Ringgold, Faith, *Tar Beach*, illus. Faith Ringgold, Crown, 1991 (hardcover), ISBN 0-517-58030-6, $15.00, unp. Ages 5–8, grades K–3.

Fantasy picture-story book. A little African-American girl, eight-year-old Cassie Louise Lightfoot, lying with her younger brother on a New York roof-top at night while her parents play cards with neighbors, imagines flying over the city, claiming the George Washington Bridge, tall buildings, and the ice cream factory for her family. Originally a quilt with the story written on fabric strips around the border, the illustrations are primitive and highly colored with strips of quilting pieces along the foot of each page. The book captures the delight and zest of a bright child in a situation that might be viewed as deprived but for her has its own city magic. Arthur Dorros's *Abuela* (no. 353) is a very similar story about a little Hispanic-American girl and her grand-mother, also set in New York City. A later picture-story book by Ringgold, *Aunt Harriet's Underground Railroad in the Sky* (1992), uses much the same illustrative technique as *Tar Beach* to tell a version of the slave escapes led by Harriet Tubman, converted into a fantasy in which Cassie and her little brother, flying among the stars, encounter a train which, every hundred years, follows the route of the Underground Railroad, and they become involved in the experience of fleeing to freedom. While an imaginative way to retell the history, the book is so full of message that it lacks the exuberance of its pred-ecessor. A history of Harriet Tubman and the Underground Railroad, includ-ing a map and a bibliography, appears at the end.

118   Robinet, Harriette Gillem, *Children of the Fire*, Atheneum, 1991 (hardcover), ISBN 0-689-31655-0, $12.95, 135 pp. Ages 8–12, grades 3–7.

Historical novel of four days in the Chicago fire that began on October 8, 1871. Orphaned, black Hallelujah, eleven, whose mother escaped from slavery in Mississippi with her child, is being raised by foster parents not far from the lakeshore of the bustling metropolis. Willful, irritated at being kept home when fires break out in the overheated city, Hallelujah mischievously runs off into the night and into what turns out to be one of the most momentous of city fires. She meets prejudice and acceptance, becomes friends with a little white girl, rescues a church full of parishioners in danger of burning to death, and saves a bagful of bank money later instrumental in rebuilding the city. Although the author's voice can be heard commenting on racial attitudes and drawing moralistic conclusions and although some incidents seem concocted, the excitement, fast action, and graphic descriptions that make the fire all too real temper the instructive tone and build credibility. A bibliography is included.

119 Rodriguez, Anita, *Jamal and the Angel*, illus. Anita Rodriguez, Potter, 1992 (hardcover), ISBN 0-517-58601-0, $14.00, unp. Ages 3–8, grades PS–3.

Picture-story fantasy set in a crowded inner city, perhaps New York, involving African Americans, as indicated in the pictures. Aunt Martha tells several young friends the story of how Benjamin, his guardian angel, helps young Jamal get the guitar he yearns for and help out the family finances at the same time. The happy, rainbow colors that encircle the angel and indicate his presence if unseen are echoed in the colorful tones of the other pictures, and they and the naive style support the story's themes of hope and perseverance in spite of setbacks. The pictures help to compensate for the predictable story. In *Aunt Martha and the Golden Coin* (1993), also a picture-book fantasy set in the inner city, Aunt Martha tells a story from her own Louisiana childhood of finding a powerful, protective magic coin. Gold tones and bold composition give the illustrations a sense of power and mystery. Although *Golden Coin* is a little more mature than *Jamal*, both books have well-worded texts, with such phrases as "I reacted instinctively," "he examined the coin and concluded," and "his face was radiant," which can tune young hearers' ears to language a cut above that of many picture books and which they should have no trouble understanding from the context.

120 Rosen, Michael J., *Elijah's Angel: A Story for Chanukah and Christmas*, illus. Aminah Brenda Lynn Robinson, Harcourt, 1992 (hardcover), ISBN 0-15-225394-7, $13.95, unp. Ages 4 up, grades PS up.

Realistic picture-story book of a friendship between an elderly black wood-carver (the historical Elijah Pierce of Columbus, Ohio) and a white Jewish boy of nine, told by the boy a year after it happened in the late twentieth century. When, for Christmas, young Michael is given a specially carved angel by old Elijah the barber, the boy is not sure whether he should keep it, since he knows his father disapproves of "graven images." After his father assures him that Elijah intends the angel as a sign of friendship, "And doesn't friendship mean the same in every religion?," Michael gives Elijah a menorah he made at Hebrew school. The text is longer than that of most picture books, and the implausibility of the story's being told by a ten-year-old (It begins, "Last year, when I was nine . . . ") is outweighed by the strength of narrative detail and the stunning, stylized artwork that catches the spirit as well as the appearance of situations and reproduces many of Pierce's carvings. A note at the beginning of the book gives information about Pierce, a lay minister as well as a barber and woodcarver, who received a "National Endowment for the Arts National Heritage Fellowship as one of fifteen master traditional artists." This is an exceptionally beautiful book that can appeal to any age reader and viewer.

121 Samton, Sheila White, *Amazing Aunt Agatha*, illus. Yvette Banek, Raintree, 1990 (hardcover), ISBN 0-8172-3575-2, $12.95, 23 pp. Ages 4–8, grades PS–3.

Brief picture-story book in which Andrew's Amazing Aunt Agatha has remarkable and amusing adventures that follow the letters of the alphabet. She (a young African-American woman) "Amazes Audiences" with sleight of hand as a magician, "Builds Boats" with Andrew's help, "Collects Clocks," and engages in various feats of strength ("Lifts Lions"), bravery ("Pets Panthers"), or diplomacy ("Quiets Quarrels"), until finally she "Yells Yahoo," while riding a bull bareback, and "Zips Zebras" into a jacket-coat, and, all the while, of course, she "absolutely adores Andrew!" Intended as reading readiness material, the nonracially specific text is expanded by colorful cartoons filled with details of each adventure or situation. This is a Ready-Set-Read book.

122 Samuels, Vyanne, *Carry Go Bring Come*, illus. Jennifer Northway, Four Winds, 1988 (hardcover), ISBN 0-02-778121-6, $13.95, unp. Ages 3–7, grades PS–2.

Amusing picture-story book of a little African-American boy caught in the bustle of preparations for his big sister's wedding, when everyone in the household has an errand for him and no one gives him time to complete the last one. The text is in short, repetitious sentences that resemble primer language. Illustrations are full of the busy activity of a large family with idealized black faces, almost all female except for overworked Leon, who is perhaps five or six. The humor should appeal to youngsters who feel unappreciated for their best efforts.

123 Sanders, Dori, *Her Own Place*, Algonquin, 1993 (hardcover), ISBN 1-56512-027-2, $16.95, 243 pp. Ages 12–15, grades 7–10.

Life story novel of an African-American girl in a small South Carolina community, who, with diligence and endurance, raises five children and makes a good life for herself despite hardships. When World War II drafts the young men of her area, Mae Lee Hudson, not yet seventeen, marries Jeff Barnes. While he is in the army, she works in a munitions plant and helps her daddy farm, saving every cent until she can buy a piece of land with a small house, a surprise for her husband when he returns. After the birth of their first child, he drifts off, returning often enough to sire four more before he disappears from her life. Although it is a struggle, Mae Lee sees that her four daughters and her son are all well brought up and get college educations. Eventually she moves to town, and after the civil rights changes of the 1960s, she does volunteer work at the hospital and makes friends among the white workers, even attending and hosting social events with mixed races. The novel has no real plot or climax, but it has many interesting scenes and does a good job of presenting the attitudes of poor Southern farmers through a period of great change. Mae Lee is a believable and memorable character. An earlier novel by Sanders is *Clover* (1990), about a ten-year-old black girl whose father is killed only hours after he marries a white woman, and the strains, misunderstandings, and gradual love that grows between the two. Especially strong is the picture of the resentment in the father's family and the close-knit community against the stepmother, who is a well-meaning but somewhat inflexible character, and the back-biting remarks that upset the child.

124 Schotter, Roni, *Efan the Great*, illus. Rodney Pate, Lothrop, 1986 (hardcover), ISBN 0-688-04986-9, $12.95, 32 pp. Ages 4–8, grades PS–3.

Realistic picture-story book set in inner-city New York about a persevering boy's efforts to make Christmas merry for his family and neighborhood. Ten-year-old Efan, who has never had a Christmas tree, is determined to have one this year to brighten the holidays for his family and the residents of drab 128th Street, especially Old Woman, who "loved Christmas better than anyone in the world." When on Christmas Eve morning he discovers that his $6.63 is not enough for a tree, he works all day for Jimmy the tree man and earns the biggest one left on the lot. He drags it home, sets it up in a trash can at the end of the street, and decorates it with pop can rings and broken glass to the joy of everyone on the block. This warm, unpretentious story about the true spirit of Christmas gives an upbeat look at life in the city. The bold, full-color, realistic paintings reveal setting, support incidents, and identify Efan and his friends as African Americans.

125 Seabrooke, Brenda, *The Bridges of Summer*, Dutton, 1992 (hardcover), ISBN 0-525-65094-6, $14.00, 143 pp. Ages 10 up, grades 5 up.

Realistic novel of a fourteen-year-old African-American girl from New York who spends the summer with her grandmother whom she has never met, a Gullah woman on little Domingo Island off the South Carolina coast. When her irresponsible mother, Ila May, goes off as a singer with a band, Princess Zarah Brown, whose given name is really Sarah Jane, has to leave her ballet lessons and friends in New York and enter an entirely different life, living in a dilapidated house with no electricity or running water, getting to know the unwelcoming old woman who is raising her little five-year-old great-grandson, Loomis, and adjusting to the unfamiliar food, different mores, and strange superstitions of the island. Despite scandalizing her grandmother, Quanamina, Zarah gradually comes to love the stubborn old owner of Domingo, to appreciate the beauty of the island, and to make friends with Benicia Saylor, a white girl from California who is visiting on Saylor's Island, the antebellum plantation island adjoining Domingo. When Quanamina dies, Zarah is ready to take charge—to sell the island to a developer and take Loomis back to New York with her. The conflicts between two extremely different ways of life are well handled, and Zarah, Quanamina, and Loomis are all interesting and believable characters.

126 Shelby, Anne, *We Keep a Store*, illus. John Ward, Orchard, 1990 (hardcover), ISBN 0-531-05856-5, $14.95, unp. Ages 4–7, grades PS–2.

In a picture-story book a little girl describes all the good things about the store her family runs: its closeness to their house, the sense it gives of family togetherness, and the way it serves as a social center for the customers. In the winter, the men pull chairs around the stove and tell stories about the old days or gently tease the children. In the summer, they sit on the porch whittling, while the women gather in the yard and string green beans or cut up apples and the children play in the field and nearby stream. Full-page, realistic pictures show a rural, roadside store, run by a handsome couple and the narrator, a little girl in pigtails. All the customers and the family are African Americans. Although the story lacks any narrative drive or tension, it gives a strong feeling of warm family life.

127 Simon, Norma, *Oh, That Cat!*, illus. Dora Leder, Whitman, 1986 (hardcover), ISBN 0-8075-5919-9, $11.95, unp. Ages 4–9, grades PS–4.

Amusing, realistic picture-story book about a present-day, urban, African-American girl and her mischievous, very active cat, a book in which story and pictures combine to capture aptly the ways of cats. Max the cat can be exasperating—cries to go out in the middle of the night, jumps into the bathtub, gets into Mom's knitting, gets "skunked," knocks over the Christmas tree—but he brings a lot of joy, too. He is a fine foot warmer at night, makes the other kids laugh with his antics, can be a welcome walking companion, and plays hide-and-seek well. He is always amazing, so that the narrator often says, "Oh, that cat!" The black-and-white drawings (possibly charcoal) perfectly extend the text to play up the humor, convey the sense of warm family life and the love between the little girl and her pet, and especially characterize Max. The pictures identify the narrator as black (the text does not indicate race) and young and the cat as a sleek black-and-white tom, show what the family does while Max snoozes, and depict him saucering downhill in the snow; these and more activities are not mentioned in the text. This is a charming story.

128 Slote, Alfred, *Finding Buck McHenry*, HarperCollins, 1991 (hardcover), ISBN 0-06-021652-2, $14.00, 250 pp. Ages 8–12, grades 3–7.

Baseball novel telling much about the African-American leagues which disappeared after Jackie Robinson integrated the sport. The narrator, Jason Ross, a baseball-card fanatic, decides on slim but persuasive evidence that the school janitor, Mack Henry, is really the great Buck McHenry, pitcher for the Pittsburgh Crawfords. Since Jason has been cut from his team in the eleven-year-old league and assigned to an expansion team that lacks a coach, he asks Mr. Henry to take on the job. Because Mr. Henry wants his grandson, Aaron, who has recently come to live with him after losing his parents and brother in an accident and is deeply depressed, to take an interest in baseball again and make friends, he goes along with the idea, not denying Jason's enthusiastic claims about his past. The plot is complicated by another new team member, Kim Axelrod, the only girl in the league, whose television-sportscaster father recognizes the story's potential and summons a camera crew to their practice. The comedy of errors works out to a happy ending telling along the way not only about the great figures in the old "colored" league, but also about the grubby and even dangerous life of a semipro baseball player of the period, a life Mr. Henry actually experienced. Although Jason and Kim are both white, emphasis is on Mr. Henry's past and on

Aaron, a potentially talented pitcher. As in many of Slote's sports novels for this age group, starting with *Jake* (1971), the setting is Arborville, thinly disguised Ann Arbor, Michigan, and the story is as much about personal relationships as about the well-described ball games.

129 Smalls-Hector, Irene, *Irene and the Big, Fine Nickel*, illus. Tyrone Geter, Little, Brown, 1991 (hardcover), ISBN 0-316-79871-1, $14.95, unp. Ages 4–10, grades PS–5.

Light-hearted and realistic picture-story book of friendship and neighborhood adventures among African-American children in Harlem in the 1950s. One Saturday morning is filled with pleasant happenings for Irene, who is seven. She gets up early and hurries to Miss Sally's to play with her best friends, Lulabelle and Lulamae. They play in the park and plant seeds in a window box, among other activities. Then Irene spies a nickel in the gutter, which the three spend on a raisin-bun at the West Indian bakery. Irene feels so good about it she even shares with mean Charlene. At the end, Irene is "feeling seven and in heaven on this summer day in Harlem." The girls' activities are simple, happy ones, true to the attitude and enjoyments of the age. Since Irene and Charlene had had a falling out earlier and Irene was ready to fight Charlene, Irene's sharing is all the more significant. Some dialect and topical references add to the sense of period. Full-color, realistic paintings show city scenes, interiors, and the girls in various activities. A pleasing, upbeat book about a spunky little girl and a Harlem without serious urban problems. In *Dawn and the Round To-It* (1993), a little girl wants someone to play but everyone in her family is too busy. Still another lively picture book for the youngest set is *Dawn's Friends* (1993).

130 Smalls-Hector, Irene, *Jonathan and His Mommy*, illus. Michael Hays, Little, Brown, 1992 (hardcover), ISBN 0-316-79870-3, $14.95, unp. Ages 3–7, grades PS–2.

Realistic picture-story book with a brief text in large print that could also serve as easy-reading material. Jonathan, shown in the illustrations as a little, chubby-faced, baseball-capped, African-American boy of four or five, tells how he and his Mommy enjoy walking through their apartment-house neighborhood, by stores, and past the park. Sometimes they take big giant steps, at other times, "itsy-bitsy baby steps," bunny hops, "crazy crisscross steps," or reggae steps, or maybe they even run, but however they go, they love it and have fun. At the end, tired out, they take "Jonathan-and-Mommy steps home." Michael Hays's off-the-page, full-color paintings depict situations and settings and show Jonathan and his Mommy as very good-looking and joyful people.

The pictures beautifully catch the happiness and affection of the simple, effectively told story.

131 Smith, Eunice Young, *A Trumpet Sounds: A Novel Based on the Life of Roland Hayes*, Lawrence Hill, 1985 (hardcover), ISBN 0-88208-198-5, $12.95, 263 pp. Ages 12 up, grades 7 up.

Biographical novel based on the youth of the eminent African-American singer of the early twentieth century. Born near the little cotton town of Curryville, Georgia, at the foot of Horn Mountain not far from Calhoun, the third of five sons of a poverty-stricken, ex-slave, cotton-farmer, Amon Sayre (the historical Roland Hayes, 1887–1977) early exhibits a strikingly beautiful singing voice and an aptitude for music. After Mr. Sayre's death in a 'coon-hunting accident, the family moves to Chattanooga, Tennessee, where Amon spends his teen years working in a foundry to supplement the mother's meager income from doing laundry. Beaten almost to death by white foundry workers who resent his being promoted to foreman, Amon quits, resumes his schooling, and is heard performing at a school program by a Professor Sterling who assumes his vocal training. After long, hard years of study, practice, and scrimping that take him eventually to Boston and the Jubilee Singers and on tours, in 1920 he leaves for Europe having been told there is no place for a black in American concert halls. The account of Amon's rise is told in gripping detail, particularly graphic being the scenes of his very hardscrabble childhood, the discrimination, the fears of the blacks for the redneck whites, especially on the part of Mrs. Sayre who had been a slave and who has a firm conviction that education is the essential path to independence and respect for her people. Foreword and afterword with information about Hayes and the way in which the author acquired her information are included.

132 Smith, K., *Skeeter*, Houghton, 1993 (hardcover), ISBN 0-395-49603-9, $13.95; (paper) ISBN 0-395-61621-2, $3.99, 208 pp. Ages 11–15, grades 6–10.

Growing-up novel in which an old African-American man becomes mentor to two white teenaged boys, teaching them not only tracking and shooting but also something of social history and respect for themselves and others regardless of race. When Joey Rider and Steve Foster first come upon Skeeter Hawkins's cabin in the Tennessee woods somewhere near Memphis, they are uncomfortable, especially Steve, who has been brought up to dislike black people and who fears his father would disapprove, but they are fascinated by his collection of guns with beautifully carved stocks, and they come back repeatedly. In the year that follows, as the boys grow much taller, get their driver's licenses, and begin to date girls, Skeeter teaches them, developing a joking, disparaging friendship with open, lively, "blabby-mouth" Joey whom he calls "Boy" and a deeper, more serious relationship with quiet, steady Steve, whom he calls "Son." As his health fails, he insists on one last major hunt to the Big Boogey swamp to get the huge buck that he says is still waiting for him there. When he suffers a heart attack and possibly is gored by the buck, the boys carry him out and stay with him until he dies, only then realizing how great their love for him has become. While Skeeter resembles the wise, old "natural man," his characterization is strong enough to overcome the stereotype, and both boys are well-drawn individuals. Information about the discrimination and danger of earlier days is brought in through Skeeter's stories, barely avoiding didacticism since the information comes from a cranky old man who always has been too proud to stoop.

133 Smothers, Ethel Footman, *Down in the Piney Woods*, Knopf, 1992 (hardcover), ISBN 0-679-80360-2, $14.00, 151 pp. Ages 9–12, grades 4–6.

Autobiographical novel of African-American family life and a girl growing up set in the Piney Woods of Georgia in the 1950s. Independent, spirited, ten-year-old Annie Rye Footman, daughter of a black sharecropper, describes a few summer weeks when she must adjust to having three older half sisters join the household and the family is terrorized by racist acts. The colloquial black dialogue seems inconsistent and often calls attention to itself and the white villain is overdrawn, but the Footmans are a convincingly warm and close family, and it is easy to like and sympathize with Annie's reluctance to share her home with relatives she barely knows. Scenes that stand out include a cross burning on the lawn and the storekeeper's threatening Mr. Footman with a pitchfork.

134 Spohn, David, *Home Field*, illus. David Spohn, Lothrop, 1993 (hardcover), ISBN 0-688-11172-6, $10.00, unp. Ages 5–10, grades K–5.

Realistic picture-story book of a present-day biracial father and son together. Early one bright Saturday morning, Matt, a young African-American boy, "gently peels open Dad's sleeping eye." Dad, white, awakens, and after breakfast, the two head for the ball field, where they practice catching and batting. Although Dad tires before Matt does, he "goes into his triple double windmill windup," and Matt gives a "mighty swing" that "sends a blast to deep center field" and smacks the barn wall. Gentle humor, especially warm, loving family relationships, unsentimental tone, and uncomplicated, unforced language combine for a convincing story for early or reluctant readers of a father-son outing that is supported by simple, framed, representational watercolors. The illustrations, not the text, establish the racial makeup. In *Winter Wood* (1991), Matt and his father work up a sweat one Saturday morning chopping wood. *Starry Night* (1992), still another strongly crafted, unpretentious father-son story, finds Matt, his older brother, Nate (also African American), and Dad enjoying a campout at the edge of the woods across the field from their farmhouse, and in *Nate's Treasure* (1991), Nate gathers for a keepsake the bones of a skunk their dog killed the year before.

135 Springer, Nancy, *They're All Named Wildfire*, Atheneum, 1989 (hardcover), ISBN 0-689-31450-7, $12.95, 103 pp. Ages 9–12, grades 4–7.

Love of horses brings together two girls in an interracial friendship: the narrator, blond Jenny Wetzel, and black Shanterey Lucas, whose families share a duplex. Both collect model horses, plastic and china, but Shanterey gives all of hers the same name, Wildfire. At school Shanterey is the object of mean tricks in which Jenny at first joins, then denounces. A neighbor, Mr. Seitz, gets a horse and welcomes Jenny to ride it but calls Shanterey a nigger and tells her to get off his land. Determined to share the horse, which they call Wildfire, Jenny waits until Mr. Seitz is away and insists that Shanterey have one ride, which she performs as if born on horseback. Mr. Seitz finds out and threatens to prosecute. Jenny's father, who ordinarily avoids conflict with neighbors, intervenes, but the Lucases have suffered other harassment, and they decide to move. Shanterey is a strong character, just touchy and defiant enough to be believable. The conclusion, while realistic, could do little for the self-esteem of an African-American child, and most of the learning and growing from the experience is Jenny's. The story, nevertheless, mirrors the experience of many blacks attempting to live in a predominantly white neighborhood. A later novel by Springer, *The Friendship Song* (1992), is a fantasy, also about a friendship between the white narrator and a black neighbor, both middle-school girls with a passion for rock music. Again, most of the development is of the white girl, who learns to love her new stepmother, a contemporary embodiment of Aengus Mac Og.

136 Steptoe, John, *Baby Says*, illus. John Steptoe, Lothrop, 1988 (hardcover), ISBN 0-688-07423-5, $13.95; Mulberry, 1992 (paper), ISBN 0-688-11855-0, $3.95, unp. Ages 1–5, grades PS–K.

Very short, realistic, almost wordless picture-story book. Two contemporary African-American brothers, one a baby, work out a way of playing side by side after the little one persuades his big brother to lift him from his playpen. Only seven words—uh, oh, here, no, okay, baby, says—used variously in dialogue, constitute the text of this charming little book, made eloquent as well as decorative by strongly composed portraits of the boys and shots of their toys in clear, muted colors. The pictures carry the story and bring the characters and this common home happening to life.

137 Stock, Catherine, *Halloween Monster*, illus. Catherine Stock, Bradbury, 1990 (hardcover), ISBN 0-02-788404-X, $11.95, unp. Ages 2–6, grades PS–1.

Realistic picture-story book, told by a little African-American boy. Because he is afraid of monsters and witches, which his next-door friend, Billy, says will be out on Halloween night, Tommy is reluctant to go trick-or-treating with Billy and his father. After Mom explains that they are "just little children all dressed up" (in a scene shown with special tenderness in the accompanying picture, a loving and understanding expression on Mom's face), together they make Tommy a monster costume. He happily joins his friend for the outing. The text treats the not unusual childhood apprehension with respect, and the soft washes show scenes of playing in leaves, making a jack-o'-lantern, and other fall activities, and relay emotions well. The large print and uncomplicated syntax make the book appropriate for just-readers. *Secret Valentine* (1991), in which a small girl tells of making valentines, including one for the little old lady next door, is another warm, mother-child story for the very young.

138 Stolz, Mary, *Cezanne Pinto: A Memoir*, Knopf, 1994 (hardcover), ISBN 0-679-84917-3, $15.00, 252 pp. Ages 11 up, grades 6 up.

Historical novel of a young slave's flight to freedom and his attempts to build his life, beginning in 1860. Deprived of his beloved Mam, who has been sold into Texas, in the company of determined, proud Tamar the cook, who taught him to read, write, and improve his English, slave boy Cezanne Pinto, about twelve, runs from the Virginia plantation of his birth. Sheltered for some months by a kind and affectionate Ontario couple whom he serves as a stableboy, he feels compelled to join the Union forces, which he does, luckily near war's end. In the cavalry, he makes friends with brash Mex-Texan Cal Trillo, returns to Texas with Trillo, becomes a cowboy on Trillo's ranch, tries unsuccessfully to find Mam, and gradually makes a life for himself. Told from the vantage of eighty years later, the book succeeds as the memoir of a very old man, since incidents can convincingly remain undeveloped and Cezanne can credibly comment on the progress of African Americans in their quest for civil rights since the emancipation of the war. The small cast of characters provides scope for developing them in dimension—Tamar, Cal, and Cezanne himself, especially. The first part of the book recalls other similar narratives, but the last part gives a limited but clear sense of the difficulties and challenges of rebuilding the western South, the beginning of the cowboy era, and the part the freed blacks played in both.

139   Stolz, Mary, *Stealing Home*, HarperCollins, 1992 (hardcover), ISBN 0-06-021157-1, $13.95, 153 pp. Ages 8–11, grades 3–6.

One in a series about a present-day African-American orphan who lives with his grandfather on the Gulf of Mexico near Bradenton, Florida. Thomas, ten, met earlier in *Storm in the Night* (1988; no. 140) and *Go Fish* (1991), and, Grandfather, a retired mailman, Joseph Weaver, enjoy a modest but satisfying life together in their small, cluttered, rundown house, playing games like scrabble and cribbage, fishing, gardening stir-fry vegetables, and following baseball on radio and occasionally at the Pirates' exhibition games. Big changes occur when prim Aunt Linzy, Grandfather's sister-in-law, who has a passion for order, moves in. She takes over Thomas's room, and his beloved cat, Ringo, as well; clears away the board games and their cherished collections; and even disparages their liking for seafood, being a vegetarian. Relief comes from an unexpected source: Aunt Linzy agrees to help Grandfather's old fisherman friend run his motel near Miami. Linzy is conventionally drawn, and Thomas is likably typical of his age yet individualized in his young-old attitudes, peculiar resentments, and desire to please Grandfather by being "gracious and understanding" to the woman displaced by age and retirement while at the same time asserting himself. Grandfather pleasingly steals the story, however, wise, witty, capable, caring, sophisticated, and always his own man in the face of Thomas's pleading and Linzy's prodding. The narrative never condescends, and the dialogue is in schooled, everyday English. The book is often very funny with humor of character, language, and situation, and is a charming and convincing story about a warm and happy, middle-class, nontraditional family. *Go Fish* (1991), illustrated by Pat Cummings and aimed at a slightly younger audience, tells how Thomas and Grandfather go fishing for trout and play the game of Go Fish, and Grandfather tells real and made-up stories. Another convincing book about two unique figures.

140   Stolz, Mary, *Storm in the Night*, illus. Pat Cummings, Harper, 1988 (hardcover), ISBN 0-06-025912-4, $12.95, unp. Ages 4–8, grades PS–3.

Realistic, contemporary, picture-story book, first in a series about Thomas and Grandfather, African Americans, who also appear in *Stealing Home* (1992;

no. 139) and *Go Fish* (1991). During a terrible thunder and lightning storm, the lights gone out, Thomas and Grandfather sit on the porch swing, listen to the night sounds, and smell the night smells. While Thomas chatters with questions to relieve his anxiety, good-humored Grandfather tells stories of how he was scared in storms when he was a boy, too. The narrative employs short sentences and simple diction, of the sort found in easy-to-reads, but it is more finely honed, more honest in tone, and more accurate to the child's point of view without being as condescending as most such books. Blue and green hues catch the psychological atmosphere as well as the physical situation. Most are portrait-like up-close views of Grandfather and Thomas, and there are some fine ones of Ringo the cat. During Grandfather's stories, Thomas and Grandfather appear in small pictures at one side, the remembered scenes appearing in larger illustrations that take up most of two pages. This is an unusually effective pairing of well-written text and skillfully executed illustrations.

141 Tate, Eleanora E., *Front Porch Stories at the One-Room School*, illus. Eric Velasquez, Bantam, 1992 (hardcover), ISBN 0-553-08384-8, $15.00, 99 pp. Ages 7–12, grades 2–6.

Realistic novel about African Americans that has no plot in itself but consists of a series of short stories within a slight frame story. Margie Carson, twelve, tells how, when she and her cousin, Ethel, seven, get bored one summer evening, her father, Matthew J. Cornelius Carson, the book's real focus, walks them to the now-closed, old brick, one-room Douglass School, where on the porch over peanut butter and crackers, rags burning in an old tub to keep the "gallinippers" from biting, he tells them wild stories about his childhood. Even as tongue-in-cheek whopper and tall tale, the humor and scariness of some happenings seem strained, and information about black heritage and history seems instructive, but some characters, like Aunt Daisy, the schoolteacher, are strong, and the sense of small-town Nutbrush, Missouri, of twenty years earlier comes through. An author's note about the school and the town that inspired the stories is an attractive feature. The book is a companion to *Just an Overnight Guest* (1980), in which a little half-white, half-African-American girl cousin comes to live with the Carsons.

142 Tate, Eleanora E., *The Secret of Gumbo Grove*, Watts, 1987 (hardcover), ISBN 0-531-10298-X, $12.95, 266 pp.; Bantam, 1988 (paper), ISBN 0-553-27226-8, $3.50, 199 pp. Ages 9–11, grades 4–9.

Realistic novel of family and community life set at the time of publication among African Americans in the coastal resort town of Gumbo Grove, South

Carolina. Eleven-year-old Raisin Stackhouse, whose father raises vegetables to sell and peddles fish and whose mother cleans condos, aspires to become a history teacher. When old Miz Effie, widow of the former pastor of New Africa Baptist Church, enlists Raisin's help in cleaning up the old church cemetery and tells her stories about the people buried there, Raisin's curiosity about Gumbo Grove's past is piqued. She sets out to investigate, in particular, the founder of Gumbo Grove, a black man buried there, and unwittingly stirs up people in town who do not want to be reminded of slave days. Eventually, with the help of her parents, young friends, and some other adults, the black community sees the value of preserving the cemetery and taking pride in their heritage. The lively, first-person narrative abounds with dialogue, teen talk, and topical references, and humor appears. Raisin is a peppery and often mischievous as well as intelligent girl. The sense of the church community is strong, and Raisin's parents are respected, hardworking, lower middle-class people, who are busy to the point of being harried, but dedicated to family and church. A subplot about Raisin's younger sister Hattie in the Miss Ebony Contest adds a personal touch and also emphasizes pride in person and heritage. Less successful because it is overlong and more obviously didactic is the school story *Thank You, Dr. Martin Luther King, Jr.!* (1990), a companion book told by Hattie's friend, Mary Elouise Avery, who is nine. Mary Elouise deplores her dark black skin and longs to be best friends with white Brandy, whose pinky-tan complexion and long blond hair she envies. With the help of Big Momma and a Black History Program, the girl comes to appreciate herself as she is and her heritage as well.

143 Taylor, Mildred D., *The Friendship*, illus. Max Ginsburg, Dial, 1987 (hardcover), ISBN 0-8037-0417-8, $13.95, 53 pp. Ages 7–11, grades 2–6.

Short, realistic account of racial tension set in a farming area near Strawberry, Mississippi, during the Great Depression, told by nine-year-old, African-American Cassie Logan, who with her family appears in the Newbery Award–winning novel *Roll of Thunder, Hear My Cry* (1976). Cassie and her three brothers observe Mr. Tom Bee, an ancient black man, stop at the store of white John Wallace and address Wallace by his first name without the prefix Mister as blacks are required to do. John's sons angrily denounce his behavior as inappropriate for a "nigger," but Tom argues that he had "saved [John's] sorry hide" when John was a child. Outside the store, Tom explains to the Logans that he not only saved John's life but also reared him, and that John had promised Tom that Tom need never call him Mister. A little later, Tom again calls John by his first name. Ashamed because other white men are present, John pulls out his shotgun and shoots Tom in the right leg. The end sees the old man dragging himself down the road, shouting "John! John!" over and over again in defiance. This tragic incident is made powerful because it is seen from the vantage of the nervous children and is very economically related. Based upon an actual incident described to the author by her father, the story is a dramatic example of unreasoning prejudice. Another illustrated short story in which the Logans appear is *Mississippi Bridge* (1990; illus. Max Ginsburg), a book with a white boy protagonist who observes discrimination against the Logans and other blacks and a terrible bus accident. The bridge serves as an ironic metaphor for race relations. *The Gold Cadillac* (1987; illus. Michael Hays), another short book, tells about a black family who undertakes a journey in their new 1950 Cadillac to the South from Toledo, Ohio, and experience racism. The journey is metaphorical of relations between the races as is that in *The Road to Memphis* (no. 144), a novel about the Logans.

144 Taylor, Mildred, *The Road to Memphis*, Dial, 1990 (hardcover), ISBN 0-8037-0340-6, $14.95, 240 pp. Ages 12 up, grades 7 up.

Historical novel, third in the series about the African-American Logans, a farm family of Strawberry, Mississippi. High school student Cassie Logan, seventeen, describes a succession of racial incidents in late 1941 culminating in a near-murder that rocks the community. In town on Saturday, Moe Turner, a friend of Cassie and her older brother, Stacey, is harassed by local rednecks. Unlike his predecessors, Moe turns on his tormentors, striking them with a tire iron and wounding one of them perhaps fatally. Knowing there will be no justice in Strawberry, Stacey, Cassie, and some friends drive Moe to the train in Memphis and to safety with the Logans' Uncle Hammer in Chicago. Their hectic and trouble-filled journey through the Mississippi night becomes metaphorical of the tribulations of blacks in America. Among other problems, Cassie is abused verbally and physically when she approaches a "whites only" restroom. The young people arrive in Memphis Sunday morning to a crowded railroad station and the news that the Japanese have bombed Pearl Harbor. Although ensuring Moe's safety is the book's main concern, other matters in addition to the racial incidents contribute tension and texture, among them black attitudes toward the war and serving in the army. While a few too many "untoward incidents" happen to the Logans and their friends by way of in- structing readers about racism, the villains are faceless and overdrawn, the journey wears thin, and Cassie "smart mouths" too often, by her own admis- sion, this substantial story shows Cassie and Stacey developing believably and gives a good sense of black-white relations at the time. Taylor's first novel about the Logans, *Roll of Thunder, Hear My Cry* (1976), is one of the most highly honored books for young people by a black writer. Its successor is *Let the Circle Be Unbroken* (1981). Several short stories, published in illustrated form, among them *The Friendship* (no. 143), flesh out the series, which includes some of the most convincing books about discrimination against blacks in the period just before World War II.

145 Taylor, Theodore, *Timothy of the Cay*, Harcourt, 1993 (hardcover), ISBN 0-15-288358-4, $13.95, 161 pp. Ages 10–14, grades 5–9.

"Prequel-sequel" to Taylor's popular *The Cay* (1969), a novel of an American boy, Phillip Enright, eleven, blinded and shipwrecked during World War II on a tiny Caribbean island with an old black man, Timothy, who teaches him survival skills and ultimately sacrifices his life to save the boy in a hurricane. In alternating chapters this new novel tells of Timothy's youth on Saint Thomas in the Virgin Islands and of Phillip's rescue, the operation that restores his sight, and his return to the cay with his father in a sort of spiritual pilgrimage dedicated to Timothy's memory. A foundling, Timothy is raised by an old island woman, an ex-slave, goes to sea at fourteen, eventually saves enough to buy and captain his own sailing schooner, and has retired when the wartime shortage of labor calls him back to work as a seaman aboard the *Hato*, the torpedoed ship on which Phillip was a passenger. Readers familiar with *The Cay* will find the fear, courage, and ultimate triumph of Phillip's risky operation, which was summarized briefly in the earlier book, developed much more fully, but the major addition is in Timothy's story, making him a more rounded and genuine character. Those unfamiliar with *The Cay* can follow the novel, but might find it lacking in unity and dramatic interest.

146 Thomas, Joyce Carol, ed., *A Gathering of Flowers: Stories about Being Young in America*, HarperCollins, 1990 (hardcover), ISBN 0-06-026173-0, $14.89, 236 pp.; Trophy, 1992 (paper), ISBN 0-06-447082-2, $3.95, 256 pp. Ages 12 up, grades 7 up.

Eleven stories of realism and fantasy compiled by an African-American writer and anthologist from several cultures about love, loss, making friends, coping with relatives, and searching for one's niche in life. Settings range from Gerald Vizenor's "Almost a Whole Trickster," which takes place among reservation Chippewas in northern Minnesota, to Joyce Carol Thomas's "Young Reverend Zelma Lee Moses," involving African-American church people in rural Oklahoma, to Maxine Hong Kingston's "Twisters and Shouters," set among Chinese Americans in San Francisco and an alternative school situation for African-American Zephyr in Al Young's "Last Chance," to Rick Wernli's futuristic "Colony." Wonder and gentle humor characterize "Christmas Story of the Golden Cockroach" by Ana Castillo, set among Chicago's Mexican-American community, and a softly lilting happiness for Alfonso in "First Love" by Gary Soto. Other writers represented are Lois Lowry and Gerald Haslam.

Styles vary, and some employ limited dialect. All give a pleasing sense of the culture and are carefully arranged for emphasis. Information about the authors is included.

147   Thomas, Joyce Carol, *Journey*, Scholastic, 1988 (hardcover), ISBN 0-590-40627-2, $12.95, 153 pp. Ages 12 up, grades 7 up.

Psycho-thriller combining fantasy and reality set in Berkeley, California, in the contemporary period. Bright, outspoken, African-American Meggie Alexander, fifteen, daughter of an army doctor and a junior-high teacher, is horrified when classmates begin disappearing and some are found dead, horribly mutilated, in Eucalyptus Forest. Meggie and her boyfriend, Matthew, investigate and are themselves kidnapped and taken to a laboratory by an unscrupulous surgeon to be used for body parts for wealthy, aged men who live, ironically, in Meggie's own neighborhood. Familiarity with a tarantula in her infancy and Meggie's quick wit and raw courage enable her to engineer her escape. The anthropomorphized tarantulas and other spiders and abundant coincidence strain belief in this otherwise engrossing, crisply written, sometimes poetic book, which poses important ethical questions.

148   Thomas, Joyce Carol, *Water Girl*, Avon, 1986 (paper), ISBN 0-380-89532-3, $2.50, 119 pp. Ages 12 up, grades 7 up.

Realistic girl's growing-up novel set at the time of publication in California's San Joaquin Valley. Life is full and mostly happy for peppery, opinionated, curious, intelligent, fifteen-year-old African-American Amber Westbrook, who enjoys her mother, plumber father, and twin younger brothers. While exploring the attic one day, she makes the startling discovery that she was given away at birth to the Westbrooks by Abyssinia and Carl Lee Jefferson. She runs away to the river to come to terms with this disturbing information. Amber is a vibrant figure and her family is pleasing and solidly middle class; however, the plot is padded, some details violate logic for a realistic work, running away "to find one's self" has become an overworked cliche, and the details about Amber's placement with the Westbrooks are left unexplained. Amber's biological parents appear in earlier books by Thomas. Her mother, Abyssinia Jackson, an aspiring medical student, is the protagonist of the first, *Marked by Fire* (1982), set in Oklahoma from 1951 to 1971. In *Bright Shadow* (1983), Abyssinia and half-Cherokee, half-African-American Carl Lee Jefferson become sweethearts; *The Golden Pasture* (1986) tells of the unhappy life Carl Lee, thirteen, has with his alcoholic African-American father and his love for a beautiful Appaloosa on his paternal grandfather's ranch near Ponca City, Oklahoma. In these books, women are strongly drawn characters, and particularly appealing is their sense of community. Deep love, violence, sorrow, and even horror appear, and important events are often accompanied by significant or even catastrophic changes in the weather, like tornadoes, or, as in *Water Girl*, by earthquakes. In spite of the author's tendency to overwrite, to make black is beautiful too obvious, and to include unlikely elements that lessen credibility, the books are consistently interesting.

149 Thomas, Joyce Carol, *When the Nightingale Sings*, HarperCollins, 1992 (hardcover), ISBN 0-06-02094-7, $13.89, 148 pp. Ages 12 up, grades 7 up.

Realistic novel with fantasy touches set in Sweet Earth near the great southern cypress and mangrove swamp. The mysterious Swamp Woman summons Queen Mother Rhythm, lead singer in the Rose of Sharon Baptist Church gospel choir, to go with her into the great Swamp, where Queen Mother Rhythm finds her estranged sister, Melissa, dying, having just given birth. The baby girl is abruptly carried off by the Swamp Woman. Years later, when Queen Mother Rhythm and a handsome young churchman, Anthony, are searching for a successor to Queen Mother Rhythm at a gospel singers' convention, they encounter a girl with a marvelous voice, Marigold, who turns out to be the long-lost niece. She has been living in seclusion on the other side of the Swamp as a slave to a woman revealed as her aunt, still another sister of Queen Mother Rhythm, and the aunt's hateful, "wanna-be-singers" twin daughters. The Cinderella-story structure makes acceptable the numerous coincidences, surrealistic elements, and hyperbole. Style employs unusual terms of phrase, startling images, African-American speech rhythms, a musical cadence, and gospel rhythms in the poems that appear here and there, all of which add to the sense of place and general attraction. The book departs from the author's better-known, realistic growing-up stories.

150 Turner, Ann, *Nettie's Trip South*, illus. Ronald Himler, Macmillan, 1987 (hardcover), ISBN 0-02-789240-9, $11.95, unp. Ages 6–10, grades 1–5.

Based on the diary of the author's great-grandmother, this historical picture-story book tells of the trip a ten-year-old girl takes with her older sister and brother to the South shortly before the Civil War. For the first time she sees slaves, naively looks for what part of them is missing to make them count as three-fifths of a person, discovers that the hotel maid in Richmond has no last name, stares in disbelief at the plantation shacks, and reacts with horror and nausea to the slave auction. Although the protagonist is white, the focus is entirely on the slave experience she observes. Written as a letter to her friend Addie, the story poses the question of what would happen to them if they "slipped into a black skin like a tight coat." Illustrations are soft but detailed black-and-white pencil drawings that give a strong sense of the place and period.

151 Tusa, Tricia, *Maebelle's Suitcase*, illus. Tricia Tusa, Macmillan, 1987 (hardcover), ISBN 0-02-789250-6, $12.95; Aladdin, 1991 (paper), ISBN 0-689-71444-0, $4.95, unp. Ages 4–8, grades PS–3.

Picture-story book fantasy about a friendship between an eccentric old African-American woman (race specified only in the pictures) and a less-than-sensible bird. Maebelle, a hatmaker, aged 108, lives in a large and rambling tree house, her dearest neighbors the birds. One fall, young Binkle the bird asks to borrow Maebelle's suitcase for the trip south, then fills it with so much stuff that he crashes on takeoff. Maebelle solves his problem without damaging his self-esteem. She decides to create a hat for the annual hat contest and sends him for such items that he finds only in the suitcase as rocks, elm leaves, gardenias, and his nest, which, including the suitcase, she fashions into a hat that wins the prize for the most original entry and is placed for perpetuity in the town museum. Binkle wings south secure that his cherished belongings are safe. The amusing story makes its point lightly and undidactically. The scrappy, freewheeling, probably crayon cartoons, which hint of Dr. Seuss, elaborate on the story to make it funnier, showing the crazy house, the outlandish array of hats, the fluttery, awkward bird, the clever old woman, and, of course, the magnificent hat, with Binkle perched precariously on top.

152 Vertreace, Martha M., *Kelly in the Mirror*, illus. Sandra Speidel, Whitman, 1993 (hardcover), ISBN 0-8075-4152-4, $13.95, unp. Ages 5–8, grades K–3.

In a picture-story book, Kelly worries because her brother looks just like their father, and her little sister has eyebrows just like their mother, but she seems to look like no one but herself. Alone in the attic, feeling sad, she tries on clothes from an old chest and discovers a photo album that shows her mother at her age wearing the same sweater and hat. Her whole family agrees that she looks just like her mother did. The illustrations, in pastel, cover about one and a third pages each and show a little African-American girl with a turned-up nose, high cheekbones, and two long braids with ribbons. Nothing else in the story is ethnic specific.

153 Viglucci, Pat Costa, *Cassandra Robbins, Esq.*, Square One, 1987 (paper), ISBN 0-938961-01-2, $4.95, 176 pp. Ages 11–15, grades 6–10.

Realistic, present-day novel of a girl's growing up and of upper middle-class family life set in the town of Hatfield, New York. Pretty, bright, mostly self-assured, brown-skinned Cassandra Robbins, the seventeen-year-old biracial narrator, is happy with life in the white family into which she was adopted at birth until handsome, African-American Josh Lindsay, her older brother's Yale roommate and son of a diplomat, comes for the summer. She resents his getting the lab job she wanted, is jealous about the attention he receives especially from the local white girls, is taken aback by antagonism from black girls and by the sudden racial slurs directed at her and him by local white mothers, in particular by the mother of a white boy she dates, and most of all is uncertain about how to handle the strong sexual attraction she feels for Josh. Confronted with the need to define her racial status and accept her sexuality, Cassandra decides finally that she must first of all take care of herself and think through her direction in life. Though the age of seventeen seems a little late for Cassandra to have to come to grips with such issues, perhaps that story discrepancy may be attributed to the relatively small-town atmosphere in which she has been living. The amount of good sense and confusion she shows through most of the book seems reasonable for a well-brought-up girl who knows she is loved and cherished by her family. While the less important figures are functional types, the Robbins family members and Josh are well drawn. This book is more skillfully crafted and more literately written than most of those in the "teen growing-up romance" genre.

154 Vigna, Judith, *Black like Kyra, White like Me*, illus. Judith Vigna, Whitman, 1992 (hardcover), ISBN 0-8075-0778-4, $13.95, unp. Ages 5–8, grades K–3.

Picture-story book of the prejudice that appears among white neighbors when an African-American family moves in next door. Learning that the parents of Kyra, her best friend at the youth center, want to move to a safer neighborhood, Christy tells her about the house for sale next to hers. After they move in, Christy's friends on the block no longer play with her. At the lawn party her parents give, many of the neighbors leave when Kyra's family arrives, and the next day their yard is trashed. Kyra's family decides to stay, despite the hostility, but some of the other houses are put up for sale. The story is from white Christy's point of view and, although it is about a genuine problem, it seems didactic as presented. The watercolor illustrations are adequate but uninspired.

155 Voigt, Cynthia, *Come a Stranger*, Atheneum, 1986 (hardcover), ISBN 0-689-31289-X, $13.95, 190 pp.; Fawcett, 1991 (paper), ISBN 0-449-70246-4, $3.95, 240 pp. Ages 11 up, grades 6 up.

Realistic growing-up novel, companion to *Dicey's Song* (1982). Set in Crisfield, Maryland, about 1980, it tells of several years in the life of life-loving, assertive, African-American Mina Smiths, who, at ten, is the second youngest in the large family of a minister. Having won a previous scholarship to ballet camp and dreaming of becoming a ballerina, Mina realizes that being dismissed from camp the second summer happened as much because of her color as because of the adolescent awkwardness her white teacher complains about. At home she experiences discrimination, too, from exploitive white parents when she baby-sits, from a teacher who resents her providing information about black contributions to United States history, and from tennis teammates. Over the next several years, Mina learns that her color, while a barrier, need not prevent happiness and that life can be satisfying if she uses her talents and reaches out to others. She maintains an A average in her classes and wins a spot on the varsity tennis team. She helps her family with an elderly neighbor and sings in the church choir. She befriends a young substitute minister, who is having a crisis in faith over the untimely death in Vietnam of a much-respected fellow track runner, encourages his wife to get her high school diploma, and staunchly supports white Dicey Tillerman when her mother dies. At the end she is so full of the joy of living that she leaps "down off her porch into the dark yard" and "danced around in circles." Scenes take on moment, and the large cast of characters seems believably real, even minor figures. The themes of family love, loyalty for one's friends, and maintaining confidence in one's self and the essential goodness of life appear without sentimentality or statement. This is a richly crafted, solid story about the growing up of an admirable young black girl who rises above society's limitations.

156 Wade, Barrie, *Little Monster*, illus. Katinka Kew, Lothrop, 1990 (hardcover), ISBN 0-688-09596-8, $13.95, unp. Ages 4–7, grades PS–2.

Realistic picture-story book of family life. When Mandy overhears her mother saying she is perfectly behaved but recognizes the affection in her voice when she adds that Jimmy, her brother, is a little monster, Mandy spends a day being deliberately naughty. The story ends with Mandy's understanding mother saying that she loves her, even when she misbehaves, and Mandy happily returns to perfect conduct. The illustrations, in pen and ink and pastel watercolors, which show the family as African-American, produce much of the humor with revealing facial expressions.

157   Walker, Alice, *Finding the Green Stone*, illus. Catherine Deeter, Harcourt, 1991 (hardcover), ISBN 0-150227538-X, $16.95, unp. Ages 5 up, grades K up.

Fantasy told in picture-story format about Johnny, who has lost his precious green stone and covets his sister Katie's. His bad temper and meanness increase until he begs her to help him find his own stone, and soon their parents and the whole neighborhood join in the search, each person displaying his own glowing green stone. Johnny finds that unkind actions and even thoughts turn the stones gray, and in the end his change of heart makes the little gray rock he holds glow with green radiance. Illustrations in bright, clear colors show idealized African Americans in parklike settings. The symbolism of the stones is so obvious that the overall effect is strongly didactic. An earlier picture-story book by Walker, *To Hell with Dying* (1988), tells how an old neighbor, Mr. Sweet, an alcoholic and diabetic, is brought back from his frequent near-death illnesses by the narrator and her siblings when they are children as they clamor over him, kissing and tickling, until he opens his eyes, sits up, and plays his old guitar for them. An adult, she returns home at news of his last attack but cannot rescue him again from death. Frankly sentimental, this is not a book that will appeal to all readers.

158   Walter, Mildred Pitts, *Justin and the Best Biscuits in the World*, illus. Catherine Stock, Lothrop, 1986 (hardcover), ISBN 0-688-06645-3, $12.95, 122 pp.; Knopf, 1990 (paper), ISBN 0-679-80346-7, $3.25, 128 pp. Ages 8–11, grades 3–6.

Realistic contemporary novel of domestic life. Ten-year-old African-American Justin, who is passionate about one-on-one basketball, chafes at being required to do "women's work," like picking up his room and helping with cooking. When his Grandpa Ward, a widower, invites him to visit his ranch in the Missouri hills, Justin accepts eagerly and soon learns important information about family history as well as about manliness. Grandpa tells him about how his spread was founded in the late 1800s by "exodusters," black emigrants from Tennessee, and about famous black cowboys. Justin sees that Grandpa takes care of his house matter-of-factly and well, including cleaning and cooking. After Grandpa takes first prize for the best biscuits at the annual cowboy festival, Justin asks Grandpa to show him how to make them. At home again, Justin surprises everyone by diligently cleaning his room and making a tasty supper, including the best biscuits in the world. The simple, straightforward narrative intends to promote pride in heritage and to enhance self-esteem. Serious and humorous moments appear, Justin is a lively protagonist, the characters are well-utilized types, the tone is consistently warm, and the tensions of home life and snatches of black history are convincing. Other upbeat novels of middle-class, African-American domestic life by Walter for slightly more advanced readers concern an impulsive, life-loving girl's problems when her older half sister moves in, *Mariah Loves Rock* (no. 159) and *Mariah Keeps Cool* (1990), and a persevering boy who feels cheated because his birthday falls on Christmas and who gets involved in preparations for Kwanzaa, *Have a Happy* . . . (1989; illus. Carole Byard), a story more concerned with promoting cultural pride than the Mariah books.

159 Walter, Mildred Pitts, *Mariah Loves Rock*, illus. Pat Cummings, Bradbury, 1988 (hardcover), ISBN 0-02-792511-0, $12.95; Troll, 1989 (paper), ISBN 0-8167-1838-5, $2.95, 118 pp. Ages 8–12, grades 3–7.

Lighthearted, realistic novel of present-day family life, with some school scenes, involving urban, middle-class African Americans (as seen in the pictures although race is not specified in the text). Although Mariah Metcalf, eleven, is chosen coach for the fifth-grade end-of-the-year volleyball match against the teachers and leads the students to victory, her elation is tempered by the news that her older half sister, Denise, sixteen, will soon be living with the Metcalfs and by the fear that she may not be able for financial reasons to attend the concert of her favorite rock star, Sheik Bashara. Still, she and her girl-pals, the Friendly Five, prepare posters to welcome the Sheik, and she and sister Lynn, fourteen, get Denise's room ready. Then Daddy gives Riah a ticket as a year-end gift, and to her delight, she discovers Denise loves rock, too. Mariah is almost a caricature of the typical eleven-year-old—brash, impulsive, willful, selfish, sassy, whiny, loving, forgiving, argumentative, loud, up and down by turns. The other family members are drawn in less exaggerated strokes, the tone is positive, the scenes underdeveloped but suitable for quick reading for the intended preadolescent audience, and the pace is fast. In *Mariah Keeps Cool* (1990), the sequel, Riah adjusts to her new half sister, prepares a birthday party for Lynn, and swims with the team the Friendly Five form.

160 Walter, Mildred Pitts, *Trouble's Child*, Lothrop, 1985 (hardcover), ISBN 0-688-04214-7, $11.95, 157 pp. Ages 10 up, grades 5 up.

Realistic girl's growing-up novel set in the early 1980s among African-American fisherfolk on tiny Blue Isle off the Louisiana coast. Pretty, fourteen-year-old Martha Dumas must choose between the traditional life for island women and her deep longing for more education. The island women, and particularly her strong-minded, midwife, wise-woman grandmother, Titay, who raised her, expect her to marry and follow in the older woman's footsteps.

High school seems an impossibility for Martha, since the nearest one is fifty miles away and they are poor, but Miss Boudreaux, her former teacher, tutors her so that she is ready for tenth grade and arranges for her to live with a physician's family in New Orleans while she is attending school. The characters are familiar types, among them the jealous school friend, the acid-tongued gossip, and the handsome stranger who represents the intellectually and technologically advanced outer world. Only Martha and Titay have dimension. Most memorable is the setting; scenes in the single store, in church, and at the fish festival with dancing and singing, the constantly present sea, the use of dialect, the grandmother's pithy, proverbial expressions, and especially the beliefs and values expressed infuse the physical and psychological atmosphere with strength.

161 Walter, Mildred Pitts, *Two and Too Much*, illus. Pat Cummings, Bradbury, 1990 (hardcover), ISBN 0-02-79220-1, unp. Ages 4–9, grades PS–4.

Realistic picture-story book of present-day African Americans (race indicated only in the pictures). When Mrs. Little cannot help Mama get ready for her ladies-only party, Brandon, who is seven, offers to watch his little sister, Gina, who is two. A series of humorous mishaps follows, after which Brandon concludes, wearily but affectionately, "She's only two, but she is too much." The story tackles a common problem for older siblings with good humor and insight, but the sentence structure and diction, which could be handled by most just-readers, often sound stilted and primerish. The full-page, full-color, representational paintings abut the text, which is printed on pastel grounds, a mode that seems to clutter the pages. Figures seem molded and pasted on the pages, caught in fixed stances, and the yellowish tone that suffuses them is more typical of yesterday's reading texts than today's picture books. Walter has also written for older readers, for whom she does better.

162 Wilkinson, Brenda, *Definitely Cool*, Scholastic, 1993 (hardcover), ISBN 0-590-46186-9, $13.95, 176 pp. Ages 8–12, grades 3–7.

Realistic school and girl's growing-up novel set in the present-day Bronx in New York City. Twelve-year-old, African-American Roxanne, who lives with her divorced mother in the grungy, noisy, robbery-prone Bailey Hills Projects, has been happy and secure in middle school and with her "homegirl," Maxine, called The Max. When she starts Riverdale Junior High in a better part of town and The Max goes to another school, Roxanne is filled with apprehensions, like making friends, wearing the right clothes, being jumped on the bus and in school, dealing with boys, especially Rolland, a classmate from nursery school who hangs around her, maintaining decent grades, and keeping to her mother's rules about hours and no kids in the apartment alone. She gradually strikes up acquaintances, is happy (though a little jealous) when Rolland becomes "tight" with Jewel, and goes up much in the other students' esteem when eighth-grader Marcus pays her attention. Mostly the book ambles along, but certain matters provide some unity: why Kenya is so frequently absent from school, why Kenya and white Pat are so close, and whether Roxanne will go along with Marcus and her new girlfriends and participate in a "hooky party" that has the kids buzzing. She learns that Pat and Kenya are tight because both are welfare-hotel kids, and that Kenya is absent because she is sorely needed at home. Marcus's pressuring her to break rules and her friendship with The Max and Rolland, who breaks up with Jewel, give her the strength to refuse to go along with the crowd. At the end, she is grateful for a caring mother and old friends. Seventh grade is not easy, but she must keep trying to do her best and make the right choices. This story of developing independence of spirit and judgment is peopled by a large cast of mostly typed characters, who are hard to keep straight because of insufficient development, and it has too many problems that seem contrived for effect and a predictable conclusion. Best are the tension of the troubled school and bus situation (kids are harassed both places) and the contemporary rap and jive talk that falls well on the ear. Wilkinson is best known for her novels about an African-American girl growing up in Georgia, *Ludell* (1975) and its sequels.

163 Wilkinson, Brenda, *Not Separate, Not Equal*, Harper, 1987 (hardcover), ISBN 0-06-026479-9, $12.89, 152 pp. Ages 10–15, grades 5–10.

Historical novel of school integration set in the small town of Pineridge, Georgia, in 1965. Malene Freeman is one of six youngsters from "better" African-American families chosen to be the first blacks to attend Pineridge High. For the most part, the slights and inconveniences they experience from white students and teachers are hurtful, but it is possible to bear them in view of the larger cause. Some incidents, however, are more serious, for example, when redneck Wiley Parker sics his dogs on Malene as she walks to school. The town erupts, however, when a bomb threat is called in at school, the principal sends the six blacks home early, and Parker "kidnaps" them at gunpoint and confines them in his garage, to be rescued by combined forces of parents and police after several hours of terror. Because the author includes much sociological background information and the characters, for the most part, are unfleshed, the book moves slowly and does not grip the emotions as one would expect. Prejudice against the blacks and to some extent among blacks on the basis of color and economics, the dilemma of sympathetic whites, and the beginning of the long hard road to opportunity in education are made very clear. The book's strength is as a limited picture of a turbulent but important period.

164 Williams, Sherley Anne, *Dessa Rose*, Morrow, 1986 (hardcover), ISBN 0-688-05113-8, $15.95, 236 pp.; Berkeley, 1987 (paper), ISBN 0-425-10337-4, $4.50, 268 pp. Ages 14 up, grades 9 up.

Historical novel of slavery in the American South. In 1847 pretty field slave Dessa Rose, maybe sixteen, sold to a trader bound for the Deep South for attacking her master who killed her sweetheart, helps in the uprising of the coffle (group of chained slaves) and is sentenced to die after the birth of her baby. While awaiting the baby, she is interviewed by an arrogant, abusive white man for information for a book on slave uprisings and is freed by slaves who escaped from the coffle. They take her to a remote, seedy Alabama plantation operated by runaways for ineffectual, white Ruth Sutton. The runaways, with Ruth's help, plan to escape and eventually head West. Ironically, even though the slaves have been most instrumental in reaching free territory, they are still under the domination of whites since Ruth must go surety for them to join a wagon train. The first part of the book is slow and perplexing, since it is set up as a kind of mystery in which, through the questions of the white researcher and Dessa's thoughts, the reader gradually learns the cause of Dessa's predicament. The last part, told by Dessa, in which the runaways sell themselves repeatedly for money to go West, seems overfilled with incidents, unconvincing, and melodramatic. But Dessa's plight catches the emotions early, and she grows and changes believably as she has more opportunity to control her destiny. While the researcher is typecast as the white villain, Ruth, and a few male slaves have dimension. Such sordid aspects of slavery as inadequate food and living quarters, whippings, and intellectual deprivation are dramatized, at times overly so, and the sexual exploitation of female slaves is emphasized. Balancing Dessa's story is that of Ruth, who has been exploited and abandoned by her husband and with whom Dessa eventually becomes friends. Through Ruth, Dessa sees that even white women of the time are powerless and subject to the domination, including sexual, of men. The book is poorly paced, but parts are deeply engaging. Sexually explicit scenes appear. An author's note about sources is included.

165 Williams, Sherley Anne, *Working Cotton*, illus. Carole Byard, Harcourt, 1992 (hardcover), ISBN 0-15-299624-9, $14.95, unp. Ages 5 up, grades K up.

Picture-story book with a simple, poetic text in contemporary black English, tracing one day of an African-American migrant family picking cotton, from the cold, dark early morning through the heat of the day until they leave the field at dusk. The narrator, Shelan, possibly six to eight, is "a big girl now," not big enough to have her own sack but big enough to help pile cotton for her Mama. She admires her Daddy, who "pick so smooth and fast," envies her older sisters who fill their own sacks, but longs wistfully for the days when she just fetched the water jug and minded the baby. Despite the picture of grueling work and Shelan's remark, "It's a long time to night," the story has a strong sense of family solidarity and pride in work. Illustrations in acrylic paints cover the wide pages in double spreads and give a feel of the huge, flat fields and the passing day. Characters are depicted realistically, without being either cartoonlike or idealized as are many picture book representations.

166 Williams, Vera B., *Cherries and Cherry Pits*, illus. Vera B. Williams, Greenwillow, 1986 (hardcover), ISBN 0-688-05145-6, $14.00; Morrow, 1991 (paper), ISBN 0-688-10478-9, $3.95, unp. Ages 4–8, grades PS–3.

Realistic picture-story book of friendship and family life. Bidemmi, a young African-American girl, loves to draw pictures with magic markers, and as she does so, she tells the narrator stories about the people she creates. Each of the four stories concerns someone bringing home cherries, which are eaten, and then the pits are planted to form a "whole forest of cherry trees right on our block." This is a warm, happy book with a strong text, longer-than-usual for a picture book, illustrated with primitive watercolors and with magic markers for Bidemmi's drawings. The bright, rainbow colors with lots of pinks support the cheery mood. Bidemmi's elastic-limbed brother has particular memorability.

167 Williams, Vera B., *"More More More," Said the Baby*, illus. Vera B. Williams, Greenwillow, 1990 (hardcover), ISBN 0688-09173-3, $12.95, unp. Ages 3–7, grades PS–2.

Very short, realistic picture-story book in which the same story is repeated for each of three babies. Each small child is caught up, swung around, kissed, and hugged in loving abandon in this order: blond, white Little Guy by his daddy; African-American Little Pumpkin by his white grandma; and Asian-American Little Bird by her mama. The children are appropriately chubby, awkward, pot bellied, and big eyed, and the adults fittingly adoring and enveloping. The boldly composed full-page, off-the-page, full-palette, color-framed gouaches enclose the text, which is integrated into the pictures not only in position but also in choice of colors. The pictures extend the text in every way. They capture the action, establish the setting, and reveal character and emotion. Their generous use of primary colors projects the affection for life of these three very short, related stories. This is a charming book for the very young.

168 Williams-Garcia, Rita, *Blue Tights*, Dutton, 1988 (hardcover), ISBN 0-525-67234-6, $12.95, 138 pp. Ages 12 up, grades 7 up.

Contemporary, realistic girl's growing-up novel focusing on African Americans in a mixed ethnic and economic neighborhood and school in New York City. Pretty honor student Joyce Collins, fifteen, is often at odds with her never-married mother, herself pregnant at fifteen; has trouble coping with her sexuality; lusts for an older man and also the handsome, big-man-in-school; would so much like to be best friends with two upper middle-class girls that she takes their snubs and ridicule; and, especially, longs to continue ballet but feels put down by her white teacher because of her "big butt." A chance encounter with an African Dance Ensemble and the lead in the Kwanzaa Suite changes her life. An understanding but demanding teacher and dedicated co-dancers encourage her and help her sort out her feelings and aspirations, so that she ends up with respect for herself and the realization that, if she works at it, she can become a fine dancer. Characters are types, and the number of problems that face Joyce seems excessive. Life for young black girls is shown as bleak but hopeful. School is raw with gossip, cliques, back-biting, and jockeying for boys and attention, and street and bus scenes show teens freely and openly engaging in sex play. The book contains frank sex; vivid, contemporary teen jargon; teen pregnancy; single-parent homes; talk of abortion. Joyce's confused and heightened emotions seem valid for her age and situation.

169 Williams-Garcia, Rita, *Fast Talk on a Slow Track*, Dutton, 1991 (hardcover), ISBN 0-525-67334-2, $14.95, 182 pp. Ages 12 up, grades 7 up.

Realistic boy's growing-up novel of home and school set in the 1980s. African-American, upper middle-class, New York City resident Denzel Watson, high school valedictorian resentful of being placed in a special preparatory program for students admitted to Princeton from substandard high schools, deliberately does poorly and sets his mind on never hitting that campus again. A month on the street selling door to door with tough guy Mello changes his attitude after he gets a terrific beating because he tries to outtrick his sales mate. He hits the books when college starts and even gets involved in an African-American student group. Denzel's maturation appears not only in the story he tells but also in the style in which he tells it. His "big mouth" moderates into a modest tone as he is forced to admit that he conned his way through high school and that he can achieve if he really puts his mind to it. Street scenes with drugs and girls alternate with home scenes, and, although most characters are types and the book flags in the middle during the selling episodes, the overall problem and Denzel himself hold the attention, and the big-city setting adds interest.

170 Wilson, Beth P., *Jenny,* illus. Dolores Johnson, Macmillan, 1990 (hardcover), ISBN 0-02-793120-X, $13.95, unp. Ages 5–8, grades K–3.

Picture-story book of a little African-American girl, early school age, whose thoughts are expressed in brief monologues with text in framed boxes inset in watercolor illustrations. Subjects include friends, relatives, school, birthday, Christmas, and fun out of doors. The only ethnically specific piece is about Martin Luther King. Friends and schoolmates include white and Asian children, but family members are all rather idealized, light-brown-skinned African Americans.

171 Wilson, Johnniece Marshall, *Oh, Brother,* Scholastic, 1988 (paper), ISBN 0-590-41001-6, $2.50, 121 pp. Ages 8–12, grades 3–7.

Lighthearted, realistic novel of African-American family life. Alex Walker, a responsible, serious-minded schoolboy of about eleven, tells how he is pushed around repeatedly by his older brother, Andrew, who slacks on his schoolwork and expects Alex to cover for him, swipes Alex's bike so he cannot do his paper route, shirks his responsibilities which then fall on Alex, hangs out with a gang that picks on Alex, and even steals Alex's hard-earned money. Neither polite words nor fists have any effect, but eventually Alex learns the reasons for Andrew's antisocial and rebellious behavior. Although he continues to have to assert himself, Alex does see light at the end of the tunnel. The book lacks a proper climax, and the parents never take as firm a stand as they might to smooth relations between the boys. It is easy to relate to Alex's problems, humor lightens the tension, and the story stays true to situations for a conscientious child who opens himself to exploitation. Except for the cover picture, the reader would hardly realize that the family is black. *Robin on His Own* (1990), set in a middle-class neighborhood in Pittsburgh, is not ethnic specific either, except for such references as skin color and the A.M.E. Church. It concerns a boy of about ten, who grapples with his grief for his recently deceased mother and the problems of a musician father who is often away on gigs, his Aunt Bella's impending marriage, and the sale of their over-large house. Predictably, his running away in the middle of the night with his dog and parakeet helps toward a solution to all his problems. Both books are pleasant, family-centered stories that leave one with a warm feeling and seem intended to show that middle-class African-American children cope with the same sorts of problems other middle-class children do. The style is straightforward, unadorned, fast moving, and filled with dialogue.

172 Wilson, Johnniece Marshall, *Poor Girl, Rich Girl*, Scholastic, 1992 (hardcover), ISBN 0-590-44732-7, $13.95, 179 pp. Ages 8–14, grades 3–9.

Realistic novel of family life and a girl's growing up set recently in a middle-class urban area. When Miranda Moses, age fourteen and a half, whines for contact lenses, her parents flat-out refuse. Mr. Moses has just started his own business, and her mother's dietician's salary barely meets expenses. Some amusing situations ensue as Miranda embarks on a series of part-time, summer jobs, including baby-sitting for exceedingly fractious twin boys; working for two weeks as a junior camp counselor; stocking produce at a grocery, where she must own up to lying about her age; and finally starting her own dog-walking business. Although an only child and overprotected, Miranda is likable but seems immature and unaware for her age. The book has an antiseptic tone, and events seem deliberately contrived to show Miranda's persistence and growing sense of responsibility. Without the cover illustration, which shows Miranda as African American, most readers would be unaware of her race. The book seems intended for preadolescent girls who wish to read about girls older than themselves without launching into the nitty-gritty of many adolescent books. Its strengths lie in its picture of sensible if one-dimensional parents, its continuous action, its sympathetic characterization of Miranda, and its warm depiction of middle-class life. There are some school scenes, and Miranda's growing understanding of her archenemy, Catriona Maryland, the daughter of a minister, adds interest.

173 Winter, Jeannette, *Follow the Drinking Gourd*, illus. Jeannette Winter, Knopf, 1988 (hardcover), ISBN 0-394-89694-7, $13.95; 1992 (paper), ISBN 0-679-81997-5, $5.99, unp. Ages 5–9, grades K–4.

Picture-story book of historical fiction about the Underground Railroad. On a plantation somewhere in the American South, historical Peg Leg Joe, a white handyman, teaches the slaves the drinking gourd song, which gives them directions to freedom by following the big dipper. An extended family, soon to be sold apart—father, mother, son, an old woman, and her grandson—remember the song and flee, hiding by day, evading capture, enduring bad weather and hunger, eventually reaching the Ohio River, over which Joe ferries them, and then from station to station to Lake Erie and Canada. The dramatic, understated, fairly brief text is enhanced by equally dramatic, strongly conceived, richly colored framed primitives. They enlarge on episodes and create atmosphere. The eyes of the fugitives stand out startlingly against the dark grounds, echoing the stars in the dipper above. The painting of the family asleep, hidden in a cornfield, is itself alone worth framing for its effective use of color and pattern. An author's note about the Underground Railroad begins the book, and the song with music concludes it.

174 Woodson, Jacqueline, *The Dear One*, Delacorte, 1991 (hardcover), ISBN 0-385-30416-1, $14.00, 145 pp. Ages 12 up, grades 7 up.

Realistic contemporary problem novel set among upper middle-class, professional African Americans in suburban Seton, Pennsylvania. Feni (Afeni) Harris, twelve, is generally happy living with her divorced mother, though she is concerned that Catherine may resume drinking, still misses her dead grandmother after four years, has few friends at her private school for well-off black children, and resists her mother's efforts to bring her out socially at the black Jack and Jill club. She hits the roof, however, when Catherine takes in surly Rebecca, the fifteen-year-old pregnant, unmarried daughter of her mother's old friend who lives in Harlem and is on welfare with her large family. With the help of Catherine's lesbian friends, Marion and Bernadette, a lawyer and teacher respectively, the two girls manage a grudging relationship that eventually ripens into friendship. When Rebecca places her baby for adoption, she at first names her Afeni, the Dear One, after Feni. Although the story moves predictably and seems to belabor alternative lifestyles, tolerance, and reasons for Rebecca's situation, each girl changes interestingly as her vistas broaden and she becomes more sure of her own sense of worth. Economic differences are stressed, as are the differences between the girls' knowledge about sex, Rebecca being far more knowing than Feni. Positively presented are the adopting parents, who appear before the baby is born, and Danny, the baby's father who never appears but calls Rebecca frequently. A brief racist scene is set in a poor-white part of town.

175 Woodson, Jacqueline, *Last Summer with Maizon*, Delacorte, 1990 (hardcover), ISBN 0-385-30045-X, $13.95, 105 pp.; Dell, 1992 (paper), ISBN 0-440-40555-6, $3.25, 185 pp. Ages 10–14, grades 5–9.

Realistic contemporary problem novel of middle-class family life set among African Americans in Brooklyn, New York. The summer before she enters sixth grade brings troubles for Margaret Tory, who is eleven years old. First, her father dies of a heart attack, and then just before she enters 6-1, tough Ms. Peazle's room, her long-time best friend—bright, peppy Maizon Singh, a neighbor girl who lives with her grandmother and to whose intellectual abilities Margaret feels inferior—wins a scholarship to a boarding school in Connecticut. When Ms. Peazle encourages Margaret to write, Margaret discovers she has a special gift for poetry and wins a city contest. Unexpectedly, Maizon comes home, having decided to drop out of Blue Hill because she feels discriminated against on the basis of color and has not made friends. Both girls soon learn there is a free school for the gifted in Brooklyn which they might attend and are pleased to be back together again. Although emotions and everyday life are convincing, characters are one-dimensional for the most part, and the ending seems pat. Margaret is likable, but Maizon stands out as a more interesting personality. The story moves fast with plenty of dialogue and conveys themes of growing up and apart, coping with loss, nurturing oneself, and accepting change—too many subjects for the foreshortened plot. The friendship between the two girls is complex enough to sustain interest. Sequels are *Maizon at Blue Hill* (1992), which shows Maizon at school, and *Between Madison and Palmetto* (1993), which continues their adventures after Maizon returns.

176 Yarbrough, Camille, *The Shimmershine Queens*, Putnam, 1989 (hardcover), ISBN 0-399-21465-8, $13.95, 142 pp.; Knopf, 1990 (paper), ISBN 0-679-80147-2, $3.99, 144 pp. Ages 8–12, grades 3–7.

Realistic novel of school and family life set in New York City in the late twentieth century. Shy and fearful African-American Angie Peterson, ten, is often ridiculed by the other students about her very dark skin and short, tightly curling hair. Her self-esteem rises when she and her best friend, Michelle, join the Arts in Action program introduced by a new teacher and practice the advice of Angie's ninety-year-old Cousin Seatta to use their "get-up" gift to do their best and let their resulting "shimmershine feelin" show and set an example for others. The book suggests too obviously and too simplistically that raucousness in schools and violence on the streets are attributable to poor self-image, lack of self-respect, and inadequate knowledge about heritage. The plot is awkwardly constructed and often seems contrived to convey the message, with some incidents interjected for thesis. Adult dialogue often turns into didactic speeches to promote pride and obviate intraracial discrimination. Inner-city dialect and Southern speech patterns contribute interest and authenticity, and the pace is fast and the tone upbeat. The author's earlier *Cornrows* (1979; illus. Carole Byard), a picture book about the origin and significance of the hairstyle, has been better received.

177 Young, Al, *Seduction by Light*, Delta, 1988 (paper), ISBN 0-440-55003-3, $7.95, 338 pp. Ages 15 up, grades 10 up.

Humorous realistic novel with fantasy elements set in the present-day Los Angeles area. African-American Mamie Franklin, about forty-five, a beautiful, sexy, ex-singer, ex-bit actress, now a domestic, tells of the tumultuous events of the last year of her life, starting with the attempted robbery of her garage. The motive behind this puzzling occurrence is not explained until the book's end but gives some unity to the otherwise disjunctive plot, which also involves the mysterious appearances of Mamie's beloved deceased common-law husband, with whom she has practical and philosophical discussions; her relationship with her movie mogul employer and his wife, the eccentric, white Carleton Chryslers; getting white Harry Silverstone, her sometime agent now a billionaire producer, to acknowledge the paternity of Mamie's bright son, Benjie, an aspiring writer; her love affair with Theo, a handsome young waiter half her age, with whom she is making love when a violent earthquake hits the Los Angeles area; and the occasional ghostly appearances of the loquacious, historical Benjamin Franklin, who helps Mamie conclude that one must make the best of whatever life offers, since the here and now is all delusionary anyway, a seduction of light. Some other characters have dimension, but essentially the book is a witty, occasionally hilarious portrait of jaunty, enduring, eminently practical, revealingly honest Mamie, whose common sense, tenacious attempts to survive while caring for an ill husband and providing for a bright son engage the reader's emotions and win admiration. Mamie is a stylish lady who even departs this life with flair. Adding spice are numerous allusions to real-life show-business figures (or obvious spin-offs) and the ways of the film capital. While reading just for plot is not especially demanding, an appreciation of texture requires application. A short story by Young appears in Joyce Carol Thomas's *A Gathering of Flowers* (no. 146).

2

African Americans: Books of Oral Tradition

178 Gianni, Gary, ret., *John Henry*, illus. Gary Gianni, Kipling, 1988 (hardcover), ISBN 0-9437-1818-X, $9.95, 30 pp. Ages 4–10, grades PS–5.

Retelling of the legend of the champion African-American steel driver. The narrative follows the story's familiar features. John Henry is born on a stormy night, hammer in hand, grows to be very tall and extremely strong, loves to work, has a series of jobs none of which seems "natural" to him, although he performs impressively at each, and longs for one where he can use a hammer. He finally finds it with the railroad, where, while constructing the Big Bend Tunnel through the West Virginia mountains, he executes tremendous feats of strength and courage and competes against a steam drill, winning by using two hammers, one in each hand, but dying soon after from overexertion. The narrative employs suspense, dialect in the dialogue, and many action words to create excitement and a good pace. The full-color, somewhat glowing paintings usually sweep across the lower portion of both pages. They depict such various jobs of John Henry as in the cotton fields, on the Mississippi steamer, and in the tunnel. Some have many details of the work and people involved and show John Henry towering above the rest. Several close-ups depict him as powerfully muscled and good looking. The contest picture shows tremendous strain on his forearms and tension around his eyes and on the facial muscles. A foreword by Sandra Dolby Stahl, of the Folklore and American Studies Department at Indiana University, tells about the origin of the legend and the ways the story has been transmitted. This impressive book is one in the Kipling Press Library of American Folktales. For comparison, see *A Natural Man* (no. 186).

179 Goss, Linda, and Marian E. Barnes, eds., *Talk That Talk: An Anthology of African-American Storytelling,* Touchstone, 1989 (hardcover), ISBN 0-671-67167-7, $24.95, 517 pp.; (paper), ISBN 0-671-67168-5, $12.95, 512 pp. Ages 12 up, grades 7 up.

Large, multigenre collection divided into seven sections: animal tales and fables, memoirs, sermons, stories of family and home, ghost and witch stories, humorous tales and anecdotes, and rhymes, rhythms, and raps. The volume offers a wealth of material but makes no distinction between such stories from the folk tradition, as the Brer Rabbit tales and reporting from ex-slaves and such literary works as stories by Nikki Giovanni and Ruby Dee and poems by well-known black writers and raps, rhymes, and song lyrics by known performers. The unifying principle seems to be that they are all in the voices of African-Americans, but even that is inconsistent, since some are translations or retellings of stories from Africa, some from the U.S. South or from Northern cities, some in the unpolished voices caught by field collectors, some in formal, structured prose. Each section is followed by one or more commentaries, not all of which are closely related to the preceding material. For the poetry in the anthology, see no. 205.

180 Hamilton, Virginia, ret., *The People Could Fly: American Black Folktales,* illus. Leo and Diane Dillon, Knopf, 1985 (hardcover), ISBN 0-394-86925-7, $18.00, 192 pp. Ages 4 up, grades PS–12.

Collection of twenty-four stories from the oral tradition, divided into four sections. The first group, featuring animals, comprises mostly trickster tales familiar as Brer Rabbit or Uncle Remus stories, but in slightly different versions using Black English but not phonetic spelling. Where a modified Gullah dialect is used, a glossary is added. The other sections are "Tales of the Real, Extravagant, and Fanciful," "Tales of the Supernatural," and "Slave Tales of Freedom." Each selection is followed by a brief commentary, usually telling of the origin of the particular version and something of the tale type and prominent motifs. A bibliography of published folklore sources is also provided. A feeling of the oral transmission comes through in the simple, direct style and dialectical language. The selection offers enough variety so the book can be read straight through, but each tale is brief enough to be read aloud or told to younger children. The illustrations in shaded black and white, many of them full page, greatly enhance the book.

181 Harris, Joel Chandler, ret., *Further Tales of Uncle Remus: The Misadventures of Brer Rabbit, Brer Fox, Brer Wolf, the Doodang, and Other Creatures*, ed. Julius Lester, illus. Jerry Pinkney, Dial, 1990 (hardcover), ISBN 0-8037-0610-3, $14.89, 148 pp. Ages 10 up, grades 5 up.

Large collection of African-American trickster tales retold in what Lester terms "modified contemporary southern black English," much easier to read than the original Harris version. It follows two earlier volumes, *The Tales of Uncle Remus: The Adventures of Brer Rabbit* (1987) and *More Tales of Uncle Remus: Further Adventures of Brer Rabbit, His Friends, Enemies, and Others* (1988). Strangely, though the character of the old slave telling stories to a white boy has been eliminated, his name is retained in the titles, an element that may make some modern readers uncomfortable. Each volume is preceded by an introduction telling something of the history of the tales or the rationale for the particular selection. Illustrations are mostly black-and-white drawings with a few double-page spreads in color.

182 Harris, Joel Chandler, ret., *Jump on Over: The Adventures of Brer Rabbit and His Family*, ad. Van Dyke Parks, illus. Barry Moser, Harcourt, 1989 (hardcover), ISBN 0-15-241354-5, $15.95, 40 pp. Ages 5–12, grades K–7.

Highly illustrated, oversized book of five African-American trickster tales, told in English far easier to read than the original version by Harris, but somewhat more dialectical than the collections edited by Julius Lester (see no. 181). The stories are preceded by a brief "Illustrator's Note," and followed by the music and words to a song, "Home," by the adapter. Illustrations are watercolors, not on every page but frequent, some black-and-white brush paintings, and some full-page or double-page color spreads. Although the text is longer than most young children can read to themselves, the wealth of pictures makes this version more suitable for reading aloud in preschool or in early grades than the more extensive Lester collections. This book follows two previous volumes, *Jump! The Adventures of Brer Rabbit* (1986) and *Jump Again* (1988).

183 Hooks, William H., ret., *The Ballad of Belle Dorcas*, illus. Brian Pinkney, Knopf, 1990 (hardcover), ISBN 0-394-8465-1, $14.95, 48 pp. Ages 7–12, grades 2–7.

Based on a conjure tale from the tidewater area of the Carolinas, this highly illustrated book tells of Belle Dorcas, a "free-issue" girl whose father, the white slave master, freed her at birth although her mother remains his house slave. Belle falls in love with Joshua, a slave, and is happy until a new master decides to sell him. She appeals to Granny Lizard, a "cunger" woman, who shows her how to change him into a cedar tree in the daytime and her lover at night. Again she is happy until the new master has the tree cut and made into a smokehouse. With advice from Granny Lizard, she rubs her cunger bag around the smokehouse at night, and Joshua appears as he does every night until they are old. The title is misleading, since the book is prose, but the story captures genuine American folklore with just enough spookiness to add flavor. Illustrations are realistic, mostly full page, done in pen and ink tinted with colored pencil or pastel.

184 Lyons, Mary E., ret., *Raw Head, Bloody Bones: African-American Tales of the Supernatural*, Scribner's, 1991 (hardcover), ISBN 0-684-19333-7, $11.95, 88 pp. Ages 10 up, grades 5 up.

Fifteen folktales, mostly from the United States with a few from the Caribbean, divided into four groups: Gullah Goblins, Ghosts, Monsters, and Superhumans. These stories appear in the words of the tellers, only slightly edited for clarity, each followed by a commentary about the origin, tale type, or interesting parallels. At the end there are notes, telling where each story was collected and by whom, a bibliography, and a list of suggested readings. These have the genuineness of unpolished field collections to interest knowledgeable readers and enough variety of spookiness and gore to enthrall a less sophisticated audience. Well-spaced type and attractive section-divider decorations keep the book from looking like a text.

185 Sanfield, Steve, ret., *The Adventures of High John the Conqueror*, illus. John Ward, Orchard, 1989 (hardcover), ISBN 0-531-05807-7, $12.95; Dell (paper), ISBN 0-440-40556-4, $3.25, 113 pp. Ages 9–11, grades 4–6.

Sixteen stories of the trickster figure of African-American folklore, John, or High John, sometimes called High John the Conqueror. This wily slave is repeatedly able to get the best of his master, usually by making the man laugh or agree to a bargain that John cleverly twists to his advantage. Although originating before the Civil War, these stories continued to be told after the end of slavery, as illustrated in the last four in the collection, in which Old Master has been replaced by Old Boss, owner of the sharecropped land. John is lazy, impudent, and irreverent, the epitome of what slaves or any oppressed people would like to be. Sanfield includes notes before most of the stories, a longer general note on the stories at the end, and a bibliography. The humor of the tales, which are brief enough for fairly young readers, should appeal especially to middle-school children.

186 Sanfield, Steve, ret., *A Natural Man: The True Story of John Henry,* illus. Peter J. Thornton, Godine, 1986 (hardcover), ISBN 0-87923-630-2, $13.95, 48 pp.; Godine, 1990 (paper), ISBN 0-87923-844-5, $9.95, 32 pp. Ages 5–11, grades K–6.

Retelling of the legend of the African-American steel-driving hero, John Henry, including the familiar features of his story. He is born during the latter part of the slavery period on a stormy night, nature heralding his distinctiveness, and is a larger than usual baby. He is musically inclined, extremely strong, larger than life-sized, holds various jobs but shows special aptitude for steel driving, performs feats of prodigious strength, marries pretty Polly Ann, who also can drive steel, has a baby boy, and takes employment with the railroad company building the Big Bend Tunnel through the West Virginia Mountains, where, as he himself predicted, he dies of overexertion after competing with a steam drill. The narrative is beyond picture-book length, almost novelette, but is slow starting because of an extended introduction about the birth night. The pacing is uneven, and background information is not worked smoothly into the story. Verses here and there, rhyming speeches of John Henry, and the repetition of the words natural man give hints of the ballad origin, and occasionally homely expressions add to the folk hero quality. Facing and balancing the text, which is framed on the left, are framed black-and-white drawings close to the viewer's plane. While overly romantic and static, they employ light and dark usefully and are most notable for their distinctive placement of objects and figures. They show John Henry's magnificently muscular build and his earnest, solid character as reflected in his face, establish the period with clothing and interiors and exteriors of dwellings, and depict important scenes. Ballad verses garnered from various sources (not given) and the traditional music conclude the book. No background notes are given. The book provides an interesting contrast to such other versions as that of Gary Gianni (no. 178).

187 San Souci, Robert D., ret., *The Boy and the Ghost,* illus. J. Brian Pinkney, Simon & Schuster, 1989 (hardcover), ISBN 0-671-67176-6, $13.99; 1993 (paper), ISBN 0-671-79248-2, $5.95, unp. Ages 4–10, grades PS–5.

Folktale adaptation set not long ago in the rural American South, a variant of a widespread tale in which the body of a dead person is reassembled gradually and the reconstituted person reveals the location of a treasure. African-

American Thomas, middle child of seven in a very poor farm family, bravely sets out to seek his fortune. Along the way, he politely shares his meager soup with a ragged old man who tells him of a haunted house reputed to have a treasure. Thomas keeps his head that night while a big, red-haired ghost reincarnates limb by limb from the fireplace. The ghost leads him to a treasure cache and instructs him to dig it up and share one-half with the poor. In addition to depicting details of action and establishing setting, the off-the-page, toned-down watercolors capture the eeriness, humor, and drama of this pleasingly amusing account of virtue and composure rewarded. The reteller's note concluding the book says the narrative is based upon two "negro [sic] short stories" eventually printed in the *Journal of American Folk-Lore* in 1906 and gives a brief history of the tale type.

188 San Souci, Robert D., ret., *Sukey and the Mermaid,* illus. Brian Pinkney, Four Winds, 1992 (hardcover), ISBN 0-02-778141-0, $14.95, unp. Ages 4–10, grades PS–5.

Retelling of an African-American Sea Island, South Carolina folktale, a Cinderella variant. Young Sukey takes refuge by the sea from her "do-nothing" new stepfather's work demands. There she is befriended by Mama Jo, a "beautiful, brown-skinned, black-eyed mermaid" with "hair as green as seaweed," who each day gives her a gold coin, which arouses her parents' greed and results in more hard work for the girl. Eventually, Mama Jo helps Sukey marry a good and handsome youth, while the stepfather's cupidity culminates in his death in the angry sea. The text is euphonious and strongly composed, employing unusual expressions and verses typical of oral story and projecting the flavor of the storytelling situation. Augmenting the text are impressive scratchboard and oil paintings whose sculptured effect creates reality and establishes the racial context and nature of the characters. The felicitous combination of text and artwork results in an especially attractive and distinctive book. An author's note about sources appears at the end.

189 San Souci, Robert D., ret., *The Talking Eggs: A Folktale from the American South,* illus. Jerry Pinkney, Dial, 1989 (hardcover), ISBN 0-8037-0619-7, $15.00, unp. Ages 4–10, grades PS–5.

Retelling of an African-American folktale, a version of the "Toads and Diamonds" kind of story. Sent to the well for water, sweet, obedient Blanche generously draws water for a thirsty, old woman and is rewarded by the gift of talking eggs which change into such marvels as beautiful dresses and a carriage. Her sister, ill-natured, lazy, jealous Rose, attempts to secure the same finery but derides the old woman, and she and her ugly mother are chased into the woods by swarms of malevolent creatures like yellow jackets and whip snakes. Impressive, full-page, detailed watercolors reveal character, establish the rural, period setting, depict the action, and provide humor and drama. They show the characters as light-skinned African Americans. The pictures of the old woman's multicolored hens and of gorgeously dressed dancing rabbits stand out. The reteller's note indicates that the story is adapted from a Creole folktale, descendant of a story brought by French immigrants, variations of which spread orally throughout the South.

190 Wahl, Jan, ret., *Little Eight John,* illus. Wil Clay, Lodestar, 1992 (hardcover), ISBN 0-525-67367-9, $14.00, unp. Ages 5–8, grades K–3.

Adapted folktale of a disobedient boy who delights in bringing troubles to his family by doing just what his mother prohibits—kicking "toad frogs," sitting backward in a chair, counting his teeth, sleeping with his head at the foot of the bed—all of which bring bad luck and near disaster. When she warns him, "Don't have the Sunday moans, for fear of Old Raw Head Bloody Bones," he deliberately groans and moans all Sunday, until he is changed into a spot of jam which his mother almost wipes away. Highly realistic illustrations spread over the double pages bleeding to the edges. The text and sometimes related pictures are superimposed and show Little Eight John as an active African-American country boy of perhaps six or eight. The story ends abruptly, as if a page or at least a phrase has been omitted.

191 Wahl, Jan, ret., *Tailypo!* illus. Wil Clay, Holt, 1991 (hardcover), ISBN 0-8050-0687-7, $14.95, unp. Ages 5–8, grades K–3.

Playfully scary folktale, in picture-book form, of an old African-American man who chops off the tail of a creature that creeps through the cracks of his cabin, then cooks and eats it. That night he wakes to hear the creature scratching its way in, demanding its "Tailypo," and he calls his dogs to chase it away. This happens a second time, but the third time his dogs do not come, because the creature has grabbed them, so it gets in and gobbles the man up. The realistic illustrations completely dominate the book, filling every page to the edges, with the brief text overprinted on them in white. Colors are appropriately dark greens and shadowy blues to suit the mood with the creature emanating a fiery orange-red.

3

African Americans: Books of Poetry

192 Adoff, Arnold, *In for Winter, Out for Spring,* illus. Jerry Pinkney, Harcourt, 1991 (hardcover), ISBN 0-15-238637-8, $14.95, unp. Ages 4–9, grades PS–4.

Some two dozen free verse poems about family life and activities through the changing seasons, like playing in the snow, digging in the earth in early spring, a monarch butterfly and fireflies, a storm, and Granny's aching ninety-two-year-old legs, from the vantage of Rebecca, the youngest child. The poems are pleasing references to family life but lack such poetic qualities as rhythm and figurative language. The scattered arrangement of the words on the page has no apparent purpose and calls attention to itself, and some of the diction seems affected. The full-page illustrations in impressionistic watercolors bolster the text and provide attractive scenes in the life of a middle-class family and identify them as African American. *Sports Pages* (1986), about young athletes engaging in different sports, is for the eight-to-twelve age range, and has similar technical limitations. Although the poems are not racially specific, the black-and-white sketches show some of the athletes as African American. While Adoff's own poems fall short, his anthologies, among them *I Am the Darker Brother* (1968) and *Celebrations* (1977), are fine collections from the best African-American poets.

193 Angelou, Maya, *Now Sheba Sings the Song,* illus. Tom Feelings, Dial, 1987 (hardcover), ISBN 0-525-24501-4, $11.95; (paper), ISBN 0-525-48374-8, $6.95, 56 pp. Ages 12 up, grades 7 up.

Free verse poem celebrating African-American women, illustrated with many drawings in sepia tones of black women of various ages and types from, the introduction says, the United States and other North American countries, South America, and Africa. The very brief text was written to accompany the artwork and, in the oversized format, is overwhelmed by it. Together, however, they make a beautiful book designed to express pride in both black heritage and femaleness. Since there is some anatomically explicit language and some of the drawings are of nudes, this "picture book" is not intended for young children.

194   Angelou, Maya, *On the Pulse of Morning*, Random, 1993 (paper), ISBN 0-6790-74838-5, $5.00, unp. Ages 12 up, grades 7 up.

Inaugural poem written for and read at the ceremony installing William J. Clinton as president. In Whitmanesque lines, it evokes the spirits of the Rock, the River, and the Tree, each standing for elements of this country and its people, celebrating the nation's endurance, the diversity of its population, and its ability to change and strive for better things. Its central message is embodied in its final lines in which, "on the pulse of this new day," the poet exhorts her audience to look about at fellows and country with calm and a strong sense of hope for a better future. Angelou is the author of a number of earlier books of poetry, among them, *I Shall Not Be Moved* (1990), a collection of thirty-three poems, some about the African-American slave experience and some portraits in free verse, among them "Coleridge Jackson," victim of an abusive boss who takes his anger out on his family, and "Born That Way," a picture of a young prostitute. The more formal poems, which are stronger on expression than on skill, too often are marred by clumsy rhyme and lines padded to make them scan, though a number have something interesting to say, for example, the seven little four-line verses of "Seven Women's Blessed Assurance," virtually doggerel taken separately, which add up to a statement about possibilities for feminist pride.

195   Bryan, Ashley, sel., *All Night, All Day: A Child's First Book of African-American Spirituals*, illus. Ashley Bryan, Atheneum, 1991 (hardcover), ISBN 0-689-31662-3, $14.95, 48 pp. Ages 4 up, grades PS up.

Twenty African-American spirituals with music. In a concluding note, Bryan indicates that these songs come from the time of American slavery and are "unique in the song literature of the world." Included are such well-known ones as "He's Got the Whole World in His Hands," as well as less familiar songs. The pieces are grouped in sets of two, each pair of which is introduced by a vibrantly colored, geometrically stylized, double-page spread depicting some aspect of the songs to come. For example, the picture for "Open the Window, Noah" shows the dove arriving with olive leaf while a black Noah waits with outreached arms. A beautiful book for all ages, upbeat and life affirming. Earlier, Bryan published two unusually beautiful books, *Walk To-*

gether, Children: Black American Spirituals (1974), and its sequel, *I'm Going to Sing: Black American Spirituals* (1982), both elegant combinations of moving poetry, music, and black-and-white, strongly executed woodcuts.

196 Bryan, Ashley, *Sing to the Sun,* illus. Ashley Bryan, HarperCollins, 1992 (hardcover), ISBN 0-06-020829-5, $15.00, unp. Ages 4–8, grades PS–3.

Twenty-three mostly free verse poems of one or two stanzas, one poem per page, beside each a vibrantly colorful, sophisticated, though primitive in style, painting, the geometric figures calling to mind stained glass windows, the segments edged with white rather than black lines. The poems offer observations about "little brother's legs [that]/ Are springs," and Granny, who "had a way with fruit trees," reactions to hurricanes, the full moon, impending rain, and reminiscences. Some poems are pensive, some pure fantasy, for example, those about mermaids and blackbird parties, some seem tied to the Caribbean in content and language although most are unlocalized, and all are gentle and project an upbeat enthusiasm about life. The colors of Bryan's pictures support the Caribbean locale, and the illustrations identify the people as black. This is a warm and happy family book, in which the richly hued pictures strengthen the poems.

197 Carlstrom, Nancy White, *Wild Wild Sunflower Child Anna,* illus. Jerry Pinkney, Macmillan, 1987 (hardcover), ISBN 0-02-717360-7, $14.95; (paper), ISBN 0-689-71445-9, $4.95, unp. Ages 4–7, grades PS–2.

In free verse with occasional rhyme, a young African-American girl's morning is described—running, rolling in the grass, picking berries, climbing trees, crossing a stream, finally falling asleep. Pinkney pictures her as a sturdy child with light brown skin, a yellow dress, and hair caught into a ribbon-tied bunch on each side of her head. Without the illustrations, there is nothing ethnic specific.

198 Cummings, Pat, *Jimmy Lee Did It,* illus. author, Lothrop, 1985 (hardcover), ISBN 0-688-04632-0, $13.95, unp. Ages 4–7, grades PS–2.

Rhymed picture-story book narrated by Angel, a young African-American girl whose brother, Artie, explains that all the messes and mischief in the house are caused by Jimmy Lee, an elusive character that Angel can never see. The situations are not ethnic specific. Bright, cheerful illustrations create much of the humor.

199   Dove, Rita, *Thomas and Beulah*, Carnegie-Mellon, 1986 (paper), ISBN 0-88748-021-7, $9.95, 79 pp. Ages 14 up, grades 9 up.

Pulitzer Prize–winning collection of forty-four short, mostly one-page, free verse poems by the 1993–1994 Library of Congress poet laureate. A celebration of African-American life and family and her own forebears, the linked poems tell of her maternal grandparents, who in the 1920s left the South for Akron, Ohio, part of the black movement north in the early twentieth century. In the opening poem, "The Event," Thomas arrives north poor but hopeful, with "good looks and a mandolin." Later he courts proper, circumspect Beulah, stylish in "pleated skirt" that fans out sharply about her. At first, she refuses even to enter his "turtledove Nash" ("Courtship"). The two marry, have four daughters, who marry and have children, and after Thomas's death, the daughters invite Beulah to a Fourth of July picnic, where memories of life with her dead husband flood over her. Not only a series of family portraits, the poems also recreate the period: "They were poor then but everyone had been poor" ("The Satisfaction Coal Company"). Entertainment consists of listening to the "old trickster" on the radio, "Kingfish addressing the Mystic Knights of the Sea" ("Lightnin' Blues"). The poems as a whole are lean on imagery and music, but a warm intimacy, gentle accuracy, and a positive, dignified tie with the past distinguish them. A family chronology is included. Among Dove's other books of poems is *Grace Notes* (1989), forty-seven short, free verse poems, a few of them prose poems, of observation and personal experience, the vast majority unrelated to race but not to gender. Most rely for their effect on pictures, which are vivid and developed with economy, but some combine the visual and auditory felicitously, and a few are memorably pithy, as in "The Wake," in which an absence is described as being "like an invitation"; "Backyard, 6 A.M.," which begins, "Nudged by bees, morning brightens to detail"; and "Canary," which says that Billie Holiday's "burned voice" ... "had as many shadows as lights," and calls her face "ruined" and her gardenia her "signature." *Selected Poems* (1993) includes the poems in *Thomas and Beulah* as well as those from two earlier books of poems, *The Yellow House on the Corner* (1980) and *Museum* (1983). Among Dove's books of fiction are *Through the Ivory Gate* (no. 26), a novel, which also reflects family history, and *Fifth Sunday* (no. 25), a collection of short stories.

200   Dragonwagon, Crescent, *Half a Moon and One Whole Star*, illus. Jerry Pinkney, Macmillan, 1986 (hardcover), ISBN 0-02-733120-2, $14.95, unp. Ages 4–8, grades PS–3.

Rhymed lullaby in picture-story book form taking the reader through one night of reality and dreams for African-American Susan. The poem follows the nighttime activities of a sailor at watch on his ship, a jazz saxophonist playing at a club, bakers "white with flour," and animals in nearby woods and distant jungles. It asks such questions as, "Will morning glories, closed up tight" hold their color through the darkness until the next day dawns, and answers each in a gentle, euphonious, and repetitive refrain. The lavish watercolor illustrations that depict scenes of nature are especially impressive.

201 Evans, Mari, *A Dark and Splendid Mass*, Harlem River, 1992 (paper), ISBN 0-86316-312-2, $8.00, 62 pp. Ages 13 up, grades 8 up.

Thirty-eight poems, mostly one page or less in length, unrhymed, and gently metered, that show evidence of careful crafting and reveal a strongly feminine slant. Most are serious, sad, or pensive in attitude, and levity, except for irony or cynicism, is notably absent. Included are blues songs, love songs, pictures of New York inner-city street people, and cries of the poverty-stricken. Some celebrate family and friends, some lament wrongs committed by individuals or society, but all honor life in terms of people. "Limited Aggression" speaks of lands with "one-armed children [who] watch" further atrocities unmoved, so used to seeing horrors they have become inured to them, and "The Elders" echoes the music and singing of a church service as it pays tribute to those who, though they walk painfully and are gray, "be our heritage" and strong moral support, a "national treasure." The book's title appears as a line in "Amtrak Suite I," where the persona on a train at dusk sees cliffs, mountains, and trees as a beautiful but fearful horde of weaponed "veterans at attention." While occasionally the pieces seem overly intellectualized, artificial in tone, exaggerated in image, or unnecessarily obscure in lines or entirety, most poems make their mark well, and some have a memorable quality. Evans has published other poetry for adults, including *I Am a Black Woman* (1970) and *Nightstar* (1981), and books for children, including *J. D.* (1973; illus. Jerry Pinkney) and *Jim Flying High* (1979; illus. Ashley Bryan), both picture-story books, and *Singing Black* (1976; illus. Ramon Price), a collection of poems.

202 Falwell, Cathryn, *Feast for 10*, illus. Cathryn Falwell, Clarion, 1993 (hardcover), ISBN 0-395-62037-6, $14.95, unp. Ages 3–8, grades PS–3.

Realistic picture-story counting book that goes from one to ten in telling how an African-American family, a mother and four children, baby along, shop for groceries, prepare the meal, with Dad helping, and joyfully eat it with, probably, an extended family. The text moves in simple rhymes from one for the grocery cart through numbering the vegetables they gather to ten for the hands who help load the car. The one-to-ten sequence repeats for the trip home and meal preparation and concludes with "ten hungry folks to share the meal!" The story's unifying concept is engaging, but best are the striking, abstract, richly colored collages of cut paper and various materials that faithfully depict the numbers and make the food look delicious. Although the faces seem stiff, they are not stereotyped. The garments are exceptionally lifelike, so real that one reaches out to touch them. The weaves give the impression of the cloth being glued to the page. This is a pleasing book about family life.

203 Falwell, Cathryn, *Shape Space*, illus. Cathryn Falwell, Clarion, 1992 (hardcover), ISBN 0-395-61305-1, $13.95, unp. Ages 4–7, grades PS–2.

Short picture-book fantasy intended to introduce geometric shapes. The partially rhymed text gives directions to and follows a nimble little African-American girl gymnast, who takes many variously colored forms from a storage box, builds with them, bounces on them, puts them on as clothes, and creates a fellow dancer out of them. The two cavort about exuberantly until it is time to stop, and the girl puts all the shapes back in the box. The narrative is sprightly, and the names of the shapes repeat in a catchy refrain. The brilliant colors of the shapes create the illusion of depth, and the text and pictures are refreshingly happy and upbeat.

204 Fields, Julia, *The Green Lion of Zion Street*, illus. Jerry Pinkney, McElderry, 1988 (hardcover), ISBN 0-689-50414-4, $13.95; Aladdin, 1993 (paper), ISBN 0-689-71693-1, $4.95, unp. Ages 4–9, grades PS–4.

A single original poem in picture-book form. While waiting for the bus on a foggy morning, a group of urban African-American children grow bored and cold; they cross a high bridge beyond which they see a large statue of a green lion. In the hazy light, they imagine it is fierce, growling, roaring, and even lunging at them, and they race for safety. Later return to find that it is really inanimate. Then they discover that they have missed the bus. The free verse employs colloquial diction for the "we" persona when describing the children but formal, mouth-filling, provocative language for their impressions of the lion. The full-page, expressive paintings extend the verse and give it life. The close-ups of the children and the lion are moving.

205 Goss, Linda, and Marian E. Barnes, eds., *Talk That Talk: An Anthology of African-American Storytelling,* Touchstone, 1989 (hardcover), ISBN 0-671-67167-7, $24.95, 517 pp.; (paper), ISBN 0-671-67168-5, $12.95, 512 pp. Ages 12 up, grades 7 up.

Large multigenre anthology of poems, rhymes, stories, memoirs, folktales, and sermons, all connected by being in "the storyteller's voice." A few of the poems come directly from the oral tradition, among them "The Ibo Landing Song," collected on Saint Simons Island in Georgia; the words of such spiri-tuals as "All God's Children Got Shoes"; and sermons, for example, "Ezekiel and the Vision of Dry Bones," transcribed in Oakland, California. More of the poems are by well-known writers, including "The Creation" by James Weldon Johnson, "Aunt Sue's Stories" by Langston Hughes, and "The Party" by Paul Laurence Dunbar. There are also such song lyrics as "Signifyin' Monkey" by Oscar Brown, Jr., and rhythms and raps, among them "Get Ready, Inc." by Douglass "Jocko" Henderson and "African-American History Rap" by Sharon Jordan Holley. The majority of the entries are prose from the oral tradition. For discussion of the book as a whole, see no. 179.

206 Greenfield, Eloise, *I Make Music,* illus. Jan Spivey Gilchrist, Black Butterfly, 1991 (board book), ISBN 0-86316-205-3, $5.95, unp. Ages 1–3, grade PS.

Very short board book in verse, one of a series, in which a little girl "make[s] good music" on the piano, her thigh, her toy drums, her thumbs, and her toy trombone and xylophone, while her mommy and daddy sing along. A happy book of warm family life for the very youngest, in which the simple story is repeated in colorful but not distinguished pictures. Others include *My Doll, Keshia* (1991), *Big Friend, Little Friend* (1991), and *My Daddy and I* (1991). The pictures identify the characters as African Americans.

207 Greenfield, Eloise, *Night on Neighborhood Street,* illus. Jan Spivey Gilchrist, Dial, 1991 (hardcover), ISBN 0-8037-0777-0, $13.95, unp. Ages 5 up, grades K up.

Seventeen original poems about family and neighborhood events among urban African Americans. In mostly songs and iambic patterns, but with in-teresting variations in tone and rhythms, the usually structured poems de-scribe children at sidewalk games, an overnight, a church service, and in a boarded-up house. Most are scenes of family or friends, happy together, but one tells of a drug dealer coming and another of an angry man speaking at a meeting. From blues to toe tappers, the rhythms are mostly upbeat, and the attitude is life affirming. The full-color, full-page paintings are realistic and close to the viewer's plane, the portrait views being especially striking. This is a beautiful book with poetry that, on the whole, is technically true as well as emotionally expressive. In *Nathaniel Talking* (1988), a beautifully expressive book illustrated realistically and powerfully by Gilchrist in black-and-white pencils, a young black boy raps, jingles, jives, rhymes, and sings his way through eighteen pensive, sad, cheerful, even exuberant poems that celebrate his life and friends as he sees them. Earlier, Greenfield published *Honey, I Love, and Other Love Poems* (1978; illus. Leo and Diane Dillon), a small but choice collection told from the young child's point of view. The poems in *Under the Sunday Tree* (1988) reflect the Caribbean region and are very attractively illustrated in colorful primitives by Mr. Amos Ferguson.

208   Hudson, Cheryl Willis, and Bernette G. Ford, *Bright Eyes, Brown Skin,* illus. George Ford, Just Us, 1990 (hardcover), ISBN 0-940975-10-6, $12.95; (paper), ISBN 0-940975-23-8, $6.95, unp. Ages 2–5, grades PS–K.

Simple rhyme of about fifty words, in picture book form, showing happy African-American children in a nursery school setting. Obviously designed to promote a positive self-image and a joyous school experience, the rhyme describes the boys and girls as having "A playful grin" and exceptionally attractive hair, features, and clothes. The large-page, realistic illustrations are attractive, but every child, except for a few who are asleep at the end, is smiling, mostly grinning broadly, even when eating and reading, producing a total effect of oversell.

209   Hudson, Wade, sel., *Pass It On: African-American Poetry for Children,* illus. Floyd Cooper, Scholastic, 1993 (hardcover), ISBN 0-590-45770-5, $14.95, 32 pp. Ages 4–10, grades PS–6.

Nineteen poems (the introductory one from oral tradition) by fourteen noted African-American poets, some older, some still writing. The poems were chosen because, although they have authors, they have a strong vocal quality and serve well to continue the "oral tradition that has been passed on by our ancestors from Africa." Hudson also says that "Each captures a special aspect of the rich African-American experience." There are such fun poems as "Peas" by Henry Dumas; such sad poems as "Incident" by Countee Cullen; such silly poems as "Prickled Pickles Don't Smile" by Nikki Giovanni; such serious ones as "Listen Children" by Lucille Clifton, which concludes the anthology and contains the book's title; and such poems of self-affirmation as the traditional "African Lullaby" and "Dream Variation" by Langston Hughes, and of self-discovery as "Midway" by Naomi Long Madgett. While almost all these selections are available elsewhere, many are infrequently reproduced. Cooper's colorful, richly emotive paintings dominate the book, whose poems for the most part provide a pleasing variety of voices and subjects.

210   Kendrick, Dolores, *The Women of Plums: Poems in the Voices of Slave Women,* Morrow, 1989 (paperback), ISBN 0-688-08347-1, $8.95, 124 pp. Ages 15 up, grades 10 up.

Nearly forty poems, all in unrhymed free verse, revealing different aspects of the lives of African-American women in slavery. "Ndzeli in Passage" tells of the terrible journey in a Portuguese slave ship; "Hattie on the Block" is spoken by a mother auctioned off with her little daughter; "A Slightly Colored Lady" is in the voice of a house slave, daughter of the white master. "Sidney Looking for Her Mother . . . " and " . . . While Her Mother Waits" are companion pieces of freed slaves, attempting to reunite. Although the author seems preoccupied by whippings that kill or maim, a few pieces are happier, like "Liza Lily in Silks," in which the black woman triumphs over her mistress, knowing that she has the real love of the man they share. The poems are in a wide variety of rhythms, and, despite occasional obscure lines, none is too difficult for high school students.

211   Langstaff, John, sel. and ed., *What a Morning!: The Christmas Story in Black Spirituals,* illus. Ashley Bryan, McElderry, 1987 (hardcover), ISBN 0-689-50422-5, $12.95, unp. Ages 4 up, grades PS up.

Five colorfully illustrated African-American spirituals with music about the major events of the Biblical Christmas story, starting with the prophecy from Isaiah through the angels' song and the birth in Luke to the coming of the wise men in Matthew; brief scripture passages introduce each song. Spirituals include "Mary Had a Baby" and "Go Tell It on the Mountain," and the collection opens with the title song. The detailed, double-spread and full-page paintings, richly hued, show the holy family as black, the three wise men of three different races. A note to teachers, parents, and instrumentalists appears at the end. In *Climbing Jacob's Ladder: Heroes of the Bible in African-American Spirituals* (1991), the selector and illustrator unite for another exceptionally beautiful combination of art, poetry, and music. The pictures, also racially specific, are less vibrantly colorful but function as eloquent complements to the nine songs about such important Old Testament figures as Noah,

Abraham, King David, and Daniel. A short italicized passage about the particular hero's accomplishments precedes the song about him.

212 Lautre, Denize, *Father and Son,* illus. Jonathan Green, Philomel, 1993 (hardcover), ISBN 0-399-21867-X, $11.95, unp. Ages 3–8, grades PS–3.

Picture-book poem of thirty-nine short lines about activities that fathers and sons do together which result in a special relationship between them. They hum together, admire the beauty of fruit trees together, and appreciate the breezes in each other's company. When the activity is abstract, the illustration shows a specific situation, for example, the father and son sitting in a porch swing, each reading a satisfying book. The poem's simple, literal, racially non-specific content is much expanded by the deep-toned, full-color, full-page paintings. They are set (according to the artist's note) among the Gullah of South Carolina and are based upon actual scenes of Gullah life—carrying bundles of wood on their heads, flying kites, walking on the beach and in the market, riding horses, and attending church. The handsome, real-life figures seem caught and fixed in place, and they have a solid feel that keeps the text from seeming sentimental. Beautifully composed, they uplift the text and make this a very attractive book.

213 Little, Leslie Jones, *Children of Long Ago,* illus. Jan Spivey Gilchrist, Philomel, 1988 (hardcover), ISBN 0-399-21473-9, $14.95, unp. Ages 5–10, grades K–5.

Sixteen verses about childhood in earlier times, mostly with rural settings, concerning such events as dressing up for church, chopping wood, feeding the hens, and listening to the grandfather clock. Usually without regular meter, they get their rhythmic quality by repeating lines and employ rhyme or near rhyme. The most telling verses seem to be specific memories—playing paper dolls, going barefoot after a rain, a little brother trying to jump over a ditch and falling in. Illustrations, covering the entire double pages with the text superimposed, show all the characters as attractive African Americans, but some readers may be disturbed by discrepancies from the words; for instance, the children are not dressed as described for church, and on their way to Sunday school they ride in a horse-drawn cart, not a buggy as the poem says.

214 Mattox, Cheryl Warren, ed., *Shake It to the One That You Love the Best: Play Songs and Lullabies from Black Musical Traditions,* illus. from the works of Varnette P. Honeywood and Brenda Joysmith, Warren-Mattox Productions, 1990 (paper), ISBN 0-9623381-0-9, $7.95, 56 pp. Ages 4–11, grades PS–6.

Collection of twenty-six African-American play songs and lullabies, words and music, accompanied by paintings selected from the artists' works, Joysmith's being richly colored, impressionistic pastels and Honeywood's decorative, two-dimensional collages, of children in various situations and attitudes. Bordering each page are photographs of multicolored weavings. The collection "is designed to help advance children's awareness in two aspects of Black culture—music and art" and merges "traditional songs with contemporary art." Opening the collection is the ring-game song, "Little Sally Walker," which is followed by others like "Hambone," "Loop De Loo," "Go In and Out the Window," and "Mary Mack," while lullabies include "All the Pretty Little Horses," "Short'ning Bread," and the concluding piece, "Kumbaya." Notes about the background of the songs appear along with directions for playing them. A table of contents and a collector's note are included. This is a remarkably handsome book.

215 McKissack, Patricia, and Fredrick McKissack, *Messy Bessey,* illus. Richard Hackney, Children's, 1987 (hardcover), ISBN 0-516-02083-8, $11.95, 32 pp. Ages 3–8, grades PS–3.

A realistic picture story in limited-vocabulary verse, a Rookie Reader, in sixty-six words listed at the end of the book. The simple, repetitive narrative describes the cluttered, sloppy state of little African-American Bessey's room, with, for example, crayoned walls, books not in their cases, "and games everywhere." Bessey is admonished by the authors to clean up, and accordingly she scrubs the walls and the floor and jams her things into the closet, thus winning the approval of the authors, who praise her. The colorful, cartoonish pictures show Bessey as a pretty, pony-bunned child, and her room filled with various toys and other items scattered about in great disarray. The text serves its purpose of providing reading material with lots of repeated words and incidents to which young readers can relate. *Messy Bessey's Closet* (1989), also a verse Rookie Reader, finds Bessey cleaning out her overstuffed closet. She gets rid of items she no longer wants by giving them away to friends. The ninety-two words are listed at the end. As in the earlier book, Richard Hackney's illustrations characterize Bessey as earnest, lively, and likable and humorously depict the mess and the process of cleaning up her closet. Bessey's friends come from various races. Rookie Reader *Messy Bessey's Garden* (1991) continues the series.

216 Medearis, Angela Shelf, *Dancing with the Indians,* illus. Samuel Byrd, Holiday, 1991 (hardcover), ISBN 0-8234-0893-0, $14.95, unp.; (paper), ISBN 0-8234-1023-4, $5.95, unp. Ages 5–10, grades K–5.

Four-line rhymed stanzas in the voice of a young African-American girl of the 1930s tell of her family's connection to the Seminole Indians, who rescued her grandfather when he was a runaway slave, and of their annual visit to the powwow to dance with the Indians and show their respect. Richly colored illustrations full of vividly impressionistic action and covering the entire page picture the Ribbon Dance, the Rattlesnake Dance, and the Stomp Dance, in which all the visitors join. Pages showing the black family in their wagon going to the dance and coming home in the early dawn are quiet contrasts. Although the story is heartwarming, the conception of the Indians may be dubious. It is not clear whether the "Fiercely painted dancers," also described as "fearless," "untamed," and whooping, are in the child's imagination or in the dance circle, a stereotype either way. The poetry has many padded lines and strained rhymes. An author's note at the end tells the family history on which this story is based.

217 Medearis, Angela, *Picking Peas for a Penny,* illus. Charles Shaw, State House, 1990 (hardcover), ISBN 0-938349-54-6, $11.95; (paper), ISBN 0-938349-55-4, $5.95, unp. Ages 5–8, grades K–3.

Described as a counting rhyme, this verse is far more interesting for the story it tells in text and pictures than it is for its technical quality, since it neither rhymes nor scans well. It recounts the childhood experiences of the author's mother in the 1930s, picking peas on their grandparents' farm for a penny a pound, then going to town in the wagon to spend their earnings, which convert to a big treat because, as one stanza says, after counting rhythmically from one to ten, "you can buy a lot with a penny during the Depression." The illustrations, black-and-white drawings with the characters' clothes and the basket rims in a single color, either green or pink, give a good sense of the seemingly endless fields and the marginal rural life, but the children and their grandparents are shown almost always smiling, unlikely in the middle of a long day in a temperature that is described as probably three digits.

218 Medearis, Angela Shelf, ed., *The Zebra-Riding Cowboy: A Folk Song from the Old West,* illus. Maria Christina Brusca, Holt, 1992 (hardcover), ISBN 0-8050-1712-7, $14.95, unp. All ages, grades K–12.

Cowboy song of the educated stranger on whom the ranch hands plan to play a trick by "lending" him the bucking outlaw named Zebra Dun. The dude turns the tables by coolly staying atop the striped horse and riding him to a standstill. The cartoonlike illustrations depict the stranger as an African American with glasses, dressed in city clothes, and carrying a carpet bag and books. An afterword by the author justifies this interpretation by telling something of the history of black and Hispanic cowboys. The endpapers give the music for the song.

219 Moss, Thylias, *Small Congregations,* Ecco, 1993 (hardcover), ISBN 0-88001-289-7, $22.95, 158 pp. Ages 15 up, grades 10 up.

Ninety poems of varying lengths by an African-American poet, about thirty of them not previously collected, the remaining selected from her published collections: *Hosiery Seams on a Bowlegged Woman* (1983), *Pyramid of Bone* (1989), *At Redbones* (1990), and *Rainbow Remnants in Rock Bottom Ghetto Sky* (1991). Reflections, observations, personal experiences, mostly free and unmusical, some prose poems, the pieces speak of matters relative to the African-American experience, like the slave boat, Medgar Evans, and racist incidents, but also of matters common to women or to those less fortunate or even oppressed. They comment on home situations, like baking and family members being together, of street violence, love, cleaning women, playing under hydrants, Christmas trees, religion, and church services—a wide variety of topics. Although some levity occurs, tones for the most part are serious, angry, intense, downbeat. The poet relies heavily on images, resulting in a surrealistic, esoteric, and ultimately self-conscious, intellectualized effect. The best crafted and most accessible poems are the shorter ones, and sections of the longer ones can stand alone worthily. Of the four earlier books, *At Redbones* and *Hosiery Seams on a Bowlegged Woman* contain the largest selection of poems apprehensible for young readers. This collection is for mature and sophisticated readers.

220   Slier, Deborah, ed., *Make a Joyful Sound: Poems for Children by African-American Poets,* illus. Cornelius Van Wright and Ying-Hwa Hu, Checkerboard, 1991 (hardcover), ISBN 1-56288-000-4, $12.95, 108 pp. Ages 4–11, grades PS–6.

Anthology of seventy-five poems by twenty-seven poets, almost all of whom are African American. Some older poets are represented, among them Langston Hughes with twelve poems, the largest number for one poet, Gwendolyn Brooks, and Countee Cullen, all by poems usually associated with them. More recent writers include Nikki Giovanni, Mari Evans, Sonia Sanchez, and Useni Eugene Perkins. The poems celebrate life, bad moments as well as good, and speak of such matters specifically African American as the nature of black nationhood and pride in blackness, but most concern common and universal problems or joys. Patterns and tones vary. The book is illustrated in color and pencil; its illustrations are enticing to the eye but also overshadow the poems and keep them from speaking for themselves.

221   Young, Al, *Heaven: Collected Poems 1956–1990,* Creative Arts, 1989 (hardcover), ISBN 0-88739-968-4, $24.95, 592 pp.; (paper), ISBN 0-88739-069-2, $17.95, 350 pp. Ages 14 up, grades 9 up.

Omnibus collection of four books of previously published poems, *Dancing* (1969), *The Song Turning Back into Itself* (1971), *Geography of the Near Past* (1976), and *The Blues Don't Change* (1982); three books of "published and unpublished poetry composed between 1956 and 1990," but previously uncollected, *By Heart* (1982–1985), *22 Moon Poems* (1984–1985), and *Sea Level* (1986–1990); and some sixty other uncollected poems written from 1956 to 1990, for a total of about three hundred by a prominent African-American poet, plus an introduction, title index, first line index, biographical information, and a list of Young's published books and screenplays. Young's poems speak personally, intimately, sometimes colloquially, sometimes formally, but always flexibly, usually in free verse, often to and about his family members, musical greats like Lena Horne, John Coltrane, Billie Holliday, and personalities like John Kennedy. He comments on incidents in his own life and from his extensive travels in such countries as Spain, Italy, and Mexico, as well as in the United States, and about the Mississippi of his origin and the Detroit of his growing up. His poems are filled with city sounds, highly visual, and often very musical in jazz and blues tones, inspired by his musical background. They tell of a friend's overdosing, the Rolling Stones being "busted" for drugs in Italy, J. R. Ewing and Donahue, sad and joyful lovers, black joys and sorrows, and general matters that have nothing to do with race or economic status—a very wide selection of subjects. Some are protests, some are polemical, and although some lose the interest, many hold up well and move quickly and smoothly to their points. Young has also written several novels about African Americans, among them the comic *Seduction by Light* (no. 177).

4

Asian Americans:
Books of Fiction

222 Betancourt, Jeanne, *More Than Meets the Eye,* Bantam, 1990 (hardcover), ISBN 0-553-05871-1, $14.95; 1991 (paper), ISBN 0-553-29351-6, $3.50, 166 pp. Ages 12 up, grades 7 up.

Contemporary realistic novel of school and community life set in Rutland, Vermont. Bright, pretty Liz Gaynor, fifteen, observes racism break out all over her community. Her parents are afraid that Ben Lee, her Chinese-American lab partner and the school's top student, will get favors from the teachers simply because Asian Americans are thought to excel in science. School bully Brad Mulville taunts Ben about his "slant eyes," calls him "Chinaman," and irrationally accuses him of ruining his truck tire. A teacher assumes Ben can converse with Dory Singh, a Cambodian refugee new in school, just because they are both Asian, and Liz and Ben resent their parents' overprotective, pushy efforts to get them to excel, especially Ben, since his parents keep urging him to live up to his Chinese heritage even though he feels more American than Chinese. When Koreans buy Stangonis's vegetable stand, the Chamber of Commerce must cope with the anti-Asian sentiment that engulfs the town. Eventually, the young people facilitate communication, the town accommodates itself to the newcomers, and a romantic attachment develops between Liz and Ben. The anti-Asian aspects seem deliberately contrived, and all characters are types, but numerous complications keep the pace up, and the various prejudices produce real-seeming hurts and tensions. School scenes are good.

223 Bezine, Ching Yun, *Children of the Pearl,* Signet, 1991 (paper), ISBN 0-451-17056-3, $4.99, 399 pp. Ages 15 up, grades 10 up.

Historical novel of Chinese immigrants from the Pearl River region to San Francisco from 1910 to 1935. The uncomplicated, linear plot follows the varying fortunes of four young people—three teenaged boys and one girl—who are sold by their families to a Western-appearing Chinese man who assures them the youths will be well cared for and will soon be rich in the Land of the Gold Mountains, as they call the United States. Quanming fares the best, growing wealthy in the employ of an uncle who has an import-export firm. Fachai, whose great ambition is to own a fishing boat and bring over his beautiful young wife, lacks the courage to take risks and remains a restaurant worker. Frail, shy Loone ends up a celebrated, affluent painter who dies of lung cancer. Beautiful Meiping, like many immigrant girls, finds herself in a brothel, from whose degradation she is saved by the love of a wealthy older white man trapped in an unhappy marriage. The intertwined fates of these four friends are played out against the enemy factions of Chinatown, an area drawn in splendor and squalor, neighborliness and viciousness. Though sometimes overextended, the book engagingly details the hardships, courage, and sometimes foolishness of the immigrants and of traditional and evolving Chinese cultures and the frequent friction that resulted, and it provides an interesting contrast with Laurence Yep's *Dragonwings* (1975) for a younger audience. Explicit sex scenes appear. The "lives and loves" popular fiction account of the Pearl River Chinese, their descendants, friends, and new friends continues with *Temple of the Moon* (1992) and *On Wings of Destiny* (1992), the former covering the years 1937 to the end of World War II, the latter carrying the story through 1977. Since the point of view switches frequently, these books are less successful as fiction, but the historical background is strong. The events take place mostly in China, Taiwan, and Hawaii, under the Communists, Chiang Kai-shek, and Japanese invasion. There are also passages about Pearl Harbor and the Japanese internment.

224 Chang, Heidi, *Elaine, Mary Lewis, and the Frogs,* illus. Heidi Chang, Crown, 1988 (hardcover), ISBN 0-517-56752-0, $8.95; Random, 1991 (paper), ISBN 0-679-80870-1, $2.50, 64 pp. Ages 7–10, grades 2–5.

Short, amusing contemporary school novel. Chinese-American Elaine Chow, six or seven and just moved from San Francisco to Iowa, feels apprehensive about her new school. But her young, snappily dressed, vivacious teacher, Ms. Bonovox, shares her liking for San Francisco and has interesting ideas. Her science project about flying objects leads to Elaine's friendship with Mary Lewis Thorp, who is crazy about frogs. Elaine gets the idea of combining frogs and flying by asking her father, whose hobby is making kites, to help the girls fashion a frog kite. The kite is a hit with their classmates, and at story's end Elaine is happily jumping rope with the other boys and girls. The kite-making gives Elaine's father an opportunity to tell something of the history of Chinese kites and the importance of them to the Chinese people, information that the girls share later with the class. The vocabulary and sentence structure of this "chapter" book are simple but fairly natural. The mood is light, and Elaine and Mary Lewis seem real and convincing foils. The class is lively and adventurous. Chang's black-and-white illustrations avoid making Elaine look exotic, and her skin tone is the same as Anglo Mary Lewis's, whose eyes are unusually round. A pleasant introduction to some aspects of Chinese culture for those just reading.

225 Chin, Frank, *Donald Duk,* Coffee House, 1991 (paperback), ISBN 0-018273-83-8, $9.95, 173 pp. Ages 12 up, grades 7 up.

In this boy's growing-up novel, twelve-year-old Donald Duk, resenting his name and his Chinese family, goes through the fifteen days of the New Year celebration in San Francisco Chinatown and in a series of hilarious scenes begins to appreciate his heritage. Part realistic action, part stream of consciousness, part dream fantasy, the novel follows Donald to lavish meals at his father's restaurant, his private school where he is the only Chinese American, and back to April 1869, when the Chinese workmen lay a record-breaking more than ten miles of track in a single day to beat the Irish crews working from the east. Surprisingly, the dreams, which include such characters from folklore as Kwang Kung and Lee Kuey, are shared by Donald's friend, Arnold Azalea, and their historical accuracy is confirmed by books the boys afterward find in the public library. Eccentric but believable characters abound: Donald's uncle for whom he is named, a Cantonese opera entrepreneur and star; his twin sisters, Penelope and Venus, in part typical American teenagers, who treat their parents with eye-rolling ironical affection; his aging dance teacher, the Chinese Fred Astaire; Mr. Doong, his tai chi instructor, who plays Spanish flamenco guitar; his mother who has learned her English and her American attitudes from television; and his father, who builds, with family help, 108 model airplanes to symbolize the 108 Outlaws of Chinese legend, loads them with fireworks, and launches them from Angel Island on the last night of the New Year celebration to fly and explode in the air. A host of minor characters throng the pages making a scene as crowded and lively as Grant Street itself, but Donald is the center, a boy angry, bewildered, mischievous, and appealing. A witty, often wild, picture of modern Chinese-American culture, published for adults but understandable to good readers of Donald's age. An earlier book by the author, *The Chinaman Pacific & Frisco R.R. Co.* (1988), contains eight short stories, skillfully written but mostly in a stream-of-consciousness, surrealistic style that makes them more difficult and with vivid sexual descriptions appropriate to only the most mature high school students.

226 Choi, Sook Nyul, *Echoes of the White Giraffe,* Houghton, 1993 (hardcover), ISBN 0-395-64721-5, $13.95, 137 pp. Ages 10 up, grades 5 up.

Autobiographical historical novel set in Pusan and Seoul, Korea, for several years beginning about 1950, sequel to *Year of Impossible Goodbyes* (1991), which occurs during World War II. For two and one-half years refugees from the fighting in Seoul, Sookan, her mother, and younger brother live in a tiny hut at the top of a mountain on the outskirts of Pusan. While the two children attend school, the mother works, and they all worry about where the rest of their family is. Each morning Sookan thrills to the sound of the voice of an old poet, whose name translates to White Giraffe, calling the sleepers to wake to a new, better life with the coming dawn. She maintains her friendship with a refugee schoolmate from Seoul, has a first romance with handsome Junho with whom she sings duets in the church choir, and keeps alive her hopes to study in the United States one day. After the armistice, they return to Seoul, where they reunite with Sookan's three older brothers in their house, which is mercifully not completely destroyed, but they discover that their father is dead. Sookan studies very hard and passes the test for school in the United States and, just before leaving, learns that Junho has entered a seminary to prepare for the priesthood. As the plane lifts for the flight out, she hears in her head the call of the poet on the mountain. The story moves without tension and has the tone of a memoir. Characters are barely developed, except for Sookan who tells her story almost in diary fashion. Few events are built up, and it is hard to keep track of time. The sense of disruption is strong, however, descriptions of nature are poetic and affectionate, and the sweet, brief romance strains against the bonds of traditional propriety.

227 Coerr, Eleanor, *Chang's Paper Pony,* illus. Deborah Kogan Ray, Harper, 1988 (hardcover), ISBN 0-06-023 1328-0, $13.00, 64 pp. Ages 4–8, grades PS–3.

Historical picture-story book, an I Can Read about Chinese immigrants in the San Francisco goldfields in the 1850s. Young Chang lives and works with his Grandpa Li, the cook at the Gold Ditch Hotel. More than anything he yearns for a pony like the one in the picture on their wall. When he cleans for kind miner Big Pete, he discovers gold flakes under the floor, and, re-minded by his Grandpa Li that the gold is really Big Pete's, gives them to the man, who buys him a pony with what he regards as Chang's share. School with the village Chinese teacher, kitchen work, taunts and ridicule from the rough miners, panning for gold, some Chinese philosophy—this sort of detail gives a limited idea of life for Chinese immigrants. Diction is satisfactory and sentences are well framed for the genre, but various incidents and the conclusion seem fabricated. The format is typical for easy-to-reads (big print, good leading), and the colored pencil illustrations in mostly clear blues and golds depict scenes well but show the characters stereotypically. A note about Chinese immigrants is included.

228   Collins, David, *Grandfather Woo Goes to School,* illus. Deborah Wilson, Milliken, 1990 (hardcover), ISBN 0-88335-784-4, $8.95; (paper) ISBN 0-88335-796-8, $4.95, 30 pp. Ages 5–8, grades K–3.

Early fiction reader about Willy, a little boy of Asian descent, who is worried that his blind grandfather, who has been invited to visit his school, will not live up to the previous exciting visitors: a bus driver, a fisherman, and a cook. He asks his grandfather to pretend that he does not know him. No one is more surprised than Willy when Grandfather Woo arrives in an army uniform bedecked with medals and tells fascinating war stories. When the other children doubt Willy's claim that this is his grandfather, the old man at first pretends not to know the boy, then, realizing that Willy has learned not to be ashamed of him, he pretends suddenly to recognize Willy by his hug. The book is clearly didactic in its frequently repetitive language, its vocabulary list at the end, and in its theme. While both Willy and his grandfather have Oriental features, there is no indication whether they are Americans of Chinese ancestry or have Korean origins or origins in some other Asian country.

229   Crew, Linda, *Children of the River,* Delacorte, 1989 (hardcover), ISBN 0-440-50122-9, $14.95; Dell, 1991 (paper), ISBN 0-440-21022-4, $3.50, 213 pp. Ages 12 up, grades 7 up.

Realistic sociological problem novel about refugees from Cambodia (Kampuchea) who settle in Oregon in 1979. In 1975, in a dramatic opening to the story, Sundara Suvann, then thirteen, flees from the Khmer Rouge with her Uncle Naro and Aunt Soka and their family, leaving her own family behind in Phnom Penh. Four years and half a world later, she gets all As in high school, plans to become a doctor, and works hard at home and in the fields picking fruits and vegetables in season to help the family meet bills and establish a good life. Her friendship with handsome, white football star, Jonathan McKinnon, who interviews her for a research paper on Cambodia, brings her into conflict with Soka, who insists that Sundara maintain traditional Khmer relations between the sexes. Characters are types and the plot is predictable, but the problems, hardships, and concerns of the relocated refugees come through vividly, in particular with respect to their need to maintain their cultural values while at the same time making necessary adaptations to American ways. This tension is personalized in the romance between the two young people.

230 Ehrlich, Gretel, *Heart Mountain*, Viking, 1988 (hardcover), ISBN 0-670-82160-8, $18.95, 412 pp. Ages 15 up, grades 10 up.

Historical novel of the four World War II years when Heart Mountain Relocation Camp in northern Wyoming housed Japanese Americans evicted from West Coast areas, confining them without any evidence or formal charges ever made against them. The point of view shifts among McKay Allison, a young rancher whose land adjoins the camp and whose brothers are in the Pacific theater; Kai Nakamura, a Ph.D. candidate Nisei who is interned with his traditional Japanese parents; Mariko, an artist who has returned from Paris to care for her philosopher grandfather, Abe-san; Bobby Korematsu, the elderly cook at the Allison ranch; Pinkey, an equally elderly alcoholic cowboy, McKay's only real ranch help; and various other local people. The broad scope covers their intersecting lives and loves; the various reactions in the camp to the unfair and unreasonable situation; the bigotry, violence, generosity, and sacrifice of the Wyoming people; and news of the war's progress as it is reported or as it affects relatives and friends. The strongest pictures are of the second-generation internees who feel caged and frustrated and of the stark beauty of the desolate area through the eyes of McKay, who loves it. Despite its length, mature high school students may find this one of the most enlightening works of fiction about the people who were not in the armed services but whose lives were inevitably changed during the period. A later work by Ehrlich, *Drinking Dry Clouds* (1991), is a collection of stories, the first four of which formed the basis for *Heart Mountain*, the next ten returning to some of the characters five years later, telling among other things of the difficulties of readjustment of McKay's two brothers, both wounded in the Pacific theater; of the death of Pinkey; of the return to San Francisco of Kai's parents, his father deteriorated into a helpless, childlike state, his mother bravely facing the need to start again; and of Bobby's nursing the three brothers and reliving his past in the stories he tells to soothe the mentally disturbed eldest.

231 Garland, Sherry, *The Lotus Seed*, illus. Tatsuro Kiuchi, Harcourt, 1993 (hardcover), ISBN 0-15-249465-0, $14.95, unp. Ages 8 up, grades 3 up.

Profusely illustrated, realistic picture-story book in which the paintings' unusual perspectives recall the work of Caldecott-winning Chris Van Allsburg. The narrator's Vietnamese grandmother saves a lotus seed from the Imperial Garden, cherishes it through the ensuing wars, and carries it on her flight to the United States. After a grandson finds it and plants it and it blooms, Ba gives each of her grandchildren a seed from the new flower in remembrance. Stately full-page, full-color landscapes, close-ups, and portraits support the pensive, poetic story of respect for tradition and the importance of heritage. Although an occasional poor word choice like "snuck" disrupts the poetic quality of the text, this is a beautiful and haunting book that also gives a little sense of Vietnam's war-torn history.

232 Girard, Linda Walvoord, *We Adopted You, Benjamin Koo*, illus. Linda Shute, Whitman, 1989 (hardcover), ISBN 0-8075-8694-3, $13.95, unp. Ages 5–9, grades K–4.

Picture-story book narrated by an adopted boy, nine-year-old Benjamin Koo Andrews, whose Korean mother left him on an orphanage doorstep. He tells about his being sent to the United States as an infant, his American family, his realization when he was in second grade that he was different and the help he got from the school counselor, the adoption of his little sister from Brazil, and how he handles insensitive questions and comments. Despite lively illustrations, the story is so heavily didactic that it seems like a case history.

233 Gogol, Sara, *Vatsana's Lucky New Year*, Lerner, 1992 (hardcover), ISBN 0-8225-0734-X, $14.95, 156 pp. Ages 8–12, grades 3–7.

Realistic contemporary novel of school and family life set in Portland, Oregon, in which the American-born daughter of Laotian immigrants learns to appreciate her culture. Vatsana Chanthavone, twelve, is good friends with a new neighbor, Becky Kamminsky, who is her age, and enjoys seventh grade, except for racist jibes like chink and gook from bully Tom Connors. Complicating her life, however, is the arrival of her refugee cousin, Ketsy, and Ketsy's mother, whose need to hang on for security to the Lao language and customs puts Vatsana off. But Ketsy's grace at Lao dancing wins admiration, and the approval of Vatsana's schoolmates and teachers of her compositions on Lao customs and the keen interest of both Ketsy and Becky in Lao ways give Vatsana the courage to stand up to Tom and help her to think better of and share her culture. The book's central idea is sound—to value one's roots whatever they are—and is doubled with Becky's pride in her Jewish heritage. Tom's racism is explained by the revelation that his father lost a leg in Vietnam, a matter that reduces his hatefulness somewhat in Vatsana's eyes, and the description of Lao customs like the *baci* ceremony and the New Year celebration add interest and texture. Sometimes the information about customs and the importance of heritage seem labored and intrusive. The book strays from Vatsana's point of view, and characters and events are just too pat. Good are the sense of immigrant adjustment problems, the teachers' sensitivity to and appreciation for other cultures, and Vatsana's parents' commonsense approach to incorporating good aspects of American culture with their inherited one. A note about sources of information is included.

234   Hoobler, Dorothy, and Thomas Hoobler, *Aloha Means Come Back: The Story of a World War II Girl,* illus. Cathie Bleck, Silver Burdett, 1991 (hardcover), ISBN 0-382-24156-8, $12.95, 55 pp. Ages 8–12, grades 3–7.

Short, easy-reading, historical novel of the Japanese attack on Pearl Harbor in December 1941. Newly arrived in Oahu, Hawaii, where her Navy lieutenant father has been posted to Pearl Harbor, Laura Barnes, perhaps twelve, soon makes friends with Japanese-American-Hawaiian Michiko and her older brother, Aoki, whose family own a grocery. Laura's mother discourages the association, fearing that it might be embarrasing to her husband considering the stressful relations between the United States and Japan. Michiko's family are staunchly patriotic, however, and compassionate, and when Laura's house is wrecked and her mother injured in the attack, Aoki gets the mother to the hospital, and Laura stays at Michiko's house until things settle down and some officers take her to her father. When Laura leaves for the United States, the girls pledge lasting friendship. Although the protagonist is Anglo, the focus is on the unreasonable suspicion and open animosity directed at Oriental-appearing people at the time. The sense of the political realities and fighting in Europe and Asia are clear if limited, the atmosphere of terror and confusion during the attack comes through, and information about geography, history, and well-known sights is worked into the story. The book seems intended for those who have just achieved some reading fluency and sometimes sounds like a social studies text. Laura seems younger in the story than she appears in the illustrations. This book is one of a series called Her Story, about "events that shaped our country through the eyes of young American girls who did more than keep the home fires burning!," also including *A Promise at the Alamo: The Story of a Texas Girl* (no. 359) and *The Trail on Which They Wept: The Story of a Cherokee Girl* (no. 437), which is about the Cherokee Trail of Tears.

235   Howard, Ellen, *Her Own Song,* Atheneum, 1988 (hardcover), ISBN 0-689-31444-2, $12.95, 160 pp. Ages 8–12, grades 3–7.

Historical novel of Chinese Americans in Portland, Oregon, in 1908. When her adoptive father suffers an industrial accident and is taken to the hospital and her foster-mother aunt is on vacation, Anglo Mellie Langford, eleven, is unexpectedly cared for by the family's Chinese laundryman, Geem-Wah. His solicitous attention, home, and relatives evoke disturbing memories from Mellie's past, and she learns that she was "bought" by his childless brother from her unmarried mother, reclaimed by white authorities, and then placed by them for adoption with the Langfords. Carefully calculated suspense about Mellie's past; warm characterizations, especially of Geem-Wah and a Chinese girl about Mellie's age; and a good sense of the antiwhite sentiment against the Chinese Americans and the danger Geem-Wah invites by helping Mellie combine for a memorable fictionalization of a real incident.

236   Hudson, Helen, *A Temporary Residence,* Putnam, 1987 (hardcover), ISBN 0-399-13312-7, $18.95, 251 pp. Ages 12 up, grades 7 up.

Historical novel of one of the relocation camps to which Japanese and Americans of Japanese ancestry were sent from the West Coast during World War II. Although the Mount Hope Assembly Center is fictional, it is based on real camps made from racetracks into which large numbers of people were moved before more permanent facilities were ready, many of them American citizens and none of them convicted of any crime. The story focuses on several people: Sam Curry, a sculptor, and his Caucasian wife, a Jewish refugee from Germany; two large families of very different social rank, the Oshimas and the Noguchis, both with autocratic fathers, wives who discover the joys of personal freedom in the confinement of the camp, and children to whom the traditional ways mean less and less as time goes on; the director, Channing Haydon, a Harvard professor of social psychology, a well-meaning but ineffectual man; and the bullying second-in-command, Schweiker. Although the camp is "temporary," they go through several seasons suffering the terrible conditions: heat, dust, cold, overcrowding, almost inedible food, indignities of sudden searches and confiscations of their meager personal belongings, illness with an inadequate hospital, hostility from the nearest town, the psychological pressures of the current frustrations, and an uncertain, often hopeless, future. While the incidents are based on fact, they pile up in the novel relentlessly, creating a tone of intense grimness not as effective fictionally as some more moderate depictions of the subject.

237   Irwin, Hadley, *Kim/Kimi,* McElderry, 1987 (hardcover), ISBN 0-689-50428-4, $14.95; Puffin, 1988 (paper), ISBN 0-14-032593-X, $3.99, 200 pp. Ages 10–16, grades 5–11.

Realistic novel of a contemporary, American-born, half-Japanese girl's search for the family of the Japanese-American father who died before she was born. Sixteen-year-old Kim Andrews knows she is loved by her white mother, stepfather, and half brother, but her mirror and the teen romances she reads by the dozens point up how different especially in appearance she is from family, neighbors, and classmates in Lanesport, Iowa. She chooses spring vacation to run away under her old name of Kimi Yogushi to Sacramento, California, where she hopes to find her father's family and where she luckily gets unexpected help from other Japanese Americans. She locates her traditional, paternal aunt and grandmother, all that are left, who hesitatingly accept her, and she learns a good deal about the internment of Japanese Americans during World War II. Although the book's didactic intent is obvious, the story balances well Kim/Kimi's love for her current family with her need to find herself in her old one and resolves her conflict sensibly by having her see that she belongs to both. The Japanese-American characters reflect different attitudes toward internment and toward assimilation. The book is more character driven than plot centered, since the plot is unconvincingly constructed and coincidence abounds, but the abundant dialogue produces a rapid pace, and Kim/Kimi's adolescent and ethnic yearnings and her ambivalent feelings about family make her real and sympathetic.

238   Jen, Gish, *Typical American,* Houghton, 1991 (hardcover), ISBN 0-395-54689-3, $19.95, 296 pp.; Plume, 1992 (paper), ISBN 0-452-26774-9, $10.00, 304 pp. Ages 15 up, grades 10 up.

Realistic novel of Chinese-American family life set for about twenty years in New York City beginning in 1947. Shy, awkward, naive Ralph Chang emigrates to the United States to get his Ph.D. in mechanical engineering. He soon suffers a crush on a secretary in the college foreign students' office; he dodders through his studies until Theresa, his capable Older Sister, who has emigrated for her M.D., takes him in hand; he dutifully marries her friend, Helen, who bears him two daughters and provides ballast; he gets his Ph.D. and eventually professorial tenure; he becomes owner of a split-level house fashionably appointed; he takes a leave from his professorship to operate a fried chicken restaurant, but he loses everything because he trusts a too-clever, American-born, chiseler Chinese; he falls into the doldrums and learns he has been cuckolded by the chiseler; he accidentally hits his sister with his car, launching her into a coma of several months' duration—all the while he and the women eschew "typical American" behavior and attitudes, ironically not realizing that they themselves have become the epitome of such as they themselves define it. Although the book begins slowly, often outruns itself, indulges in overwriting, and comes to an abrupt, open ending, many scenes are extremely funny with comedy ranging from slapstick to satire; the subplots of the women's affairs lend spice and counterpoint Ralph's story; and the speed with which Chinese attempting to retain their native culture become acculturated Americans provides the main irony.

239 Kadohata, Cynthia, *The Floating World,* Viking, 1989 (hardcover), ISBN 0-670-82680-4, $17.95, 196 pp. Ages 15 up, grades 10 up.

Growing-up novel of Olivia, a Japanese-American girl in the 1950s, from the time she is twelve until she is twenty-one. The floating world is the unstable land of motels, run-down temporary houses, gas stations, restaurants, and highways that she experiences and leaves behind as she moves with her family—her mother, her stepfather, her three younger brothers, and most of all, her maternal grandmother—in their continual search for jobs and better luck. Although the grandmother dies in a motel bathroom when Olivia is not yet thirteen, she dominates the girl's life, a malevolent figure, prone to rages in which she boxes the children's ears or locks them outside, yet she seems somehow a stronger role model than Olivia's unhappy mother or her stepfather, who is kind and loving but a failure. Characterization is vivid, and the story is told with ironic humor in pieces that seem slightly disjointed, perhaps because some parts were first published as short stories, but that also echo the unstable nature of her life. Although their Japanese-ness is part of their problem, it is a novel of dislocation more than prejudice. The setting is the West Coast, Nebraska, and Arkansas.

240 Kadohata, Cynthia, *In the Heart of the Valley of Love,* Viking, 1992 (hardcover), ISBN 0-670-83415-7, $20.00, 224 pp. Ages 14 up, grades 9 up.

Futuristic novel set in 2052 in Los Angeles, a city so riddled with crime and disease that mere survival is an art. The narrator, eighteen-year-old Francie, is an orphan whose Japanese-American mother and father of mixed Chinese and African-American descent both died five years earlier of widely prevalent cancer. She lives at first with Annie, her aunt, and Annie's boyfriend, Rohn, a couple deeply in love who laugh and dance despite the hardships. When Rohn is arrested in a black-market deal and disappears, Annie is devastated, and Francie, not really knowing what to do, enrolls in college, where she works on the school paper and becomes deeply involved with Mark, a loving young man, and a group of misfits who congregate in the journalism office. What happens in the story is far less important than the tone, which reflects the gritty life of shortages, deteriorating buildings and public services, and police and government that are both repressive and corrupt. Yet somehow the attitude remains hopeful, in the voice of Francie who sees the world from an oddly skewed perspective, both cynical and innocent. Because whites have long since become a minority, Francie's ethnic background is not especially important to the action. The picture of this country halfway through the

twenty-first century is so much a projection of all that is wrong today inten-
sified that it is both frightening and believable.

241 Kline, Suzy, *Song Lee in Room 2B,* illus. Frank Remkiewicz, Viking,
1993 (hardcover), ISBN 0-670-84772-0, $11.95, 56 pp. Ages 5–9,
grades K–4.

Easy fiction chapter book in the Horrible Harry series, this one starring the
little Korean girl, Song Lee, who proves to be kind and to have an imagination
and a sense of humor. Too shy to speak in front of the class in the assignment
to tell about their favorite vacation spots, Song Lee solves her problem by
making and hiding behind a cardboard cherry-blossom tree and talking about
her former home in Seoul. On Saint Patrick's Day, after Song Lee refuses to
tell about Harry's secret contribution to the green smorgasbord (strips of cel-
ery filled with peanut butter and dotted with raisins to represent ants), Mary
squashes a handful of green clay on her head. Song Lee pretends she was
making a hat so that Mary will not be scolded. Usually perfectly behaved,
Song Lee disobeys the fire drill rules to run back and save Chungju, the
salamander she has donated to the classroom. Like the other Horrible Harry
stories, this is narrated by Harry's friend and admirer, Doug. Song Lee is also
featured in *Horrible Harry's Secret* (1990), in which Harry, the class cut-up,
falls in love with Song Lee, reforms to gain her approval, and even calls off
his feud, temporarily, with Sidney because she does not like fighting. Although
Song Lee seems to fit the stereotype of the well-mannered Asian child, she is
also fun loving and often delighted with Harry's clowning. Unusually lively
and genuine stories for the early-reading group.

242 Konigsburg, E. L., *Up from Jericho Tel,* Atheneum, 1986 (hardcover),
ISBN 0-689-31194-X, $14.95, 192 pp. Ages 10 up, grades 5 up.

Lighthearted mystery-fantasy novel set for several weeks in the 1980s in a
mobile-home park on Long Island, New York. Anglo Jeanmarie Troxell, the
narrator, and Korean-American Malcolm Soo, both eleven, dig to bury a Dal-
matian in the clearing behind their park and fall through the ground into a
shaft at the bottom of which is a room bathed in an amber-rose light. They
meet the aging spirit of a dead actress named Tallulah, in speech and manner
the replica of historical Tallulah Bankhead, who sends them on a number of
tasks to prove their worthiness for their ultimate quest, which is to find her
valuable lost necklace. At the end, both children have had many adventures
which have increased their self-confidence. Both are stereotypically presented,
Jeanmarie being inclined to overdramatize and dominate and Malcolm being
almost fanatically neat and organized, aware that he is expected by society to

be an overachiever, and aspiring to become a Nobel Prize winner in physics or chemistry. The action is fast, and the dialogue is abundant and snappy and filled with contemporary comments. Best are the details that reveal preadolescent thinking and behavior and the striking turns of phrase, quips, wordplay, and one-liners.

243 Kraus, Joanna Halpert, *Tall Boy's Journey*, illus. Karen Ritz, Carolrhoda, 1992 (hardcover), ISBN 0-87614-746-5, $13.95, 48 pp. Ages 5–10, grades K–5.

Realistic novelette of a present-day Korean village boy's adjustment to life in the United States. After his grandmother dies, over the boy's protests his soldier uncle puts parentless Kim Moo Yong, about eight, on a plane for the United States, telling him to "be tall, inside." Adopted by an American scientist and his wife, the boy is determined to go home. He tries to run away, refuses food, and generally proves difficult, until his American father's colleague, Mr. Cho, also from Korea, becomes his mentor, explains American ways to him, encourages him to make friends, and urges him to take advantage of this opportunity for a good life. Although some humor appears (his new mother gives the boy a broom to ward off tigers), this serious story moves without suspense and buildup. Kim is stubborn and determined, the Americans steadfastly patient, and Mr. Cho unceasingly reasonable. The book, an almost clinical account of adjustment, never fully engages the reader's emotions, and there are disconcerting gaps in the narrative. But it does introduce young readers to the trauma of relocation and what might be expected if a family adopts such an orphan. Ritz's full-color paintings depict people and incidents and add interest. The story is based on the experiences of the author's own adopted son and other children like him.

244 Lee, Gus, *China Boy*, Dutton, 1991 (hardcover), ISBN 0-525-24994-X, $19.95, 322 pp.; NAL-Dutton, 1991 (paper), ISBN 0-451-17434-8, $5.99, 400 pp. Ages 15 up, grades 10 up.

Somewhat autobiographical novel of a Chinese-American boy's coming of age set in 1953 and 1954 in the mixed-ethnic Panhandle section of San Francisco. Kai Ting, seven, is the last child and only son of a respected Chinese family whose father was a colonel in World War II and whose mother fled with his three older sisters from the Japanese to California, where Kai was born. A shy, thin, undersized, easily intimidated boy, traumatized by the loss of his beautiful, indulgent mother to cancer, abused by his white stepmother, Edna, who resents his Chinese-ness, Kai is regularly beaten up by street kids, in particular by the notorious bully, black Big Willie Mack, who derisively dubs him "China Boy." After a particularly brutal encounter, a kindly Hispanic auto mechanic, Hector Pueblo, advises Mr. Ting to send Kai to the YMCA to learn boxing for self-defense. The men there, realizing Kai's predicament, advise him in combining street-fighting tactics with boxing strategy, and in a terribly bloody battle, he triumphs over Willie, and thus over all Willie's kind, including his bully stepmother, to whom, upon coming home bloodied and dirty, he announces, *"I ain't fo' yo' pickin-on, no mo'!,"* employing the diction of the streetwise and asserting his self-hood at the same time. Although the book outruns itself and the author seems overly clever and self-indulgent stylistically, the major figures in the large, ethnically mixed cast are well fleshed, especially Mah-mee, his mother; Tony Barraza, his ex-pugilist instructor; Colonel Ting, the gallant, patrician, amazingly unaware father; and the astonishingly resilient Kai himself. Humor relieves the stark harshness of the boy's life, in particular that arising from the tension between the boy's frequent naive misperceptions and the mature I-narrator's hyperbolic recollections.

245   Lee, Marie G., *Finding My Voice*, Houghton, 1992 (hardcover), ISBN 0-395-62134-8, $13.95, 165 pp. Ages 11–17, grades 7–12.

Realistic novel of present-day school and home life for a Korean-American girl in Arkin, Minnesota. In her senior year, pretty Ellen Sung, daughter of a doctor, confronts important matters, among them whether to adhere to her strict parents' wishes and study hard, go to Harvard for pre-med like her older sister, and not date until college; as well as how to deal with racial slurs. Ellen learns to take situations one by one and becomes increasingly mature in her attitudes. After thought and investigation, she chooses Harvard because she thinks it is best for her. She goes to parties and out on dates with handsome, popular Anglo Tomper Standel without her parents' knowledge, until Tomper persuades her to take him to meet her parents. The racial aspect culminates in a melodramatic scene that strikes a false note. At a year-end party, a jealous, prejudiced Anglo girl hits her with a bottle and severely lacerates her face. The sensitive, honest, literate, first-person narrative and Ellen's believable development help to compensate for the conventional incidents and stock cast. Ellen learns to stand back, be objective, and make rational decisions. The sense of conflicting generational expectations and goals is very strong.

246   Lee, Marie G., *If It Hadn't Been for Yoon Jun*, Houghton, 1993 (hardcover), ISBN 0-395-62941-1, $13.95, 134 pp. Ages 8–12, grades 3–7.

Realistic school novel set in present-day Minnesota. Korean-born, American-adopted Alice Larsen, twelve, would prefer to forget her cultural origins. When Yoon Jun Lee, a Korean immigrant, comes to her small town, his presence reminds her that she, too, looks different and has a different background. Her minister father even wants her to do "good works" by befriending the lonely, ridiculed boy. When the two are paired by lottery for International Day and must prepare Korean foods and a report on Korea, Alice gains a broader sense of self as well as cultural understanding, gets an opportunity to help Yoon Jun, and even finds she likes and admires him. The plot seems too neatly set up, especially the pairing and the episode in which Yoon Jun saves Alice from being hit by a car, and characters are types. But the racial attitudes and slurs like "gook" are sound, and the basic idea of the importance of learning about one's heritage has value. The book is mostly dialogue, events move fast, and the sense of seventh-grade life, while conventional, is clear. The presentation of Native Americans as school problems and outcasts is unfortunate, but the addition of a despised Native American girl to the cast, like Yoon Jun from a poor, hardworking family, sets Alice's economic and social privilege in relief. Unfortunately, the girl is presented as not likable and also negatively as a smoker.

247   Levine, Ellen, *I Hate English,* illus. Steve Bjorkman, Scholastic, 1989 (hardcover), ISBN 0-590-42305-3, $12.95, unp. Ages 4–9, grades PS–4.

Realistic picture-story book about Chinese immigrants in New York City. Recently arrived from Hong Kong with her family, third-grader Mei Mei resists learning English, refusing to respond to her teacher or to use the language herself, continuing to think always in Chinese. Even the efforts of the Chinatown Learning Center fail to penetrate the wall she builds around herself linguistically. But one day, a bright, lively, blond, young teacher named Nancy arrives, reads to Mei Mei and tells her stories, then takes her for a long walk down the street, chattering so happily and exuberantly that her enthusiasm catches Mei Mei. The naturally ebullient little girl responds. Mei Mei "talked for twenty-two minutes without stopping. In English," until both she and Nancy are laughing "so hard neither one could say a word in English or Chinese." The story's strength lies in the way it humorously catches the immigrant's natural fear of losing the symbol of what one has held dear and safe—language. The loose, colorful, cartoonish watercolors in details and tone support the story's sense and help keep it light.

248   Lim, Shirley Geok-lin, Mayumi Tsutakawa, and Margarita Donnelly, eds., *The Forbidden Stitch: An Asian American Women's Anthology,* Calyx, 1989 (hardcover), ISBN 0-934971-10-2, $26.95; (paper), ISBN 0-93491-04-8, $14.95, 290 pp. Ages 14 up, grades 9 up.

Large collection of poems, stories, artwork, and reviews, the first anthology, the introduction says, ever published entirely of works by Asian-American women. The artwork, in a variety of media, which takes up thirty-five pages, is the least impressive, partly because none is reproduced in color, and the twenty-eight pages of reviews have limited interest, but the thirty-three poems and fifteen stories show talented work from a large number of authors. Some are established writers, many have had pieces published in literary periodicals or relatively obscure magazines, and a number see their work in print for the first time in this volume. They are more similar in their femaleness, which is the concern of many of the selections, than in their ethnic backgrounds, being from Asian countries with very different cultures or being second-, third-, or even fourth-generation Americans. Although the works vary greatly, almost all are written with skill; the prose is probably more easily approachable for high school students than the poetry. This is a good representation from a widely diverse group; author biographies and an extensive bibliography are included.

249 Lo, Steven C., *The Incorporation of Eric Chung*, Algonquin, 1989 (hardcover), ISBN 0-945575-18-1, $14.95, 199 pp. Ages 12 up, grades 7 up.

Hilarious, realistic novel of a young immigrant from Taiwan who, after studying computing at Texas Tech, becomes embroiled in a scheme to exploit the China market in the 1980s by a fast-talking acqaintance and a Texas billionaire. Although he has never been to China and understands the Communist bureaucracy even less than the American corporate world, Eric Chung finds himself the Chinese Expert in the doomed venture. Eric is an appealing mixture of innocence and cynicism, and he reports the corporate maneuvers with bewildered wonder and sharp humor. The tone is breezy and informal, and the structure skips back and forth through the 1970s from his arrival in the United States to his present position as president of Coldwell Electronics International, Inc., a job from which he expects daily to be fired. While the satirical picture of American business is the strongest element, there are also poignant pictures of workers laid off without compassion and of the young Asian university students, baffled by Western ways, clinging together on the alien campus.

250 Louie, David Wong, *Pangs of Love*, Knopf, 1991 (hardcover), ISBN 0-394-58957-2, $19.00, 225 pp. Ages 14 up, grades 9 up.

Eleven short stories, about half of them with Chinese-American characters, notably the title story, which details the strains between the narrator, a young man, and his immigrant mother with whom he lives. The two can hardly communicate, since she speaks no English and knows American life only through television, which she cannot understand, and his Chinese is limited to the vocabulary of a five-year-old, the age at which he switched to English. In "Inheritance," a modern, educated young woman, pressured by her father and her husband, a graduate student from Communist China, to have a child, worries that she may have inherited her mother's bitter and abusive temper. Some of the stories are touching, including "Birthday," in which a man tries to fulfill a promise to his ex-girlfriend's young son. All show sharp insight into personalities and the conflicts of families and relationships, without obscurity or explicit sexual scenes.

251 McHugh, Maureen F., *China Mountain Zhang,* Tor, 1992 (hardbound), ISBN 0-312- 85271-1, $19.95; (paper), ISBN 0-812-50892- 0, $3.99, 312 pp. Ages 15 up, grades 10 up.

Futuristic novel set mostly in New York City, but also in China, on Baffin Island, and on Mars, in the twenty-second century. The United States has become a second-rate backwater, politically controlled by China, the dominant world power with a highly repressive social order. Zhang, whose name in Mandarin translates as "China Mountain," is actually the son of a Chinese man and a Latino woman, but they had him gene-altered before his birth so that he would appear to be entirely Chinese, since that is the preferred ethnic background, and he operates as an ABC (American-born Chinese), hiding his true heritage and his real name, Rafael. He also has to hide, for the most part, his homosexuality, although in New York it is not as dangerous as in puritan- ical China, where a person can be shot for deviation. Through a series of mishaps and blunders, among them a six-months' duty at a research station north of the Arctic Circle, he is accepted to study engineering at Nanjing University, a rare and highly coveted opportunity. After successful completion of his course, he returns to New York, much to the astonishment of all since the chances for advancement and wealth are much greater in China. The combination of decaying streets, subways, and buildings in New York and brilliant technological innovations, including exciting human-powered kite races over Manhattan and illegal cybernetic speakeasies in Beijing, is entirely convincing, as is the struggling commune on Mars, connected to the main story when one of the men there becomes Zhang's long-distance tutorial stu- dent. The strongest element is the characterization, which is very believable and well developed. Zhang's sexual orientation, which is erotic, is treated sympathetically, though his acts are not described in detail, and it serves as one of the many hurdles the intelligent ABC must cope with in a highly bureaucratic and inefficient society. His desolation when his tutor and gay lover in China commits suicide, because he fears he has been discovered, is moving. Obviously, this aspect may present a problem in some school libraries, but mature students will find the novel both amusing and compelling.

252 Miklowitz, Gloria, *The War between the Classes*, Delacorte, 1985 (hardcover), ISBN 0-385-29375-5, $13.95; Dell, 1986 (paper), ISBN 0-440-99406-3, $3.50, 158 pp. Ages 11–17, grades 7–12.

Realistic contemporary school novel set in a mixed ethnic area, perhaps in Los Angeles. Amy (Emiko) Sumoto, a seventeen-year-old Japanese-American of modest means, is madly in love with handsome, well-to-do, white Adam Tarcher, although she knows her strict parents disapprove and expect her to marry a Japanese, especially her father, a victim of internment during World War II. Amy becomes more decisive and assertive with respect to her classmates and parents, and Adam becomes less self-assured and macho through a class project, the Color Game, originated by social studies teacher Otero, which, dividing the students into groups by socioeconomic status and sex, is designed to show how human relations are determined by wealth, color, and gender. Unfleshed and unindividualized characters, a studied social mix, an overly obvious didactic intent, a pedestrian style, and a predictable outcome are somewhat offset by the sense of the father's lingering resentment, the closeness of Amy's family, the emphasis on respect and tradition, and the cultural dilemma of Asian-American youth.

253 Mills, Claudia, *A Visit to Amy-Claire*, illus. Sheila Hamanaka, Macmillan, 1992 (hardcover), ISBN 0-02-76991-2, $14.95, unp. Ages 4–8, grades PS–3.

Realistic contemporary picture-story book set in an unspecified area, in which the text gives no indication of race, but the pictures show the characters to be Japanese Americans and the protagonist's family to be biracial, the father a white man. On a visit to her cousin, Amy-Claire, seven, biracially depicted Rachel, five, wants to have Amy-Claire's exclusive attention as she did the previous year. She stays aloof while Amy-Claire, an only child, plays big sister with Rachel's little sister, Jessie, two. Rachel's disappointment grows and her jealousy builds until she sees that she can play big sister, too, increasing the fun for all. This story of sibling rivalry that develops into family love is repeated in off-the-page, double-spread, realistic oil paintings that are especially notable for their strong composition, warmth of family relations, and stunning portraits of family members.

254 Mochizuki, Ken, *Baseball Saved Us,* illus. Dom Lee, Lee & Low, 1993 (hardcover), ISBN 1-880000-01-6, $14.95, unp. Ages 6–13, grades 1–8.

Picture-story book of historical fiction set in a World War II Japanese-American internment camp. A Japanese-American boy of about ten tells how he and his parents and older brother are rudely and rapidly evacuated to an unspecified location in the American desert, where they and other evacuees suffer from homesickness, heat, cold, lack of sanitary facilities, overcrowdedness, and boredom. When his older brother becomes rebellious, his father organizes the internees to construct a baseball field and set up teams. The game gives the people something to focus on and pass the time. For the narrator, baseball also builds his self-esteem. He saves an important game with a long ball, and, returned home after the war with his skills enhanced, he becomes known as "Shorty" instead of "Jap" and again he saves an important game. The success-story aspects seem tacked on. The callous and swift uprooting of the families and the understated description of camp conditions are sufficient to grab the emotions. Supporting the boy's account and increasing the reader's sense of outrage are the dark and brooding, starkly realistic scratchboard and oil paintings, which ironically are sometimes reminiscent of Holocaust pictures. The baseball scenes are also very convincing and evocative of the game. An author's note about the incarceration of the Japanese Americans introduces the book. His own family, according to the book jacket, were sent to the Minidoka camp in Idaho.

255 Namioka, Lensey, *Yang the Youngest and His Terrible Ear,* illus. Kees de Kiefte, Little, Brown, 1992 (hardcover), ISBN 0-316-59701-5, $13.95, 134 pp. Ages 8–12, grades 3–7.

Amusing novel of a tone-deaf boy in a musical family, recent immigrants to Seattle from Shanghai. Yingtao Yang, nine, is the youngest child of a symphony violinist and his concert pianist wife. Since his siblings are all musically gifted (Eldest Brother plays the violin and leads their quartet, Second Sister plays the viola, and Third Sister plays the cello), Yingtao is thought to be lazy or deliberately contrary when he cannot play his part. Only Third Sister, ten, realizes that Yingtao cannot hear the beautiful music. Together, they work out a plan whereby their talented friend, Matthew Conner, will play the second violin part from behind a screen at the recital through which their father hopes to recruit more students. When the hoax is revealed, Mr. Conner, who has scorned his son's interest in music, is convinced of Matthew's ability, and Mr. Yang is willing to allow Yingtao to play baseball, assured by the other father that the boy has real skill. Much of the humor comes from misunderstandings of common American phrases by the Chinese and the cultural differences on both sides. Although Yingtao's misery and guilt at his musical failure are well evoked, the story is mostly light, and family love prevails over difficulties.

256 Narahashi, Keiko, *I Have a Friend*, illus. Keiko Narahashi, McElderry, 1987 (hardcover), ISBN 0-689-50432-2, $13.95, unp. Ages 3–8, grades PS–3.

Picture-story book in which a very young boy records all the things his shadow does with him during the day until it disappears at night. The very simple text ends, "He is yesterday's night left behind for the day." Full-page and double-page watercolors with large areas of subtly shaded single colors show the child to be an Asian American with a chubby baby face. Especially interesting are the pictures at the beach, with the wavery shadow swimming beneath the boy and standing in the shallow waves near the sand.

257 Ng, Fae Myenne, *Bone*, Hyperion, 1993 (hardcover), ISBN 1-56282-944-0, $19.95, 199 pp. Ages 14 up, grades 9 up.

Realistic contemporary novel set in San Francisco's Chinatown about Chinese immigrants and their Chinese-American children. Two generations of a family struggle to coexist: Leila, the narrator, a teacher and the eldest daughter, who finds herself, paradoxically, increasingly controlled by her parents and increasingly in control of them; Ona, the second daughter, who commits suicide; Nina, the youngest, who escapes to New York and becomes a tour guide; Mah, an eccentric, hardworking seamstress, by turns demanding, self-sacrificing, self-pitying; Leon, Leila's stepfather, father of Ona and Nina, a seaman who fails at every land enterprise he embarks upon and yet retains the girls' love and respect; and Mason, Leila's lover and eventual husband, a sensible, kind auto mechanic, who understands the family, loves them, and endures them. The story unfolds backward in a series of sparely written, powerful vignettes about the family's life. It is held together by two intertwined questions: Why did beautiful, young Ona take her own life, and what was her father's part in precipitating the event? The answers lie in the generational culture clash, as strong blood and traditional bonds rub against new inclinations. Character revelation excels; the abundant ironic humor sets the terrible tragedy and the family's struggles in relief; and the camaraderie, the abrasiveness, the poverty, the gossip, the supportiveness, the vanity, the pride, the jealousies, the caringness of the Chinatown Chinese are worked into the story in such a way that the reader truly believes them. The story is slow starting but is worth the effort.

258   Okimoto, Jean Davies, *Molly by Any Other Name,* Scholastic, 1990 (hardcover), ISBN 0-590-42993-0, $13.95, 276 pp. Ages 12–14, grades 7–9.

In this girl's growing-up novel, Molly Jane Fletcher, adopted shortly after birth by a white couple, knows only that she is Asian until her last year in a Seattle high school, when she decides to look for her birth mother. Most of the story details the trauma to her devoted, intelligent adoptive parents; to her genetic mother, Karen, and to Karen's husband and mother, all of whom are threatened by opening old wounds; and to Molly herself, who hates to cause them pain but feels compelled to discover who she is. She is supported emotionally by Roland Hirada, a fourth-generation Japanese American whom she considers almost a brother before he starts taking out another girl. She turns to Joe Abrams, the handsome leader of the cheering team until, predictably, she discovers Joe is too fast for her and that she and Roland really love each other. After more than half the book, the point of view switches from Molly to Karen, an artist of Japanese extraction now living in Halifax, Nova Scotia, with her husband and ten-year-old son. A short third section details their happy meeting. Although the novel is at pains to tell that not all reunions with birth parents are happy, Molly's quest turns out almost too well, but it is balanced by the emotional turmoil of all the adults involved and the inability of both Karen's husband and her mother to accept the outcome.

259   Pettit, Jayne, *My Name Is San Ho,* Scholastic, 1992 (hardcover), ISBN 0-590-44172-8, $13.95, 149 pp. Ages 8–14, grades 3–9.

Historical novel of a Vietnamese refugee in 1975. Nine-year-old San Ho lives in the little village of Mi Hung near Saigon where he has never known anything but war. He is taken by his widowed mother for safety to a refugees' home in Saigon, and three years later he is airlifted to Philadelphia where his mother lives with her American Marine husband. At first, San Ho is intimidated by the strange language, food, and customs, but his teacher is kind, his stepfather, Stephen, who is comforting, gets him a bike and teaches him baseball, and his skill at math and athletics wins him friends at school. San Ho tells his story years later, after he has become a high school teacher of history in New England, in mostly a matter-of-fact voice that is not uniformly engaging, approaches recitation, and often seems instructive of the plight of the Asians. Even the racial incident of the destruction of San Ho's mother's garden lacks emotional impact. The best part is the first third, which is set in Vietnam and tells about the slaying of the schoolteacher and the precarious, mid-war life in the village.

260 Porte, Barbara Ann, *"Leave That Cricket Be, Alan Lee,"* illus. Donna Ruff, Greenwillow, 1993 (hardcover), ISBN 0-688-11793-7, $14.00, unp. Ages 4–10, grades PS–5.

Realistic, contemporary, picture-story book set somewhere in the United States among a Chinese-American, middle-class family. Young Alan Lee hears a cricket in the house and, in spite of suggestions from his parents otherwise, persists until he catches it. He wants to cage it as his Great-Uncle Clemson says people did back in China when he was a boy. Alan soon feels that the cricket is not happy in its jar because it does not sing. He releases it and is gratified when he hears its familiar chirping once again. Great-Uncle Clemson assures him, "It's a lucky house that has a cricket" chirping in it. The story is high in family and cultural values and compassion, without being didactic, and it is complemented by subtly shaded pastels and colored pencils patterned after Chinese panel art. Each right-hand page has a picture-panel showing one or more scenes, and the text is arranged in a corresponding panel on the left-hand page, with the result that this is an aesthetically as well as emotionally pleasing book.

261 Rattigan, Jama Kim, *Dumpling Soup,* illus. Lillian Hsu-Flanders, Little, Brown, 1993 (hardcover), ISBN 0-316-73445-4, $15.95, unp. Ages 5–8, grades K–3.

Picture-story book of the New Year's celebration of a large, mostly Asian family in Hawaii, who gather at the home of their Korean grandmother on Oahu. The narrator, a little girl named Marisa, wants to be part of the making of the traditional dumplings for the first meal of the new year for all her aunts, uncles, and cousins—some Chinese, some Japanese, some Hawaiian, some even whites—a meal to ensure that they will eat well all year. Although her clumsily wrapped dumplings do not look quite right, her grandmother cooks them anyway and makes sure everyone has at least one of hers along with the others. The lively illustrations capture the excitement of the children, allowed to stay up after midnight to join the first meal, and the love and happiness in the extended family of mixed ancestry as is the population of Hawaii. Included is a brief glossary of terms used in the various languages of the family.

262 Roland Donna, *Grandfather's Stories from the Philippines,* illus. Ron Oden, Open My World, 1985 (hardcover), ISBN 0-941996-07-7, $4.50; (paper), ISBN 0-941996-08-5, $4.50, 25 pp. Ages 4–10, grades PS–5.

Realistic picture-story book. When Grandfather, who lives in the Philippine Islands, comes to America to visit his family here, young "Juan, Petra, and

Lidia sit by his side and learn about the land and the people who live on the islands of the Philippines." This quotation summarizes the action of the book and gives a feel for the diction, vocabulary level, and tone. Grandfather tells the children about the mountains, the crops, the settlement by the Spanish, entertainments, typhoons, different occupations, and the like. In the illustrations, scenes involving the family are in color, while those showing Grandfather's accounts are mostly in black and white. They show appropriate scenes; for example, when the text discusses farms, the illustration shows a farmer plowing with the carabao, and accompanying the story of the Spanish landing, there are ships and workers unloading them. All are decidedly representational, since the book's purpose is to instruct. This is more a social studies text than a work of literature. By the same writer and illustrator are *Grandfather's Stories from Cambodia* (1984), *Grandfather's Stories from Mexico* (no. 374), and *Grandfather's Stories from Viet Nam* (no. 263, illus. Kevin Rones), which are similar.

263 Roland, Donna, *Grandfather's Stories from Viet Nam*, illus. Kevin Rones, Open My World, 1985 (paper), ISBN 0-941996-11-5, $4.50, 25 pp. Ages 4–10, grades PS–5.

Realistic picture-story book whose intent is to inform. Grandfather often tells young Vinh and Lang and their parents stories about their homeland which the children left with him and their parents as refugees when they were very young. He tells of Vietnamese history, about working on a rubber plantation with their father, and about gathering latex. Their mother also keeps alive former traditions, like occasionally wearing Vietnamese dress and serving a certain noodle soup, and their father plays a traditional guitarlike instrument. The three-quarter page pictures, alternating black and white and color, go along with the easy-reading text. See also by Roland *Grandfather's Stories from Mexico* (no. 374), *Grandfather's Stories from the Philippines* (no. 262), and *Grandfather's Stories from Cambodia* (1984), all in a similar vein.

264 Sakai, Kimiko, *Sachiko Means Happiness*, illus. Tomie Arai, Children's Book, 1990 (hardcover), ISBN 0-89239-065-4, $13.95, 32 pp. Ages 5–8, grades K–3.

Picture-story book set in a presumably American large town or city. When her aging grandmother no longer recognizes her and denies being a grandmother, saying she is five years old, Sachiko is angry and lets the old woman walk off until she stops, bewildered, and starts to cry. Then Sachiko realizes that her grandmother is like a lost child and, gently suggesting that she stay at her house for the night, leads her home. The quiet emotion of the understated pictured story is complemented by beautiful illustrations of a gray-haired woman and a black-haired girl with very similar Japanese features in full-page spreads and, on the facing pages beside the text, scroll-like oblongs filled with flower designs and Oriental motifs.

265 Sasaki, R. A., *The Loom and Other Stories,* Graywolf, 1991 (paper), ISBN 1-55597-157-1, $10.00, 112 pp. Ages 14 up, grades 9 up.

Nine sensitive, evocative stories, almost all about the Terasaki family, Japanese Americans in the San Francisco of the twentieth century. The title story concerns the mother, a bright, hopeful little girl, and follows her through her childhood, her 1939 graduation from the University of California, the World War II internment camps, marriage to a *kibei,* a man born in America but sent back to grow up in Japan, and the childhood of her four daughters, during all of which she suppresses her own nature to become a sweet, traditional creature. The gift of a loom from a grown daughter frees her self-expression. She weaves dull gray browns, embedded with brilliant reds, greens, and yellows that show only in bright sunlight. Other stories concern her daughters, mostly Jo, the youngest, who becomes a writer, lives in Japan, and returns to help with her father's terminal illness. While the tone of the collection as a whole is poignant, much of it is very funny, detailing hilarious situations and invoking sharp irony. The ethnic experience, the efforts to become "real" Americans, the call of cultural roots—all are reported with sympathy and insight. Although published for adults, the collection offers nothing unsuitable for high school students.

266 Savin, Marcia, *The Moon Bridge,* Scholastic, 1992 (hardcover), ISBN 0-590-45873-6, $13.95, 232 pp. Ages 9–14, grades 4–9.

Historical novel set in San Francisco, centering on the internment of Japanese Americans in World War II. After the bombing of Pearl Harbor, her classmates turn nasty and call ten-year-old Mitzi Fujimoto names because she is of Japanese descent. Ruthie Fox, white and also ten, comes to her defense, thereby losing her longtime best friend, Shirl, whose father is an army man, and gaining Mitzi as a new one. For four months, they spend every spare moment together. In April, when the United States government decrees that Japanese Americans should be relocated from the West Coast, Mitzi and her family have to leave their grocery store and move, first to a camp and then inland to Arkansas, as Ruthie later learns. At first, the two girls correspond, but when Mitzi no longer replies, Ruthie has no address to which to send letters. Three years and four months pass with no word from Mitzi, until, the war over, she writes, and the two girls make plans to meet at a place they both loved, the bridge in the Tea Garden in Golden Gate Park. Ruthie realizes that Mitzi has suffered in ways she can never understand, and Mitzi fears she may never catch up in school. Both girls wonder whether their friendship can endure, and both look forward to better times. The style is mundane, tension is minimal, too much of the book is given over to the girls' playtimes together, and the characters are stereotypes. The book's strongest point is in bringing out in a limited way the unreasonable hatred and fear directed toward the Japanese Americans and the speed and callousness with which they were evacuated. A historical note is included.

267 Say, Allen, *The Lost Lake,* illus. Allen Say, Houghton, 1989 (hardcover), ISBN 0-395-50933-5, $14.95; (paper), ISBN 0-395-63036-5, $4.80, 32 pp. Ages 6–9, grades 1–4.

Picture-story book narrated by Luke, who spends a boring summer with his father in the city until they go on a camping trip to the Lost Lake, where Dad and Grandpa used to camp. After a long backpack, they reach the lake, no longer a secret but swarming with people. Disgusted, Dad takes off cross-country, finding a pleasant stream which Luke likes, but moving on until they camp after dark, then wake in the morning to find they are overlooking a beautiful, pristine lake all their own. The father-son relationship is nicely handled, with Luke somewhat ironic but hoping to please and the father well-meaning but obviously unused to having a child on his hands. Illustrations are full-page paintings in bright colors framed by ample white space, giving a sense of the clear air and fresh water in the natural settings. Luke, who is probably eight to ten, and his father are pictured as Asian Americans.

268 Schotter, Roni, *A Fruit & Vegetable Man,* illus. Jeannette Winter, Little, Brown, 1993 (hardcover), ISBN 0-316-77467-7, $15.95, unp. Ages 4–8, grades PS–3.

Realistic picture-story book. Young Asian immigrant Sun Ho and his sister enjoy watching old Ruby Rubenstein stock the shelves of his popular fruit and vegetable store and meet his customers on Delano Street in New York City. Sun Ho even accompanies Ruby to the market and learns shelving and sales techniques. When Ruby falls ill, the boy and his family keep the store going, and, since he is confident that all will be well with his business in their hands, Ruby and his wife retire to the mountains. The fruit and vegetable store becomes Sun Ho's family's enterprise. Pleasing if predictable, the story projects a warm and uplifting tone. The full-color, deep-toned, double-framed pictures establish the physical setting of the commercial district and the lushly stocked store and also the mixed-ethnic social climate. The enticing pictures have the quality of fine greeting cards, and several could suitably be framed. Sun Ho's country of origin is not indicated.

269 Sinykin, Sheri Cooper, *The Buddy Trap*, Atheneum, 1991 (hardcover), ISBN 0-689-31674-7, $13.95, 129 pp. Ages 8–12, grades 3–7.

Contemporary realistic problem novel set in Wisconsin. Since he is an accomplished classical flutist, adopted Korean orphan Cam Whitney, twelve, prefers music camp but goes to regular camp to please his parents. His worst fears are soon realized. During the annual war games, he is forced to become a double agent to protect his flute from bullies. The experience not only brings home to him how much he loves his music but also plunges him into an unaccustomed leadership role and gives him insights into antisocial behavior. Ample action keeps the pace moving, and the climax is tense, but the story's focus is more on the moral issues and the reasons behind such behavior. Characters are types, including the overly fat boy, the cerebral boy, the bully who has been brutalized by an alcoholic father, and the always sunny counselor. Cam's race is minimally exploited, though his fears that he will be scorned and derided because of it remain constant.

270 Tamar, Erika, *The Truth about Kim O'Hara*, Atheneum, 1992 (hardcover), ISBN 0-689-31789-1, $14.95, 187 pp. Ages 11–14, grades 6–9.

Contemporary, realistic, psychological problem novel set in Greenwich Village, New York City. Although fifteen-year-old Anglo Andy Szabo tells what happens, at the story's center is beautiful, brilliant Vietnamese Kimberly O'Hara, with whom Andy is madly in love and who was introduced in *It Happened at Cecilia's* (1989). Kim seems happy with her family, Vietnam vet father, younger half-sister, and adopted mother, but when Andy gets to know her better, he realizes she is overly compulsive about school and proper behavior and is always tightly controlled—attitudes that frustrate Andy when he asks her for dates and pressures her for sex and she refuses. After she falls apart at the homeless shelter where he tutors, then freezes on a French test and runs away, Andy learns her painful story. When she was a small child in Vietnam, she pretended to be Kim O'Hara, Mr. O'Hara's Vietnamese illegitimate daughter, in order to get a home, and has tried to be perfect in order to compensate for living a lie. Story's end finds Andy hoping she will seek counseling. The main characters are drawn with clarity; no easy solutions are proposed to Kim's problem; and blame is not directed at anyone. Some events are too pat, but the interest level remains high, Andy's school friends are believable, and the trusting and warm relationship between Andy and his family and the air of acceptance between Andy's friends and Kim are pleasing features.

271 Tan, Amy, *The Joy Luck Club*, Putnam, 1989 (hardcover), ISBN 0-399-13420-4, $18.95, 288 pp.; Ivy, 1989 (paper), ISBN 0-8041-0630-4, $5.95, 332 pp. Ages 14 up, grades 9 up.

Realistic novel of contemporary Chinese-American life in San Francisco with internal stories going back to mid-twentieth-century China. The Joy Luck Club is a social-support group of four Chinese women born before World War II, who have immigrated to the United States. Each tells her story in several segments, either by herself or as remembered by her daughter. Interspersed among these accounts are the narratives of their four daughters. Since the stories deal with some of the same events but seen from a different vantage, the book becomes a highly textured, subtle, occasionally hilarious, always revealing study in character, in efforts made to reconcile traditional Chinese culture with American ways, and in the bonds and conflicts between mothers and daughters of diverging circumstances. The many counterpointing episodes and the large cast are sometimes confusing, but unity is achieved by the frame account of just-deceased Suyuan Woo, who abandoned her baby twin daughters while fleeing from Japanese soldiers and whose daughter, Jing-Mei, visits China to meet her recently located older half sisters. Although it was a Book-of-the-Month Club selection, to be avoided is *The Moon Lady* (1992), a revision for younger readers of a China-set chapter from *The Joy Luck Club*. The narrative is condescending and overly long, and experts criticize the illustrations as unauthentic.

272 Tan, Amy, *The Kitchen God's Wife*, Putnam, 1991 (hardcover), ISBN 0-399-13578-2, $22.95, 320 pp.; Ivy, 1991 (paper), ISBN 0-8041-0753-X, $5.95, 532 pp. Ages 14 up, grades 9 up.

Historical novel whose main portion is a long flashback to World War II in China. China-born Winnie Louie, now in her seventies and living in San Francisco, tells her American-born daughter the story of her tragic marriage in a sexist culture to an abusive man, the deaths of their three children, and her struggles to survive poverty and his nearly psychopathic cruelty, endure the chaos of the Japanese invasion, and find happiness with a loving, American-born Chinese minister. This highly detailed account (which recalls the broad-spectrum Russian novel), often sexually frank, combines mystery, horror, violence, suspense, warmth, even hilarity to present a fascinating picture of a turbulent period in Chinese history, the problems of immigrant acculturation, relations between the immigrant generation and the American-born generation, in particular mothers and daughters, all from the point of view of what emerges as a sometimes foolish, sometimes smart, very tough woman, a true survivor. There is a commonsense naivete about Winnie and her life that gives the book unusual charm. This book is more mature in substance than the author's *The Joy Luck Club* (no. 271) but less complex in structure.

273   Terris, Susan, *The Latchkey Kids,* Farrar, 1986 (hardcover), ISBN 0-374-34363-2, $10.95, 167 pp. Ages 9–11, grades 4–6.

Realistic novel of family life for middle readers about eleven-year-old Callie and her friendship with Nora Chen, which gets her into trouble but eventually solves her problems. Because her father, suffering from severe depression, has lost his job, Callie's mother returns to work, and Callie finds herself a latchkey child, responsible for her much younger brother, Rex, picking him up at his school, taking him home, locking them both in their new San Francisco apartment, and waiting tensely for her mother and father, who no longer act like themselves. Her loneliness is eased by a developing friendship with a classmate, Nora Chen, newly arrived from Hong Kong. Nora also has family responsibilities, but the two discover a place they can be together and keep Rex happy in the half-built apartment house next door, where construction is temporarily suspended. After Rex almost falls through a heating vent, Callie is badly injured saving him and is rescued by Mrs. Chen, Nora's Ah-Ma or grandmother. By mutual agreement, Mrs. Chen becomes Ah-Ma to Callie and Rex, and although Callie's father is not cured, he has begun to make an effort, and the future looks bright. The protagonist and her brother are white, but the Chen family plays a prominent role in the plot, and their cultural differences in expectations for the children are important. The family strains imposed by a mentally ill parent are well depicted, and Callie's misery and resentment are realistic. Nora, almost too good and understanding, is made human by her love of mischief.

274   Thomas, Joyce Carol, ed., *A Gathering of Flowers: Stories about Being Young in America,* HarperCollins, 1990 (hardcover), ISBN 0-06-026173-0, $14.89, 236 pp.; Trophy, 1992 (paper), ISBN 0-06-447082-2, $3.95, 256 pp. Ages 12 up, grades 7 up.

Eleven stories of realism and fantasy, from several cultures, about love, loss, making friends, coping with relatives, and searching for one's niche in life, intended as a "sampling of the rich colors and voices that make up today's America." Three are by Asian-American writers. Maxine Hong Kingston's "Twisters and Shouters" involves an off-center philosophical conversation between bus riders on their way to a party in Chinese-American San Francisco. Poignancy characterizes the romance of the Korean-American girl in "Autumn Rose" by Kevin Kyung and sad perplexity the Japanese-American girl's view of mixed-racial events in Jeanne Wakatsuki Houston's "After the War." Other settings include an Indian reservation in northern Minnesota, rural Oklahoma among African-American church people, and Chicago's Mexican-American community. Other writers represented include Gary Soto, Lois Lowry, Al Young, Rick Wernli, and the anthologist herself. All the stories give a pleasing sense of the culture and are carefully arranged for maximum effect. Information about the authors is included.

275 Tompert, Ann, *Will You Come Back for Me?*, illus. Robin Kramer, Whitman, 1988 (hardcover), ISBN 0-8075-9112-2, $13.95; (paper) ISBN 0-8075-9113-0, $5.95, unp. Ages 3–6, grades PS–1.

Picture-story book of Suki, who is apprehensive at the prospect of attending a day care center when her mother starts to work, even dreaming that her stuffed bear, Lulu, has a traumatic first day at Brown Bear's School for Teddies. Gently, her mother assures her that there is nothing to fear, that she will always come back for her because she belongs in her heart. The illustrations, slightly cartoonish, show Suki and her mother as Asian Americans and the other nursery school children as ethnically mixed. The warm mother-daughter relationship tempers the obviously didactic purpose of the story.

276 Tran, Kim-Lan, *Tet: The New Year,* illus. Mai Vo-Dinh, Simon & Schuster, 1993 (paper), ISBN 0-671-79843-X, $4.95, 23 pp. Ages 5–10, grades K–5.

Realistic picture-story book about Vietnamese immigrants to the United States. As the festival of Tet, the Vietnamese New Year, approaches, Ms. Kim, an English language teacher, encourages her children to talk about how they celebrate the occasion, both previously in Vietnam and now in America, works with them to prepare to celebrate together, and invites them to her house for the festival, where she explains what she has done to get her home ready. When very homesick, dispirited, newly immigrated Huy Ly does not come, she issues a special invitation to him and his father, and both attend. The obviously informational text works well in instructing in a social studies way and also in conveying a limited sense of cultural loss and immigration shock. The point of view shifts disconcertingly, however. It begins with Huy Ly and switches to Ms. Kim, a matter that changes the book's emphasis and tone and almost eliminates identification with Huy Ly. The full-color watercolors establish setting, depict characters and incidents, and show the objects used at various stages for Tet. Amplifying them are small, colored photographs of, for example, the interior and exterior of an American Vietnamese store and scenes with Tet materials in a home. A glossary is included.

277 Turner, Ann, *Through Moon and Stars and Night Skies,* illus. James Graham Hale, Harper, 1990 (hardcover), ISBN 0-06-026189-7, $13.00, unp. Ages 4–8, grades PS–3.

Picture-story book of a little Asian boy, probably Vietnamese, who flies from his native country, holding the pictures he has been sent of his new adoptive parents, their white house, their red dog, and the room prepared for him with a teddy-bear quilt. At first, he is afraid of everything, but as reality begins to match his pictures, he starts to accept his new home and the love of his new parents. A simple, quiet story illustrated with muted, gentle watercolors, it resists the opportunity to underscore its meaning with any didactic statement.

278 Uchida, Yoshiko, *The Bracelet,* illus. Joanna Yardley, Philomel, 1993 (hardcover), ISBN 0-399-22503-X, $14.95, unp. Ages 5–9, grades K–4.

Historical picture-story book of the evacuation of people of Japanese ancestry from the West Coast during World War II, as seen through the eyes of a second grader. Japanese-American Emi, seven, watches the family possessions being carted away, misses her father who has been sent to a prison camp, and feels the loss and dislocation of a situation she cannot understand. Just as she, her mother, and her sister, Reiko, are about to leave for the train station taking only what they can carry with them, Emi's friend, Laurie Madison, comes with a present, a bracelet to remember her by. Somewhere during the journey from Berkeley to the racetrack where they are housed in a horse stall, Emi loses the bracelet. At first she is devastated, but eventually she realizes that Laurie's gift of friendship and reassurance will stay with her whatever happens. An afterword tells of the historical relocation and its injustice, but the story itself wisely remains simple, from the point of view of a young girl. The illustrations are highly realistic, with the different clothing, postures, and Japanese faces individualized and the grim camp appropriately stark and dusty.

279 Uchida, Yoshiko, *The Happiest Ending,* Atheneum, 1985 (hardcover), ISBN 0-689-50326-1, $13.95, 111 pp. Ages 9–11, grades 4–6.

Historical novel in which Japanese-American Rinko Tsujimura, twelve, tries to save Teru Hata, who is coming from Japan, from marrying Mr. Kinjo, who is twice her age and has paid her passage to join her mother. In the process, she learns that some arranged marriages, like that of Mrs. Sigino, her Japanese language teacher, are failures, and some, like that of her parents, are successful, and that love and happiness depend more on the characters of the individuals than upon age. Life in Berkeley, California, in the 1930s, is evoked with understanding and humor, and Rinko, the first-person narrator, experiences both the frustrations and the pride of her ethnic background as an American-born child of immigrant parents. Earlier books featuring Rinko are *A Jar of Dreams* (1981), which deals with the anti-Oriental prejudice of the period, and *The Best Bad Thing* (1985), in which she helps Mrs. Hata, a widow with two sons, and discovers that things that seem bad at first sometimes turn out to be good.

280 Uchida, Yoshiko, *Picture Bride*, Northland, 1987 (hardcover), ISBN 0-87358-429-5, $14.95, 216 pp. Ages 15 up, grades 10 up.

Historical novel of Hana Omiya, a young Japanese woman who comes to Oakland, California, in 1917 to marry Taro Takeda, a man whom she has never met. At first, she is dismayed to find that he is older and far less affluent than she has been led to believe, but realizing she cannot back out of the marriage without disgracing the man, the relatives in Japan who acted as go-betweens, and her own family, she bravely makes the best of the situation. Her greatest challenge is to forego the romance offered by Taro's friend, Kiyoshi Yamaka, a lively young man to whom she is greatly attracted and who dies in the 1918 flu epidemic. She also suffers a miscarriage, hostility from the white community, and her husband's resentment at her better ideas and management ability. Eventually she even must accept the estrangement of her beloved daughter, who marries a white American, and, not long after that, deportation to an internment camp in Utah during World War II. Throughout it all, she represses her resentment and curbs her naturally outgoing personality, trying to be a good, traditional wife. The picture of what life must have been like for many Japanese-American women in the early part of the twentieth century is moving, and Hana is an appealing character, strong despite her subordinate role and enduring in the face of personal and cultural difficulties. A number of secondary characters are also memorable.

281 Watanabe, Sylvia, *Talking to the Dead and Other Stories*, Doubleday, 1992 (hardcover), ISBN 0-385-41887-6, $20.00, 127 pp. Ages 14 up, grades 9 up.

Ten stories of Japanese Americans in a mixed-ethnic neighborhood in the town of Luhi in Hawaii. Each story is complete in itself, but all are tied together by setting and characters, the protagonists in a particular story being, for example, people on the periphery in others. The effect is to give less a sense of plot problems resolved, although that happens, as of the culture of a close-knit area—of several generations grappling with changing circumstances, attitudes, and beliefs. Here are conniving and domineering wives and mothers, faithless husbands, children staying or leaving, perhaps in rebellion, healers, prayer ladies, sons called to war, daughters on the stage. In "Anchorage," a girl helps her grandmother contend with her father's Alzheimer's disease. "The Caves of Okinawa" finds a mother interfering with her husband's plans to help their son flee to Canada to evade Vietnam, where eventually the young man dies. In the title story, a young woman apprenticed to a traditional "laying out" woman removes her mentor's body from its coffin in the dead woman's son's mortuary to give it the burial she knows the old lady would have wanted. Subtle humor, particularly of irony and character, and unexpected turns combine with a clear, understated style.

282 Watanabe, Sylvia, and Carol Bruchac, eds., *Home to Stay*, Greenfield Review, 1989 (paper), ISBN 0-912678-76-3, $12.95, 321 pp. Ages 14 up, grades 9 up.

Thirty-one short stories from twenty-nine Asian-American women writers with Chinese, Vietnamese, Japanese, Filipino, Hawaiian, Asian-Indian, and Korean backgrounds. The stories "have arisen smack-dab out of the mainstream of American tradition. Their cross-cultural perspectives address what is increasingly becoming common American experience. In new ways, in their many voices, these stories tell and re-tell the old American story of coming home to stay." The opener is an excerpt from Maxine Hong Kingston's *China Men*, but the rest are complete in themselves and often carry the air of personal or heard experience. Vietnamese-American Elizabeth Gordon tells how she and her mother came to America, brought by her U.S. soldier father, and her difficulty in determining her race for school forms in "On the Other Side of the War: A Story." Chinese-American Gish Jen (no. 238) writes of an amusing music lesson, after which an umbrella causes a car accident. Sarah Lau's story tells of a Chinese-American mother's anger and frustration as her Americanized daughters grow away and leave home, and Wakako Yamauchi describes a dysfunctional Japanese-American farming family in the Imperial Valley of California in "And the Soul Shall Dance." Some stories reflect anti-Asian sentiment, for example, "Wilshire Bus" by Hisaye Yamamoto; "Changes" is set in the Tule Lake Japanese Relocation Center where the Anglo writer, Marnie Mueller, was born when her C.O. father was working there. The book also contains stories by Fae Myenne Ng (no. 257), Amy Tan (nos. 271, 272), and Sylvia Watanabe (nos. 281, 282). This is a choice, varied, skillfully written and arranged collection. Biographical information is included.

283 Whalen, Gloria, *Goodbye, Vietnam,* Knopf, 1991 (hardcover), ISBN 0-679-82263-1, $13.00, 135 pp. Ages 9 up, grades 4 up.

Historical novel about Vietnamese refugees in the 1970s. Thirteen-year-old Mai tells how her father, mother, grandmother, and younger brother and sister flee by night from their Mekong Delta village with meager supplies and almost no money to escape the oppressive regime. At the sea, they board an over-loaded, leaky, old boat, paying for their passage with their father's skill as a mechanic. In spite of disease, intense heat, very little water and food, great apprehension, and a captain almost ignorant of navigation, they arrive in Hong Kong. There they live under unbelievably cramped conditions in a warehouse, in constant fear of being sent home, until the news arrives that relatives in the United States will sponsor their emigration to America and sets them on their way. The plot is predictable from other refugee stories, and characters are types to advance the plot, the most memorable being the cranky grand-mother, who once secures their safety by bribing an official with a duck she smuggled out, and an all-wise, extremely capable woman doctor who travels with them. The thousand-mile voyage is foreshortened, and the disappoint-ment and discomforts of the warehouse camp are minimally described. The book's strength lies in its clear, if limited, sense for middle-grade readers of the hardships, fortitude, and endurance of these people in their quest to be free from tyranny.

284 Williams, Vera B., *"More More More," Said the Baby,* illus. Vera B. Williams, Greenwillow, 1990 (hardcover), ISBN 0688-09173-3, $12.95, unp. Ages 3–7, grades PS–2.

Very short, realistic picture-story book in which the same story is repeated for each of three babies. Each small child is caught up, swung around, kissed, and hugged in loving abandon in this order: blond, white Little Guy by his daddy; African-American Little Pumpkin by his white grandma; and Asian-American Little Bird by her mama. The children are appropriately chubby, awkward, pot bellied, and big eyed, and the adults fittingly adoring and en-veloping. The boldly composed full-page, off-the-page, full-palette, color-framed gouaches enclose the text, which is integrated into the pictures not only in position but also in choice of colors. The pictures extend the text in every way. They capture the action, establish the setting, and reveal character and emotion. Their generous use of primary colors projects the affection for life of these three very short, related stories. This is a charming book for the very young.

285   Yep, Laurence, ed., *American Dragons: Twenty-five Asian American Voices,* HarperCollins, 1993 (hardcover), ISBN 0-06-021494-5, $15.00, 237 pp. Ages 12 up, grades 7 up.

Anthology of mostly short stories, with some poems and several excerpts from novels, by writers whose ethnic roots are from China, Japan, Korea, Vietnam, Thailand, and Tibet. There is a general preface and an introduction to each section, as well as a brief biographical note at the beginning of each piece, an afterword, and a recommended bibliography. Quality is uneven; in general, the prose is more impressive than the poetry. Of the six sections— Identity, In the Shadow of Giants (about parents), The Wise Child, World War II, Love, and Guides—the strongest is the last, about grandparents, which contains several skillful stories: "Yai," by Visalaya Hirunpidok, "There's No Reason to Get Romantic," by Ann Tashi Slater, "Jijan," by Rebecca Honma, and the futuristic "Black Powder," by William F. Wu. All the pieces in the World War II section are by Japanese Americans, reflecting the particular pain suffered by their people at that time. Young readers may be especially attracted to the ironic humor of the excerpt from Lensey Namioka's novel, *Who's Hu?* and Cherylene Lee's "Hollywood and the Pits." Among other well-known writers is Maxine Hong Kingston, whose "A Sea Worry" is set in Hawaii. This is a valuable collection for junior high and high school ages. For the poems in the book see no. 338.

286   Yep, Laurence, *Dragon War,* HarperCollins, 1992 (hardcover), ISBN 0-06-020302-1, $14.95, 313 pp. Ages 11 up, grades 6 up.

Concluding novel in a fantasy series starring dragons, magicians, a monkey wizard, and other figures from Chinese folklore, modified with new adventures and modern dialogue. In the first two books, *Dragon of the Lost Sea* (1982) and *Dragon Steel* (1985), narrated by Shimmer, the exiled Dragon princess, she and an orphan boy, Thorn, seeking to restore the inland sea of her people, capture the witch, Civet, who stole the sea. They travel to the realm of the sea dragons where they join forces with Indigo, a human slave girl of the dragons, learn of the internal conflicts among the factions of the dragons, and become embroiled in the fight against the terrible krakens rising from the Abyss. In the third book, *Dragon Cauldron* (1991), narrated by Monkey, they seek to repair the magic cauldron which was cracked when they stole it from the king of the sea dragons, planning to use it to restore the Inland Sea. When they take it to the Smith and the Snail Women, other mythological figures, Thorn allows himself to be imprisoned in the cauldron metal as the only way to mend it. Before they can use it, however, it is stolen by the Boneless King, who plans to use it to enslave all the creatures of the world. In *Dragon War,* the final book of the series, also narrated by Monkey, they are caught in the war between dragons and humans, lose and regain the cauldron numerous times, finally defeat the Boneless King, restore the Inland Sea, and rescue Thorn from the cauldron. It turns out that Thorn is really the lost heir to the throne, and he assumes kingship with a vow of peace between humans and dragons. Action is unflagging and the scenes of the many realms through which the characters pass are highly imaginative, but the fantasy is not entirely convincing, partly because it is difficult to imagine dragons, even the water-loving, non-firebreathing Chinese variety, performing many of the actions described and partly because the fantasy limits are too fluid to provide the necessary narrative tension, since many of the characters can change shape at will. The language is late twentieth century, and the dialogue, particularly that of Shimmer and Monkey, is continually wisecracking in nature.

287   Yep, Laurence, *Mountain Light,* Harper, 1985 (hardcover), ISBN 0-06-026758-5, $11.95, 281 pp. Ages 10–14, grades 5–9.

Historical novel starting in China during the Red Turban revolt of 1855 and ending in conflicts in the California goldfields between rival groups of Chinese immigrants. Having left home for adventure to join the rebellion against the ruling Manchus, nineteen-year-old Squeaky falls in with the Gallant, an old, respected warrior, and his daughter, Cassia, members of a clan feuding with his native village, and their friend Tiny, a Stranger, one of the Hakka people unaccepted although they have lived in the province for several centuries. After the Gallant is killed and Tiny's wife is murdered in the growing persecution of the Strangers, Squeaky and Tiny travel to America to join Cassia's brother, Foxfire. The bitter feuds, which defeat the revolt in China and follow the immigrants to America, are the most interesting and revealing historical elements, but the extreme hardships of the ocean voyage are vivid and plenty of action and narrow escapes in both China and California keep the action lively. This is a sequel to *The Serpent's Children* (1984), which deals with the childhood and early adult years of Cassia and Foxfire, who migrates to America. Both narrative and dialogue are in modern English giving no feeling for the period of the setting in time.

288 Yep, Laurence, *The Star Fisher,* Morrow, 1991 (hardcover), ISBN 0-688-09365-5, $12.95, 150 pp.; Puffin, 1992 (paper), ISBN 0-14-036003-4, $3.99, 160 pp. Ages 8 up, grades 3 up.

Biographical novel of a Chinese-American family in the hills of West Virginia in 1927. Resilient Joan Lee, fifteen, tells how she and her brother, energetic Bobby, ten, and her sister, willful Emily, eight, and their immigrant parents travel by train from Ohio to the small town of Clarksburg where Papa sets up a laundry in an abandoned schoolhouse. Mama has trouble with the English language and American ways, and the family encounters troubling prejudice until help comes from unexpected sources and Mama learns to bake apple pies. Although the star fisher legend seems intrusive and the story lacks the freshness of the author's earlier historical novel, *Dragonwings* (1975), which gives a strong picture of prejudice against immigrants in the early twentieth century, or his novel of contemporary family life *Child of the Owl* (1977), about a girl and her immigrant grandmother, both books set in San Francisco, *The Star Fisher* projects a good sense of the family's values and problems. The book is based on the author's own family experiences.

5

Asian Americans: Books of Oral Tradition

289 Birdseye, Tom, ret., *A Song of Stars,* illus. Ju-Hong Chen, Holiday, 1990 (hardcover), ISBN 0-8234-0790-X, $14.95, unp. Ages 4–10, grades PS–5.

Retelling of an Asian legend of the Milky Way and other constellations. When Princess Chauchau, the weaver daughter of the Emperor of the Heavens, and her lover, the kind herdsman, Newlang, spend so much time together that they neglect their duties, they are condemned by her father to meet only once a year, on the seventh day of the seventh month. When, on that day, the river (the Milky Way) separating them rises in a raging torrent, the emperor relents and allows magpies to form a bridge of birds to unite them. The illustrations employ conventional romantic poses and expressions for the lovers (in keeping with traditional Oriental art), and the stylized, jewel-toned, shimmering, paper-cut illustrations flow along with the narrative and catch its sentimental spirit. The pictures of the emperor in particular stand out; they aptly express his power, majesty, and love for his children. A reteller's note gives the background and briefly describes the modern Chinese and Japanese festivals that commemorate the legend.

290 Blai, Xiong, ret., *Nine-in-One, Grr! Grr!,* ad. Cathy Spagnoli, illus. Nancy Hom, Children's Book, 1989 (hardcover), ISBN 0-89239-048-4, $13.95, 32 pp. Ages 5–8, grades K–3.

Folktale of the Hmong people of Laos which explains why the world is not overrun by tigers. When the first tiger asks the god Shao how many cubs she will have, he tells her nine in one year, but only if she remembers his words. To aid her memory she sings, repeatedly, "Nine-in-one, Grr! Grr!" and then is tricked by the Eu bird into reversing it to "One-in-nine, Grr! Grr!" The full-page illustrations are flat, as if made by applique embroidery in glowing colors, and are elaborately framed with wide strips of geometric patterns. Illuminated initial letters on text pages echo the colors and designs of the facing pictures.

291 Bryan, Ashley, ret., *Sh-Ko and His Eight Wicked Brothers,* illus. Fumio Yoshimura, Atheneum, 1988 (hardcover), ISBN 0-689-31446-9, $13.95, unp. Ages 4–8, grades PS–3.

Retelling of a Japanese folktale. Sh-Ko is ridiculed by his eight older brothers for his ugliness. His kindness to a supernatural rabbit they treated cruelly is rewarded with a magical gold thread, which enables him to win the hand of a princess. Related in good storytelling flavor, the tale combines the widespread motifs of the despised youngest who succeeds because of his virtue and the grateful, helpful animal, but it also has enough twists and turns to make it seem completely fresh. It is accompanied by lively, amusing, delicately shaded brush sketches on salmon-colored paper. The pictures create the Oriental atmosphere, point up situations, and keep the story from becoming too serious.

292 Carrison, Muriel Paskin, ret., *Cambodian Folk Stories from the Gatiloke,* Tuttle, 1987 (hardcover), ISBN 0-8048-1518-6, $15.95, 139 pp. Ages 11 up, grades 6 up.

From a translation by the Venerable Kong Chhean, fifteen stories of the ancient Theravada branch of Buddhism, told for many centuries in the oral tradition and first written down in the late nineteenth century. Although used in the Buddhist tradition to teach, the stories differ from Aesop's fables, more familiar didactic tales of the European literary tradition, in being usually longer and in featuring fools and rascals who do not necessarily receive their punishment in this life, it being assumed that they will be dealt with justly in their next reincarnation. Those faults especially warned against are the failure to reason carefully, a lack of respect for women, and the abuse of power by those of high status. A foreword describes the Gatiloke and the development of the Cambodian literary tradition; a long appendix tells about the history and social traditions of Cambodia, followed by a glossary and a bibliography.

293 Compton, Patricia A., ret., *The Terrible EEK: A Japanese Tale Retold,* illus. Sheila Hamanaka, Simon & Schuster, 1991 (hardcover), ISBN 0-671-73737-6, $14.95, unp. Ages 4–8, grades PS–3.

Retelling of a Japanese folktale revolving around a simple verbal misunderstanding. On a dark and rainy night in the mountains, a father's statement that his greatest fear is a leak sets off a chain of funny misadventures that saves him and his household from a thief and a wolf. Sturdy, full-color, heavy-palette, close-to-the-viewer oils catch the humor of the ironic situations, give some sense of the culture, and make this a very attractive book.

294 Demi, ad., *A Chinese Zoo: Fables and Proverbs,* illus. Demi, Harcourt, 1987 (hardcover), ISBN 0-15-217510-5, $14.95, unp. Ages 4 up, grades PS up.

Thirteen fables based on ancient Chinese sources. The short, unadorned narratives employ anthropomorphized, typecast animals as characters, and move unrelentingly with little dialogue to the moralistic conclusion. They caution against being greedy, judging by appearances, and not trusting to chance, among other practical advice for getting on in life. Each fable and its picture take up two pages, the text hugging the sides of the fan-shaped illustration. The fans portray the action of the stories in delicately drawn, finely detailed, full-color Chinese brush watercolors on a buff-toned background. They shimmer and glow and give the effect of real fans. Their amusing touches relieve the basic seriousness of the stories which are pleasingly told in slightly formal tones. The morals of each tale appear as proverbs at the bottom curve of each fan. Less graciously beautiful as a whole but still outstanding is *Demi's Reflective Fables* (1988), which contains thirteen more fables, these decorated by circular pictures, some completely filled with colorful figures and background color, others presenting characters and objects on white grounds, to give the impression of designs on ancient Chinese mirrors. Author's notes conclude both books.

295 Demi, ret., *The Magic Boat,* illus. Demi, Holt, 1990 (hardcover), ISBN 0-8050-1141-2, $15.95, unp. Ages 4–8, grades PS–3.

Retelling of a Chinese folktale. Chang, an honest, hardworking lad, saves an old man's life and is rewarded with a magic dragon boat. Tricked out of it by wicked Ying who uses it to become prime minister, Chang is helped by talking animal friends to regain it from Ying and the greedy emperor, who, respectively, are turned into an old gray wolf and a big wild pig in punishment. Adorning the gracefully told story are equally graceful, delicately detailed watercolors done in pale tones except for accenting orangy-reds and golds. The pictures repeat the story and depict trees, animals, buildings, and costumes that localize the tale. The red dragon that forms the boat and the golden phoenix on which the old man appears are especially striking. Further enhancing Demi's reputation for capturing the essence of Chinese culture in adaptations of old stories are *Chen Ping and His Magic Axe* (1987), *The Empty*

Pot (1990), and *The Artist and the Architect* (1991), the latter an open-ended look at human nature, where the reader or hearer must decide whether the main character forgives or seizes the opportunity for revenge. In each book, the basic style of illustrating is the same, but the shapes of the pictures vary to suit each book, making them all exceptionally beautiful.

296   Garland, Sherry, ret., *Why Ducks Sleep on One Leg,* illus. Jean Tseng and Mou-sien Tseng, Scholastic, 1993 (hardcover), ISBN 590-45697-0, $14.95, unp. Ages 3–8, grades PS–3.

Retelling of a Vietnamese folktale explaining an observable characteristic of ducks. Because the Jade Emperor, the ruler of all gods and spirits, has created them with only one leg, the original three ducks have trouble getting food, flying, and avoiding being stepped on. They petition the Jade Emperor's earthly delegate, the village guardian, for one more leg each. Denied their request on the grounds that the Jade Emperor might be offended, they ask the guardian for the three extra legs of an incense pot that he is about to discard. Since these legs are of gold, the ducks must conceal them while they sleep, and that is why ducks sleep on one leg to this day. This charmingly told *pourquoi* is enhanced by humorously detailed, full-color, off-the-page paintings. They establish the Oriental setting with houses and dragons, for example, and cleverly characterize the irascible, self-important village guardian and the humble, determined little ducks.

297   Ginsburg, Mirra, ad. *The Chinese Mirror: A Korean Folktale,* illus. Margot Zemach, Harcourt, 1988 (hardcover), ISBN 0-15-200420-3, $12.95; (paper), ISBN 0-15-217508-3, $4.95, unp. Ages 5–8, grades K–3.

Retold folktale of a Korean villager traveling in China who sees a mirror for the first time and, delighted by the friendly face he sees, buys it, brings it home, and hides it. His wife, seeing him taking it out secretly and laughing, peeks at it after he goes out and is heartbroken to see a beautiful young woman who she assumes is a new wife. Her mother-in-law sees an ugly crone, her father-in-law an old neighbor, and their little son a bully who has stolen the pebble he holds. A passerby, outraged, strikes the bully, smashing the mirror to hundreds of shiny splinters. The folktale is illustrated with watercolors in the style of two eighteenth-century Korean painters. The retelling, in simple, direct sentences, draws no moral.

298 Hamanaka, Sheila, ret., *Screen of Frogs,* illus. Sheila Hamanaka, Orchard, 1993 (hardcover), ISBN 0-531-05464-0, $15.95, unp. Ages 4–10, grades PS–5.

Retelling of a Japanese folktale. Rich, lazy, spoiled Koji sells off his inherited lands to pay debts he incurs on extravagant purchases until he has only his great house and one mountain and lake left. One day, by the lake, he is accosted by a huge frog who begs him not to make all the wildlife in the area homeless by selling the remaining land. Troubled and anxious by what he has heard, Koji sells his personal property until he has left only his futon and an old, blank screen. In gratitude, frogs cover the screen with paintings of frogs in all sizes and vibrant colors. Much sobered, Koji devotes himself to working in the fields and cherishes the screen, from which, on his death years later, the painted frogs fade, leaving the screen blank. This simple story, which promotes respect for nature and pleasure in ordinary, everyday work on the land, is extended by brightly colored acrylics and collages. Facial features, costumes, houses, interior objects, and black lines that recall calligraphy establish the setting, and many witty touches relieve the story's seriousness and keep it from sounding didactic. Some paintings are delicately impressionistic, while others, like that of the big, pleading frog and the expressionistically decorated screen, are bold close ups.

299 Han, Oki S., ad., and Stephanie Haboush Plunkett, *Sir Whong and the Golden Pig,* illus. Oki S. Han, Dial, 1993 (hardcover), ISBN 0-8037-1344-4, $13.99, unp. Ages 5–9, grades K–4.

Korean folktale of a trickster tricked. Sir Whong, a man of wealth, generosity, and impeccable taste, is visited by a stranger who asks for a loan of 1,000 nyung, a great deal of money. He offers as collateral a pig made of gold, which he represents as a family treasure worth many times the amount he is asking. Sir Whong agrees, but some months later, when he looks at the pig, he sees that the color has faded and realizes that he has been cheated. He waits until the village has a big ceremony for a wedding, attended by people from some distance around, and in the middle of the reception he begins to wail and lament that he has lost or been robbed of the pig and fears the owner will be terribly upset. News gets back to the stranger, as Sir Whong has foreseen, and the unscrupulous man sees a way in which he can get much more money. He calls upon Sir Whong, says that fortune has smiled upon him, that he is able to repay the 1,000 nyung and wants his pig back. Sir Whong graciously complies, and the stranger leaves, confounded. The large watercolor illustrations show details of Sir Whong's artfully elegant home and of village life, particularly of the preparations and celebration of the wedding. Many of the pictures are enclosed in elaborate frames of traditional designs, flowers, or ducks swimming among water plants.

300 Haugaard, Erik, and Masako Haugaard, rets., *The Story of Yuriwaka,* illus. Birgitta Saflund, Roberts Rinehart, 1991 (hardcover), ISBN 1-879373-02-5, $12.95, 42 pp. Ages 9–12, grades 4–7.

Subtitled "A Japanese Odyssey," this hero tale is an outgrowth of the stories of Odysseus brought to Japan in the sixteenth century, but long transformed into a part of the Japanese oral tradition. The Emperor of Kyushu, beset by sea raiders, sends for Yuriwaka, the strongest man in the kingdom, who lives with his wife, Lady Kasuga, as governor in the district of Bungo. He sets off with three ships, fights for three years, and sails for home, having lost two of his ships but also having destroyed the pirates of Shiragi. Two jealous officers steal his iron bow as he sleeps, maroon him on a small, rocky island, and report that he is dead. Lady Kasuga, who refuses to marry one of the officers, is placed under arrest. When eventually he is rescued by fishermen, Yuriwaka has no way to prove who he is and works in the stables until, in an archery contest, he is the only one able to wield the iron bow and thereby claims his rightful place. Although the shipwrecked hero, the faithful wife, and the exceptional bow are the only portions of the story that retain close resemblance to the *Odyssey,* the story in itself is a stirring hero tale with details and social mores distinct from those of the Western world. The handsome book has three double-page illustrations in color, four full-page, black-and-white paintings, and numerous smaller pictures and decorations throughout, all using Japanese costume and design.

301 Heyer, Marilee, ret., *The Weaving of a Dream,* illus. Marilee Heyer, Viking Kestrel, 1986 (hardcover), ISBN 0-670-80555-6, $12.95, unp. Ages 5–11, grades K–6.

Elaborately illustrated Chinese folktale, retold in a more detailed and literary version than the same tale, *The Enchanted Tapestry* (no. 316). The old woman trades rice money for a beautiful painting she sees in the marketplace and becomes obsessed by the brocade copy of it she weaves at the suggestion of her youngest son. Her tears and blood from her eyes fall into the weaving and become part of the river and the glowing sun. When a sudden wind blows the brocade away, first the eldest, then the second son set out to recover it but are discouraged by the hardships predicted by a fortune-teller. When the youngest son learns that he must knock out his front teeth to bring a stone horse to life, he does not hesitate, nor does he flinch when he rides through fire and freezing water, until he gets to Sun Mountain. There the fairies beg one more night to copy the weaving and hang up a shining pearl to give them light as they work. The red fairy abandons her copy and weaves her own likeness into the old woman's brocade. When the son returns and the weaving becomes real, he and his mother find the red fairy sitting by the fish pond. Printed on heavy, large, shiny pages, the illustrations are extremely detailed, with patterns of fabrics, designs of pottery and architecture, and embellishments of birds, flowers, and lizards adding to the richness of the pictures. This is an interesting comparison of interpretation with the San Souci book.

302 Hong, Lily Toy, ret., *How the Ox Star Fell from Heaven,* illus. Lily Toy Hong, Whitman, 1991 (hardcover), ISBN 0-8075-3428-5, $14.95, unp. Ages 4–10, grades PS–5.

Chinese folktale telling how people acquired beasts of burden. Once all the oxen lived with the Emperor of All the Heavens in his Imperial Palace, and people, who had great difficulty planting and harvesting their crops, often went five days without a meal. The emperor, seeing that this was wrong, sent his messenger, the Ox Star, with a proclamation saying that people should eat at least once every three days, but the Ox Star got the message garbled and announced to the people that they should eat three times every day. In anger, the emperor stripped the Ox Star of his fine robes and threw him out of heaven along with the other oxen to earth, where they have labored for humans ever since. The highly stylized illustrations, which resemble woodblock pictures, are predominately the blues, greens, and browns of earth, with highlights of brilliant reds and golds in the imperial costumes and the noserings of the oxen. They are done, a note tells the reader, in gouache and airbrushed acrylics.

303 Hong, Lily Toy, ret., *Two of Everything,* illus. Lily Toy Hong, Whitman, 1993 (hardcover), ISBN 0-8075-8157-7, unp. Ages 5–9, grades K–4.

Chinese folktale of a poor farmer who digs up a brass pot and discovers that anything dropped in it is reproduced, so that his purse becomes two purses, his coat two coats, and so on. Difficulty arises when his wife, peering into the pot, loses her balance and falls in, so that he suddenly has two identical wives. When he trips and falls into the pot himself, his duplicate appears and he is in despair, but his clever wife sees that now there are two couples, so each man can have his own wife, and since they can double anything they drop in the pot, there will always be enough for all. The amusing illustrations, done with airbrushed acrylics and gouache, are largely in tans, browns, blues, and purples, with landscapes in shades of green, all in flat, unshaded planes. Figures of the people, the hills, and the pot are in rounded shapes, reminiscent of the style of Wanda Gag.

304 Johnston, Tony, ad., *The Badger and the Magic Fan: A Japanese Folktale,* illus. Tomie dePaola, Putnam, 1990 (hardcover), ISBN 0-399-21945-5, $13.95, unp. Ages 4–8, grades PS–3.

Retelling of a humorous Japanese folktale. A mischievous badger turns himself into a little girl to steal a magic fan from three *tengu* (goblins) and uses it to make a rich girl's nose very long. When doctors, a witch, and eminent thinkers cannot repair it, the girl's father promises her in marriage and half his wealth to the man who can make her nose short again. The badger does so with the fan, but before they can be married, the *tengu* recover the fan and cause his nose to grow to the sky where bridge makers use it to support their construction. This "it-serves-him-right" story moves pleasingly with just enough cultural explanation worked into the narrative. The framed, colorful illustrations are done in the naive style typical of dePaola. They create the culture by using slanted eyes, kimonos, chrysanthemums, and the like, and emphasize the comic aspects, such as making the noses grotesquely long.

305 Kendall, Carol, ret., *The Wedding of the Rat Family,* illus. James Watts, McElderry, 1988 (hardcover), ISBN 0-689-50450-0, $13.95, unp. Ages 7–10, grades 2–5.

Chinese folktale of the pompous and self-important rat couple who want to marry their daughter to the greatest in the world. They apply first to Sun, then Black Cloud, then Wind, and finally to Wall, each of which admits that the next is stronger, until Wall points out that eventually a rat can destroy any wall. Not discouraged, the couple decide that cat is more powerful than rat, and so arrange a marriage to one of the cat family. After elaborate preparations, the bride and her parents go with a large entourage to the bridegroom's house, where the cat family promptly devours them. Only the poor cousins, too thin, overworked, and shabby to be part of the wedding party, survive and thrive. Although obviously a variant of the same tale as *The Greatest of All* (no. 306), the disastrous marriage to the cat provides a very different tone, and the large illustrations feature extravagant costumes and traditional Chinese figures, like the dragon representing Black Cloud and the *oni* as Wind. Scenes of preparations for the wedding and the procession to the cat's house have dozens of rats dressed in colorful robes, carrying decorative banners and streamers, and riding in sedan chairs. Still other versions of the tale are *The Moles and the Mireuk* (no. 307), *The Mouse Bride* (no. 500), and *The Mouse Couple* (no. 515).

306 Kimmel, Eric A., *The Greatest of All*, illus. Gloria Carmi, Holiday, 1991 (hardcover), ISBN 0-8234-0885-X, $14.95, unp. Ages 3–8, grades K–3.

Japanese folktale of a mouse from the emperor's palace who refuses to allow his daughter to marry a humble field mouse, wanting only the greatest of all to be her husband. He applies in turn to the emperor, the sun, the cloud, the wind, and the wall, with each one sending him on to a greater power, until the wall confides that the field mouse, who tunnels into him and will some day bring him down, is stronger than he. The daughter marries the field mouse, and all are happy. The inventive illustrations, all set formally on light, brick-colored pages with both pictures and text framed by the background color, show the mice in traditional Japanese costume, but without Disney-like cuteness. For the same basic story, see *The Wedding of the Rat Family* (no. 305), *The Moles and the Mireuk* (no. 307), *The Mouse Bride* (no. 500), and *The Mouse Couple* (no. 515).

307 Kwon, Holly H., ret., *The Moles and the Mireuk*, illus. Woodleigh Hubbard, Houghton, 1993 (hardcover), ISBN 0-395-64347-3, $14.95, unp. Ages 4–8, grades PS–3.

Retelling of a Korean folktale. In this version of a widespread story, a mole father seeks the most powerful being in the world as a husband for his beautiful daughter, only to learn from the huge, wise, old statue called the Mireuk that moles are the most feared and respected of creatures. Two-dimensional, cartoonish, poster paintings in mostly primary colors add details to the story and play up the ironic humor. The ethnic atmosphere is limited to the pictures of the Mireuk and the temple it stands beside. See also Judith Dupre's *The Mouse Bride* (no. 500), Carol Kendall's *The Wedding of the Rat Family* (no. 305), Eric A. Kimmel's *The Greatest of All* (no. 306), and Ekkehart Malotki's *The Mouse Couple* (no. 515), which are all essentially the same story as this one.

308 Lee, Jeanne M., ret., *Toad Is the Uncle of Heaven*, illus. Jeanne M. Lee, Holt, 1985 (hardcover), ISBN 0-03-004652-1, $13.95, unp. Ages 5–8, grades K–3.

Vietnamese folktale of the lowly toad who, in a long drought, decides to call upon the King of Heaven to send rain. On his journey he is joined by a swarm of bees, a rooster, and a tiger, all of whom aid him when he is about to be thrown out, and he so impresses the king that he is granted an audience and is called by the respectful title, Uncle. Illustrations are brilliant, mostly separate figures set in large expanses of flat color, yellow or blue in the early pages, purple at the king's palace. Human figures are stylized and stiff, but the toad has varied expressions.

309 Merrill, Jean, ad., *The Girl Who Loved Caterpillars,* illus. Floyd Cooper, Philomel, 1992 (hardcover), ISBN 0-399-21871-8, $14.95, unp. Ages 8–12, grades 3–7.

Retelling of a twelfth-century Japanese tale, variously classified as fiction or folktale. Because pretty Izumi, the daughter of a noble, has from childhood been fascinated by worms, toads, snakes, and especially caterpillars, she is scorned by neighbors and others of her rank. A young nobleman, hearing of her deep interest in and knowledge of such creatures, fashions a "large and marvelously lifelike" mechanical snake as a gift for her. She replies wittily to the attached note, then again wittily to the note of the nobleman's captain who observes her inspecting a horde of the furry creatures. He feels her heart and mind are focused on them and leaves amused and pondering. She remains engrossed in her caterpillars. The slightly formal language supports the basic seriousness of this story whose open-endedness is explained in an afterword. What happened to Izumi may have appeared in a now-lost next chapter. Opulent, one-and-a-half page oil wash paintings decorate the book and make it very handsome. The pictures of the characters are often fine portraits. Slightly fuzzy, using costumes and such artifacts as vases, they excel in creating a feel of old Japan. They also support well the theme of respect for nature's small, seemingly ugly creatures.

310 Morris, Winifred, ret., *The Magic Leaf,* illus. Ju-Hong Chen, Atheneum, 1987 (hardcover), ISBN 0-689-31358-6, $13.95, unp. Ages 4–8, grades PS–3.

Retelling of a Chinese folktale of the droll or numbskull variety. A silly young man is reputed to be a fine swordsman and a scholar. Since, however, he lacks practical good sense, he loses his sword and is unable to buy even a pair of shoes. When he reads in a book about a leaf of invisibility and then thinks he has found one, he enters the mayor's garden to view the prize peonies and is thrown in jail, only to have the good fortune of being tried by a judge, who, though learned, is no smarter than he. The story makes its point about the difference between learning and sense lightly, its humor pleasingly complemented by lively watercolors in blue and green tones. They reveal the man's foolish nature and underscore the point with wit and spirit. The text also reads well in Morris's retelling of another droll, *The Future of Yen-Tzu* (1992), about a youngest son who, hoping for a better future, sets out for the palace and discovers that the future holds surprising twists and turns. Friso Henstra's washes picture incidents but are often confusing since objects cannot be clearly differentiated, and thus as a whole the book is less successful than *The Magic Leaf*.

311   O'Brien, Anne Sibley, ad., *The Princess and the Beggar,* illus. Anne Sibley O'Brien, Scholastic, 1993 (hardcover), ISBN 0-590-46092-7, $14.95, unp. Ages 5–9, grades K–4.

Korean folktale of a princess who weeps so much that her father declares she must marry Pabo Ondal, a beggar who lives like an animal in the mountains. Banished from court, the princess finds the hut of Ondal, who treats her kindly and from her learns to dress decently, to read and love poetry, and to ride and hunt skillfully. At her urging, he competes in the Festival of the Hunters, amazing all by his daring exploits. She then insists that he compete in the Festival of the Scholars, where he wins the poetry contest and explains to the king that he owes everything to his wife. Bidden to come forward, the princess is reaccepted by her father, but she chooses to live away from court with her husband. The Weeping Princess is an interesting combination of a strong woman directing the fortunes of her husband and a submissive wife using her abilities not for her own advancement but for his, as her culture dictates. The rich illustrations, done with pastels and colored pencils, reflect the clothing, hairstyles, and customs of the Yi Dynasty, which is known as "Traditional" Korean culture.

312   Pan, Cai-Ying, ad., *Monkey Creates Havoc in Heaven,* illus. Xin Kuan Liang, Zhang Xui Shi, Fei Change Fu, and Lin Zheng, Viking Kestrel, 1987 (hardcover), ISBN 0-670-81805-4, $9.95, unp. Ages 8 up, grades 3 up.

Story of the Chinese mythological Monkey King, based on the sixteenth-century novel, *The Pilgrimage to the West* by Wu Cheng En. Seeking more power, the Monkey King gets the special as-you-wish magic staff that can be transformed into many shapes and sizes. When he learns of this, the Celestial Emperor decrees that Monkey become Master of the Imperial Stables, the lowest-ranking position in Heaven where he can be kept under surveillance. At first flattered, Monkey discovers his lowly status, frees the imperial steeds, and assaults those sent to arrest him. He continues to create havoc, eating the divine peaches of eternal life, devouring the golden pills of immortality, fighting off an army of 10,000 troops, and, when he is finally captured, resisting death by swords, axes, and fire. Finally, Buddha Hu Lai agrees that, if he can somersault out of his hand, Monkey will become Celestial Emperor, but this he cannot do. He is imprisoned in the mountain of Wu Hong, where he remains for 500 years, at last being released to guard the monk Tripitaka on his journey to the West. The illustrations are brilliantly colored and highly stylized. Some are full page; others are in small boxes, like comic strips, several on a page, with background sheets in a variety of colors. All are full of action and detail. This is beautiful and unusual book.

313 Paterson, Katherine, ret., *The Tale of the Mandarin Ducks,* illus. Leo Dillon and Diane Dillon, Lodestar/Dutton, 1990 (hardcover), ISBN 0-525-67283-4, $14.95, unp. Ages 3–10, grades K–5.

Japanese folktale of a mandarin duck captured and caged by a cruel lord who covets his rich plumage. When the duck sickens with grief and a kitchen maid releases him, the angry lord blames his one-eyed steward and demotes him to kitchen helper, where he falls in love with the maid. Seeing their happiness, the lord orders their execution, but two mysterious strangers arrive with a message from the emperor saying that the death penalty is now forbidden. They lead the maid and the steward to a hut in the forest, where they are treated royally. The next morning, the strangers are gone, but a pair of mandarin ducks standing before the hut bow, then fly away. The text is longer and more descriptive than the typical folktale, with the characters given names and literary details added. The illustrations are gorgeous, filling the large pages with text passages inset, often in frames. The figures echo not only the costumes but also the postures of Japanese paintings, and many traditional stylistic features are included, among them vases of flowers in the foreground and arched bridges and gnarled trees in the background. Another folktale earlier translated by Paterson is *The Tongue-Cut Sparrow* (1987), retold by Momoko Ishii and illustrated by Suekichi Akaba.

314 Rappaport, Doreen, ret., *The Journey of Meng,* illus. Yang Ming-Yi, Dial, 1991 (hardcover), ISBN 0-8037-0895-5, $13.95, unp. Ages 5–12, grades K–7.

Chinese legend of a loyal wife whose scholar husband has been seized by the emperor's soldiers and enslaved on the Great Wall. As winter comes, she sews him warm padded clothing and, although she has never been away from home, sets off to take them to him. After great hardships and some magical intervention which allows her to fly like a bird, she arrives at the wall only to learn that her husband has died from the toil. Her great anger erupts like a tornado and destroys great sections of the wall, revealing her husband's bones. The emperor sends for her, falls in love with her beauty, and demands that she give herself to him or die. She bargains to get a funeral of honor for her husband, then denounces the tyranny of the emperor and leaps from the Great Wall into the sea, where her ground-up bones turn into thousands of little, silvery fish. The female hero, while a true Oriental wife, is a figure of strength and determination, a good addition to a largely male heroic literature. The ink and watercolor paintings are graceful and decorative.

315 Sadler, Catherine Edwards, ret., *Heaven's Reward,* illus. Cheng Mung Yun, Atheneum, 1985 (hardcover), ISBN 0-689-31127-3, $11.95, 37 pp. Ages 9–13, grades 4–8.

Six tales from China, some of unknown origin, some of known authorship but long adopted into the oral tradition. As a foreword points out, the opening story, "Heaven's Reward," reflects Confucian philosophy, while "The Little Goddess," "The Poet and the Peony," and "The Magic Pear Tree" represent Taoist ideas which elevated the role of women and challenged traditional roles in society. "The Greedy Brother" is a peasant tale much like some from European collections, and the final story, "The Wild Goose," has been adapted to reflect the Communist point of view. Each tale is illustrated with a graceful full-page or double-page black-and-white drawing. An earlier collection by the same reteller and illustrator team is *Treasure Mountain* (1982), which contains six folktales from Southern China.

316 San Souci, Robert D., ret., *The Enchanted Tapestry,* illus. Laszlo Gal, Dial, 1987 (hardcover), ISBN 0-8037-0306-6, $11.95, unp.; 1990 (paper), ISBN 0-8037-0862-9, $4.95, unp. Ages 4–11, grades PS–6.

Chinese folktale of the beautiful tapestry woven by an old woman with three sons. The older two are selfish, lazy young men, but the youngest is a hardworking, devoted boy. Despite the urging of the older sons, who want to sell her work for their own profit, the weaver continues to toil for months on a single tapestry, while the youngest son cuts wood to feed the family. When the tapestry is almost completed, it is blown away. The mother urges first the eldest, then the second son to seek it, but each is discouraged by the hardships foretold by a sorceress they meet, and each takes the bag of gold she offers instead. Knowing his mother will die without the tapestry into which she has woven her dreams, the youngest son sets off, braves all the dangers, and endures the hardships until he reaches the fairies of Sun Mountain, who return the weaving to him, but not before one has fallen in love with him and has woven a picture of herself into the tapestry. When he returns, his mother recovers, the tapestry grows to a real landscape into which the two step, and he meets there the fairy whom he marries. The delicately detailed watercolor illustrations are done in misty shades, predominately browns and blues, with highly stylized mountains, trees, waves, and oriental faces. They often suggest silk screens or paneled hangings and beautifully complement the fluently told story. Compare with *The Weaving of a Dream* (no. 301).

317 San Souci, Robert D., ret., *The Samurai's Daughter,* illus. Stephen T. Johnson, Dial, 1992 (hardcover), ISBN 0-8037-1135-2, $13.95, unp. Ages 4–10, grades PS–5.

Retelling of a Japanese legend. In medieval Japan, Tokoyo, the daughter of an exiled samurai (knight), brought up in the samurai tradition though female, chooses to join her father in exile, sails to his offshore, island prison, slays a terrible serpentine monster in a furiously fought undersea battle, and rescues a statue of the emperor from the monster's cave, thus restoring the emperor's sanity and her father to his rightful position. Told in formal, fluid style, the story is enhanced by dramatic, dignified, abstract paintings, whose solid composition and deep tones underscore the magnitude of the intrepid heroine's feat. This is an especially happy combination of storytelling and illustration. The reteller's note gives sources. Less successful (although more can usefully be said about it) is the retelling by the same writer and illustrator of another Japanese tale, *The Snow Wife* (1993). This story emphasizes the importance of keeping one's word and revolves around the widespread supernatural wife motif. Mosaku, a young Japanese woodcutter, sees a beautiful woman in white leaning over the body of his dying, elderly coworker and promises her never to reveal what he has seen. Later he marries and unwittingly tells his wife of his strange experience, and his wife, the woman of the vision, returns to the Wind God's realm. He undertakes a long journey fraught with many difficulties and eventually wins her, returning home with his snow wife, now fully mortal. The romantic text flags sorely during the journey and has a jarringly didactic section. The metaphysical elements are both strengthened and deemphasized by the handsome, full-color, full-page watercolors. For example, the picture of the snow woman bending over the old woodcutter projects a pleasing ethereal quality, but the pictures of the man and woman ogres the young man meets and the Wind God are more comic than the text suggests. No source is given for the story.

318 Shute, Linda, ret., *Momotaro the Peach Boy,* illus. Linda Shute, Lothrop, 1986 (hardcover), ISBN 0-688-05863-9, $13.95, unp. Ages 5–10, grades K–5.

Japanese folktale of the boy found by an old couple in a peach, who grows to be a kind and generous young man and a great hero who defeats the wicked demons or *oni* that have been attacking and robbing the people. As he sets off on his journey to Onigashima Island, Momotaro shares his food with a dog, a monkey, and a pheasant, all of whom help him in his battle against the evil *oni*. A long note at the end discusses the sources for the story, the costumes and weapons pictured, and the traditional role of the dog, monkey, and pheasant in Japanese folklore. It also gives a brief glossary of the Japanese terms used. Momotaro and his parents are ordinary-looking peasants. The animals are without clothes when they first encounter the boy, but as soon as they join in the quest they assume clothing. The *oni* look like red and blue goblins wearing loincloths.

319 Snyder, Dianne, ret., *The Boy of the Three-Year Nap,* illus. Allen Say, Houghton, 1988 (hardcover), $15.45, ISBN 0-395-44090-4, 32 pp. Ages 5–8, grades K–3.

Japanese folktale of a lazy but clever boy, who tricks the rich merchant into repairing his mother's house by pretending to be a god and is himself tricked by his even cleverer mother into having to take a job and marry the merchant's daughter. The illustrations, some of which resemble traditional Japanese paintings, are formally framed with heavy black lines within white borders, but the characters are depicted with playful exaggeration to match the mood of the story.

320 Tompert, Ann, ret., *Bamboo Hats and a Rice Cake,* illus. Demi, Crown, 1993 (hardcover), ISBN 0-517-59272-X, $13.00, unp. Ages 5–10, grades K–5.

Japanese folktale of the old man who takes his wife's heirloom wedding kimono, their only possession of value, to market, hoping to buy rice cakes for New Year's Day and thereby bring good fortune for the year. He trades the kimono to a neighbor for the fans she failed to sell at the market, the fans for a little gold bell, the bell for five bamboo hats. On the way home in the snow, he passes the six statues of Jizo beside the trail. He apologizes for not having rice cakes to leave for an offering, tries to brush the snow from the statues, and then remembers his bamboo hats. To the heads of five statues he ties the hats from the market, and on the sixth he puts his own hat. That night, after he and his wife have gone to bed hungry, the statues appear and leave an enormous rice cake on their doorstep. This variation of the trading-down story has a particularly Japanese cast, with the old wife approving of her husband's kindness instead of berating him for his foolishness, as in many versions. The illustrations on the oversize pages have wide, white margins at the top and bottom, symbolizing, according to an illustrator's note, heaven and earth, with man in the middle, an arrangement of harmony. On the side of each page is the Japanese character for a significant word, for example, rice cake or kimono, and that character is used instead of the corresponding English word in the text. Pictures of market scenes and the New Year celebration are busy, with many little figures surrounding the central person of the incident, while others use the spare decorative pattern of traditional Oriental painting.

321 Tompert, Ann, ret., *Grandfather Tang's Story: A Tale Told with Tangrams,* illus. Robert Andrew Parker, Crown, 1990 (hardcover), ISBN 0-517-57487-X, $15.00, unp. Ages 3–8, grades PS–3.

Chinese folktale of two fox fairies, good friends but rivals in shape-changing. They try to outdo each other, transforming themselves into a rabbit, a dog, a squirrel, a hawk, a turtle, a crocodile, a goldfish, and finally a goose, each move allowing one to threaten or to escape the other. When one sees his friend flying away with the wild geese, he also becomes a goose until his friend is shot by a hunter. He then turns himself into a lion, scares away the hunter, and nurses his friend back to health in their original fox shapes. The folktale is accompanied by tangrams, pictures made from the seven geometric shapes of an ancient Chinese puzzle game in which the standard pieces must be rearranged, touching but not overlapping, to form new pictures. The whole is framed by a story of Grandfather Tang telling the tale to Little Soo and arranging his tans as he talks. Besides the tangrams, which accompany each shape-change of the foxes, illustrations in ink lines and pastel watercolors decorate pleasantly. The possibility of using tangrams with a flannel board should make this appeal to storytellers, and older children may find a challenge in making new pictures with the tan pieces.

322 Torre, Betty L., ret., *The Luminous Pearl: A Chinese Folktale,* illus. Carol Inouye, Orchard, 1990 (hardcover), ISBN 0-531-05890-5, $14.95, unp. Ages 4–8, grades PS–3.

Retelling of a story from John Minford's translation of *Favourite Folktales of China,* published in 1983 by New World Press. The Dragon King's beautiful daughter insists that she will marry only a man proved to be honest and brave, and she tests two brothers by sending them after a luminous, night-glowing pearl. The elder, selfish and greedy, returns with vast wealth, including a magnificent pearl whose sparkle disappears at night. The younger brother, who has taken time to help a village in flood, returns with a black pearl that seems drab but dazzles in the night sky like a million stars. Although some language seems off-key—the wedding feast is described as "scrumptious," for instance—the story consistently holds the interest as it follows the worldwide pattern of the triumph of the virtuous youngest. Cultural touches give the tale an Oriental quality and are picked up and extended in the almost luminescent, detailed paintings. The views of the Dragon King's underwater realm reveal its splendor and wealth, and some comic features relieve the story's basic seriousness.

323 Uchida, Yoshiko, ret., *The Magic Purse,* illus. Keiko Narahashi, McElderry, 1993 (hardcover), ISBN 0-689-50559-0, $15.95, unp. Ages 5–9, grades K–4.

Japanese folktale of a poor young farmer who, on his way to the Iseh shrine, gets lost and finds himself in the Black Swamp. There he is approached by a beautiful young girl, who begs him to take a message to her parents in the dreaded Red Swamp, from which no man emerges alive. Pitying her, he agrees, and she gives him a magic purse which, no matter how much he spends, will always be full again in the morning as long as he leaves one coin in it. With difficulty, he makes his way to the Red Swamp where an old man meets him, takes him in a boat to a golden room where he and his wife wait upon him, feed him lavishly, and give him a tray of golden coins, before returning him to the edge of the swamp. He goes on to the shrine, gives thanks to the gods, and returns to his village where he builds a big house, buys land and farm animals, and lives prosperously and generously, never forgetting the young girl of the Black Swamp. The wide pages are filled with watercolor illustrations especially effective in portraying the murky waters and the dark tree trunks of the Black Swamp and the ominous orange-red glow of the terrible Red Swamp.

324 Uchida, Yoshiko, ret., *The Two Foolish Cats,* illus. Margot Zemach, McElderry, 1987 (hardcover), ISBN 0-689-50397-0, $12.95, unp. Ages 3–8, grades PS–3.

Japanese folktale of two cats who quarrel over which will get the bigger rice cake. On the advice of the badger, they travel to the old monkey of the mountains, who settles their dispute by taking a bite from first one cake, weighing the result, then nibbling on the other, until both cakes are gone. Illustrations seem to be in India ink and watercolor, with many of the scenes looking like art from Japanese scrolls with gnarled tree trunks and graceful, bare branches. An unpretentiously attractive book.

325 Vuong, Lynette Dyer, ret., *The Golden Carp and Other Tales from Vietnam*, illus. Manabu Saito, Lothrop, 1993 (hardcover), ISBN 0-688-12514-X, $15.00, 128 pp. Ages 9 up, grades 4 up.

Six stories of romance, magic, and wrongs righted retold from several written Vietnamese sources. The title tale tells of a comedy of errors resulting from impersonations, while in "A Friend's Affection" a young mandarin rejects his profligate friend in order to redeem him. A youth is tricked into accomplishing impossible tasks, his virtue rewarded by marriage to the king's daughter, in "The Ogre's Victim." "Tears of Pearl" is about an ill-fated romance between a human and a sea fairy; "Third Daughter" is a Cinderella-type story; and "Second in Command" relates the adventures of a warrior maiden. These stories of dragons, ogres, jungles, and wealthy houses and poor are fast moving, lively, and filled with color but contain more dialogue, emotion, and details of place and story than are typical of tales from oral tradition, and hence some might deem them fantasy. Full-page, framed, full-color paintings, one for each story, depict important scenes and help create setting. The book includes very interesting endnotes; there is a pronunciation guide.

326 Wall, Lina Mao, ret., *Judge Rabbit and the Tree Spirit: A Folktale from Cambodia*, ad. Cathy Spagnoli, illus. Nancy Hom, Children's 1991 (hardcover), ISBN 0-89239-071-9, $13.95, 32 pp. Ages 4–10, grades PS–5.

Cambodian folktale retold in both English and Khmer. A mischievous banyan tree spirit tricks a pretty young wife whose husband has gone to war by impersonating the husband. When the husband returns and she is unable to identify him, Judge Rabbit solves her dilemma by luring the spirit into a bottle. Although they have an ordinary greeting-card quality, the bright, decorative watercolors are framed by cultural motifs; establish the setting with garb, trees, houses, and the like; depict important scenes; and contribute humor. The English text is presented on the left-hand pages, the Khmer on the right, integrated skillfully into the illustrations. A note about the figure of Judge Rabbit, the center of a cycle of stories, is included.

327 Wang, Rosalind C., ret., *The Fourth Question: A Chinese Tale*, illus. Ju-Hong Chen, Holiday, 1991 (hardcover), ISBN 0-8234-0855-8, $14.95, unp. Ages 4–9, grades PS–4.

Retelling of a Chinese folktale which suggests that unselfishness will result in prosperity and happiness. A virtuous young man journeys to the Wise Man of Kun-lun Mountain seeking answers to four important questions, three of other people and one of his own. Given permission to ask only three, he chooses those of the other people, and, home again, finds his generosity rewarded with a beautiful bride and wealth. Although late twentieth-century thinking might lead some to question the philosophy behind the story (which appears elsewhere also in ancient thought, for example, in Old Testament teaching), the story is pleasantly told with just enough detail, a light spirit, and a good pace. The illustrations recall the work of Tomie dePaola, being flatly stylized and slightly comic. They are in soft pink and green tones, with such Oriental touches here and there as calligraphy and facial features.

328   Watkins, Yoko Kawashima, *Tales from the Bamboo Grove*, illus. Jean Tseng and Mou-sien Tseng, Bradbury, 1992 (hardcover), ISBN 0-02-792525-0, $14.95, 49 pp. Ages 9–12, grades 4–7.

Six Japanese folktales, told to the author by family members and friends when she was a child in Korea. Although "Why Is Seawater Salty?" is well known from various oral traditions, the others are less familiar and, in their bittersweet endings, several seem more typically Japanese. The retellings are slightly literary, with given names for most of the characters and more description than in the usual folktale. The illustrations are full-page black-and-white paintings, with calligraphy titles inset like scrolls.

329   Yacowitz, Caryn, ad., *The Jade Stone: A Chinese Folktale*, illus. Ju-Hong Chen, Holiday, 1992 (hardcover), ISBN 0-8234-0919-8, $14.95, unp. Ages 4–8, grades PS–3.

Retelling of a Chinese folktale about the primacy of destiny. The Great Emperor of All China orders famous stone carver Chan Lo to fashion a Dragon of Wind and Fire from a large chunk of green and white jade. When Chan Lo produces a fish sculpture because that is all that the stone wishes to become, the angry monarch imprisons the artisan until the emperor himself hears fish sounds from within the stone. The horizontally arranged ink and watercolor paintings done on rice paper "evoke the look of ancient hand-colored oriental wood-block prints" and extend the story with many deft cultural touches and a charming, gentle whimsey. Reteller's and illustrator's notes are included.

330   Yep, Laurence, ret., *The Man Who Tricked A Ghost*, illus. Isadore Seltzer, Bridgewater, 1993 (hardcover), ISBN 0-8167-3030-X, $15.95, unp. Ages 5–9, grades K–4.

Ghost story retold from a Chinese folktale first recorded in the third century A.D. A young man named Sung meets the ghost of a warrior wearing antique armor and learns that, having heard of his boast that he does not fear ghosts, it is headed for his home to kill him. Pretending that he, too, is a ghost, Sung tricks it into showing him many of its disguises, each of which he assures the ghost will not frighten Sung, until he finally learns the ghost's secret. If it is spat upon, it can no longer change shape. Sung waits until it has changed itself into a ram and spits, then sells the sheep and ends up free of danger and rich. The illustrations are bold and brilliantly colored, covering the entire oversized pages with text inset in boxes. The central double-page spread is without words, showing four of the hideous disguises assumed by the ghost.

331 Yep, Laurence, ret., *The Shell Woman and the King,* illus. Yang Ming-Yi, Dial, 1993 (hardcover), ISBN 0-8037-1394-0, $13.95, unp. Ages 5–10, grades K–5.

Chinese folktale, from an eighteenth-century collection, about a woman from the sea, a shape-changer who can become a shell and travel about in the water. She marries a good man named Uncle Wu, but the greedy king hears about her and sends soldiers to seize them both. Enchanted with her beauty, he demands that she become his queen, threatening to kill Wu if she does not either marry him or obtain three wonders for him. She is able to produce the first wonder, hair from a toad, invisible to the king, and the second, the arm of a ghost, which she lures to a picnic in the graveyard. When the king then demands luck by the bushel, she brings a large dog, which she says must be fed some fire. After wolfing down a number of burning branches, the dog starts to cough and spit out flames, until the king and his palace are consumed. The Shell Woman points out that he did not specify what sort of luck he wanted. She and Uncle Wu leap upon the dog's back and ride to their home. The large pages are beautifully illustrated with ink and watercolor paintings, especially effective in the misty seascapes and scenes of the burning palace; the text is superimposed on patterned paper reproduced from silk used to mount scrolls.

332 Yep, Laurence, ret., *Tongues of Jade,* illus. David Wiesner, Harper Collins, 1991 (hardcover), ISBN 0-06-022470-3, $19.89, 194 pp. Ages 8–12, grades 3–7.

Chinese folktales collected in the United States, all except one found in Oakland, California's Chinatown during the 1930s by Jon Lee as part of a WPA project. The seventeen stories are divided into five sections: Roots, Family Ties, The Wild Heart, Face, and Beyond the Grave. Each section is introduced by a short discussion of what significance the tale might have had for the early immigrants. Sometimes the connections seem strained; others are easy to understand, for example, the attitude toward parents, as in "The Little

Emperor," and the need to save face, as in "The Teacher's Underwear." The only one not from the original Lee collection is "The Ghostly Rhyme," a whimsical story of a scholar whose ghost haunts his village, seeking the final line of a poem that he cannot remember, a tale collected in San Francisco's Chinatown by Wolfram Eberhard. The title comes from the ancient practice of covering the dead with pieces of jade, in the belief that jade has the power to preserve the body, a practice reflected in the horror story, "Eyes of Jade." Each tale is accompanied by a handsome black-and-white illustration using half a page divided vertically, giving the impression of an Oriental scroll. A companion volume is *The Rainbow People* (1989), which contains twenty tales also from the Jon Lee WPA collection. Only one, "Slippers," is set in the United States, about a lonely bride in a small California Chinatown in the days when few Chinese could bring their wives with them. A number of the tales are similar to familiar European folktales, but many, including "The Ghost's Bride" and the title story, seem peculiar to Oriental culture. Yep has retold the stories in his own voice, using modern English, serious but not formal.

333 Young, Ed, ret., *Lon Po Po: A Red-Riding Hood Story from China*, illus. Ed Young, Philomel, 1989 (hardcover), ISBN 0-399-21619-7, $14.95, unp. Ages 4–10, grades PS–5.

Retelling of a Chinese folktale, which, according to the book jacket, "comes from an ancient oral tradition and is thought to be over a thousand years old," and was translated into this version by Young himself. Interestingly, it seems more like the old European story about the wolf and the seven little kids than that of Red Riding Hood. *Lon Po Po* tells of three sisters who are left home while their mother visits their grandmother and who must outwit a wily wolf who pretends to be their grandmother, their Po Po. The simple, directly told story is made suspenseful and dramatic by highly atmospheric watercolors and pastels fashioned after Chinese panel art. Their subtle coloring and patterning, especially of wolf shadows and wolf and human eyes, enhance the conflict. They increase in significance with repeated viewings. Another Chinese folktale retold and illustrated by Young is *Red Thread* (1993). In old China, proud young Wei Gu learns from a matchmaker that he will some day marry the ugly baby girl being carried on the back of an old, blind market woman. Aghast, Wei hires a servant to kill the child, but years later learns he has indeed married the girl whose feet the matchmaker said were bound to his by the mystical red thread of destiny. Panoramic, subtly shaded, off-the-page, full-color views of markets and houses and up-close portraits intrigue the eye and support the inevitability of the prophecy, as does the red line that appears on every page separating the illustration from the several lines of text at the bottom. A beautiful book that conveys a good sense of the cultural worldview even though the crease mars some scenes.

6

Asian Americans: Books of Poetry

334 Demi, ad., *Dragon Kites and Dragonflies: A Collection of Chinese Nursery Rhymes*, illus. Demi, Harcourt, 1986 (hardcover), ISBN 0-15-224199-X, $14.95, unp. Ages 3–8, grades PS–3.

Twenty-two traditional Chinese rhymes, adapted from translations. In high-spirited, bouncy rhythms and mostly regular rhymes, the verses tell of celebrating the New Year, silk worms, acrobats, a wedding, kites, getting up in the morning, the punishment of a naughty boy, dragon boats, and other events in the child's life, although one rhyme tells how the emperor built the Great Wall to keep the Tartars out. Two-page spreads, enlivened with shimmering reds and glowing yellows, are filled with multitudes of tiny detailed figures. Panoramas presenting little scenes within each picture, extending the rhymes and offering a wide variety of viewing pleasure, make the book very attractive. A note at the beginning gives sources. *Demi's Dragons and Fantastic Creatures* (1993) presents nineteen Chinese folklore animals in stunningly colorful, full-page spreads; their significance is summarized in amusing, brief verse couplets. Notes are included.

335 Foster, Sesshu, *Angry Days*, West End, 1987 (paperback), ISBN 0-931122-46-5, $5.95, 69 pp. Ages 15 up, grades 10 up.

Twenty-one poems divided into three sections. The first section concerns life in Los Angeles; the second is mostly about Central America; and the last, entitled "The World We Give Our Children," is about or to family members: Marina (evidently the author's daughter), his father, and his stepmother, among others. All are in free verse, with no rhymes or regular meter. One long piece, "Grandpa," printed all in caps in paragraph form, addresses Marina and tells about the author's father, a rolling stone and alcoholic, who "was always good at things that were real nice for one day" and warns that she may inherit his desire to be "free," an attitude others deem impractical and irresponsible. The final long poem, "Visitation," is about a return to the site of a World War II Japanese relocation camp. Although the author is a Japanese American, several of the poems deal with Hispanic characters and settings. The poems have much to say, and there are occasional lines of vivid imagery, but they are often marred by polemic, the anger clear but the rhetoric jarring.

336 Lim, Shirley Geok-lin, *Modern Secrets*, Dangaroo Press, 1989 (paper), ISBN 1-871049-00-B, $11.25, 126 pp. Ages 15 up, grades 10 up.

Nearly one hundred poems, mostly short, by an author born in Malacca, Malaysia, of Chinese-Malayasian heritage, who got her Ph.D. at Brandeis University and has taught at several institutions of higher education in the United States. Technically skilled, the poems employ a large variety of strict poetic forms and free verse and deal with many different subjects. A few, like "Bukit China," about lighting a joss stick after her father's death, "Returning to the Missionary School," and "Visiting Malacca" are set in Malaysia. More are concerned with academic life, which she sometimes embraces and sometimes views cynically. She wonders whether or not "life in libraries" among walls of books that appear to talk to each other has been a waste in "A Woman Speaks of Grandchildren" and decides that she wants to have "yeasty thighs" and sit comfortably with her grandchildren about her. Some are about writing and writers, including a scathing comment on the intellectual insulated from life, addressed to Wallace Stevens, in "I Defy You," and an angry denunciation of confessional women poets in "Mean Confessions." Some are about problems in the lives of women, or short, tightly written portraits of individuals or animals, like one about a female panther at night, who is motionless, "except for the wired force" in her head. Although many contain obscure lines, which puzzle even after repeated readings, most have enough force and energy to attract young readers, and her control of the medium is worth careful study. Frequently, even in free verse poems, she uses rhyme, either in a last couplet or a final word that picks up an earlier line end, to bring a sense of closure. Some of her most moving poems are the most tightly restricted in form, for example, "Pantoun [*sic*] for Chinese Women," an intricately constructed poem about the preparation made by the father and paternal grandmother to murder a newly born infant because she is a girl. Her earlier collection, *No Man's Grove* (1985), which contains a variety of sonnets and two villanelles, makes more use of rhyme and near-rhyme than her later work. Some poems from that book and from *Crossing the Peninsula* (1980) have been reprinted in *Modern Secrets*.

337   Lim, Shirley Geok-lin, Mayumi Tsutakawa, and Margarita Donnelly, eds., *The Forbidden Stitch: An Asian American Women's Anthology*, Calyx, 1989 (hardcover), ISBN 0-934971-10-2, $26.95; (paper), ISBN 0-93491-04-8, $14.95, 290 pp. Ages 14 up, grades 9 up.

Large collection of poems, stories, artwork, and reviews—the first anthology, according to the introduction, ever published entirely of works by Asian-American women. The artwork, in a variety of media, which takes up thirty-five pages, is the least impressive, partly because none is reproduced in color, and the twenty-eight pages of reviews have limited interest, but the thirty-three poems and fifteen stories show talented work from a large number of writers. Some are established authors, many have had pieces published in literary periodicals or relatively obscure magazines, and a number see their work in print for the first time in this volume. They are more similar in their femaleness, which is the concern of many of the selections, than in their ethnic backgrounds, being from Asian countries with very different cultures or being second-, third-, or even fourth-generation Americans. Although the works vary greatly, almost all are written with skill; the prose is probably more easily approachable for high school students than the poetry. This is a good representation from a widely diverse group. Author biographies and an extensive bibliography are included.

338   Yep, Laurence, ed., *American Dragons: Twenty-five Asian American Voices*, HarperCollins, 1993 (hardcover), ISBN 0-06-021494-5, $15.00, 237 pp. Ages 12 up, grades 7 up.

Anthology of poems and short prose pieces by writers whose ethnic roots are from China, Japan, Korea, Vietnam, Thailand, and Tibet. Most of the poems, all of which are unmetered and unrhymed, are about older relatives; Amy Ling's verse portraits of her two grandmothers, one in Taiwan and one Pennsylvania Dutch, are especially memorable. In "Desert Flowers," Janice Mirikitani explores the irony of her mother in a World War II relocation camp making crepe paper flowers for American Legion poppy day. Three poems are about fathers. In "A Father's Wishes—" Chinese-American Alan Chong Lau starts with a birthday letter from his father and tries to make sense of their strained relationship, ending by asking his father whether he can still tell him he loves him. Japanese-American Janice Mirikitani directs "For My Father" to her strawberry-farmer parent, who, cold-eyed, whipped his children for stealing strawberries from the stem, fruit "we could not afford" for their morning meal at home. In "Translations," Wing Tek Lum, a Chinese American from Hawaii, writes of the Chinese attempt to placate the whites by giving them what they thought they wanted and sums up that section of his long poem by noting that Cantonese lacks a term for fortune cookie. For the short stories in the volume see no. 285.

7

Hispanic Americans: Books of Fiction

339 Alvarez, Julia, *How the Garcia Girls Lost Their Accents,* Algonquin, 1991 (hardcover), ISBN 0-945575-57-2, $16.95, 290 pp.; Plume, 1992 (paper), ISBN 0-452-26806-0, $9.00, 304 pp. Ages 15 up, grades 10 up.

Realistic, episodic novel of Dominican-American girls' growing up and family life covering about thirty years, beginning in 1956. Moving backward in time, each of the fifteen chapters can stand alone, but together they tell how Papa (Carlos) Garcia, a doctor, fleeing dictator Trujillo's secret police, brings his wife and four daughters to New York City. The girls attend Catholic schools, boarding school, and colleges, and all but the youngest become professionals, ironically continuing to be regarded as Hispanics in the States but as *Americanas* on the island. Although the girls are well drawn, from child psychologist Carla through emotionally unstable Sandra and writer and teacher Yolanda to iconoclastic, mischievous Sofia, the parents are more memorable, indulgent, stern, macho Papi, always concerned that his girls not become "loose women," and seemingly fluttery Mami, always the patient family ballast. Zippy in style, the book exudes the flavor of family life both in the United States and on the island. It is sometimes bittersweet and often very funny, in telling of their "turbulent lives—so many husbands, homes, jobs, wrong turns among them," and provides a perceptive look at the position of women in the late twentieth century. The most vivid parts take place on the island—the dozens of cousins in this well-off family sneaking out from the family compound for forbidden fun, the voodoo Haitian maids, the dreaded secret police—experiences that continue to shape the girls' lives long after emigration and color their impressions of themselves as women and of men. Pride in family and heritage are important, and the title symbolizes the girls' gradual Americanization. Alvarez has also published *Homecoming* (1984), a book of poems, some of which reveal the ethnic point of view.

340 Anaya, Rudolfo A., *The Farolitos of Christmas: A New Mexico Christmas Story*, illus. Richard C. Sandoval, New Mexico Magazine, 1987 (paper), ISBN 0-937206-06-7, $6.95, 32 pp. Ages 4 up, grades PS up.

Realistic, family, picture-story book set among Mexican Americans in the village of San Juan in the Sangre de Cristo Mountains of New Mexico in recent years. Because Father is away at his job in another village and the *abuelo* (grandfather) is ill, nine-year-old Luz fears that her family will have no *luminarias* (bonfires) in front of their house to provide light for the *pastores* (shepherds) to perform the Christmas Nativity story. Buying sugar for her mother gives her the idea of using paper bags and candles to make little lanterns, or *farolitos*, as her *abuelo* calls them, stabilizing the lights with sand. The day before Christmas, she and her friend, Reina, make dozens, placing them along the path and on the adobe wall all the way to the road. At dark on Christmas Eve, they light them until 100 shine in the night, attracting people from all over the village. The *pastores* decide that these are the best *luminarias* in the village and perform there. The emotionally engaging story is complemented by primitive, stylized paintings whose static quality gives the fiction a legendary aspect, while their bright tones underscore the joy of the season. There is a strong sense of New Mexican custom, combining popular American ways with old Hispanic ones, while such old Indian customs as the Winter Deer Dance, are mentioned in conversation. Spanish words appear, for which there is a glossary at the beginning of the book.

341 Anzaldua, Gloria, *Friends from the Other Side*, illus. Consuelo Mendez, Children's Book, 1993 (hardcover), ISBN 0-89239-133-8, $13.95, unp. Ages 5–9, grades K–4.

Bilingual picture-story book of a friendship between a Mexican-American girl in South Texas and a *mojado*, a Mexican boy who has secretly crossed into the United States with his mother looking for a better life. Prietita defends Joaquin, the boy who comes to sell firewood, against neighborhood bullies and escorts him back to his tumbledown shack, beginning a strong friendship. When a neighbor woman shouts that the Border Patrol is coming, Prietita runs with Joaquin to warn his mother and leads them both to the house of the herb woman, where they hide until the patrolmen have left. Illustrations, done in watercolors, graphite and colored pencils, and collage, are richly colored with realistic Chicano faces and dilapidated buildings bravely decorated with religious pictures and calendars. A strong narrative to counter the hysteria against illegal immigrants.

342 Bethancourt, T. Ernesto, *The Me Inside of Me*, Lerner, 1985 (hardcover), ISBN 0-8225-0728-5, $10.95, 155 pp. Ages 12–14, grades 7–9.

Realistic novel of Fred (Alfredo) Flores, a Mexican-American boy of Santa Amelia, California, who, because of a plane accident to his family, becomes a very wealthy orphan. With one more year of high school to complete, he decides on a whim that he wants to go to Stanford University, and his guardian, an Anglo lawyer who was his grandfather's friend, gets him into an expensive and exclusive prep school specializing in preparing students for prestigious colleges. He immediately makes a bad impression by driving an overly flashy convertible and dressing in the wrong sort of clothes. His roommate, Roderigo Alondra y Castillo, known as Snotty Roddie, son of a Central American dictator, is hostile and frames him by planting drugs beneath his mattress. His only friends are Lenny Rosenfeld, a Jewish boy, son of a movie magnate, who is marking time until at twenty-one he will inherit from his mother the controlling stock in the company and can fire his father, and an African-American girl, Natalie Simpson, who is afraid of letting her family down by becoming involved with a non-black boy. With their help, Fred eventually overcomes the petty and corrupt politics of the school, learns to be true to himself, and goes to art school in New York, to develop his real talent. The strongest elements in the novel are the way attitudes toward Fred change when people, those newly met and old friends in Santa Amelia, discover he is wealthy, and his relationship to the lawyer, which remains ambiguous; he never is sure whether the man sent him to the school, knowing he would not fit in, to teach him how to survive, as he says, or expecting him to fail miserably, as Freddie suspects. The pace is lively, and Freddie is a believable character.

343 Bruni, Mary Ann Smothers, *Rosita's Christmas Wish*, illus. Thom Ricks, TexArt Services, 1985 (hardcover), ISBN 0-935857-00-1, $13.95, unp. Ages 5–10, grades K–5.

Picture-story book of *Los Pastores*, a play about the journey of the shepherds to Bethlehem to adore Baby Jesus, performed in San Antonio, Texas, by members of Our Lady of Guadalupe parish. The action follows nine-year-old Rosita through the exciting Christmas Eve celebration in which neighbors and friends act the parts of shepherds and the devils who try to prevent their arrival at the manger. Through the chance illness of the woman to act the part of Gila, the young shepherdess, Rosita's friend Debbie takes the part, and since Rosita knows the music and dances just as well and is dressed similarly, she is welcomed as a second Gila. The drama itself, a version of a medieval folk play brought to Mexico by Franciscan friars, ends with a song and dance of the *palomita*, the little white dove, performed by both girls. Music and words of the song are given at the end of the book, along with a glossary of the many Spanish terms used in the story. Illustrations are lavish, graceful paintings apparently done with charcoal and watercolor, showing the Mexican-American community and the characters acting the *pastorela*.

344 Bunting, Eve, *How Many Days to America? A Thanksgiving Story*, illus. Beth Peck, Clarion, 1988 (hardcover), ISBN 0-89919-521-0, $14.95, unp. Ages 5–9, grades K–4.

Picture-story book of a family from an unidentified Latin American country escaping in an overloaded fishing boat to America. They are boarded by thieves, reach a shore only to be driven away by soldiers who give them water and fruit but will not let them land, and finally arrive at a place where they are welcomed and given a Thanksgiving dinner. The narrator is an unnamed little boy, traveling with his parents and younger sister. Since the country of their origin and that from which they are turned away are not named and the only clue is the Hispanic cast to their features, the story must be viewed as a generic refugee tale. The theme of welcoming the oppressed is commendable, but, in light of the experience of Haitians and other boat people, may give a false impression of the actual prospects for such escapees. The illustrations are done mostly in muted tones of misty seascapes.

345 Buss, Fran Leeper, with Daisy Cubias, *Journey of the Sparrows*, Lodestar, 1991 (hardcover), ISBN 0-525-67362-8, $14.95, 155 pp. Ages 12 up, grades 7 up.

Starting with the intense suffering of their escape from Mexico into the United States nailed in crates, this novel follows the fortunes of Maria Acosta, fifteen, her pregnant older sister, Julia, and their little brother, Oscar, illegal immigrants from El Salvador. Their father and Julia's husband having been killed by the *Guardia*, repressive political police, they have made their way with their mother and baby sister, Theresa, by foot through Guatemala, hoping to reach safety together, but Theresa's illness has forced the mother to stay in Mexico. Bruised, penniless, and disoriented, the three siblings arrive in Chicago where other Salvadorans, some as poor and vulnerable to deportation as they are, aid them, as do some legal Americans, and Julia's baby is born. When a letter from Mexico tells them that their mother has been seized and deported, Maria goes alone to retrieve Theresa, a terrifying journey during which she narrowly escapes rape, drowning, and apprehension by the immigration authorities. The harrowing tale is lightened by Maria's sweet romance with Tomas, who was nailed in the same crate, and her struggles between her attraction to him and her culturally required modesty make her a convincing teenager. Although Maria occasionally loses faith, religion plays an important part in the lives of the almost hidden community of refugees. Their nearly hopeless plight and their brave struggles elicit strong emotion, and, although the political reasons that they might be deported are touched on only lightly, U.S. government policy is clearly pictured as wrong.

346 Castillo, Ana, *So Far from God: A Novel*, Norton, 1993 (hardcover), ISBN 0-393-03490-9, $19.95, 251 pp. Ages 15 up, grades 10 up.

Realistic contemporary novel set near a little town in New Mexico not far from Albuquerque, involving Mexican-American descendants of the early Hispanic settlers. The narrative covers about a quarter century in the life of steadfast and resourceful Sofia, who, after she is abandoned by her gambler husband, runs a meat market to support herself and her four daughters: Esperanza, a college-educated television newswoman who dies a prisoner of terrorists in Saudi Arabia in the Gulf War; Caridad, a "loose woman," who after being terribly mutilated and left for dead, becomes a healer and mystic who launches herself from a cliff to her death; Fe, ambitious equivalent of a yuppie, who dies of industrial poisoning; and La Loca, the "crazy one," who is "resurrected" from an epileptic seizure and is henceforth regarded as holy, has visions and premonitions, and dies of AIDS, source unknown. The author as knowing and yet naive narrator tells all as she sees it, even the frequent suprareal, paranormal, and outrageous, with good humor, understanding, and deliberate verbosity that lays open the difficulties of life for Latina women and the gender conflicts they face with men who try to maintain their traditional Latino masculine roles but fail due to circumstances. In spite of the obvious tragic elements, this saga of five less than fortunate women, the men in their lives, and their neighbors is often very funny. The occasional Spanish is easily deduced from context. Earlier novels are *Sapogonia: An Anti-Romance in 3/8 Meter* (1990) and *The Mixquiahuala Letters* (1986; 1992), an epistolary novel. Both books are more complex in structure and more mature in substance but embrace matters similar to those in *So Far from God*.

347 Cervantes, Esther DeMichael, and Alex Cervantes, *Barrio Ghosts*, illus. Steve Healy, New Readers, 1988 (paper), ISBN 0-88336-315-1, $6.65, 79 pp. Ages 10 up, grades 5 up.

Five short stories of fantasy involving ghosts, each told in the "I" person by different late teens of Mexican-American background and set in a present-day Los Angeles barrio. In one, Franky Mendoza encounters a phantom car and a ghostly namesake, while in others, dead rock musician Cruz returns to enlist Luci's help in completing an important project and changes her life; Ruben meets La Llorona, the weeping woman of Mexican legend; grounded Tomas changes bodies with his cat in order to keep tabs on his girl and finds out she is not worth his attention; and Tina wins the part of "The Little Match Girl" for the Christmas program with the help of Danny, the resident high school ghost. Intended as high-interest, low-vocabulary reading, the stories accentuate plot and move fast with plenty of action and dialogue, uncomplicated sentences, and undemanding diction with a smattering of Spanish words explained in a glossary. Teen interests like clothes, the opposite sex, music, and cars are stressed, but such traditional values as the integrity of the family, honoring elders, and obedience also figure strongly. The black-and-white drawings depict story situations. (New Readers is a division of Laubach Literacy International.)

348 Christopher, Matt, *Centerfield Ballhawk*, illus. Ellen Beier, Little, 1992 (hardcover), ISBN 0-316-14079-1, $11.95, 59 pp. Ages 7–11, grades 2–6.

Early reader about kids' league baseball. Motherless Jose Mendez, the nine-year-old outfielder for the Peach Street Mudders, tries valiantly to raise his batting average, hoping to please his father who was a minor leaguer known for his strong bat. His efforts usually backfire, and he becomes increasingly depressed when his sister, Carmen, eleven, stars as batting champ of her softball team, until his father attends one of the Mudders' games in which Jose's outstanding fielding wins his admiration. Although the style is simple, designed for an early reading level, a good knowledge of baseball is required to make sense of the games which are described in detail. Nothing except his name indicates that Jose is of Hispanic descent, not even the illustrations which picture an integrated team but do not distinguish Jose from boys surnamed McGee and Chong.

349 Cisneros, Sandra, *Woman Hollering Creek and Other Stories*, Random, 1991 (hardcover), ISBN 0-394-57654-3, 165 pp.; Vintage, 1992 (paperback), ISBN 0-679-73856-8, 165 pp. Ages 15 up, grades 10 up.

Twenty-two stories of Mexican Americans, some a brief page, others as long as twenty-five pages. These are divided into three sections, the first dealing with the growing-up experience, the next about tragedies of early adulthood, and the third and longest group, titled "There Was a Man, There Was a Woman," concerned with love, marriage, and other relationships, all told with a sharp, sometimes cynical, often humorous clarity. Most are set in Texas and feature women, some assertive, some enduring, each strong in her own way. The title story is about an abused wife escaping back to Mexico. The Hispanic ethnic experience is central to most of the pieces, with a strong thread of religion, poverty, and male dominance, and the struggle against all three. Mature students will be caught up in the emotions of believable characters. Stories in an earlier book by Cisneros, *The House on Mango Street* (1989), are most closely connected, tracing the growing up of a Mexican-American girl with her two brothers and little sister, and while also vivid and uncompromising, demand less sophistication in a reader.

350 Corpi, Lucha, *Delia's Song*, Arte Publico, 1989 (paper), ISBN 0-934770-82-4, $9.50, 191 pp. Ages 15 up, grades 10 up.

Realistic period novel of a Mexican-American woman's coming to terms with self and society. Delia Trevino leaves her male-dominated family in Los Angeles for the University of California-Berkeley campus in 1968, at the height of the grape boycotts and the Third World Liberation Front student activism that leads to police brutality and jailings of students, the most exciting and enlightening part of the novel. Among the protestors is bright, dedicated Jeff Morones, whom at the end of the novel Delia openly acknowledges she loves after a hiatus of about ten years in their relationship. In between she secures her Ph.D. in literature, fights increasingly troubling nightmares, which she comes to see as psychological workings-through of fears and worries, and learns to accept the unfortunate but real position as second to her deceased brothers, gains some longed-for approval from her mother, and realizes that the factionalism of the Third World is unfortunate and real. The novel employs flashbacks, flash forwards, different points of view, and stream of consciousness, in addition to linear narrative, and the in-her-head portions have a gripping, poetic pulse. The book captures the dilemma of many contemporary women as well as that of many Chicana women. There is some explicit sex.

351 Corpi, Lucha, *Eulogy for a Brown Angel*, Arte Publico, 1992 (hardcover), ISBN 1-55885-050-3, $17.95, 189 pp. Ages 14 up, grades 9 up.

Realistic mystery-detective story set in Los Angeles and the San Francisco area of California in 1970 and almost twenty years later. Gloria Damasco, the young Hispanic-American wife of an Oakland doctor and a Chicana activist, is visiting a writer friend during the Los Angeles Chicano civil rights march and finds at the edge of the site of the conflict between police and activists the dead body of a small, four-year-old boy, Michael David Cisneros. After he gives Gloria information about the slaying, young Mando of the Santos gang is also found dead. There follows an increasingly tangled and frustrating set of events, involving street gangs, Chicano reporters, international intrigue, and dark Cisneros family secrets. Although the hard work and friendship of policeman Matthew Kenyon restores Gloria's confidence in the good faith, at least, of some Anglos, Kenyon dies, having pursued all leads to no avail. Years later, still haunted by the boy's body, Gloria succeeds in unmasking the killer. Numerous conventions keep the plot boiling to the not unexpected, dramatic conclusion, but the poignancy of the first death and the well-delineated Mexican-American climate, including some history of Mexican Americans, gives the book a humanistic tone. Events deal mostly with better-off or wealthy Hispanic Americans and give a sense of the underclass distrust of the Anglo power structure among them. This is a Sisters in Crime mystery.

352 Delacre, Lulu, *Vejigante Masquerader*, illus. Lulu Delacre, Scholastic, 1993 (hardcover), ISBN 0-590-45776-4, $14.95, unp. Ages 5–10, grades K–5.

Bilingual picture-story book of Ramon, a young Puerto Rican boy, who makes his own costume so he can join the masqueraders celebrating in Ponce all through February, wearing horned masks, carrying *vejigas*, or inflated cow bladders, and playing good-natured pranks. Although his costume is ripped by a mean goat on his first day, his mother helps him mend it, and he wins the respect of the older boys. An opening note explains about *vejigantes* and a page at the end describes other masqueraders from Spain and Latin America. Two pages show how to make a mask, followed by a page of glossary, bibliography, and traditional *vejigantes* chants. Illustrations, done in watercolor with colored pencils and pastels, give a vivid idea of the excitement and action of the carnival.

353 Dorros, Arthur, *Abuela*, illus. Elisa Kleven, Dutton, 1991 (hardcover), ISBN 0-525-44750-4, $14.00, unp. Ages 4–9, grades PS–4.

Picture-story book fantasy set in contemporary New York City. Little Hispanic-American Rosalba, the narrator, and her mostly Spanish-speaking *abuela* (grandmother) take the bus to the park where they feed the birds. Rosalba imagines she and her *abuela* fly with the birds over the city, the docks, the Statue of Liberty, the airport, and into the clouds, joyfully free and together. The elation of the adventures real and imagined and the love the two have for each other conveyed by the simple, poetic text are perfectly caught and extended by the colorful, primitive collages. This is an unusually charming and attractive book, whose highly detailed pictures offer sweeping views of the city, unusual perspectives, and hundreds of tiny scenes for many hours of viewing pleasure. A glossary of Spanish words and phrases is included. For comparison, see Faith Ringgold's *Tar Beach* (no. 117).

354   Fernandez, Roberta, *Intaglio: A Novel in Six Stories*, Arte Publico, 1990 (paper), ISBN 1-55885-016-3, $9.50, 159 pp. Ages 14 up, grades 9 up.

Six stories, all narrated by Nenita ("the girl") Cardenas, eldest of three daughters in a Mexican-American family, about the women who affect her life as she grows up. The first, ostensibly about a second cousin, Andrea, is really about sibling rivalry, brought out and resolved after many decades. "Esmeralda" is about Veronica, a girl of stunning beauty, who is sent to live with relatives because she has fallen in love with a sweet and innocent young worker, only to be raped in her new town. Two are about witches, or at least women with extraordinary powers. In "Filomena," Nenita goes with the older woman to Michoacan to participate in the traditional Tarascan rituals of the Day of the Dead, an experience which she finds spiritually moving and which helps her to face the death of Filomena's son, whom she has greatly admired. All are interesting stories, skillfully written, reflecting customs and attitudes peculiar to the Hispanic culture, but collectively they can be called a novel only by stretching the definition of the genre. Although three family trees are included, it is difficult to sort out the connections among the various women. A glossary of some of the many Spanish words and phrases is included.

355   Gonzelez, Ray, ed., *Mirrors beneath the Earth: Short Fiction by Chicano Writers*, Curbstone, 1992 (paper), ISBN 1-880684-02-0, $13.95, 331 pp. Ages 14 up, grades 9 up.

Thirty-one stories, almost half by women, mostly realistic, by Mexican-American authors both well known and more newly published. Only a few stories do not occur in the United States, for example, "Mrs. Vargas and the Dead Naturalist" by Kathleen Alcala, set in Mexico, and "Days of Invasion" by Juan Felipe Herrera, set partially in Central America. Almost all reflect some aspect of the Hispanic experience in this country, from national holidays in "Family Thanksgiving" by Nash Candelaria and "Fireworks" by Danny Romero to the Alamo in "The Ghost of John Wayne" by the compiler. The prevailing tone is grim, relieved by occasional lighter and even some funny pieces, among them "The Marijuana Party" by Mary Helen Ponce, in which three women approaching middle age decide to do something daring to enliven their dull lives. The stories are followed by brief biographical sketches of the authors.

356 Hammond, Anna, and Joe Matunis, *This Home We Have Made/ Esta Casa que Hemos Hecho*, illus. with photographs, Crown, 1993 (hardcover), ISBN 0-517-59339-4, $14.00, unp. All ages, all grades.

Picture-book fantasy. The story was written to accompany the illustrations, which are photographs of portions of a forty-six-foot-long mural in New York City's South Bronx, created by "formerly homeless children who were living in the building on which the mural was painted in the summer of 1991." The story appears on each page first in English and then in Spanish. In it, a little homeless girl tells how one night she leaves her mother and brother sleeping under a stairway and creeps out to look at the stars. She sees a wagon go by, pulled by a strange green animal and carrying a building that would be nice to live in. Invited to join the "building parade," she goes along, with dancers, animals, and musicians that gradually grow in number. Eventually, the building is given to two angels in the sky, one of whom tucks it safely into a snowy globe, which the angels hand to the children and becomes their home. The surrealistic, deep-color paintings catch the otherworldliness of the story and the wistful yearnings of the dispossessed for a better life without sentimentality but with great emotional impact, conveying the message in the distorted pictorial style of Diego Rivera. They show the little girl and some other figures as Hispanic (it seems); some other persons appear to be black. The entire mural is shown in foldout pages at the end of the book. This is an unusual, somewhat puzzling, touching book. There is an authors' note at the end about how the book came to be.

357 Havill, Juanita, *Treasure Nap*, illus. Elivia Savadier, Houghton, 1992 (hardcover), ISBN 0-395-57817-5, $13.45, unp. Ages 4–8, grades PS–3.

Realistic picture-story book of a present-day Hispanic-American family. One afternoon, when it is too hot for Alicia to nap and too hot for her Mama to sew, both relax while their fan blows cool air over ice cubes at them. Mama tells the story Alicia loves, of how in Mexico years ago a little girl named Rita went with her Mama to visit her Grandfather in the mountains, where after a happy reunion, they say goodbye and Grandfather gives Rita a "treasure" of a serape, a bird cage, and his *pito* (flute). Later Rita and her family emigrate to the United States. She becomes Alicia's great-grandmother, and the treasure Grandfather gave her becomes Alicia's mementoes of the past. This pleasing story of family history and pride in heritage has abstract, quiet watercolors for Alicia's part and primitives highly patterned with tropical details and bright colors for Mama's story. This is a simply told, effectively illustrated book.

358 Hernandez, Irene Beltran, *Across the Great River*, Arte Publico, 1989 (paper), ISBN 0-934770-96-4, $8.50, 136 pp. Ages 12–14, grades 7–9.

Realistic novel about a Mexican family who secretly cross the Rio Grande hoping to find a better life and discover both trouble and kindness. Narrated in first person by Katarina Campos, a girl probably no more than ten, their adventures include her departure with her parents and her little brother, Pablito, from their village by night, the disappearance of her father and the wounding of her mother by gunshot as they board a rowboat, and their arrival at the isolated ranchito of Anita, an obese old woman healer, the first of a series of people, both Hispanic and Anglo, who help them. Besides their fear of being deported as illegals, they are stalked and her mother seriously injured by a tattooed smuggler who has seen a shining stone carried in the pouch the mother wears around her waist. The stone, which Kata has cleverly protected by transferring the pouch to her own waist, hiding it and retrieving it in tense situations, proves to be the solution to their troubles, when Anita sells it for enough for bus fare back to their village, where they find Kata's father, and enough left over to buy some land and farm animals. Although Kata hopes to return to Anita some time in the future, their odyssey does not result in their being Americans. The gold nugget, which the father simply dug out of a rock without knowing it was valuable, is a plot weakness, and a subplot of the kindly doctor, his waspish wife, and his loving nurse is contrived, but the fears and hardships of the children and their mother are exciting and realistic.

359 Hoobler, Dorothy, and Thomas Hoobler, *A Promise at the Alamo: The Story of a Texas Girl*, illus. Jennifer Hewitson, Silver Burdett, 1992 (hardcover), ISBN 0-382-24147-9, $12.95; (paper), ISBN 0-382-24154-1, $4.95, 57 pp. Ages 8–12, grades 3–7.

Short, easy-reading historical novel, a simple account of the battle of the Alamo in San Antonio, Texas. Events are seen from the viewpoint of young Maria Hernandez, the Mexican-Texan daughter of a blacksmith involved in the battle. The action starts at Christmas in 1835, just after the Texans under Sam Houston and Jim Bowie have defeated Mexican General Cos. Soon rumor has it that General Santa Anna, president of Mexico, is mobilizing, and Bowie sends for reinforcements. The old Spanish mission called the Alamo is fortified; Maria and her father help make cannonballs. Men arrive under William Travis, who becomes the commander, and Davy Crockett, and others come until they total somewhat fewer than two hundred. Maria, her mother, and father join the resisters in the fort; her father later rides for help and thus survives. Bowie falls ill, and after Santa Anna attacks, Maria manages to get through the lines to his house to get the portrait of his dead wife and children as she had earlier promised. The final struggle occurs on March 6, when the much outnumbered group is overwhelmed and everyone is slain, except for the women and children. Forty-six days later, however, Maria is gratified when Santa Anna's forces are defeated at the San Jacinto River and Texas is free of Mexican rule. The story often sounds like a social studies text but serves to introduce the happening. Starting the book, however, with a chapter mostly devoted to the Mexican-Texan nine-day Christmas celebration and ending it with directions on how to make a piñata trivialize the historical event. Suspense is minimal but adequate to hold the interest. Bowie is presented as a sad, tragic figure and Crockett as a fun-loving, guitar-playing folk hero. Certain well-known aspects are not overlooked—Santa Anna's reputation for cruelty, his Death Song, his red flag that means no quarter, no prisoners, and Travis's line in the sand. A map and a note indicating how much of the story is actually historical would be welcome. A few black-and-white woodcuts show scenes and add interest. Others by the Hooblers in the Her Story series about important historical events include *Aloha Means Come Back: The Story of a World War II Girl* (no. 234), about Pearl Harbor, and *The Trail on Which They Wept: The Story of a Cherokee Girl* (no. 437), about the Cherokee Trail of Tears.

360 Hughes, Dean, *Nothing but Net*, illus. Dennis Lyall, Knopf, 1992 (hardcover), ISBN 0-679-93373-5, $6.99; (paper), ISBN 0-679-83373-0, $2.00, 108 pp. Ages 8–11, grades 3–6.

Realistic sports novel set in a desert town in southern California. African-American Miles Harris is clearly the most competent basketball player on the Angel Park Lakers coed team in the twelve-and-under league, but mean, snide Coach Donaldson rides him and refuses to let him play in his natural way, denigrating him as a "street player" and a show-off. Miles, who is sure that the coach's hostility is racially based, considers leaving the team, and when Mexican-American Kenny Sandoval describes to his father the team's situation, losing because the coach refuses to play Miles, Mr. Sandoval encourages Kenny to stand up to the coach on behalf of Miles and the team. Kenny does, the coach puts him in charge of practice, the team gathers around Kenny and Miles, who gives them pointers he has learned, and two games later the Lakers, who have a miserable record, win their first game. This story of the importance of standing up for what one believes takes place almost entirely on the court and is filled with rapid action, descriptions of plays, and jargon. The style is not elegant but neither is it stilted or patronizing, and those who like sports stories written by someone in the know or those sports enthusiasts who read reluctantly and need enticing will find this a very enjoyable book. This book, which is one in the Angel Park Hoop Stars series, contains a glossary and diagrams of plays.

361   Hurwitz, Johanna, *Class President,* illus. Sheila Hamanaka, Morrow, 1990 (hardcover), ISBN 0-688-09114-8, $12.95, 85 pp. Ages 9–11, grades 4–6.

Brief, amusing school novel tracing how Julio Sanchez becomes fifth grade class president, gaining self-confidence and the respect of his classmates. Their new teacher, Ernesto Flores, has a number of unusual ideas, among them that the students should elect their own leader. Everyone expects Cricket Kaufman, the smartest girl, to win, including Cricket, who nevertheless tries to influence the electorate by passing out free chocolate bars. Julio himself backs Lucas Cott, his best friend, and he becomes his campaign manager. After Arthur Lewis's new glasses are broken in the noontime soccer game, Julio volunteers to be his Seeing Eye Boy, walks him home, and convinces the class that they should pay for Arthur's new glasses with a bake sale. He also copes with the terrible Cott twins at the sale, convinces the principal to reinstate the newly outlawed soccer-at-noon game, and in other ways proves his leadership, so that when Arthur nominates him and Lucas withdraws his own name even some of the girls vote for him and he beats Cricket. The story, like its predecessor which features Lucas and Cricket, is very light, but there are some appealing scenes in the Hispanic-American Sanchez family home where Julio's mother, his grandmother, and his two older brothers all give plentiful advice.

362   Marzollo, Jean, *Soccer Sam,* illus. Blanche Sims, Random, 1987 (hardcover), ISBN 0-394-88406-X, $6.95; (paper), ISBN 0-394-88406-X, $3.50, 48 pp. Ages 6–8, grades 1–3.

Realistic picture-story book intended as an easy-to-read book. Sam's cousin, Marco, is homesick for a while after he arrives by plane from Mexico to stay the year. After he teaches Sam and the other second graders to play soccer and they defeat the third graders handily, Marco feels better about himself and agrees to teach the third graders, too. Text and illustrations are adequate for what they are intended to do. For the most part, the text is smoothly constructed, and the pictures pick up the action, show the characters, and have a comic flavor. A few Spanish words add atmosphere. This is a Step into Reading Step 3 Book.

363 Mohr, Nicholasa, *Going Home*, Dial, 1986 (hardcover), ISBN 0-8037-0269-8, $11.89, 192 pp. Ages 9–11, grades 4–6.

Growing-up novel of the summer a young girl from New York spends with her great uncle in the Puerto Rican village from which her grandparents came. The narrator, eleven-year-old Felita Maldonado, is often at odds with her mother, who has become obsessively protective, and her two brothers, who are assigned to keep a close eye on their younger sister. When she stays with her Tio Jorge in Barrio Antulio, she is at first homesick and bored, but she becomes involved in a church young people's group and in painting the sets for their historical pageant, and, despite the resentment and mean tricks of some of the local girls, she makes many friends and learns to love her family's homeland. Often angry at the way girls are restricted in the Hispanic culture of New York, Felita finds they have even less freedom in Puerto Rico. Felita's attraction to her boyfriend, Vinny, from Colombia, her squabbles with her brother, Tito, and her troubles with the girls in the village are standard fare in stories for this age group, but the contrasts between the two cultures and between the Puerto Rico the old people remember and the one they find when they return give the novel some depth.

364 Mora, Francisco X., *La Gran Fiesta*, illus. Francisco X. Mora, Highsmith, 1993 (hardcover), ISBN 0-917846-19-2, $19.00, unp. Ages 3–8, grades PS–3.

Picture-story book of fantasy set in an unidentified Spanish-speaking area, that cautions against being greedy. Crow persuades some gullible but accommodating birds to help him decorate his big tree for La Gran Fiesta de Navidad (Christmas) "in the Northern tradition," with fruits, cookies, candies, and the like, intending to eat all the goodies himself. He urges them to bring more and more until the tree is so heavy it collapses. As the birds help Crow clean up the mess, it grows dark, and they notice that the "stars twinkled and the moon glowed at the top" of the little tree the birds have, making it much more beautiful than Crow's laden one. The story is simple and straightforward, with some Spanish words explained at the end, and moves as expected. The decorative, two-dimensional, full-color, posterlike pictures are cheery and bright, almost like Christmas cards, and they follow the text, adding details of story and setting.

365 Mora, Pat, *A Birthday Basket for Tia*, illus. Cecily Lang, Macmillan, (hardcover), 1992, ISBN 0-02-767400-2, $13.95, unp. Ages 2–6, grades PS–1.

Picture-story book of a young Mexican-American girl, Cecilia, who plans a surprise for the ninetieth birthday of Tia, her great-aunt. Cecilia fills a basket with all the things she likes best: the book her aunt reads to her, the mixing bowl in which her aunt makes cookies, a flowerpot so they can grow flowers together, a teacup so her aunt can make her hot mint tea, and finally her red ball, so they can play together. When Tia arrives, the surprise party includes musicians and many friends and family members, and the understanding aunt thoroughly appreciates Cecilia's basket. Throughout, the cat, Chica, shares the secret. The simple story is accompanied by bright, simple illustrations made from cut paper with dyes, giving a good sense of Cecilia's excitement and happiness.

366   Nodar, Carmen Santiago, *Abuelita's Paradise*, illus. Diane Paterson, Whitman, 1992 (hardcover), ISBN 0-8075-0129-8, $13.95, unp. Ages 5– 8, grades K–3.

Picture-story book of the reminiscences of Marita's grandmother, her *abuelita*, of her native Puerto Rico. After her grandmother's death, Marita sits in the rocking chair where Abuelita used to hold her and remembers the stories of her *paraiso*, her homeland, where she helped her father in the sugar cane, watched the honeycreeper bird come right in the window to get sugar from the table, stuffed pillows with chicken feathers as her father played his lute on the porch in the evenings, and rode through the rain forests and the mountains on the mule. With her mother, Marita rocks and remembers her grandmother's stories, and they feel her love continue to embrace them. The illustrations of a lush, Eden-like country are appropriate to a land of memory, and the attachment of the child to her grandmother makes a warm, supportive story.

367   Ortiz Cofer, Judith, *The Line of the Sun*, University of Georgia Press, 1989 (hardcover), ISBN 0-8203-1106-5, $15.95, 291 pp.; 1991 (paper), ISBN 0-8203-1335-1, $12.95, 304 pp. Ages 14 up, grades 9 up.

Realistic novel of family life set in the mid-1900s in the village of Salud, Puerto Rico, and then in a Puerto Rican barrio in Paterson, New Jersey. The first half is the turbulent story of a young island man; the second half concerns his slightly younger sister as told by his niece, her daughter. Wild, blacksheep Guzman gets in trouble as the lover of El Cabra (the witch) and emigrates to mainland United States, where he escapes from a fenced migrant labor camp to the New York City subways and, more than a dozen years later, on Christmas Eve, turns up at the apartment of his shy, beautiful, responsible sister, Ramona, where he is instrumental in saving her life and those of her children and returns, broken in body, to the island. Marisol's account, based on her mother's stories, her grandmother's letters, overheard conversations, and her imagination, elevates Guzman to an almost romantic hero status, although she admits at the end that there may be some lies involved. Life on the island—the gossip; the church; the women who are self-appointed guardians of morality; cockfighting and gaming; the male-dominated, patriarchal society; the work-laden, child-ridden women—is vivid, the best part of the unevenly told story. It forms an ironic contrast to that of the immigrants in El Building, the only place where Ramona feels secure because she is hemmed in by her own people but where Marisol feels inferior, suffocated, and even the object of racial dislike from neighboring blacks. Suspense comes from interpersonal relationships in the first half, while overt action produces tension later when the barrio men plan a labor strike, the women hold a spiritist meeting, police cars prowl the neighborhood, lights blinking, and a terrible fire forms the climax. Guzman's uncanny instinct for survival enables him to do just that, but Ramona remains vulnerable and unable to fit into the mainland culture, both spiritually and practically, even though her navy husband has the financial means to provide a good life in the suburbs. Marisol, on the other hand, appreciates her island origins and culture but is also happy with the English language and mainland culture. In addition to the setting, many figures in the large cast stand out for their dimension.

368 Paredes, Americo, *George Washington Gomez: A Mexicotexan Novel*, Arte Publico, 1990 (hardcover), ISBN 1-55885-012-0, $9.50, 302 pp. Ages 15 up, grades 10 up.

Historical novel of Mexicotexans on the Lower Rio Grande from about 1915 to 1940, focusing on a very bright Mexican-American youth named George Washington Gomez, from just before his birth until he is about twenty-five. The only son of a pacifist, ironically slain by *gringos* for suspected sedition, George, known to his family as Gualinto, is raised by his Uncle Feliciano (the book's most memorable figure, an ironic combination of realism and idealism), who devotedly cares for his widowed sister's family and puts the boy through college in hopes that he will help his people in some profession, only to find that Gualinto turns his back on his kind, marries an Anglo woman, and intends to raise his family as Anglos. Although this never completely finished novel often tells rather than shows and although the author's comments intrude, it makes vividly evident the widespread, deep-seated prejudice against the Mexicotexans and their feelings about the Anglos who have taken their land, ridicule them, and relegate them to the bottom of the social order, often denying them simple justice. Gualinto represents the hopes of a better life for all through educating the brightest and also the all too understandable callousness of those educated in the Anglo system toward their people. The book has a very ironic, pessimistic ending. The school scenes are graphic, the home scenes memorable; excellent use is made of detail.

369 Paulsen, Gary, *The Crossing*, Orchard, 1987 (hardcover), ISBN 0-531-05709-7, $11.95, 128 pp.; Dell, 1990 (paper), ISBN 0-440-20582-4, $3.25, 114 pp. Ages 12 up, grades 6 up.

Realistic, sociological problem novel, a very dark, sober, almost depressing account of a few days in the life of homeless Manny Bustos, a fourteen-year-old Juarez, Mexico, street boy. While on the take, Manny strikes up an unlikely friendship with an American army sergeant, an emotionally disturbed, alcoholic Vietnam War veteran, who saves the boy from alley killers, and as he dies, passes his wallet to Manny so he can buy his escape from poverty and degradation to the United States. Although it is unclear how Manny will accomplish the crossing at El Paso, Texas, and although the American becomes a stereotypical hero, the story envelops the reader from start to finish with its vivid sense of the dangers of street life and the hopelessness of the boy's existence. The economical, understated style increases the tension.

370 Paulsen, Gary, *Sisters/Hermanas*, Harcourt, 1993 (hardcover), ISBN 0-15-275323-0, $10.95, 65 pp.; (paper), ISBN 0-15-275324-9, $3.95, 65 pp. in English, 65 pp. in Spanish. Ages 12 up, grades 7 up.

Short, realistic, bilingual novel of two Texas girls, both fourteen. One, Rosa, is the child of deep poverty and is an illegal immigrant from Mexico; the other, Traci, is a beautiful, blond daughter of privilege. Rosa works the streets at night to pay for her tawdry motel room and slick clothes to attract men and for money to send home to her mother in Mexico City. During the day, she dreams of gracing the cover of a magazine like *Glamour*. Traci, on the other hand, has almost from infancy been groomed by her ambitious mother for beauty, popularity, and a wealthy marriage. Currently she is being prepped for the top cheerleading spot on her high school team. The girls meet at the very end of the book quite by chance in a mall clothing store, where Traci sees Rosa cowering under the dress racks, seeking refuge from the authorities. Traci tries unsuccessfully to shield her, recognizing that "we are the same. That girl and I—we are the same," a statement her mother hotly denies, but Traci instinctively knows is true. This open-ended story is almost all highly understated narrative, the only dialogue being between Traci and her mother. Many small details of everyday life point up the contrast between the two girls at the same time as they bring out their similarities. Rosa's portion is told very closely from her point of view and is much more sympathetic and personal, whereas the parts about Traci are distanced from the reader. Not until the very end, when she delivers her redeeming speech, does seemingly superficial Traci rise in the reader's esteem. Although it glosses over the dangers of street life, the book presents a bleak commentary not only on the situation of illegal immigrants but also on the position of women in American society, regardless of economic status or ethnic origin.

371 Poey, Delia, and Virgil Suarez, eds., *Iguana Dreams: New Latino Fiction*, HarperCollins, 1992 (hardcover), ISBN 0-06-055329-4, $25.00, 376 pp.; (paper), ISBN 0-06-096917-0, $12.00, 376 pp. Ages 15 up, grades 10 up.

Nearly thirty short stories by contemporary writers of Mexican-American, Cuban-American, Dominican-American, Puerto Rican–American, and Chilean-American backgrounds, ten of them women. Skillfully crafted and sparingly worded, they speak of children going to confession and exasperating the priest, returning to the island, a cleaning woman and her employer who are close friends, sheepherders and their camp tender, a circus elephant who kills his tender, war in Korea, marriage, drug dealers and cops, death, growing up, cultural assimilation, clinging to culture, anger, love—a wide range of subjects, people, and tones by well-known and lesser-known authors, among them Jose Antonio Villarreal, Rudolfo Anaya, Rolando Hinojosa-Smith, Sandra Cisneros, Julia Alvarez, Ana Castillo, Virgil Suarez, and Pablo Medina. This is a choice, enlightening, consistently interesting, literate but never stuffy collection whose purpose "to showcase writers from all Latino cultures" and "whet readers' appetites and enrich their imaginations" is amply accomplished. The book is hefty, but the stories taken individually catch the attention early and move well.

372 Reiser, Lynn, *Margaret and Margarita/Margarita y Margaret*, illus. Lynn Reiser, Greenwillow, 1993 (hardcover), ISBN 0-688-12239-6, $14.00, unp. Ages 3 up, grades PS up.

Lighthearted, realistic picture-story book set in an urban area. Two little girls, Margaret, who speaks only English, and Margarita, who speaks only Spanish, go to the park with their mothers and meet. Language proves no barrier as they play together with their pet rabbit and cat respectively, each picks up some words in the other's language, and they and their mothers become friends. The book is entirely dialogue, English on the left for Margaret and her mother, and Spanish on the right for the other two. The pictures are amusing black-and-white cartoonish sketches, in which the figures are given color so they stand out. The illustrations change to full color when the girls play together and revert to black-and-white panoramas of the city with patches of color when the two families leave to go home.

373 Rohmer, Harriet, and Cruz Gomez, ads., *Mr. Sugar Came to Town/ La Visita del Sr. Azucar*, illus. Enrique Chagoya, Children's Book, 1989 (hardcover), ISBN 0-89239-045-X, $12.95, 32 pp. Ages 4–8, grades PS–3.

Realistic picture-story book "adapted from a puppet show produced by the Food and Nutrition Program of the Watsonville, California, Rural Health Clinic as part of its outreach program to farmworkers and their families. The puppet show was performed in the migrant labor camps of Watsonville, California." Young Hispanic-Americans Alicia and Alfredo have always loved Grandma Lupe's meals, especially her tamales, until Mr. Sugar cruises the neighborhood with his traveling truck of goodies. Repeatedly over the next days, they stuff themselves with his sweets, until they become fat, lazy, hyperactive, and slothful in school and their teeth decay. Finally Grandma Lupe unmasks Mr. Sugar as a fraud, and the children eat her nutritious meals again. This intentionally didactic story is pleasingly written in English and Spanish on each page and supplemented by full-page, cheerfully colored, pencil-and-pastel, decoratively framed paintings. The pictures show the characters and situations and deliberately overdramatize them and the emotions.

374 Roland, Donna, *Grandfather's Stories from Mexico*, illus. Ron Oden, Open My World, 1986 (hardcover), ISBN 0-941996-09-3, $4.50, 25 pp. Ages 4–10, grades PS–5.

Realistic picture-story book in which a grandfather, who lives in Mexico, visits his Mexican-American grandchildren and tells them stories about their homeland. A silversmith in Taxco, he tells about his wares, Indians of old Mexico, the arrival of the Spaniards, the land and climate of Mexico, present-day ways of life, clothing, entertainments, and the blending of indigenous and Spanish cultures. Full-color pictures alternating with black-and-white tones fill the upper two-thirds of each page, while the easy-reading text in large, black print takes up the rest. The book is intentionally didactic and stresses the typical aspects of Mexican life both in the narrative and in the pictures. Objects are easily identified, but the figures are stiff. Occasionally, the setup works against sense; for example, on one page the text emphasizes the people's liking for bright colors for fiestas, but the accompanying illustration is entirely in black and white. Others in the series are *Grandfather's Stories from the Philippines* (no. 262), *Grandfather's Stories from Viet Nam* (no. 263), and *Grandfather's Stories from Cambodia* (1984), all similar in style, content, and format. All assume that the immigrants want to know about and have pride in their native cultures.

375   Roth, Susan L., *Another Christmas*, illus. Susan L. Roth, Morrow, 1992 (hardcover), ISBN 0-688-099942-4, $15.00, unp. Ages 4–10, grades PS–5.

Realistic picture-story book set in recent years in Puerto Rico. The Christmas after Grandpa dies, Ben's family spends the holidays in Puerto Rico, in a little family inn in a "pink and yellow village by a bright turquoise beach." Grandma surprises everyone by preparing a celebration that combines such familiar aspects of Christmas on the mainland as a tree and gingerbread men with local customs, for example, a nativity scene with the wise men on horses instead of camels and playing a tape of "Feliz Navidad," to which she and Ben dance. This pleasing family story featuring an inventive Grandma calls attention to the likenesses and differences between northern mainland and Hispanic, tropical practices, and it captures the happy, sharing, loving elements of the season. The highly decorative, abstract, cut-paper collages are like a series of eloquent Christmas cards and support the seasonal feeling. The predominately primary colors catch the mainland festival feeling rather than an island one, since the tones are not quite right for Puerto Rico, even the more tropical portions.

376   Soto, Gary, *Baseball in April and Other Stories*, Harcourt, 1990 (hardcover), ISBN 0-15-205720-X, $14.95, 111 pp.; Odyssey, 1991 (paper), ISBN 0-15-205721-8, $4.95, 137 pp. Ages 10–14, grades 5–9.

Eleven realistic short stories set among contemporary Mexican Americans in Fresno, California, revolving around sports, family, first love, school, and other matters of importance to middle-schoolers. The concerns may be serious, at least to the young people involved, but the prevailing mood is light and upbeat. Although personal names, references to Mexico and places there, immigrating, and occasional Spanish words identify the culture, the subjects are typical of working-class American children anywhere. In the title story, two brothers fail to make Little League, but the more persevering younger one establishes himself as a catcher on a pick-up team. In other stories, a broken bike chain almost causes Alfonso to miss his first date; Manuel stars at pantomiming "La Bamba" in spite of himself; straight-A Lupe, never good at sports, becomes marbles champion; Veronica loses the head of the gorgeous Barbie doll she wanted so badly; and Victor wishes he had not bragged that he knew French in order to show off before his girl. A glossary of Spanish words is included. A companion volume is *Local News* (1993). For older readers, Soto has published *Living up the Street: Narrative Recollections* (1985), lively essays of his own personal experiences in growing up as a Mexican

American in Fresno. A short story by Soto, entitled "First Love," appears in Joyce Carol Thomas's *A Gathering of Flowers* (nos. 146, 174).

377 Soto, Gary. *The Cat's Meow*, illus. Carolyn Soto, Strawberry Hill, 1987 (paper), ISBN 0-89407-087-8, $4.95, 64 pp. Ages 6–10, grades 1–5.

Amusing, contemporary, talking-animal fantasy in a family story context. Mexican-American Nicole, eight, is astonished when one Saturday morning her beloved white cat, Pip, speaks to her in perfect Spanish. Pip informs Nicole that she learned Spanish from Mr. Langer, the avid reader just around the block, who speaks a different language on each day of the week. Nicole and Mr. Langer become good friends through Pip, but when a snoopy lady from the house behind blabs to the media about Pip's talent, Mr. Langer moves out to avoid the hoopla, taking Pip along. Several weeks later, Nicole discovers a black cat in her yard. This cat, who speaks to Nicole in both French and Spanish, says that her name is Pip and that she can also speak four other languages. In addition to the extraordinary premise that a cat can learn human languages laboratory style with earphones, much of the humor comes from the characterizations: serious, solicitous Nicole, who tells this consistently interesting story straightforwardly with lots of lively dialogue; practical Pip; eccentric Mr. Langer; and Nicole's fun-loving, often giddy parents, seemingly awkward yet really very clever at the business of parenting. The book is not ethnic specific except for several references and the Spanish words.

378 Soto, Gary, ed., *Pieces of the Heart: New Chicano Fiction*, Chronicle, 1993 (paper), ISBN 0-8118-0068-7, $10.95, 179 pp. Ages 12 up, grades 7 up.

Fifteen realistic short stories of contemporary Mexican-American life in the American Southwest, one each by such Chicano writers as Sandra Cisneros, Ana Castillo, Danny Romero, and Victor Martinez. In the introduction, Soto comments that the stories are probably autobiographical and that each has a "dark kernel" at its center, observations well taken. Although some stories are lighter, the general picture of Hispanic-American life is bleak—of unending toil to make ends meet; far too many mouths to feed; men striving to retain the macho tradition; women catering to them and struggling, health broken; young people either growing away or straining to reconcile new ways with traditional ones; and prejudice from Anglos. "Enero," which tells of Constancia, pregnant with her eleventh child, who grieves for the impending loss of her eldest from tuberculosis, and "The Baseball Glove," about a boy from a comfortable Chicano family, who, while picking chiles for a baseball glove, acquires more money than he needs when wetbacks abandon their sacks and run away during a police raid, are examples of the ironic drama in these stories.

379 Soto, Gary, *The Skirt*, illus. Eric Velasquez, Delacorte, 1992 (hardcover), ISBN 0-385-30665-2, $14.00, 74 pp. Ages 6–10, grades 1–5.

Realistic chapter-book novel of family life set in present-day Joaquin Valley, California. Friday afternoon, Mexican-American Miata Ramirez, nine, leaves on the school bus the Mexican skirt she needs for the *folklorica* dance after church on Sunday and enlists the aid of her best friend, Ana, in recovering it. After library on Saturday morning, they squeeze into the schoolyard, retrieve it from the bus, and squeeze back out, almost under the eyes of Miata's father, a welder who is repairing a bus, only to discover that Miata's mother has a new skirt for her. Miata proudly wears both on Sunday, the new one atop the old, which had been her mother's back in Mexico. The diction and sentence structure are easy but not babyish, and Miata and her friend are obvious foils: Ana, shy and organized; Miata, forgetful and impulsive. The closeness of the middle-class Hispanic family comes through strongly, and the closeness of the Hispanic community, in a limited way; pride in culture is strong but not labored.

380 Soto, Gary, *Taking Sides*, Harcourt, 1991 (hardcover), ISBN 0-15-284076-1, $15.95, 138 pp. Ages 8–12, grades 3–7.

Realistic novel of school and family life set at the time of publication in Sycamore, a pleasant suburban community south of San Francisco, California. Eighth-grader Lincoln Mendoza, a Mexican-American basketball star, faces several problems: adjusting to his new, mostly white school, Columbus Junior High; maintaining friendships at Franklin Junior High in the barrio Mission District in San Francisco, where he used to live; squaring things with his old pal, Tony, whose feelings he has hurt over a television set stolen from his former apartment; convincing Monica Torres to be his girlfriend; playing against his old teammates in the year's big game; and, most important of all, deciding who and what he is and where his loyalties really lie. The setting, reinforced with many Spanish words and phrases, defines Linc's situation, and the battle on the court between the two teams forms an exciting backdrop for the climax of Linc's internal struggle, where he decides that he must be true to himself. Other elements to commend the book are the well-drawn, single-parent family, the strong sense of pride in heritage, the urban crime problem, and the discomfort of being in an ethnic minority. Action is plentiful, the dialogue convincing, and the characterization adequate. In the sequel, *Pacific Crossing* (1992), Lincoln and Tony spend the summer living with host families in Japan. A glossary of Spanish terms is included.

381   Stanek, Muriel, *I Speak English for My Mom*, illus. Judith Friedman, Whitman, 1989 (hardcover), ISBN 0-8075-3659-8, $11.95, unp. Ages 4–8, grades PS–3.

Picture-story of Lupe Gomez, a young Mexican-American girl in Chicago, who must translate for her Spanish-speaking widowed mother until the threat of her factory closing makes the mother decide to enroll in a night school English program. The relationship is warm and mutually supportive, although Lupe admits that sometimes she would rather play than accompany her mother on errands. Illustrations are in shaded black and white with a red-brown border of what looks like Mexican Indian designs. Lupe and her mother are attractive but not idealized.

382   Suarez, Virgil, *Latin Jazz*, Morrow, 1989 (hardcover), ISBN 0-688-08475-3, $18.95, 290 pp. Ages 15 up, grades 10 up.

Historical novel in the voices of five Cuban Americans in a family scattered from the prison of La Cabana on the island to California. The only first-person sections are those of Hugo Carranza, who left college to fight in the revolution but has been imprisoned for years by Castro's forces because he opposed the takeover by communism. Other sections focus on his father, Esteban, now a widower, who lives with his daughter in Los Angeles; his wife Concha, whose memory holds the family together; his son-in-law Angel Falcon, who was a pharmacist in Havana and now works tirelessly driving an ice cream truck; and Angel's son, Diego, a nightclub band leader whose wife has just left him for his best friend, the band's keyboard player. The trigger for most of the action is the storming of the Peruvian embassy in Miramar, Havana, by Cubans seeking asylum, a crisis that leads to the Mariel boat lift of thousands to Key West, Florida, in 1980. Hugo escapes from prison and mingles with the other refugees, seeking a young woman, Lucinda, who also fought with the guerilla revolutionists, and eventually gets to Florida, where his father, with Diego, has come with two other older Cubans hoping to find their families. Although replete with exciting events, explicit sex scenes, and considerable humor, the strength of the book lies in the picture of the three generations of Cubans, all displaced, the older ones because they have lost their homes and professions, the younger ones, like Diego, because they are essentially rootless, and how they are still held together and supported by strong family feeling. A wealth of interesting characters fill minor roles. A later novel by

Suarez, also with historical aspects, *The Cutter* (1991), is set almost entirely in Cuba, although the whole story concerns efforts of the main character, Julian Campos, to get to the United States, a goal he achieves in the last eight pages. It contains vivid scenes of the cutting of sugar cane by forced "volunteers" and of the bleak and suspicion-ridden life common under the communist regime.

383   Taha, Karen T., *A Gift for Tia Rosa*, illus. Dee deRosa, Dillon, 1986 (hardcover), ISBN 0-87518-306-9, $13.95, 40 pp.; Bantam, 1991 (paper), ISBN 0-553-15978-X, $2.75, 36 pp. Ages 4–9, grades PS–4.

Realistic picture-story book set in a present-day urban, Mexican-American neighborhood, or, since the text does not specify the area, possibly a Mexican one. Eight-year-old Carmela dearly loves her elderly neighbors, Tia Rosa and Tio Juan. She is saddened to hear Father say that Tia Rosa is so sick that she probably will not live long. Carmela spends every moment she can with Tia Rosa in her bedroom, knitting a scarf for Father for Christmas while Tia Rosa works on a blanket for a grandchild-to-be. After Tia Rosa dies, Carmela shows her love for her lost friend by finishing the blanket for the new baby girl. The simple, directly told story, whose language is easy enough for early readers, is high in family and neighborly warmth and closeness. The realistic, uncluttered paintings show the family and friends in various typical situations. The cheery colors and upbeat floral and geometric designs on clothing support the theme that love and caring continue even after death. The characters' faces are individualized and expressive.

384   Taylor, Theodore, *Maria: A Christmas Story*, Harcourt, 1992 (hardcover), ISBN 0-15-217763-9, $13.95, 84 pp. Ages 8–12, grades 3–8.

Brief novel of a girl's struggle to represent her Mexican-American people with a float in the annual Christmas parade of San Lazaro in California's San Joaquin Valley, set presumably in the 1960s. When her friends, daughters of wealthy ranchers, discuss their families' plans for expensive, custom-designed floats, Maria Gonzaga impulsively announces that Rancho Gonzaga, a small truck farm, will also enter this year. Then she must find money for the entry fee, persuade her hardworking father, and think of an idea that will cost almost nothing. Finally, she settles on a simple Nativity scene built out of old barn wood, with Maria and her brother, Rafael, as Mary and Joseph, and their ox and hinny as the animals, all pulled on a flatbed wagon by their Hispanic neighbors—a float whose sincerity shames the lavish entries. Although the story is simply told, the characters are well developed, particularly Maria's father, whose *orguillo*, pride in his heritage, drives him to agree to the entry and bully his reluctant son to take part, and Maria, who understands her father's initial anger and Rafael's fear of humiliation, yet stubbornly persists in her effort. Prejudice against Mexican Americans is shown more as a dismissal of their importance in the community than in any active harassment.

385 Temple, Frances, *Grab Hands and Run*, Orchard, 1993 (hardcover), ISBN 0-531-05480-2, $14.95, 165 pp. Ages 8–14, grades 3–9.

Realistic novel of contemporary Salvadoran political repression and the flight of refugees to the United States. When the motorcycle of Jacinto Ramirez, a political activist, is found mysteriously abandoned, Jacinto's son, Felipe, the twelve-year-old narrator, his daughter Romy, eight, and their mother, Paloma, do as he had instructed and "grab hands and run" for Canada and safety. With only bare essentials and a good supply of various currencies he has accumulated, always remembering to stay together, be calm, and look like simple travelers, they journey by bus, on foot, by boat, and by truck following the advice of trusted helpers whose names they memorized before leaving, through Guatemala into Mexico, and across the Rio Grande into the United States, where they are apprehended and taken to a Texas detention center. They face deportation, and Felipe seriously considers voluntarily returning to find and help his father, but a kind priest investigates and learns that Jacinto is dead, and they elect to continue north. The book's end finds them relocated in a farming area of Wisconsin, where they receive papers admitting them to Canada. Although the trip has enough ticklish spots to hold the reader, the little group seems amazingly fortunate. Political realities are seldom brought to the fore and then mostly in overheard conversation, for the children's safety not sensibilities, but Felipe once finds human bones that Jacinto explains might be the result of dismemberment and Felipe knows he faces certain induction into the army if they stay. Romy emerges as a spunky star, and Paloma shows true grit (the child reader may not pick up on some of the hazards she faces but the adult does). The book is mostly plot, and the author has attempted to do too much for the book's bed, but the story functions satisfactorily as an introduction to a terrible and festering problem. Temple's *Taste of Salt* (1992) eloquently describes political repression in modern Haiti.

386 Trambley, Estela Portillo, *Trini*, Bilingual, 1986 (hardcover), ISBN 0-916950-62-X, $19.00, 247 pp.; (paper), ISBN 0-916950-61-1, $12.00, 247 pp. Ages 14 up, grades 9 up.

Realistic novel of about twenty years in the life of a Tarahumara Indian–white woman, set in the mid-twentieth century mostly in Mexico. Half-orphaned Trini, thirteen, shares with her father the dream of one day owning land. She marries her father's one-time helper, Tonio, a life-loving philanderer, bears him a daughter, moves to Juarez when he gets his U.S. green card, makes a dangerous and physically painful crossing to El Paso to bear her son on American soil, and with the help of a kind Mexican-American couple finds a tiny patch of ground where she can finally realize her dream. No fairy-tale success story, Trini's life is full of poverty and trouble, but for the most part she remains indomitable. Trini is supported by various women, many of them complete strangers, and thus the book becomes a feminist statement about necessary sisterhood. Trini's father; her first and only real love, Sabochi, an Indian headman; and the railroad worker who helps her get land are the few good men in the story, whose steadiness and decency contrast with the many cruel, selfish, insensitive, macho males who people the pages. The United States represents salvation, but at the end Trini deplores the shallow materialism that lures her children, because for her, as they have always been, the elemental virtues of land, family, and work are most important. At the age of thirty, she mirrors Mexican-American poor women, old before their time, overburdened with children, putting up with the whims of irresponsible, drinking, womanizing men—just managing. Still, Trini wins respect merely for surviving. The writer's loving descriptions of the mountains, rocks, winds, and the very soil, the land from which Trini comes and which she passionately loves, substantiate the theme of the importance of the earth for existence. The plot holds, the characters are three dimensional, the setting is alive, and, even though the overuse of Spanish and Indian words sometimes makes reading tough going, the persevering reader will find this moving account of Mexican and Mexican-American poor well worth the effort.

387 VanEtten, Teresa, *Dead Kachina Man*, Sunstone, 1986 (hardcover), ISBN 0-86534-072-2, $10.95, 131 pp. Ages 12 up, grades 7 up.

Realistic mystery-detective novel set in New Mexico in the late twentieth century. Investigating the mysterious death of famous kachina carver Ray Hava of the San Jaime Pueblo plunges Mexican-American police captain Dominique Rios into a frightening and amazing series of events, including conflict with tribal policeman Ed Cruz, Cruz's son, and other pueblo dwellers and threats against his own life, not to mention drugs, pornography, blackmail, closet skeletons, shady characters, colorful townspeople, long-lost relatives who reappear, a little romance, and a chain of murders—conventional elements skillfully concocted and woven together to keep the plot boiling. The emphasis is on thrills, but some sense of the natural terrain, the social problems caused by the intrusion of white culture, and Native cultural ambience comes through. See also Teresa Pijoan de Van Etten, *Spanish-American Folk-*

tales (no. 397), and Teresa VanEtten, *Ways of Indian Magic: Stories Retold* (no. 468).

388 Weiss, Nicki, *On a Hot, Hot Day*, illus. Nicki Weiss, Putnam, 1992 (hardcover), ISBN 0-399-22119-0, $13.95, unp. Ages 1–6, grades PS–1.

Picture-story book with a very simple, occasionally rhyming text following the activities of a mother and her daughter through the year. On a summer day, "they spray their arms and toes and knees/ And pretend they're wading in the icy seas." In rainy fall they drink cocoa in the luncheonette, in winter they read together in the big green chair, and in spring they smell the herbs planted on the windowsill. Each season ends with Mama doing something loving with her child: "Mama swings her Angel"; "Mama hugs her Angel"; and finally, at every season, "Mama loves her Angel." The illustrations, many of which show the same urban block in different activities, are in pastel colors with accents of bright clothing and the very black hair of the mother and child. Although the characters have light brown skin, the only indication that they are Hispanic comes from the names on the store buildings: El Bodegero on the grocery store and Pepe's Luncheonette.

8

Hispanic Americans: Books of Oral Tradition

389 Aardema, Verna, ret., *Borreguita and the Coyote: A Tale from Ayutla, Mexico*, illus. Petra Mathers, Knopf, 1991 (hardcover), ISBN 0-679-80921-X, $15.00, unp. Ages 4–8, grades PS–3.

Retelling of a Mexican folktale in which Coyote the trickster is foiled, making use of a number of familiar motifs. Four times, Borreguita, a clever little lamb, tricks Coyote, who intends to eat her. She persuades him to wait until she is fatter, fools him into diving for a cheese (really the moon) instead of dining on her, tricks him into believing he is holding up a mountain while she runs away, and, finally, charges full tilt into his mouth, giving him a horrible mouthache. This version of the classic story of the triumph of the weaker through wit and sheer audacity is supported by playful, full-color paintings that show the action and settings and perfectly catch the nature of the characters. The text has a pleasing storytelling quality.

390 Ada, Alma Flor, ret., *The Rooster Who Went to His Uncle's Wedding*, illus. Kathleen Kuchera, Putnam, 1993 (hardcover), ISBN 0-399-22412-2, $14.95, unp. Ages 5–8, grades K–3.

Latin American folktale first heard by the reteller in Cuba. Built on the cumulative pattern of the more familiar English tale, "The Old Woman and the Pig," it tells of the rooster who, with his beak newly polished, starts for his uncle's wedding and muddies it by gobbling a single golden kernel of corn from a puddle of mud. He asks the grass to clean his beak, only to be refused, "No, I won't. Why should I?" He appeals to the lamb to eat the grass, the dog to bite the lamb, the stick to hit the dog, the fire to burn the stick, and so on until the sun agrees to do his bidding because he has always greeted it with his bright song. Quickly all the other creatures reverse their refusal, and he arrives at the wedding clean and in time for the banquet. The illustrations, predominately orange, green, and bright blue, feature a stylized rooster and are done with prints made from a zinc plate engraved with a dry point needle, then filled in with brilliant colors.

391 Baden, Robert, ret., *And Sunday Makes Seven*, illus. Michelle Edwards, Whitman, 1990 (hardcover), ISBN 0-8075-0356-8, $13.95, unp. Ages 5–9, grades K–4.

Folktale set in Costa Rica, about two villagers, Carlos, kind but very poor, and Ricardo, rich and selfish, each of whom has a large brown mole on the end of his nose. Once Carlos, gathering wood in the forest, loses his way and, climbing a tree, spots a light and follows it to a house where he sees twelve ugly witches dressed in black dancing in a circle and singing, *Lunes y martes y miercoles—tres!* (Monday and Tuesday and Wednesday—three!) over and over. Suddenly, without thinking, Carlos sings out loudly, *Jueves y viernes y sabado—seis!* (Thursday and Friday and Saturday—six!). The witches drag him into the room, cheer his wonderful new rhyme, and sing the new version tirelessly. Then they reward him by touching the end of his nose and removing the wart. He finds himself on the edge of the forest, his burro loaded with twelve bags of gold. Ricardo, hearing of his good fortune, insists that Carlos take him to the witches' house, where he joins in their song by loudly supplying the last line, *y domingo, siete!* (And Sunday, seven!). The witches, furious that he has added an unrhyming line, put a second mole on his nose and send him off with no money. The cartoonlike illustrations are set on every other page inside a wavy white margin; the text is set on opposite pages inside a wavy black line frame. This is a lively, amusing book.

392 Cruz, Martinez, Alejandro, ret., *The Woman Who Outshone the Sun*, illus. Fernando Olivera, Children's, 1987 (hardcover), ISBN 0-89139-101-4, $13.95, 32 pp. Ages 5–11, grades K–6.

Legend of the Zapotec Indians of Oaxaca, Mexico, retold in a highly illustrated, bilingual edition. An amazingly beautiful woman, Lucia Zenteno, arrives in the village and is treated with suspicion and fear. The river falls in love with her, flows through her shining black hair, and, when she is driven from the village, goes with her. In the drought that follows, the people repent, seek her out, and beg her to return. Back in the village, she combs the water, fish, and otters from her hair and then disappears forever. The full-page pictures, in bright reds, fuchsias, blues, and greens, are in a semiprimitive style. The initial letters and small illustrations on the text pages add to the total brilliant color suitable to the title.

393 Hayes, Joe, ret., *La Llorona, The Weeping Woman: A Hispanic Legend Told in English and Spanish*, illus. Vicki Trego Hill, Cinco Puntos, 1987 (paper), ISBN 0-938317-02-4, $4.95, unp. Ages 5–12, grades K–7.

Retelling of what is "truly the classic folk story of Hispanic-America," related first in English and then in Spanish on each page, aptly accompanied by brooding, sepia-toned, mostly full-page illustrations depicting characters, incidents, and setting. Haughty village girl Maria declares she will marry only the handsomest man in the world. After she weds a handsome ranchero and has two children and he leaves her for an elegant lady, she becomes enraged, throws the children into the river, drowning them, and, distraught at her deed, dies on the river bank. It is said that to this day she walks the night, sobbing and calling for her children. The realism of the illustrations actualizes the events and theme. Facial close-ups dramatize the emotions, her pride, anguish, and despair. The text has a pleasing storytelling quality. A note on storytelling introduces the book; a note about the widespread legend of the weeping woman appears on the back cover. Far less successful on the whole is *Mariposa, Mariposa* (1988), for K–3, which explains why butterflies flit from flower to flower. The quality of the text of this light, cumulative Hispanic tale far exceeds that of Lucy Jelinek's pictures. Their yellows and pinks and crinkly, comic lines cheapen the book.

394 Kimmel, Eric A., ad., *The Witch's Face: A Mexican Tale*, illus. Fabricio Vanden Broeck, Holiday, 1993 (hardcover), ISBN 0-8234-1038-2, $15.95, unp. Ages 5–11, grades K–6.

Retelling of a folktale from both the Hispanic-Mexican and central Mexican–Mazahua Indian traditions. Young gentleman Don Aurelio stops for the night at a large, isolated homestead, where he falls in love with a beautiful young witch who saves his life. She accompanies him home, and they plan to marry, but when he fails to obey her and destroy her human face, he loses her forever. Although an introductory note clearly identifies the tale as Indian, the characters, details, illustrations, and overall tone emphasize the Hispanic tradition. Amplifying the detailed, engrossingly told story of the importance of trust in love are full-color, mostly double-spread, very handsome, impressionistic paintings. Sources are given.

395   Mora, Francisco X., ret., *The Legend of the Two Moons*, illus. Francisco X. Mora, Highsmith, 1992 (hardcover), ISBN 0-917846-15-X, $19.00, unp. Ages 4–8, grades PS–3.

Retelling of a Mexican folktale that explains why the moon appears in the sky and also in bodies of water. When Chucho the dog accepts the invitation of Perico the parrot to spend the night in Perico's tamarindo tree, Chucho discovers two moons in the sky. Perico decides to capture one, flies to the sky, pulls one loose, and flies back. Because the moon is so heavy, he falls with it into the *cenote* (pool) near by, where it continues to glisten. The text is simply stated, with some Spanish words (glossary at end), moves fast, and is easy to follow. The decorative, slightly comic, posterlike illustrations are clear and bright, retell events, add details, particularly of setting and character, and give the book a joyful atmosphere. Less successful is *The Coyote Rings the Wrong Bell: A Mexican Folktale* (1991), a wordless book in which a clever rabbit outwits a coyote. The illustrations, also by Mora, are similar in color and technique to those of *Two Moons* but do not tell the story well. The text fortunately appears in small print at the end of the book. The book concludes with a bibliography of Mexican folktales.

396   Mora, Francisco X., ret., *The Tiger and the Rabbit: A Puerto Rican Folk Tale*, illus. Francisco X. Mora, Children's, 1991 (hardcover), ISBN 0-516-05137-7, $12.95; (paper), ISBN 0-516-45137-5, $5.95, unp. Ages 4–8, grades PS–3.

Retelling of a Puerto Rican folktale in which a cunning trickster rabbit three times outwits a powerful but gullible tiger. The story is told entirely in pictures, which depict the most significant events but are not good in conveying motives and building to climax. Fortunately, a sprightly and detailed version of the tale, with dialogue, appears at the end of the book. When Señor Tiger threatens to eat him, Señor Rabbit convinces the tiger that he can save the tiger from a coming hurricane by lashing him to a tamarind tree, then persuades Señor Tiger that a cheese factory exists at the bottom of a lagoon into which the tiger jumps and almost drowns, and, finally, maneuvers the tiger into allowing the rabbit to ride him like a horse. The pictures accompanying this lively and drolly humorous story with parallels in the Brer Rabbit series are amusing, two-dimensional, posterlike, sparsely detailed, full-color paintings. If they fall short in narrative quality, they catch the story's sense of fun. Information about storytelling and a bibliography of books about storytelling and about Puerto Rican and Hispanic folktales are included.

397 Pijoan de Van Etten, Teresa, ret., *Spanish-American Folktales*, illus. Wendell A. Hall, August House, 1990 (paper), ISBN 0-87483-155-5, $9.95, 128 pp. Ages 9 up, grades 4 up.

Lively retellings of twenty-eight, mostly lighthearted Hispanic-American folktales from New Mexico, with notes about the sources and background of the tales concluding the book and several amusing black-and-white line drawings. Some stories, like "The Flea" (a riddle story), "The Dead One Fell" (a ghost story about assembling a dead body piece by piece), "The Animals' Escape" (which resembles "The Brementown Musicians"), and "The Ant" (which recalls "The Ant and the Grasshopper"), have familiar European counterparts. Many stories revolve around witches, magic, the despised triumphing, and the proud and avaricious getting their comeuppance. Talking animals are prevalent, the wily Coyote appears, and the thrusts of many stories are pragmatic morals, for example, "Wise Stones," which implies that life is what one makes it, and "Leticia's Turtle," about sharing with those less fortunate. Most exalt the lowly, hard work, and using one's wits—the peasant virtues. See also Native American Indian stories collected and retold by the same writer, under Teresa VanEtten, *Ways of Indian Magic: Stories Retold* (no. 468) and under Teresa Pijoan, *White Wolf Woman: Native American Transformation Myths* (no. 527).

398 Rohmer, Harriet, ad., *Brother Anansi and the Cattle Ranch/El Hermano Anansi y el Rancho de Ganado*, illus. Stephen Von Mason, Children's Book, 1989 (hardcover), ISBN 0-89239-044-1, $12.95, 32 pp. Ages 4–8, grades PS–3.

Retelling of an African-American tale collected in Nicaragua about Anansi the trickster-spider, a figure from Africa known also in the Caribbean and North and Central America. When Brother Anansi learns that Brother Tiger has won "half a million" on the lottery, he convinces his friend to "go in for cattle raising" on a "nice green pasture" he owns. After they prosper, Brother Anansi tricks Brother Tiger out of his half of the cattle, until Brother Tiger has only one cow left. The understated story moves with a good pace and plenty of flavor, employing such modern details as the lottery and current "big business" practices like exporting to the United States and South America and such distinctive expressions as "big man cow" and "everything was going pretty." Adding to the fun are full-page, brightly colored, two-dimensional, comic, acrylic and colored pencil pictures. They show Brother Anansi as a long, lanky, orangy-brown-skinned, probably Hispanic, man, with a hint in his overextended limbs of a spider; Brother Tiger as a slow-witted, yellow-and-orange jaguar (jaguars are called tigers in Central America); the cows as a motley mixture; and the setting of palm trees and exotic flowers and greenery. The text appears on the page first in English and then in Spanish, with one or two green leaves separating them, a pictorial element that foreshadows the conclusion. This highly amusing book ends with a note about the origin of the story, the informant, and the artist. A brief, italicized introduction aimed at the young reader or hearer and telling about the origin and nature of Anansi precedes the narrative.

399 Rohmer, Harriet, ad., *Uncle Nacho's Hat/El Sombrero del Tio Nacho*, illus. Mira Reisberg, Children's Book, 1989 (hardcover), ISBN 0-89239-043-3, $12.95; (paper), ISBN 0-89239-112-X, $5.95, unp. Ages 4–8, grades PS–3.

Adaptation of a Nicaraguan folktale, told in English and Spanish on the same page, about the need for looking at circumstances in new ways. When his niece, Ambrosia, gives Uncle Nacho a new hat, he tries unsuccessfully several times to get rid of the old, holey one. Seeing him dejected because his hat keeps coming back, Ambrosia suggests he put his mind on the new one instead. Flattened primitive paintings in brilliant, clear tropical colors and motifs enhance the fun of this comedy of errors with a pleasant moral; a delightful book.

9

Hispanic Americans: Books of Poetry

400 Castillo, Ana, *My Father Was a Toltec*, West End, 1988 (paper), ISBN 0-931122-49-X, $6.95, 75 pp. Ages 15 up, grades 10 up.

Forty-six original poems, about one-third in Spanish, in various forms but mostly free, some employing colloquial or street talk, others more formal, educated diction, that speak of the Mexican-American woman's experience. Autobiographical, the poems are in tones that vary from hurting to wistful to explosive as they tell of growing up in Chicago where her father was a member of the Toltec street gang and where on the streets she defends herself, blade ready, by hurling insults like "Dago bitch" in return for "Dirty Mexican bitch," through the mature realization of how her origins in a Latino macho household have molded her, to strongly feminist poems not always ethnic specific, and to the final piece, "In My Country," which is a very touching, expressive if overlong picture of a utopian world. The English poems (this reader is not fluent enough in Spanish to comment on the ones in that language) are pleasingly crafted and always provocative in substance. Previous collections are *Otro Canto* (1977), *The Invitation* (1979), and *Women Are Not Roses* (1984), and she has published novels, including *So Far from God* (no. 346). See Joyce Carol Thomas's *A Gathering of Flowers* (nos. 146, 274) for "Christmas Story of the Golden Cockroach," a short story by Castillo.

401 Cisneros, Sandra, *My Wicked Wicked Ways*, Third Woman, 1987 (paper), ISBN 0-943219-01-9, $8.95, 103 pp.; Turtle Bay, 1992 (hardcover), ISBN 0-679-41821-0, $15.00, 103 pp. Ages 15 up, grades 10 up.

Sixty poems, divided into four groups, the first being about life in a barrio of a Texas city. The second contains and is named for the title poem, the wicked ways being the life of a single daughter with six brothers, who leaves home to adventure on her own, learn about love and loneliness, and write poetry. The third section consists of poems written in or about France and Italy—Other Countries—and the last, The Rodrigo Poems, about an ex-lover. Although occasionally obscure, the poems project strong emotion: anger, tenderness, depression, longing. Only the first section is specifically about the Mexican-American experience, although the position of a woman in the Hispanic culture is implicit in a number of the other poems. All are in unrhymed, nonmetric verse.

402   Delacre, Lulu, comp., *Las Navidades: Popular Christmas Songs from Latin America*, illus. Lulu Delacre, Scholastic, 1990 (hardcover), ISBN 0-590-43548-5, $12.95, 32 pp.; (paper), ISBN 0-590-43549-3, $3.95, 32 pp. Ages 5–12, grades K–7.

Twelve songs of the Christmas season from Latin American countries, most of them from Puerto Rico or Mexico, in highly illustrated picture-book form. Besides the songs in Spanish and in English translation by Elena Paz, the book provides musical arrangements by Ana-Maria Rosado. Songs celebrate the joys of the season in food and nature, the Annunciation, the journey to Bethlehem, and the arrival of the Three Kings. Each song is accompanied by an illustration, usually full page, in slightly muted colors, possibly done with colored pencil, and an explanation of its meaning in the country of its origin. An earlier collection by the same illustrator-translator-arranger team is *Arroz con Leche: Popular Songs and Rhymes from Latin America* (1989), a more general selection of children's rhymes in a similar format, which also includes directions to the games that are played with some of the songs.

403   Duran, Roberto, Judith Ortiz Cofer, and Gustavo Perez Firmat, *Triple Crown*, Bilingual, 1987 (paper), ISBN 0-916950-71-9, $10.00, 167 pp. Ages 14 up, grades 9 up.

Collection of about 150, mostly one-page, free verse poems, almost equally divided between three Hispanic-American poets: Mexican-American Duran, Puerto Rican–American Ortiz Cofer, and Cuban-American Perez Firmat, whose offerings include seventeen poems in Spanish. Duran's sharply expressed, pithy, often epigrammatic poems reflect work in the San Joaquin Valley, street culture, brown-white relations, prison life (he is an ex-convict), and Chicano family life, and play with word sounds and meanings. Ortiz Cofer's poems are longer and frequently draw scenes—mother home alone and dancing to a mariachi record, the writer in the confessional, immigration processes, the poet's grandmother walking in a pasture, and street people seen in the morning "sucked like leeches to the walls" of buildings in the city center, having barely survived the night streets. Although not exclusively, for the most part, her Hispanic heritage pervades her writing. Perez Firmat expresses mixed feelings about being of two cultures and often mingles Spanish and English as a literal representation of his mixed heritage. He speaks of his family, his writing, remembered scenes, but mainly of the ambiguity of cultural blending in poems that vary from a few lines to a full page, in tones pensive to satirical, but all with a decidedly intellectual bent.

404 Gonzalez, Ray, ed., *After Aztlan: Latino Poets of the Nineties*, Godine, 1992 (hardcover), ISBN 0-87923-931-X, $22.95, 258 pp.; (paper), ISBN 0-87923-932-8, $14.95, 258 pp. Ages 14 up, grades 9 up.

More than 130 poems by thirty-four "of the best contemporary Chicano and Puerto Rican poets writing in the United States today," one-half of whom are women, each represented by up to six poems. The poems were selected to display

> the current state of Latino writing and . . . [to show] that these writers have created a complex, vibrant literature . . . and share the common concerns of all Latino writers—finding ways to overcome political barriers placed upon them, preserving the traditions of a culture that stresses close familial ties, and most of all, showing how Hispanic literature has become a true part of 'mainstream' American arts and letters.

Such well-known authors as Victor Hernandez Cruz, Gary Soto, and Ana Castillo appear, as well as less familiar ones, including Rebecca Gonzales, Demetria Martinez, and Ernesto Trejo. As is to be expected with such a collection, the quality is uneven, but that inconsistency is balanced by the wide variety of tones and subjects. Most are informed by the past or present Latino situations, for example, "Grandmother's Father Was Killed by Some Tejanos" by Leroy Quintana, "People of the Harvest" by Naomi Quinonez, "Tomatoes" by Luis J. Rodriguez about migrants, and "The Purpose of Altar Boys" by Alberto Rios, but many speak of matters common to human life. A glossary of terms and Spanish words would be helpful. Biographical information is included.

405 Gonzalez, Ray, *Twilights and Chants*, James Andrews, 1987 (paper), ISBN 0-9614643-1-3, $8.95, 97 pp. Ages 15 up, grades 10 up.

Sixty poems by a Mexican-American poet that find their stimulus in his personal experience and observations (on the beach in "The Opinion at Point Loma"), literary life ("The Echo of the Voice," for Pablo Neruda), history

("Cortez the Killer"), and places ("March Sequence, Las Cruces, New Mexico"). There are love songs, poems about the Rio Grande and Mexico, lizards, cottonwoods, and a dying woman who saves candles. Most are freely constructed and have unobvious rhythms, but some are musical and even chantlike with repetition and listing, and most draw their images from nature. Some are frustratingly obscure, and the best ones are the shorter ones, in particular those about the animals in the Denver zoo, wolves, and the desert and the Southwest that appear in the center section of the book.

406 Mora, Pat, *Communion*, Arte Publico, 1991 (paper), ISBN 1-55885-035-X, $7.00, 91 pp. Ages 14 up, grades 9 up.

Sixty mostly short, free verse poems of observation and personal experience, a few tightly metered but mostly unrhymed, by a Mexican-American poet. The interests that inform her poems range from the elderly in nursing homes to people and scenes observed on trips to India (among them the Taj Mahal, about which she ironically comments, "Like love it rises" . . . while women pound wash in the river near by) and Pakistan, butterflies in the desert, a Huichol Indian flood and creation myth, nuns, abusive husbands, children departing from Mexico for the States, young people losing the old stories and language, rebellious teens, relationships between men and women and between women—a wide range of subjects only some of which are ethnically specific. Subtly musical, simple in structure but not simplistic, layered in meaning but not pretentious, the poems use images drawn from the real world she sees. Some terms are strikingly sensory. A particularly memorable poem is the poignant and rallying "Strong Women," an internally and externally rhymed feminist statement in tightly metered iambs, which concludes: "Strong women, teach me courage to esteem." Two earlier collections by Mora, *Borders* (1986) and *Chants* (1984), are similar, although her work shows developing skill. *Borders* is divided into four sections, the first and longest about the Mexican-American immigrant experience. The strongest poems are in the second section, about family, which give vivid portraits or tell little, memorable stories, and in the third, where the poems are highly erotic without indulging in any explicit sexual imagery. Poems in *Chants* are more closely tied to the desert land, Aztec and Maya Indian heritage, and Mexican culture. Some revolve around old, or still sustained, beliefs, like witches and devil children. Some speak of the condition of women in a man-dominated, macho-driven culture. Some mother-daughter poems are wrenching.

407 Ortiz Cofer, Judith, *Terms of Survival*, Arte Publico, 1987 (paper), ISBN 0-934770-73-5, $7.00, 64 pp. Ages 14 up, grades 9 up.

Fifty short (less than a page in length) poems by a Puerto Rican–American poet that reflect the area, ways, and beliefs of the island culture with a strong, feminine viewpoint. She opens with "Quinceanera," spoken by a girl on reaching the cultural milpost of the fifteenth birthday: "My dolls have been put away," as though they were dead children that she will take with her to marriage. The poet talks of the evil eye and saints; makes envy concrete with "It is a green snake," a best friend's necklace; describes a witch as having a face brown and wrinkled "like ripples on a muddy pond," a woman who has dealings with both God and the devil, one who absolutely must be avoided; and comments on marriage, liberty, and the relationships between women of several generations. She speaks of the importance of continuity, calling it "dangerous . . . to forget the climate of your birthplace" and turn a deaf ear to the words of dead relatives that come to you in your dreams, and of the healing power of the earth, of how, in her fertile interior, "the earth brews" whatever cures humans need. The poems spare words, the images often reflect the tropics and the land, the emotion is understated and reflective, and the rhythms are subtle. Ortiz Cofer has also published a novel, *The Line of the Sun* (no. 367), and *The Latin Deli: Prose and Poetry* (1993).

408   Rodriguez, Luis J., *The Concrete River*, Curbstone, 1991 (paper), ISBN 0-915306-42-5, $9.95, 125 pp. Ages 14 up, grades 9 up.

Forty-three poems, all in free verse except for a few printed in paragraph form, divided into five sections: Prelude to a Heartbeat, Dancing on a Grave, Always Running, Music of the Mill, and A Harvest of Eyes. Subjects are contemporary, urban, and gritty: unemployment, violence, drug use, smoky bars. Many are set in Watts and East Los Angeles, where the author grew up, some in East Harlem, a few in Chicago, where he now lives. Some, especially those in Dancing on a Grave, are marred by political polemic or inappropriate pretentious terms. Most powerful are those set in foundries and among the workers of steel mills, which ring with the conviction of firsthand experience, and some based on his own family, like "Deathwatch," about his father, and "The Bull's Eye Inn," where his ex-wife waited on tables, stand out. Images are frequently striking, and the predominant tone is angry. Most of the pieces are easily accessible by high school students.

409a   Soto, Gary, *Neighborhood Odes*, illus. David Diaz, Harcourt, 1992 (hardcover), ISBN 0-15-256879-4, $15.95, 68 pp. Ages 8 up, grades 3 up.

Twenty-one short-lined poems in free verse and fairly large print, most of them two or three pages long, about childhood interests and everyday activities in a Mexican-American community. For the most part, the subjects and events are not ethnic specific. The children enjoy life with one another and with their families as, among other matters, they go to the park on Sunday after church, buy snow cones from the truck, poke fun at the errors in family photos, snitch pomegranates, run through the sprinkler, and thump the guitar. Although some poems are overextended and lose the reader's interest, the picture of daily life, spiced with mouth-filling and atmospheric Spanish terms, seems strong and true to childhood. Moods vary, but the general tone is up-beat and joyful. The decorative black-and-white silhouettes add a special at-traction. A glossary of Spanish words is included. For middle-schoolers and up is *A Fire in My Hands* (1990), twenty-three poems less strictly formed but on similar subjects and themes, preceded by an author's essay about his poetry and followed by a series of questions and answers about where he gets his ideas and so on. Both books offer much reading pleasure. Anecdotal notes precede each poem.

409b   Soto, Gary, *Who Will Know Us?: New Poems*, Chronicle, 1990 (paper), ISBN 0-87701-673-9, $8.95, 69 pp. Ages 15 up, grades 10 up.

One of several books of poems, including *Black Hair* (1985) and *Home Course in Religion: New Poems* (1991), intended for adults but for the most part accessible to mature high school students and about matters within their appreciation. Soto speaks in subtly rhythmical, sometimes internally rhymed free verse about growing up Catholic and Mexican American in California's San Joaquin Valley, his schooling, being a son, husband, and father, traveling, home life, ancestors, and young sex. Some poems are pensive, some wry but never bitter, some wistful, some joyful—various moods, tones, and layers of meaning appear—and hold up to the end. Most have one or two lines that puzzle, but the author's voice is straightforward and honest and only somewhat tied to ethnic origin. Some poems in *Home Course* are longer and require more application, and religion and family continue to be major concerns.

410   Weissman, Ann, ret., *The Castle of Chuchurumbel*, illus. Susan Bailyn, Hispanic Books Distributors, 1987 (hardcover), ISBN 968-6217-00-2, $8.95, unp. Ages 3–7, grades PS–2.

Exuberant Mexican and southwestern United States nursery rhyme that moves cumulatively and repetitively, like "The House That Jack Built," told with a good beat first in English and then in Spanish on each page. Unclut-tered, pastel-colored pictures in comic style show the various items as the rhyme progresses, the figures free on the pages. The castle is shown first, then the keys to open the doors, the cord for the keys, and so on through water, fire, and different animals, until at the end the owners of the castle are intro-duced. An opening note says that the rhyme has been adapted somewhat from the oral form and probably originated in Spain.

10

Native-American Indians: Books of Fiction

411 Alexie, Sherman, *The Business of Fancydancing: Stories and Poems*, Hanging Loose, 1992 (hardcover), ISBN 0-914610-24-4, $18.00, 84 pp.; (paper), ISBN 0-914610-00-7, $10.00, 84 pp. Ages 14 up, grades 9 up.

A collection of five short stories and forty patterned and prose poems revolving around contemporary Spokane Indian reservation life in eastern Washington State. Alexie reflects predominately the viewpoint of a young, Native American male on such disturbing aspects as welfare, drinking, lost hopes, and on such lighter matters as male bonding in basketball tournaments and powwows. Typical in tone and thrust of the five stories is the opener, "Traveling," which describes a police search of a car filled with Indians on the way home from the Kamiah All-Indian Six-Foot-and-Under Basketball Tournament, a piece that operates with wry humor on top and sad regrets underneath. "Translated from the American" is a brief exchange between a traditional grandmother and her college-educated son that reveals ironic aspects about acculturation. In "Special Delivery," a comedy of behavioral errors and misconceptions ensues as Thomas-Builds-the-Fire tries to make the story he carries in his head come true, while "Gravity" shows a son returned to the reservation after months in the city enjoying basketball shots with his father. "Father Coming Home" tells of the fear of a boy after his father cuts his knee in half with a chainsaw at work. The overall tone is upbeat, in spite of the often deplorable conditions they expose, and the sense of place and local problems owing to loss of cultural identity and unemployment is very strong. The dialogue is extensive, as are the narrative details, humor abounds, and the storytelling flavor prevails. For the poems in this book, see no. 543.

412 Alexie, Sherman, *The Lone Ranger and Tonto Fistfight in Heaven*, Atlantic Monthly, 1993 (paper), ISBN 0-87113-548-5, $21.00, 223 pp. Ages 14 up, grades 9 up.

Twenty-two spirited and revealing short stories by a Spokane–Coeur d'Alene author that mingle the despairs, hopes, and joys of growing up as an Indian on the reservation today. While drunkenness and poverty are rampant, respecting one's heritage and one's self as a person as well as an Indian can be redemptive. The personas speak in tones from wry and self-deprecating to angry and polemical to amused and even raucous, but always with vivid details of family life on the reservation. The title story tells of a stormy Anglo-Indian marriage. In "Every Little Hurricane," young Victor witnesses a fistfight between his two uncles, and "Witnesses, Secret or Not" tells of the close, warm relationship between a father and son who drive to the city so that the father can repeat for the detective the little he knows about an Indian's mysterious death. Peopling these pages are basketball heroes, seen as the equivalent of yesterday's warriors; white policemen who shake down Indians; bright Indian children belittled by white teachers; and educated Indians who return to the reservation and do not know what to do with themselves there—stories of yearnings and aspirations with self-preservation as the main goal. Many moments of camaraderie, affection, mutual support, and even sacrifice occur at weddings, homes, automobiles, powwows, even in taverns. Some pieces are not short stories in the usual sense but are vignettes strung together, and a few prose poems are included, but Alexie excels with the anecdote and is good with the unexpected twist. The style is rapid, occasionally raunchy, vibrantly visual, often playful, sometimes pithy, mostly exciting and engaging. The story titles catch the interest immediately. Alexie has also written poetry; see nos. 543, 544.

413 Allen, Paula Gunn, ed., *Spider Woman's Granddaughters: Traditional Tales and Contemporary Writing by Native American Women*, Beacon, 1989 (hardcover), ISBN 0-8070-8100-0, $19.95, 242 pp.; Fawcett, 1990 (paper), ISBN 0-449-90508-X, $12.00, 256 pp. Ages 14 up, grades 9 up.

Twenty-four short stories by and about women and women's concerns. Seven come from various oral traditions, and seventeen are realistic short stories or biographical accounts by such writers of the nineteenth and early twentieth centuries as Ella Deloria, Pauline Johnson, Pretty Shield, and Humishima (Mourning Dove) as well as by such well-known late twentieth-century writers as Louise Erdrich, Leslie Silko, and the editor, and newer voices, including LeAnne Howe. Gunn says that these are "women's war stories or woman-warrior stories . . . about women who have entered battle, and have suffered defeat and captivity . . . who do not give up hope, even when they are dying, their children are stolen, they are subject to emotional and physical battery; who continue to resist." Beauty, generosity, conflict, sorrow, deprivation, and love of people and life mark these carefully selected, artfully arranged, engrossing stories about traditional and contemporary women in families and by themselves. An introduction, notes on the stories and about the authors, a glossary, and a short bibliography are included. For the oral tradition stories in this book, see no. 480.

414 Bragg, Bea, *The Very First Thanksgiving: Pioneers on the Rio Grande*, illus. Antonio Castro, Harbinger House, 1989 (paper), ISBN 0-934173-22-1, $7.95, 57 pp. Ages 7–11, grades 2–6.

Short historical novel told mostly in dialogue set in northern Mexico and what is now southwestern Texas from January to the end of April 1598. Two fictitious Anglo-Indian orphan brothers, Manuel, twelve, and Fernando, nine, and their performing goat, Captain-General Martinez, join the historical expedition of the Spanish explorer, Don Juan de Onate, in crossing the Chihuahuan desert of northern Mexico. After days of terrible thirst and parching heat, the 400 people and 7,000 animals arrive at the Rio Grande near present-day El Paso, Texas, where Onate claims the region for Spain. He holds a thanksgiving feast in which the Indians of the region also take part, a festival that preceded the one at Plymouth by almost a quarter century. The style is lively and occasionally amusing but otherwise pedestrian, and plot and characters are conventional. The book emphasizes the difficulties of the trek in praise of the Spaniards' feat, but no attention is given to the impact on the Indians, except to mention that they might be fierce and obstruct the journey and to point out that many die in the Spanish silver mines. In fact, one reason the boys join is to avoid being put to labor in the mines. Sepia-toned illustrations add much to an understanding of the story and place. A historical note and a glossary are included.

415 Brant, Beth, *Mohawk Trail*, Firebrand, 1985 (hardcover), ISBN 0-932379-03-6, $15.95, 94 pp.; (paper), ISBN 0-932379-02-8, $6.95, 94 pp. Ages 15 up, grades 10 up.

Thirteen stories and three poems celebrating this Mohawk-Anglo poet's origins, the working class, and women, among them several pieces about homosexuals. More character sketches or narrative essays than short stories in the usual sense, they tell of Brant's own family tree and her people's coming to Detroit from Canada, discrimination against Indians and women in the

Detroit workforce and assembly line, life in the Great Depression, whites carrying off Indian children in the 1890s and an Indian lesbian losing hers to a white husband, dancers, laborers, a mental patient, housewives, mothers, simple people trying to live good lives under difficult circumstances—these and other selections are generally serious, even sad or plaintive. Humor is scarcely represented; one rare instance is "Indian Giver," in which to have a big Christmas tree for the family, Grandpa cuts off the branches intending, unsuccessfully as it turns out, to glue them back on after he gets the trunk in the house. While concepts and experiences are for the most part mature, the storytelling is straightforward, sentences are uncomplicated, and diction and use of detail are concrete and relaxed. The eight short stories in *Food and Spirits* (1991) focus on Indian homecomings, for example, those of Violet who returns to a little town in northern Michigan to visit her grandmother after leaving her abusive husband; of David who comes home to his family to die of AIDS; and of eighty-year-old Elijah who travels from his Ontario reserve to visit his beloved twin granddaughters in Detroit. The preface, entitled "Telling," is an emotional prose-poem about child abuse. Brant has also edited *A Gathering of Spirit* (1984), a large, varied anthology of poems, essays, short stories, letters, and miscellaneous writings by sixty Indian women from different walks of life, some lesbian, some incarcerated, some educated, some not, each eloquent in her own way as she speaks about Indian women and women's lives. Bibliographies and biographical information are included.

416 Bruchac, Joseph, *Dawn Land*, Fulcrum, 1993 (hardcover), ISBN 1-55591-134-X, $19.95, 317 pp. Ages 12 up, grades 7 up.

Novel combining realism, legend, and fantasy set among the western Abenaki sometime between the last Ice Age and the coming of the first European settlers in the area that is now Vermont and northern New York state. Essentially a quest story, the novel follows Young Hunter, an orphan of one of the thirteen villages of the Dawn Land People, or as they call themselves, the Only People. Called by some inner voice and by Bear Talker, the Oldest Talker of the village who speaks with spirits, and by Medicine Plant, the Oldest Talker of the village of the Salmon People, he sets out to face some great evil approaching from the north and west, armed with the secret weapon, the Long Thrower, a bow which is unknown to most of the Only People, and accompanied by his three dogs. Eventually he saves a young woman of the Long House People and is adopted into their group, but he still must face the evil, which he now recognizes as huge stonelike Ancient Ones, man-eating survivors of the first creation, who destroy the bison and other animals with fire and pose a threat to all the peoples in their path. They employ a terrible animal, perhaps based on a saber-tooth tiger, and a renegade human from Young Hunter's own village, Weasel Tail, who acts as their "dog," scouting, killing, and kidnapping for them. In a final confrontation, Young Hunter uses his bow to kill their beast and starts an avalanche that buries the Ancient Ones and also Weasel Tail, who redeems himself by a final courageous act. Throughout are inserted legends of the Abenaki illustrating their values and mores which are interesting but slow the action. The tone throughout is that of legend, and the dialogue is in the language of the Noble Redman, but readers caught up in the story may accept it as appropriate to the setting in time.

417   Cannon, A. E., *The Shadow Brothers*, Delacorte, 1990 (hardcover), ISBN 0-385-29982-6, $14.95, 179 pp.; Dell, 1992 (paper), ISBN 0-440-21167-0, $3.50, 179 pp. Ages 12 up, grades 7 up.

Realistic novel set at the time of publication in Lake View, Utah. Anglo Marcus Jenkins, sixteen, and his Navajo foster brother, Henry Yazzie, also sixteen, have been inseparable ever since Henry came to live with the Jenkinses when he was seven. Marcus is content to play second fiddle to top-student Henry, who also beats Marcus handily at running track. Life changes abruptly for both when Henry falls for beautiful Anglo Celia Cunningham and Frank, a star Hopi runner, enrolls in school and challenges Henry's athletic supremacy. Henry's discovery that Celia, a talented artist, has painted his portrait as a heavily tanned Anglo and an accident to his real father send Henry back to the reservation for the summer, perhaps forever, but not before the two boys acknowledge that they may be of different cultures, but they still have deep affection for each other. The author skillfully juxtaposes normal adolescent growing pains of sweethearts and school with the additional crises of Henry's need to establish his ethnic identity and Marcus's need to find out who he really is. Marcus's account of events is now-sounding and sometimes witty and amusing, not always honest about himself, but convincing in its picture of family relationships, school situations, recreation, and his growing understanding of how Henry is both like him and different from him. Although Henry is too remote and inarticulate, Frank rings false, and Celia is predictable, the story moves along well, and both main characters though types are credible.

418   Conley, Robert J., *Mountain Windsong: A Novel of the Trail of Tears*, University of Oklahoma Press, 1992 (hardcover), ISBN 0-8061-2452-0, $19.95, 240 pp. Ages 14 up, grades 9 up.

Historical novel taking place over about five years in the mid-1830s mainly in North Carolina and Oklahoma. In a frame story set in recent years on the Cherokee reservation in North Carolina, a Cherokee grandfather tells his young grandson the story of two early nineteenth-century Cherokee lovers,

Waguli (Whippoorwill) and Oconeechee, who are parted by the Cherokee removal. The bulk of the novel gives details of the removal, personalizing events through what happens to the two young people. About to be married, the pair are parted by chance; Waguli is taken away captive from North Carolina by U.S. soldiers, brutalized, incarcerated, and eventually transported to Oklahoma where he falls into degradation, alcoholism, and violence. Oconeechee searches for him for four years, before encountering an old white man who has lived among the Cherokees, Gun Rod. He journeys west to Oklahoma, sobers Waguli up, and brings him back to her. The modern narrative provides the writer an opportunity for commentary that the historical part can not, sets the historical events in relief, and strengthens it by playing down the sometimes sentimental "poor Indian princess" stereotype. The details of the removal are presented in ghastly clarity, and the unfortunate postremoval internal dispute among the Oklahoma Cherokees is not ignored. Interrupting both narratives are passages from such source materials as the Treaty of New Echota, American Bureau of Ethnology reports, and a letter protesting the removal from Ralph Waldo Emerson to President Martin Van Buren. These are interesting in themselves and contribute texture and authenticity but are not integrated into the story. A note about historicity and a map would be useful.

419 Conley, Robert J., *Nickajack*, Doubleday, 1992 (hardcover), ISBN 0-385-41695-4, $15.00, 182 pp. Ages 12 up, grades 7 up.

Historical novel set in 1841 and laid against the turmoil among the Cherokees after their removal to Oklahoma. During the trial in which he is sentenced to hang for the murder of a fellow Cherokee, young family man Nickajack flashes back several times to the strife between the United States and Georgia governments and the Indians that led to the division of the Cherokee nation into the Ridge group, who capitulated and left on their own for Oklahoma, and the Ross group, who were determined to remain on ancestral lands and were forcibly evacuated on what became known as the Trail of Tears. Apolitical and interested only in ensuring the safety of his family, Nickajack emigrates with the Ridges, who also include his best friend, Coffee Soldier; and the two families start a new (and well-described) life as pioneers in the West. After the Rosses arrive, they instigate bitter strife with the earlier emigrants. Attacked by Ross men, Nickajack kills one in self-defense but is convicted of murder by a predominately Ross court and is hanged. At the book's very end, grief stricken and distraught, Coffee Soldier kills a Ross man, leaving the reader to understand that the terrible intratribal hatred will continue. This is a stark, poignant, economically told book of how U.S. treachery divided a once-thriving nation of Indians and of how that division, in turn, destroys the life of an honorable, peaceful man who is to be taken as symbolic of others like him. A few real figures make cameo appearances, but all important story characters are fictitious. Conley, himself Cherokee, has written other fiction about Indians, including *Ned Christie's War* (1990), a novel whose main character was historical and which takes place twenty-five years after the American Civil War when the U.S. government is trying to force the Cherokee nation to allow Oklahoma to be admitted to the Union as a state.

420 Conley, Robert J., *The Witch of Goingsnake and Other Stories*, University of Oklahoma Press, 1988 (hardcover), ISBN 0-8061-2148-3, $18.95, 165 pp.; 1991 (paper), ISBN 0-8061-2353-2, $9.95, 184 pp. Ages 13 up, grades 8 up.

Eighteen stories by a Cherokee author of realism and fantasy (magic, witches, shape changing, and the like) involving Cherokees in Georgia before the Trail of Tears, in Oklahoma afterward, and in modern times. The stories are intended "to show not only something of the range of Cherokee history but also something of the variety within contemporary Cherokee culture." Yellow Bird creates himself as a man and as a Cherokee as he thinks through the story of his people in the selection bearing his name. Some stories take their genesis from white prejudice, among them the dramatic "The Night George Wolfe Died," "Wili Woyi," and "The Hanging of Mose Miller," while witchcraft drives "Wickliffe" and the title story. A set of lively pieces about modern Indians revolves around a hell-raising Cherokee named Calf Roper. Although history is sometimes inserted with a heavy pen, whites are too obviously and overly villainized, and some pieces approach the tone of "dime westerns," the stories move fast, except in the informative parts, and the diction is not difficult. The result is a lot of good reading that amply accomplishes the book's purpose. The introductions, one of which is by Cherokee Chief Wilma Mankiller, are very helpful.

421 Cook-Lynn, Elizabeth, *From the River's Edge*, Arcade, 1991 (hardcover), ISBN 1-55970-051-3, $17.95, 147 pp. Ages 15 up, grades 10 up.

Realistic novel set in the late 1960s among the Sioux (Dakota) of South Dakota near the Missouri River not far from Pierre. The basic plot of the story takes place mostly in a courtroom and concerns the lawsuit brought by the prosecuting attorney on behalf of sixty-something Dakota John Tatekeya against a white rancher for stealing forty head of John's cattle, only three of which have been located, their brands altered. John endures the humiliation of the trial, where the defense calls witnesses to subvert his case by attempting to show incompetence, repeated drunkenness, and so on. John wins the suit, and he is awarded damages for the three cattle, but ironically almost immediately his haybarn and stacks burn, undoubtedly torched by the rancher, and since the rancher is appealing the verdict, it is unlikely John will ever collect. A subplot revolves around the relationship between John and his beautiful, thirty-year-old mistress, Aurelia Blue, who, realizing John is aging, ironically takes up with the young Indian who testified most hurtfully against John because his own brother assisted the rancher in the rustling. The novel is engrossed with the continuing irony behind Indian-white relations, and through John's flashbacks as the trial progresses suggests that historically Indians have been confronted by such dilemmas as that facing John, where the white law, presumably intended to help, will inevitably weaken or even destroy him, and will continue to erode the old intratribal and familial relationships. John's musings on the vicissitudes of history give the impression that the author herself is speaking and lend the book a didactic tone that is augmented by the sometimes ponderous style. Nevertheless, the book exerts a strong emotional appeal because John is presented so sympathetically and because his plight is made so clear, and hence that of Indians generally.

422 Cook-Lynn, Elizabeth, *The Power of Horses and Other Stories*, Arcade, 1990 (hardcover), ISBN 1-55970-050-0, $17.95, 131 pp. Ages 12 up, grades 7 up.

Fifteen very short stories, preceded by one poem, by a Crow-Creek-Sioux author mostly about present-day Sioux that embody such symbols of traditional culture as horses, family, and land and emphasize the disintegration of the native social fabric because of the impact of white culture. Stories tell how old Joseph becomes despondent when his son dies in World War I and his body is not returned for a traditional burial and how the unexpected visit of a pushy white minister to a Sioux family goes humorously awry. Other stories describe the bitter quarreling of the drunken cross-blood children of an abusive white father when they gather for his funeral, the return of Young Nephew from Saigon and war to wage a different battle for survival on the Sioux reservation, and the death of talented poet Magpie, who is shot by parole officers for allegedly resisting arrest. More character sketches than conventional short stories, these mostly serious accounts employ a matter-of-fact, understated style rather than projecting the intimacy and fluidity of the storyteller. The dialogue is sparing, occasional characteristic Indian expressions and Sioux terms contribute to the setting and reinforce attitudes, and the total effect is an ironic lament about the barrenness of existence for contemporary Sioux.

423   Deloria, Ella Cara, *Waterlily,* University of Nebraska Press, 1988 (hardcover), ISBN 0-8032-4739-7, $25.00, 244 pp.; (paper), ISBN 0-8032-6579-4, $8.95, 244 pp. Ages 14 up, grades 9 up.

Historical novel of Dakota (Sioux) life from the woman's perspective. Set in the mid-nineteenth century in what later becomes South Dakota, just before the white invasion, it follows twenty years in the lives of two women, Blue Bird and her daughter, Waterlily. When Blue Bird is in her late teens and has given birth to Waterlily, her improvident, jealous husband "throws her away publicly." Back with her own people, she marries Rainbow, as steady and gentle as her previous husband had been unreliable and disagreeable, and she has a happy life and more children. Waterlily grows up, protected, happy, indulged, and in her late teens she is "bought" (the highest type of marriage) by Sacred Horse, a stalwart youth the counterpart of her stepfather in character. She goes to live with his people, and although she never feels fully at home there, she is reasonably content. When Sacred Horse dies in a smallpox epidemic spread by blankets dropped by passing white soldiers, she returns to her people, gives birth to a son, and marries a handsome, young singer, the cousin of her late husband. The uncomplicated, linear plot is the mechanism for presenting a range of situations intended to show how cultural ideals shaped everyday lives, in particular, how social behavior was mandated by kinship and marriage. For example, women, like Blue Bird and Waterlily, achieve honor by putting children, husbands, and male relatives first. Characters are ciphers, with little personality, and the author can often be heard explaining the reasons behind certain behaviors. Deloria was herself Sioux, fluent in the language, and an ethnological scholar determined to preserve in print the values of Dakota traditional life and to promote appreciation for them. Material for the book came from her own remembered experiences, interviews, and extensive studies and translations. Published for the first time about fifty years after it was written and not the blend of history, culture, and fiction that late twentieth-century literary tastes demand, the book is nevertheless a sympathetic, fascinating look at the lives of nineteenth-century Native-American women. A preface, biographical sketch, and afterword are included.

424   Dorris, Michael, *Yellow Raft in Blue Water,* Holt, 1987 (hardcover), ISBN 0-8050-0045-3, $16.95, 356 pp.; (paper), ISBN 0-446-38787-8, $8.95, 372 pp. Ages 14 up, grades 9 up.

Realistic novel of self-discovery, essentially the same story told by three generations of Montana Indian women in one family, Rayona, fifteen, Christine, her mother, in her early forties; and Aunt Ida, the woman who Christine thinks is her mother but really is her aunt. Events take place mostly on the reservation east of Havre but also in Seattle where Christine bears Rayona, comes to accept her failed marriage to an African-American, learns that she has but a short time to live, and decides to return to the reservation so that Rayona can stay with Aunt Ida. Abrupt shifts and a sudden conclusion make the novel more demanding than it needs to be, and some events strain credulity, but the narratives, told from youngest to eldest, characterize the women well and illuminate resentments, misunderstandings, dissensions, heartaches, and loves—the ironies that underlie family relationships. Although reservation life is important to the story, more vital to an appreciation of events is their condition of being women. Key episodes and people as seen from the different perspectives unify the book and play up the humor, sadness, stupidity, self-sacrifice, and deep love that appear. Although the personalities and circumstances change, the pattern of life repeats. The particular Native-American group is not specified in the book but may be Gros Ventre or Assiniboine-Sioux. Dorris has also published *Morning Girl* (1992), about Caribbean Indians at the time Columbus arrives. Dorris and his wife, Louise Erdrich (nos. 425, 548), have collaborated on *The Crown of Columbus* (1990), a 382-page sometimes humorous, often satirical, mystery-detective novel, more complicated in structure and probably better for very capable and more sophisticated readers, about the discovery of a lost diary of Christopher Columbus. It has an astonishing conclusion. For comparison, see Gerald Vizenor's *The Heirs of Columbus* (no. 469).

425   Erdrich, Louise, *Tracks,* Holt, 1988 (hardcover), ISBN 0-8050-0895-0, $18.95, 226 pp.; HarperCollins, 1989 (paper), ISBN 0-06-097245-9, $9.95, 226 pp. Ages 15 up, grades 10 up.

Realistic novel of life among Chippewa (Ojibwa) Indians on their reservation in North Dakota from 1912 to 1924. The story alternates between the first-person accounts of old Nanapush, clever, keen-witted tribal elder and storyteller, and teenaged, mixed-blood Pauline, who is torn between the old beliefs and Catholicism. Events revolve around imperious Fleur Pillager, a tall, beautiful Chippewa woman, who is admired, feared, hated, and respected both for herself and for her suspected witch powers, and the attempts of the Indians to hold on to their land and the best of their old ways in the face of the rapid changes caused by the coming of the whites. Though published later, the books *Love Medicine* (1984; rev. exp., 1993) and *The Beet Queen* (1986), both involve some of the same characters as *Tracks. Tracks* is the shortest and simplest in structure. The other two have several narrators each, employ larger casts of characters, and span fifty and forty years, respectively, and hence are considerably more complex. Each of the three books can stand by itself, has rich characterizations, and involves love, hate, revenge, compassion, greed—

the basic emotions—shown mainly from the woman's point of view and told in fluid, descriptive, concrete prose. Taken together, the three form a panorama of change and adjustment among interrelated and interconnected Indians, biracials, and whites in the northern Midwest for the first three-quarters of the twentieth century. A fourth book in the series is *The Bingo Palace* (1993). With Michael Dorris (no. 424), she has published *The Crown of Columbus* (1990).

426 Glancy, Diane, *Trigger Dance*, University of Colorado Press/Fiction Collective Two, 1990 (hardcover), ISBN 0-932511-35-X, $18.95, 137 pp.; Fiction Collective, 1990 (paper), ISBN 0-932511-36-8, $8.95, 137 pp. Ages 14 up, grades 9 up.

Twelve short stories and sketches and the title novella about Native-American Indians, mainly Cherokee in present-day Oklahoma, some in the author's voice, most in an omniscient third, most serious and reflective but never dense, some wryly funny, about Indians trying to sustain their heritage in an Anglo-dominated world. The stories speak of managing with children after a failed marriage to an alcoholic; aged Anna America's feelings, memories, and tribulations as she awaits death in a nursing home; Roan and his sons confronting Grandpa's request to be cremated, all the while Roan is certain the world will soon end; Aunt Parnetta's struggles with her new refrigerator; old Joseph Stink, one-time writer, who continues to learn a new word every day—a kaleidoscope of colorful characters and ironic situations, mostly in a family setting. These carefully honed stories show that the author knows how to make her point and when to stop after she does. The title novella is particularly noteworthy. Thirteen more very short stories and prose poems and the title novella (in several disconnected sections) appear in *Firesticks* (1993). Some are surrealistic, most are cryptic or nearly cryptic, and the whole does not have the accessibility or direct appeal of *Trigger Dance*. There is some explicit sex.

427 Gregory, Kristiana, *Jenny of the Tetons*, Harcourt, 1989 (hardcover), ISBN 0-15-200480-7, $13.95, 119 pp.; (paper), ISBN 0-15-200481-5, $4.95, 119 pp. Ages 12 up, grades 7 up.

Historical novel of the American West set in the Idaho Tetons in the late 1870s. Fictitious Carrie Hill, fifteen, tells how she is orphaned in an Indian raid on her family's wagon train and is sent to live with historical trapper Beaver Dick Leigh and his real-life Shoshone wife, Jenny. In her year and a half with them, Carrie becomes hardened to the trail, grows to love Jenny, Dick, and their children, sees all but Dick die of smallpox, falls in love with and marries a young trapper, and above all gains respect and admiration for Indian ways and beliefs. The motivation for the plot strains belief—that Carrie would agree to live with Dick when she refuses to continue west with the settlers. The title implies that Jenny is the book's focus, and indeed history suggests (to judge from the author's notes) that a story about her built upon the scant information available could be enthralling, but she is only fleshed conventionally and is kept subordinate to Carrie, who is also drawn in cliched terms. The plight of the Native-American Indians at the hands of the whites becomes apparent from events, and selections from Beaver Dick's diaries, which introduce each chapter, afford fascinating glimpses into the lives of the mountain men who lived and worked among the Indians. An introduction, epilogue, short glossary of Shoshone words, maps, and a bibliography are included. To be avoided is *The Legend of Jimmy Spoon* (1990), also based on memoirs, a trite, stereotyped, and sometimes inaccurate story of a white runaway boy among the Shoshone people of historical Chief Washakie in the mid-1800s.

428   Hale, Anna W., *Mystery on Mackinac Island*, illus. Lois McLane, Harbinger House, 1989 (paper), ISBN 0-943173-34-5, $8.95, 182 pp. Ages 8–11, grades 3–7.

Contemporary, realistic mystery-detective novel set on resort Mackinac Island in Michigan's Straits of Mackinac. Intelligent, independent, capable, Native-American Hunter Martineau, thirteen, is determined to win the $100 reward for apprehending the thief who is stealing rented bicycles from tourists. He wants the money to continue living in the cabin he had shared with his just-deceased grandfather, the Old Chief. With the help of his young tourist friends Rusty and Jancy, luck, and plenty of snooping about the island, Hunter brings to justice the island trashman, Kirby Tyson, who has been smuggling his ill-gotten bikes to the mainland. Such stereotyped characters as Hunter's unfortunate, drunken father and the wise old woman librarian, and conventional Gothic incidents, including a haunted house, eerie cries in the night, numerous red herrings, and a villain easy for the reader to spot, do not diminish the story appeal. While one might quarrel about the ethnic aspects, plenty of action holds the interest, Hunter is admirable, and the island setting is strongly drawn and worked well into the story. The appearance of an Odawa (Ottawa) chief in a dream instructing Hunter to return the binoculars he "borrowed" and to set his moccasins on the right path seems didactic and too fortuitously "Indian" for complete credibility. A bibliography of books about Mackinac Island is included.

429   Highwater, Jamake, *The Ceremony of Innocence*, HarperCollins, 1985 (hardcover), ISBN 0-06-022302-2, $12.95, 186 pp. Ages 12 up, grades 7 up.

Historical novel set in Montana and California in the late 1800s and early twentieth century, continuing the story of Amana, a Blackfeet Blood woman, begun in *Legend Days* (1984) and concluded in *I Wear the Morning Star* (1986); the three books together are known as The Ghost Horse Cycle. At the end of *Legend Days*, Amana is left a widow when her husband is trampled to death during a buffalo hunt. The second book takes her from near-starvation and begging at Fort Benton through marriage to a French-Canadian trader (with whom she has a daughter, Jemina) who deserts Amana, through the painful problems of Jemina's marriage to a handsome circus rider, Cherokee Jamie Ghost Horse, and the birth of two grandsons, Reno and Sitko, during the Great Depression. The third book, told by Sitko, a talented artist, details the problems that arise for Amana who has trouble hanging on to her cultural heritage because she has been displaced to the San Fernando Valley in California and the movie realm. It pursues the problem the family face because of Jamie's alcoholism, which eventually shatters the group, and Sitko's own unhappiness in boarding school from racism and from lack of self-worth. Although the three books appear regularly on recommended lists, they are severely marred by structural defects, inept pacing, cliched diction, overwriting, melodrama, and stereotyping of characters and incidents. Best are the descriptions of traditional customs and the picture of the devastation that hits Indian areas and the Indians' descent into poverty and degradation following the white conquest. In an overly obvious monomythic sequel, *Kill Hole* (1992), homosexual Sitko is captured in the desert by a Pueblo-like group, forced to undergo trials both physical and spiritual, and emerges with a broader sense of self.

430   Highwater, Jamake, *Eyes of Darkness*, Morrow, 1985 (hardcover), ISBN 0-688-41993-3, $13.00, 191 pp. Ages 12 up, grades 7 up.

Biographical novel based on the life of Charles Alexander Eastman, a Santee Sioux born in 1858, who attended white schools, became a physician, worked among his people, and wrote his autobiography. The novel begins just before the assassination of Chief Sitting Bull and the massacre at Wounded Knee in the last days of 1890 in the area of what is now the Dakotas. The story starts with Alex East (as he is called in the novel) working at a government agency, then flashes back after Wounded Knee to his birth and youth among the nonreservation Sioux; his rearing by his grandmother and uncle; through the return from white society of his father, who had been presumed dead, is now a Christian, and sends him to white schools; and ends with East's ministering to the wounded of both races after the massacre. The novel stays close to the main incidents of Eastman's life chiefly as given in his books *Indian Boyhood* (1902) and *From the Deep Woods to Civilization* (1916), even reproducing some language verbatim. Although the novel has many graphic moments and gives a feel for Sioux traditional life and for prejudice against Indians, it is superficial in characterization, occasionally overwritten, and inclined to be polemic. Moreover, it is less emotionally engaging than Eastman's own writings, which, though employing the style of early twentieth century and in the early parts inclined to be a bit patronizing toward the Indians, are not difficult. Because of their understatement and telling detail, Eastman's works carry a conviction that the novel does not approach. No list of sources is given in Highwater's book, and a map and a brief chronology would be helpful.

431   Hill, Kirkpatrick, *Toughboy and Sister*, McElderry, 1990 (hardcover), ISBN 0-689-50506-X, $12.95, 128 pp. Ages 8–12, grades 3–7.

Survival novel of two Athabascan Indian children, Toughboy, eleven, and Sister, nine, who spend a summer alone at a remote cabin. The motherless youngsters are happy with their father, even though he sometimes stays away drinking for days. One day, at their Yukon River summer fishing camp, he leaves and returns drunk. They cannot get him from the boat where he is sprawled, and the next day he is dead. In the storm that follows, the inexpertly tied boat is swept away. Not until after school starts in the fall does old Natasha, the village wise woman, arrive to investigate. When she sees how well they have managed, she decides that they are old enough to care for themselves and says they can live with her. Although the language is easy, the story is not oversimplified or written down to a young audience. The children's often clumsy efforts to cope with their dwindling food supply and a marauding bear are far more realistic than in most Robinsonnades, and their mutual dependence, occasional squabbling, and dread of being separated and sent to distant relatives make them believable and appealing characters. In a sequel, *Winter Camp* (1993), Toughboy and Sister go with Natasha to her isolated cabin to run her trapline, as she used to do years before. When Nelson, a visiting prospector, is injured by a moose, she takes his dog team and heads for McGrath, seventy-five miles away, to get help, although the temperature is dropping rapidly, leaving the children with the old man getting weaker and the thermometer at more than fifty below zero. Both children make mistakes that could be fatal, but with hard work and Nelson's advice they hold out until the air rescue helicopter arrives to fly them out. Although the children are individualized and believable protagonists, the two old people are the strongest characters, both longing for the old ways, genial, supportive Nelson contrasting with cranky Natasha. Speculation by both Toughboy and Sister about which is preferable, the traditional way symbolized by the dog team or the new way of the helicopter, adds depth to the survival story.

432   Hillerman, Tony, *Sacred Clowns*, HarperCollins, 1993 (hardcover), ISBN 0-06-016767-X, $23.00, 305 pp. Ages 14 up, grades 9 up.

Mystery novel set on the Navajo reservation and the Tano Pueblo in New Mexico. The story features Tribal Police Officer Jim Chee and Lieutenant Joe Leaphorn, who working together solve murders at a Tano ceremonial and at a Navajo boarding school, cases that at first seem unrelated but prove to be tied together by the making and selling of fake Native-American artifacts. This is one of several novels about the two, notably *Coyote Waits* (1990), in which they investigate on separate paths the murder of a fellow officer. Chee has arrested an aging Navajo shaman who seems to have no motive and about whose guilt there is some question. The unraveling of the complicated mystery involves a university history professor, a graduate student, the remains of a turn-of-the-century bandit who might have been Butch Cassidy, a Vietnamese refugee family, and a modern young Navajo woman attorney. Others include *Skinwalkers* (1988), which deals with the Navajo belief in witches; *A Thief of Time* (1988), about physical anthropologists and illegal pot hunters in the Anasazi ruins; and *Talking God* (1989), which is set mostly in Washington, D.C., and concerns artifacts in the Smithsonian Institution. All are notable for treating Navajo traditions and beliefs with respect. In some, the plot problem or a subplot hinges on the curse of alcohol to reservation people.

433   Hirsch, Ron, *Seya's Song*, illus. Constance R. Bergum, Sasquatch, 1992 (hardcover), ISBN 0-912365-62-5, $14.95, unp. Ages 4–10, grades PS–5.

Realistic picture-story book set among the Klallam (S'Klallam, Clallam) Indians of the Pacific Northwest. As she walks through the countryside at different seasons, a little Klallam girl describes what she sees, using the Klallam words her Grandmother (Seya) taught her for creatures and objects like salmon, blackberries, and whales. She also speaks of traditional activities for each time of the year. This is a quiet, pensive book without tension or climax. The parenthesized Klallam words, which interrupt the sequence of thought and seem overly intrusive, make the book into a kind of vocabulary lesson. The full-color paintings mirror the activities in the text and are especially striking for the animals, like the elk, which seems so magnificently mighty and so lifelike in appearance one can almost feel the hair on his hide, and for those where Northwest coast traditional motifs appear. A glossary of native words is included as well as a note about the Klallam.

434   Hobbs, Will, *Bearstone*, Atheneum, 1989 (hardcover), ISBN 0-689-31496-5, $12.95, 144 pp.; Avon, 1991 (paper), ISBN 0-380-71249-0, $3.50, 154 pp. Ages 10–14, grades 5–9.

Realistic, contemporary boy's growing-up and adventure novel set mostly in the high mountains of western Colorado. Parentless, fourteen-year-old, Ute-Navajo Cloyd Atcitty, considered intractable at the boarding school to which the Ute tribe has sent him, is taken by a social worker to live temporarily with an old rancher-miner, Walter Landis. Although he enjoys the hard work and loves his blue roan horse, Cloyd's resentment spills over and he destroys Walter's cherished peach trees. The old man repairs the rift by taking the boy into the mountains to help reopen his old mine. Accidents and hair-raising adventures met with physical strength and good judgment elevate the boy's self-esteem to the extent that in the fall he does better in school and elects to stay on the ranch. The characters, events, and conclusion are conventional for the western-ranching-survival genre. The boy's feelings at being displaced from the southern Utah area he loves and his intense desire to live up to the secret name he adopts and to learn more about his heritage are credible if not original. Excitement abounds, and the passages in the mountains convey the beauty and power of the higher elevations. In the sequel, *Beardance* (1993), Cloyd accompanies Walter to his mine in the San Juan Mountains, where he tries to help orphaned grizzly cubs and strengthens his cultural identity.

435   Hogan, Linda, *Mean Spirit*, Atheneum, 1990 (hardcover), ISBN 0-689-12101-6, $19.95, 375 pp.; Ivy, 1992 (paper), ISBN 0-8041-0863-3, $4.99, 375 pp. Ages 14 up, grades 9 up.

Historical novel involving real people and events set in the oil country of northern Oklahoma near Guthrie. This broad-canvas story has a large cast of colorful characters, mainly mixed bloods and half bloods of Osage descent, and plenty of local flavor. In the early 1920s, oil-rich Indians become the target of white intimidation and exploitation. The book is set up as a kind of mystery—who is behind the series of unexplained murders of Indians, the latest the shooting-slaying of beautiful, wealthy, Osage Grace Blanket? Into the web of intrigue are drawn the entire town of Watona, Indian and white, including Grace's lovely daughter, Nola, who at thirteen marries her white guardian's son, Will, for her physical protection; and Stacey Red Hawk, idealistic Sioux agent for the United States Bureau of Investigation. The story unravels slowly, murder compounding murder, red herrings galore, with deceit, bribery, and unconscionable acts among local officials and in high places, and unselfish heroism among Indians, until finally John Hale, rancher and oil man, presumed friend of the Indians, stands exposed. The novel's main force comes from the sense of the times, laying open the utter disregard on the one hand not only of Indian rights but also of Indians as people, and on the other the Indians' realization that the law which seemingly is to protect their rights is in actuality void, and thus resignation and acceptance become essential for their survival. Other characters that stand out are Indian landowners Moses and Belle Graycloud, who are reduced to financial penury by white duplicity; Michael Horse, educated veteran and prophet; Baptist minister Joe Billy and his white wife; and historical John Stink, who becomes a living ghost, all of whom eventually take to the hills for refuge. The book moves unevenly with many changes of scene, uneven pacing, disturbing shifts, and undisciplined use of detail, and the characters are so numerous they are hard to keep track of; however, the novel excels as a heart-wrenching, temper-arousing look at a terrible period in American history. Brief author's note about historicity at the end. For Hogan's poems and short stories, see *Savings: Poems* (no. 555) and *Red Clay: Poems and Stories* (no. 436).

436   Hogan, Linda, *Red Clay: Poems and Stories*, Greenfield Review, 1991 (paper), ISBN 0-912678-83-6, $9.95, 81 pp. Ages 14 up, grades 9 up.

Four short stories and twenty-six mostly one-page poems, with introductions, by a Chickasaw writer. The four pleasingly written stories are strongly Oklahoma localized, speaking of horse trading, night riders, night fishing, and a visit to an old grandmother who cleverly confuses a white woman. The stories move fast, concern Hogan's ancestors and the region in which they farmed, and give a glimpse into the hard times of the Depression and the land grabbing that followed on the discovery of oil in Indian territory. The first short story, "The Black Horse," which was told and then written down by Hogan's father, has an oral storytelling flavor. The second story, "That Horse," which is Hogan's elaboration upon the first story, is more literary. The two provide an interesting contrast in styles. The poems, which represent "an identification with my tribe and the Oklahoma earth," speak with understatement and much visual and auditory imagery of various animals, the birth of a colt, hackberry trees, ponds, canyons, grandparents, and other family members. They are clear, skillfully composed, and telling. Hogan has also published other collections of poems, for example, *Savings: Poems* (no. 555), and a novel, *Mean Spirit* (no. 435).

437   Hoobler, Dorothy, and Thomas Hoobler, *The Trail on Which They Wept: The Story of a Cherokee Girl*, illus. S. S. Burris, Silver Burdett, 1992 (hardcover), ISBN 0-382-24333-1, $12.95, 57 pp. Ages 8–12, grades 3–7.

Easy-reading historical novel of the forced removal of the Native-American Cherokees in 1837. Soldiers come to the Georgia plantation of the father of Sarah Rogers, who is ten or twelve, Christian and white-educated, and put the family out for a white farmer who has won their land in a lottery, which is happening to other Cherokees as well. Historical Chief John Ross informs the people that, in spite of his best efforts, President Martin Van Buren refuses to stay the evacuation begun under President Andrew Jackson. The people must leave hastily, and the bulk of the book describes the long, sad, hard journey to Oklahoma and the difficulties of resettlement there. Personalizing the event are such details as Sarah's having to leave behind party dresses and her piano, the burning of her old grandmother's lodge by soldiers while whites watch, the pandemonium of being herded into a stockade, lack of food and water, cold, illness, crossing the Ohio and the Mississippi rivers, and the death of the grandmother, a sad occasion for Sarah but only one of many on this trek of 115 days during which one-quarter of the Cherokees die. On a psychological level, Sarah comes to hate the white culture she has assimilated, and she insists on being called by her Cherokee name of Tsaluh, until in Oklahoma the historical Cherokee leader Sequoyah, developer of the Cherokee alphabet, visits the Rogers family and helps her to see the importance of being guided by the best of both her cultures. Part of the Her Story series, based on important events in American history, the book serves its purpose of being an easily assimilated overview of the Trail of Tears. There is enough excitement and emotion to hold the interest, but an instructive tone sometimes intrudes, and characters and incidents are minimally developed. A map would be helpful, although several black-and-white illustrations that depict characters and incidents add interest, but the writers do not indicate how much of the story is historical. Unfortunately, the last pages, about how to make a medicine belt like the one Sarah's grandmother made for her, have the effect of lessening the horror of this dark period in American history of which the story otherwise gives a good feeling in its limited way. Others by the Hooblers in the same series include *A Promise at the Alamo: The Story of a Texas Girl* (no. 359) and *Aloha Means Come Back: The Story of a World War II Girl* (no. 234), about Pearl Harbor.

438 Hotze, Sollace, *A Circle Unbroken*, Houghton, 1988 (hardcover), ISBN 0-89919-733-7, $13.95, 202 pp.; Clarion, 1988 (paper), ISBN 0-395-59702-1, $4.95, 202 pp. Ages 12 up, grades 7 up.

Historical novel of Native Americans that begins in 1845. After living happily for seven years near the Black Hills as the daughter of a Sioux chief, a seventeen-year-old captive, white Kata Wi, formerly Rachel Porter, is recaptured by bounty hunters and returned to her embittered minister father in Saint Joseph, Missouri. Her inability to renounce completely a way of life she cherished as her father demands and hurt by the disparaging remarks of white women about her background and Indians in general, Rachel decides to return to the Sioux. The book's weakest aspects are its plot, which goes as expected, and minimal characterization. Its strengths come from its stark picture of the problems that repatriated whites had in adjusting and of the vivid contrast in the ways of life and especially in spiritual values between whites and Native Americans. Some romance, some pathos, and some excitement are woven into the story.

439 Humphrey, William, *No Resting Place*, Delacorte, 1989 (hardcover), ISBN 0-385-29729-7, $18.95, 256 pp.; Delta, 1990 (paper), ISBN 0-317-99667-3, $10.95, 256 pp. Ages 14 up, grades 9 up.

Historical novel of the forced removal of the Cherokees from their ancestral lands in Georgia to Oklahoma in the mid-1830s. The events are recounted by thirteen-year-old Amos Smith IV on the occasion of the Texas Centennial of independence in 1836, as told to him by his father, the great-grandson of Amos Ferguson, later known as Amos Smith I. The grandson of highly respected, half-blood Abel Ferguson, Georgia Cherokee landowner, and son of David, a prominent physician who emigrated to Oklahoma earlier, Amos and his grandparents become part of the group led by Chief John Ross, who suffered unspeakable indignities and untold losses in life and fortunes when the United States government evacuated them west. The account is history only somewhat relieved by personalizing and is many times overwritten for effect. Its strength lies in its arousal of horror and outrage at how the Cherokees, and those who tried to help them in their suffering, were treated. A map and a chronological table would have been helpful, and the lack of a note about historicity is a grievous omission. As it is, the uninformed reader has no way of knowing how much, which parts, and which figures are true. In many ways, this is a very powerful book, one that neither glorifies the Indians nor completely vilifies the whites, but still it makes the point very clearly that a grave injustice was done to the Cherokees.

440   Kesey, Ken, *The Sea Lion: A Story of the Sea Cliff People*, illus. Neil Waldman, Viking, 1991 (hardcover), ISBN 0-670-83916-7, $14.95, 48 pp. Ages 8–12, grades 3–7.

Long picture-story fantasy set among a tribe of Native-American Indians called the Sea Cliff People in the Pacific Northwest at an unspecified time. Despised for his small size and crippled back and leg, orphaned Eemook, a slave, tribal spoon maker, and skilled carver, yearns to be worthy of Shoola, the chief's daughter. When a terrible storm hits, a majestically large, handsome, regally garbed stranger wearing a gleaming shell pendant, bursts into the longhouse and engages in a duel of shadow-making with Eemook's guardian, the tribal herb woman, intent on stealing away Shoola. Eemook saves her by declaring a potlach at which every man must sacrifice his most prized possession, initiating the exchange by contributing his own precious, elaborately carved spoon handle, and thus forcing the stranger to relinquish the magical shell of power. The tribe rises against the man and his companion dark demons, forcing them over the cliffs and into the sea, from which the stranger emerges as the hairy-maned Lion of the Sea. The following spring all the maidens of the tribe, except Shoola, give birth to babies covered with golden hair, who become the bellowing Sea Lion People. Kesey's improvisation on the Celtic Selkie legend for a Native-American *pourquoi* is moderately successful. Diction is uneven, occasionally striking in imagery, sometimes trite and even ponderous. The basic story of the triumph of the despised is dramatic with conflict after the stranger arrives, but the story is slow starting and unevenly paced, and it offers no surprises. The depiction of the Native People is questionable even for fantasy, and the "pop art" illustrations make use of Pacific Coast motifs but often quite literally overwhelm the text, being superimposed upon it in pink, blue, and orange tones that distract.

441   Lesley, Craig, *River Song*, Houghton, 1989 (hardcover), ISBN 0-395-43086-6, $18.95, 307 pp.; Dell, 1990 (paper), ISBN 0-317-99666-5, $8.95, 307 pp. Ages 15 up, grades 10 up.

Contemporary novel about Nez Perce Indians mainly along the Columbia River in Oregon, sequel to *Winterkill* (1984). Danny Kachiah and his son, Jack, seventeen, whom Danny has reclaimed from Jack's stepfather now that Danny's ex-wife is dead, drift from job to job, fighting fires, picking fruit, whatever comes along, while Jack rodeos, trying to make good at Danny's own sometime unsuccessful calling. Determined to give Jack a sense of cultural heritage, Danny settles in with an old salmon fisherman, Willis Salish, at the same time attempting to lay to rest disturbing ghosts from his past, straighten out fishing rights for the Indians, and come to terms with Pudge, a longtime girlfriend. Pride in heritage is important in this book, the characterizations are strong, the episodes stand out, and the story excels in showing prejudice against Native Americans and their resentment at having lost their lands and not being given equal treatment under the law. Some myths are interwoven into the action, a few ceremonies take place, and some fascinating history, especially in the portions about Chief Joseph and his people, is included.

442 Lesley, Craig, ed., *Talking Leaves: Contemporary Native American Short Stories*, Laurel, 1991 (paper), ISBN 0-440-50344-2, $10.00, 385 pp. Ages 14 up, grades 9 up.

Thirty-eight short stories from almost as many Native-American Indian writers of different tribal backgrounds, arranged alphabetically by writer. Established and award-winning authors represented are Joy Harjo, James Welch, and Gerald Vizenor; less well-known or rising ones include Kathleen Hill, Elizabeth Woody, and Greg Sarris. The opening story, by Paula Gunn Allen, "The Deer Woman," suspensefully reworks the traditional plains legend, with an unexpected twist, and Anna Lee Walters's "Bicenti" works on the nerves with weird happenings among present-day, educated Indians in Santa Fe. In a story by Roberta Hill Whiteman, fifteen-year-old Indian Phoebe encounters prejudice and callousness from her employers when she works as a summer girl for a wealthy couple in Lake Forest, Illinois. A young Klallam sailor is sentenced to the brig, where he is verbally abused and degraded by a racist sergeant, and finds consolation in memories of forest and elders in a story by Duane Niatum. In a short piece by Vickie Sears, a little Assiniboin foster girl gains self-esteem by associating with a seventy-year-old woman powwow dancer. The stories reflect suburbia, Alaskan village life, the Colorado territory at the time of Black Kettle, the White Earth reservation in Minnesota—a variety of settings and subjects. Chapters from longer works appear, including "Queen of Diamonds" from Michael Dorris's *Yellow Raft in Blue Water* (no. 424) and "She Is Beautiful in Her Whole Being" from *The Ancient Child* (no. 448) by N. Scott Momaday. If some selections lose their punch or peter out, the vast majority stay interesting; as a whole, this is a satisfying representation of contemporary Indian short fiction. An introduction by the editor and biographical notes at the end are included.

443 Levin, Betty, *Brother Moose*, Greenwillow, 1990 (hardcover), ISBN 0-688-09266-7, $12.95, 213 pp. Ages 9–12, grades 4–7.

Historical novel of the settlement of New Brunswick and Maine in the very late 1800s. Two orphaned white girls, Nell and retarded Louisa, from a Nova Scotia children's home, both about twelve, are helped by Native American

Joe Pennowit, a lumberman and woodsman, and his grandson, Peter, thirteen, to reach their home in the Maine woods. Without Joe's courage, determination, outdoor skills, and persistence, the little party would not have survived the rigors of their overland journey by horse and wagon and foot through the dense woods and the unexpectedly early winter, the numerous wettings, harsh winds, ice, snow, and lack of food and shelter. Although the reader is asked to identify with Nell, from whose vantage the third-person narrative progresses, Joe dominates the book. At first apparently a murderer who happens to help the girls, it is later revealed that he killed for Nell's sake and that he is a genuinely good, honest, unself-pitying man of hard life, who though admired by many who have come to know him is still mostly tarred with the negative brush typical of the period. The narrative is uneven and episodes are inadequately exploited, but the flavor of the deep woods is strong, racial attitudes clear, and Louisa's retardation well handled. The title comes from Louisa's name for a moose captured and tamed by Joe which dies tragically. An author's note about orphan placement and Native Americans of the period is included.

444 Lipsyte, Robert, *The Brave*, HarperCollins, 1991 (hardcover), ISBN 0-06-023915-8, $14.95, 195 pp. Ages 12 up, grades 7 up.

Sports novel. Touchy, belligerent, seventeen-year-old Sonny Bear has been left by his erratic mother on the Moscondaga Reservation with his great-uncle, Jake, who has taught him boxing and has tried to teach him traditional lore and control of his violent temper. Disgusted with the hand-to-mouth life, Sonny leaves to join the army but, right off the bus in New York City, he is waylaid by a young African-American drug dealer, Stick, and his pretty blond accomplice, Doll. Soon he is arrested by Police Sergeant Alfred Brooks, sent to a juvenile correction facility, knifed and hospitalized. Brooks gets him into Donatelli's Gym, run now by Henry Johnson, where his training partner is fat, black Martin Witherspoon. The rest of the book details his intense training, his first fights, his fury when Brooks is shot and crippled by Stick, and his apprehension, with Martin's help, of Stick who has long eluded police. Although the main focus of the book is on boxing, the stories of the Running Braves, which Jake tells the boy, and the difficulties of a modern half-Indian in a rough urban culture serve to give meaning and motivation to the novel. The gym, Brooks, and several other characters earlier appeared in *The Contender* (1967). A sequel, *The Chief* (1993) is narrated by Martin, Sonny Bear's self-appointed "writer," who is now in college but still follows Sonny, Jake, and Alfred (in his wheelchair) to the small-town, often rigged, fights. Sonny and Martin fly to Las Vegas and, partly through luck, they get a chance at an important fight and, eventually, at the championship. Trouble, in the shape of gambling interests trying to build a casino on the reservation, finally arouses

Sonny's latent pride in his heritage and, after Jake is shot, he makes a much publicized three-hundred mile run from the governor's office to the longhouse of the reservation to rally his people and insist on their rights. Although the book ends before the big fight, Sonny's chances look good, Martin has material for his book, and Jake has prevailed in awakening Sonny to the importance of his background. Lipsyte's writing is tight, fast paced, and compelling, with good character development and strong sensory descriptions of the training and the fights.

445 Luenn, Nancy, *Song for the Ancient Forest*, illus. Jill Kastner, Atheneum, 1993 (hardcover), ISBN 0-689-31719-0, $14.95, unp. Ages 4–10, grades PS–6.

Picture-story book of fantasy in which an animal interacts with humans. Concerned by a troubling dream foretelling the end of the forest and its creatures, Raven beseeches the world spirit for a song of power to prevent the dream from coming true. He sings it for the brown people (shown as Indians in the pictures), who do not believe that the forest can ever end. Years later, a new people arrive (shown as whites), who push the first people out and, unheeding of Raven's song, clear the land. Only a little modern girl named Marni listens and convinces her father, a logger, who appeals to his fellow workers. The recalcitrant landowner hesitates, but when the trees themselves take up Raven's song, the owner and crew run away in terror. The patently didactic text, which leaves the reader hanging, has a certain choppiness that impedes the narrative flow disconcertingly. The strongly composed, muted oils employ Northwest Indian motifs and various techniques, like inserts, to augment the storytelling and create setting. They make the book visually very attractive.

446 Lyon, George Ella, *Dreamplace*, illus. Peter Catalanotto, Orchard, 1993 (hardcover), ISBN 0-531-05466-7, $15.95, unp. Ages 4–10, grades PS–5.

Realistic picture-story book about the prehistoric Anasazi Indians. A young girl of six or seven tells how she and her family drive "up a steep road, hike a paved trail . . . [that is] all plain as beans" until she is on the ancient site and hears the guide describe the archaeological aspects and the ancient inhabitants. During the guide's talk, what the girl sees in actuality fades away and she imagines the ancient ones going about their everyday lives, making pots, dancing, grinding corn, fetching water, and the like, until it is time to leave and she comes back to reality. The understated, impressionistic text employs distinctive phrases and Indian words, giving a limited sense of what the times were like without sounding instructive. Fleshing out the text are equally impressionistic, full-color paintings of the Mesa Verde ruins. The imagined pictures have a hazy quality at first, becoming more definite as the girl moves into the made-up world, while the here-and-now ones remain representational. The pictures convey an excellent sense of place, with striking views of the ruins up close, in kivas, and from a bird's-eye vantage. The ancient figures and activities seem compatible with archaeological discoveries and present-day Pueblo behavior. A note about the Anasazi and sources of information for both story and pictures and a map of major Anasazi sites would be helpful.

447 Meyer, Carolyn, *Where the Broken Heart Still Beats*, Harcourt, 1992 (hardcover), ISBN 0-15-200639-7, $16.95, 196 pp.; (paper), ISBN 0-15-295602-6, $6.95, 196 pp. Ages 8–12, grades 3–7.

Biographical novel based on the fragmentary historical facts known about Cynthia Ann Parker. Captured by Comanches from her pioneer home in West Texas in 1836, when she was nine, Parker was recaptured near the Pease River by Texas Rangers in 1860. The story focuses on her life after her return to white relatives with her infant daughter, Topsannah or Prairie Flower, and their efforts to force her to give up her name, Naduah, and her Indian ways and allegiance. Told in alternate chapters of third-person narration and entries from the fictitious journal of her twelve-year-old cousin, Lucy Parker, the novel records her longing for her two sons, now Comanche warriors, and her Native-American people and her misery among her white family, who are mostly well meaning but, except for Lucy, without sympathy or understanding of her great loss. Because of the Civil War, her uncle is unable to keep his promise that she will be allowed to visit her Indian family, and after the death of her young daughter she gives up hope and soon dies. The story, whose details have been almost entirely invented, is strongly sympathetic to her love for the Comanche life and critical of the obtuse bigotry of the white people, especially the older women. Although white by ancestry, Cynthia Ann is pictured as Native American by training and affection.

448 Momaday, N. Scott, *The Ancient Child*, Doubleday, 1989 (hardcover), ISBN 0-385-27972-8, $18.95, 315 pp.; HarperCollins, 1990 (paper), ISBN 0-06-097345-5, $11.00, 336 pp. Ages 15 up, grades 10 up.

Realistic novel set in rural, western Oklahoma and on the outback of the Navajo reservation in Arizona. After his Anglo adoptive father dies, Kiowa-born, Anglo-raised Set, a world-famous painter, reclaims his heritage and self-esteem with the help of a strong-willed, beautiful, seemingly ageless

Kiowa-Navajo girl of nineteen named Grey, who has been taught medicine secrets by her very old great-grandmother. The book is made powerful and also complicated by the mingling of Wild West legends about Billy the Kid and Navajo and Kiowa beliefs, myths, and history. Although it is a significant statement about present-day conditions for Native-American Indians and the continuity of culture, the book is less accessible for high school youth than the author's earlier Pulitzer Prize–winning *House Made of Dawn* (1966), about a young Tanoan man's efforts to find his cultural identity after he returns from World War II, and *The Way to Rainy Mountain* (1969), which combines Momaday family history and Kiowa history, legends, and beliefs.

449   O'Dell, Scott, *Streams to the River, River to the Sea*, Houghton, 1986 (hardcover), ISBN 0-395-40430-4, $14.95, 176 pp. Ages 12 up, grades 7 up.

Biographical novel of Sacagawea, the young Native-American woman of the Agiduka Shoshone people who accompanied the Lewis and Clark expedition to the Pacific Coast in the first decade of the nineteenth century. Starting when she is thirteen, it tells of her capture and enslavement by the Minnetarees from the east, near what is now Mandan, North Dakota, and how she is won in a gambling game by Charbonneau, a half-French, half-Sioux trader, as his second wife. When Captain William Clark hires her husband as a guide, he knows that Sacagawea is the best part of the bargain, and he delays the trip until her baby is born. Near Three Forks, Montana, the headwaters of the Missouri, they meet her brother and through him get horses to cross the Rocky Mountains. The narrative closely follows the journals of the expedition, but speaks in the voice of the Indian woman and adds her deep love for Clark, which may well have been true, since he proposed to take her back to Saint Louis. Aware, however, that whites who marry Indians are looked down upon, she takes her young child and heads back to her people, no longer feeling bound to Charbonneau, who has proved treacherous on the trip. The understatement and emotional restraint of the protagonist seem appropriate in a woman who endured great hardship and won the respect of the explorers.

450   O'Dell, Scott, and Elizabeth Hall, *Thunder Rolling in the Mountains*, Houghton, 1992 (hardcover), ISBN 0-395-59966-0, $14.95, 128 pp. Ages 8–12, grades 3–7.

Historical novel telling of the doomed but heroic trek of the Nez Perce led by Chief Joseph in 1877 in an effort to evade the American soldiers who were trying to force them onto a reservation. Told in the first person by Sound of Running Feet, daughter of Joseph, it details their almost incredible journey, with children and old people, much of it with many wounded, from the Wallowa Valley in what is now eastern Oregon through the Bitterroot Valley and the Yellowstone Park region, across the rugged Absaroka Mountains and northward in Montana to the Bear Paw Mountains, in an effort to reach the "Old Lady's country," Canada, to which Sitting Bull and his people had earlier escaped. A foreword by Hall, O'Dell's wife who shared in the research and completed the manuscript after his death in 1989, says that most of the characters are actual historical figures and that the narrative closely follows the journey and battles as recorded by both the Nez Perce and U.S. Army personnel. This is both its strength and weakness as fiction. Much of the power of the story comes from the reader's realization that this really happened, but at the same time foreknowledge of the outcome robs it of suspense and the possibility of a happier outcome.

451 Osofsky, Audrey, *Dreamcatcher*, illus. Ed Young, Orchard, 1992 (hardcover), ISBN 0-531-08588-0, $14.95, unp. Ages 4–7, grades PS–2.

Realistic picture-story book set in a northern woodland "in the moon of the raspberries in a time long ago." An Ojibwa baby sleeps snugly in a cradleboard while Mother goes about her tasks. The baby's big sister weaves a dream web to attach to the cradleboard loop. It catches "dark dreams" so that the little one sleeps the night through peacefully. Ed Young's full-color, mystical pastels depict scenes from traditional, northern, everyday Indian life, accentuating the setting with many Ojibwa motifs drawn from nature. The softly rendered impressionism of the pictures complements the melody and dreaminess of the simple, spare text.

452 Owens, Louis, *The Sharpest Sight*, University of Oklahoma Press, 1992 (hardcover), ISBN 0-8061-2404-0, $19.95, 263 pp. Ages 15 up, grades 10 up.

Realistic mystery novel in a family and community setting about Choctaws living in the California mountains and in Mississippi. Mundo Morales, young Hispanic-Indian deputy in the village of Amaraga, California, investigates the disappearance of his childhood friend and deranged Vietnam buddy, part Choctaw Attis McCurtain, who is eventually found dead, having drowned in the local river. All the while Mundo seeks to keep Attis's father, Hoey, from murdering the man Hoey thinks is responsible for his son's death. Hoey, who has mystical powers, is also determined to send his other son, Cole, back to their Choctaw relatives, especially Uncle Luther, also a mystic, where he will be close to their roots. An atmosphere of foreboding and things inexplicable predominates from the very beginning, where Mundo has a vision of Attis in the river, to the end, where his old dead grandfather appears occasionally to give advice and where Cole and Hoey return to Mississippi for good to find Uncle Luther awaiting their arrival, having in his mysterious way known when they were coming. Old beliefs come through strongly, and white greed, materialism, and disdain for Indians play a role. The action drops in the middle, the mysticism sometimes annoys, and the conclusion may not please the reader, but it fits the story as it unfolds. The sense of mixed Indian, Hispanic, and white small-town life is vivid. There is explicit sex, and earthy language is used occasionally.

453   Owens, Louis, *Wolfsong*, West End, 1991 (paper), ISBN 0-931122-66-X, $12.95, 249 pp. Ages 15 up, grades 10 up.

Realistic, contemporary novel set in Washington's northern Cascades Mountains. Stehemish (Salish Native-American Indian) Tom Joseph, one of the few boys from the tiny town of Forks ever to win a scholarship, comes home from college in California. He has returned to attend the funeral of his Uncle Jim, the last tribal singer in the region. A personal problem soon develops when his girl is promised to the son of the "town owner." Then he becomes involved in a public controversy—since logging wanes, the town sees economic opportunity in an open-pit copper mine to be built in the protected wilderness. The book moves slowly but relentlessly to the inevitably tragic conclusion, as Tom, unable to find value in the outer world and discovering the Indian one gone, takes matters into his own hands. Important ideas appear, including local versus multinational ownership, conservation versus economics, Indian spirituality versus Anglo pragmatism, accommodation, assimilation, pride in heritage, and prejudice against Indians. Except for the major ones, most of the characters are functional and indistinguishable from one another; Tom is too inarticulate and reactive for sympathy; and he and his brother, Jimmy, a young, fat, near-alcoholic, represent two kinds of modern Indians, the former idealistic, the latter acculturating for expediency. Although the novel overextends itself, it is never dull, and descriptions of the forests are beautiful.

454   Pitts, Paul, *Racing the Sun*, Avon, 1988 (paper), ISBN 0-380-75496-7, $3.50, 150 pp. Ages 8–12, grades 3–7.

Boy's growing-up novel set in Salt Lake City, Utah, in recent years. The story revolves around a Native-American Indian, suburban family's gaining respect for their Navajo heritage. Twelve-year-old Brandon Rogers is not sure he likes having his ailing paternal Grandpa Redhouse, a reservation Indian, living with them. Grandpa shares his room, gets him up in the dark for dawn runs, and keeps him awake in the evening with his night chants. But Brandon gradually comes to love the old man and to admire his inner strength and accepting ways. The boy begins to enjoy racing the rising sun so much that he persuades his closest pal to participate. He learns to appreciate the Navajo customs that his university professor father, especially, seems ashamed of. When the old man senses that his death is near and asks to go home, Brandon, knowing his parents would disapprove, draws money from his college account and on his own takes his grandfather by bus to the reservation, where near his children and grandchildren and on his own soil the old man dies. The way Brandon's nuclear family comes to accept Grandpa Redhouse in their home and to gain a realization of the importance of the larger family unit and respect for tradition seems natural, and the message that Indians can live among Anglos and respect and even maintain many of the old ways is worked into the narrative without explicit statement. Dialogue is often too witty and grownup sounding for Brandon and his friends, like an adult speaking, or the wiseacre chatter of a television family. A predictable but pleasing aspect is the reconciliation between the grandfather and Brandon's father. The mother is the strong, sensible modern Navajo woman, center of life but not stereotyped. Details of family life are typical of the suburban middle class, and there is abundant humor. Also by Pitts is *The Shadowman's Way* (1992), in which a Navajo boy of thirteen befriends a white youth, who becomes the object of racial intolerance from Navajo classmates. A fast-moving style, some contrivance, and a limited sense of reservation town and school life are found in the book.

455 Polacco, Patricia, *Boat Ride with Lillian Two Blossom*, illus. Patricia Polacco, Philomel, 1988 (hardcover), ISBN 0-399-21470-4, $14.95, unp. Ages 5–8, grades K–3.

Fantasy picture-story book set in Michigan, probably in the early twentieth century. Mabel, playing along the shore of Kalaska Pond with her older brother, William, who is fishing, and their pet goat, Banana Joe, keeps asking questions, "What makes it rain? Where does the wind come from? Why does the moon look so cold," to which William always answers, "I dunno, Sparky." An old Indian woman appears and takes them for a wild ride in their airborne rowboat through the skies where they see the wolves whose howls cause the wind, the great spirit caribou that gallops across the sky with the sun in his antlers, the polar-bear spirit that carries the moon through the heavens, and other wonders of nature myth. Although the explanations are similar to those in some Native-American tales, they are not presented as genuine legend, and the fantasy setting distinguishes them from documented folklore. Illustrations are in vivid color, with the red-haired children in straw hats and the old Indian realistically wrinkled until, in the boat ride through the sky, she becomes young and beautiful.

456 Prusski, Jeffrey, *Bring Back the Deer*, illus. Neil Waldman, Harcourt, 1988 (hardcover), ISBN 0-15-200418-1, $13.95, unp. Ages 4–10, grades PS–5.

Fantasy picture-story book of Native-American Indians, probably intentionally generic. When his father does not return from the hunt and the family needs food, an Indian youth, who is being instructed in beliefs by his aged grandfather, embarks on the hunt, both actual and symbolic ritual, evidently. He follows his father's footprints, encounters a wolf by a stream, spots a buck, and trails it, as does the wolf. He races the wolf for the buck, knife at the ready, and suddenly finds himself at home. The wolf becomes the figure of his father, and the buck blends with the figure of his grandfather. The story's point is not clear, the tone is instructive of Indian life in many places, and the language is often cliched. The abstract illustrations are sometimes elegant. They emphasize the mystical aspects, with romantic paintings, silhouettes, and little animal figures and symbols patterned after ancient Indian artwork. The pink tones do not fit, but the portraits of the grandmother and the wolf and the silhouette of the buck's horns are magnificent.

457 Roesch, E. P., *Ashana*, Random, 1990 (hardcover), ISBN 0-394-56963-6, $19.95, 401 pp.; Ballantine, 1991 (paper), ISBN 0-345-37298-0, $5.99, 414 pp. Ages 15 up, grades 10 up.

Historical novel beginning in the 1790s and extending into the third generation that tells of the Russian conquest and settlement of the coast of Alaska by the Russian-American Trading Company. The main characters, general outlines of the story, and the significant details of the conquest are true. Along with many of her tribe, fifteen-year-old Ashana, the narrator daughter of the *queshqa* (chief) of her clan of Athabascan Indians of the Kenai Peninsula in Alayeksa (Alaska), is taken hostage by the Tahtna (Russian) invader, Aleksandr Baranov, to his headquarters on what is now Kodiak Island and is forced to become the concubine of the proud, ambitious, power-hungry governor and trading-company director. She bears him two children, both of whom are raised as Russian nobles, although she tries persistently to keep them aware of their Native-American antecedents. In spite of numerous indignities and with the help of some devoted friends, Ashana maintains her self-respect and many of her ways and even smuggles guns to her people. Helped by her girlhood husband to escape, she is kidnapped again by Baranov's men, along with her children, and she lives out her life on remote Kodiak, a grand lady to her people if despised by the Russians. This broad-spectrum story features a large but distinctive cast, the most memorable of whom are the indomitable princess, the brutish yet vulnerable and strangely likable Baranov, and their son, who epitomizes the dilemma and condition of half bloods. The novel sets in stark relief the suffering of the Indians in the face of Anglo greed and inhumanity, particularly the rape and brutalizing of the women, and the chasm between the worldview of the two peoples which emerges through numerous incidents and conversations. This is a long book, but the uncomplicated, linear structure is easy to follow. Maps, a historical introduction, and a bibliography are included.

458   Roop, Peter, and Connie Roop, *Ahyoka and the Talking Leaves*, illus. Yoshi Miyake, Lothrop, 1992 (hardcover), ISBN 0-688-10697-8, $12.00, 60 pp. Ages 7–10, grades 2–5.

Short historical novel about Sequoyah's invention of the Cherokee alphabet in the early nineteenth century. The story is told from the vantage of, but not by, his daughter, Ahyoka, who, according to this story, conceived the basic idea for the alphabet. After her disapproving mother divorces her father for irresponsibility by putting his things outside the house because he devotes all his time to trying to devise "talking leaves," Ahyoka joins him in leaving their Williston, Alabama, hill home and trekking westward. She has given the special silver bracelet he made for her to a white trader in return for a spelling book from which she gets the idea to use shapes for sounds rather than draw pictures to stand for entire words as he has been doing. This is a pleasing, straightforward, unadorned account of an eight-year-old girl's belief in her father and, though slim, it has emotional appeal. Based on a meager primary source statement that Sequoyah's daughter aided him in his labors, it is intended for early or reluctant readers to read for themselves. The black-and-white illustrations seem uninspired and do little except picture characters and situations. Included are the alphabet, an authors' note about Sequoyah, and a bibliography of sources.

459   Spinka, Penina Keen, *White Hare's Horses*, Atheneum, 1991 (hardcover), ISBN 0-689-31654-2, $12.95, 154 pp.; Fawcett, 1992 (paper), ISBN 0-449-70407-6, $3.99, 161 pp. Ages 10–15, grades 5–10.

Historical novel set for about five years around 1520 in the coastal mountains of central California among the Chumash Native Americans, told from the standpoint of a young girl growing up at the time, and offering a possible way wild horse herds started in the West. Intelligent, impulsive, outspoken, eleven-year-old White Hare looks forward to a happy life with her close-knit family and loyal neighbors and to marriage some day with perceptive, sturdy Dancing Bear. As the years pass, she grows into womanhood sensing also that she has special powers. These are put to good use when, in her late teens, a small party of Aztecs with horses secured from the Spaniards threaten to conquer and enslave her people. Visions and trances enable her to steal the animals and take them over the mountains where she releases them to multiply on the plains. A heavy, awkward style that sometimes assumes an instructive tone, disconcerting grammatical and typographical errors, anachronistic comments about the position of and attitudes toward women, dubious assumptions about mother-goddess worship, a plot that wavers between being historical or merely period, and mystical experiences, including out-of-body ones, that are ineptly introduced and obtrusive—in spite of such problems, the book grows in tension and offers a convincing and fascinating picture of Chumash tribal life, and these are strong points in its favor. An author's note points out that the places described in the Santa Monica Mountains are actual and descriptions of life in the village are accurate to what is known of Chumash society. The "prequel" is *Mother's Blessing* (1992), in which five hundred years earlier another independent Chumash girl attempts to fulfill a prophecy that she will become a great leader.

460 Strete, Craig Kee, *Big Thunder Magic*, illus. Craig Brown, Greenwillow, 1990 (hardcover), ISBN 0-688-08853-8, $12.95, unp. Ages 4–10, grades PS–5.

Humorous, picture-story fantasy about three friends, Nanabee the sheep, Thunderspirit, a small, timid ghost, and the Great Chief, the Pueblo Indian to whom Nanabee belongs. When Great Chief decides to go to the city, he takes Nanabee with him, leaving Thunderspirit so lonely he cannot sleep. He takes off after them and finally finds Nanabee in the zoo, from which he releases him, and they all go back home, Great Chief wondering why he ever left in the first place. Underneath the humor lies a comment about city life compared with life in the country, as well as reflections on friendship and on being satisfied with what one has. Thunderspirit changes; loyal and able, he takes charge at the zoo, using his thunder and lightning to release the magic in his seemingly nondescript medicine bag to blow the lock right off Nanabee's cage, and then tells Great Chief it is time to go home. The final picture shows him curled up beside Nanabee's stomach, secure and comfortable with his best friend again. Almost every illustration is constructed with hundreds of tiny dots to form the shapes. Colors are mostly tawny desert shades and blue-greens for thunderspirit's work. They pick up the satire and comedy, show movement well, picture the desert setting, and, though they stereotype the Great Chief, they add a special attraction to the book.

461 Strete, Craig Kee, *Death Chants: Short Stories*, Doubleday, 1988 (hardcover), ISBN 0-385-23353-1, $12.95, 180 pp. Ages 14 up, grades 9 up.

Thirteen short stories and two novelettes of fantasy having to do with Native American Indians and death. Atmospheres vary—from amusing to outrageously funny through the weird and surreal. A five-year-old Navajo girl of 1845 enters the future thirty years hence in search of the grave of her husband. A Pueblo psychic is ferried by army helicopter to a Vietnam wilderness that does not exist. Other stories involve a futile attempt to save a girl's life with a sandpainting; the holding of the first wardance, which ends matriarchy and ushers in patriarchy; an aged white movie director and his Indian star, who rehash their dozens of films together; and young Elk Boy, who, tired of arguing over whether or not a companion is really dead, picks up a huge rock and kills him. Included also is an original story about how Coyote the trickster and his wife create the world and death. Extensive dialogue, undemanding, concrete diction, short paragraphs, and unusual twists contribute to a rapid pace, and the conclusions are consistently unexpected and usually ironic. As well as providing top-notch escapist entertainment, the stories comment on the human condition and also on some aspects of Indian and white relations.

462 Strete, Craig Kee, *Death in the Spirit House: A Novel*, Doubleday, 1988 (hardcover), ISBN 0-385-17826-3, $14.95, 179 pp. Ages 10 up, grades 6 up.

Survival adventure-thriller set in the wilderness of a mountain called Spirit House somewhere in present-day Colorado. The Native-American tribal area and the tribal descent of the protagonists are not specified. Red Hawk, a murderer disowned by his Indian family for wantonly slaying wildlife, escapes to the mountain intent on killing a huge black cougar. He meets Harvard-educated, white-raised, Indian John Skydancer, a lawyer for a company seeking to evade responsibility for the radiation poisoning of Indians, whose plane has crashed on the mountain. After the cougar, who represents the spirit of the mountain, kills Red Hawk, the fearful and morally ambivalent Skydancer pulls himself together, utilizes the contents of Red Hawk's pack, slays the cougar, which ironically ensures his spiritual as well as physical survival, and decides to remain in this land of his origins. These and other characters, among them the woods-wise sheriff and Red Hawk's traditional parents, are types that suit the genre. White business interests are shown as utterly unprincipled and morally depraved as represented by Skydancer's employer and his beautiful, unscrupulous, oversexed daughter. Sensationalism occurs at every turn, and Indians are romanticized, but for pure suspense entertainment the book excels. There is some sex. The language is not difficult, and the book is fast paced. Strete also published *Paint Your Face on a Drowning in the River* (1978), in which an Indian youth yearns to leave the reservation, as well as other fiction concerning Indians.

463 TallMountain, Mary, *The Light on the Tent Wall: A Bridging*. illus. Claire Fejes, University of California Press, 1990 (paper), ISBN 0-935626-34-4, $12.00, 95 pp. Ages 12 up, grades 7 up.

Eight short stories and essays, along with fifty-five poems, by an Athapascan-Irish-American poet. TallMountain's writing derives mainly from her life's experience. It is highly visual and moves with carefully controlled emotion. She speaks of her Alaskan childhood, her uprooting to the continental United States as the adopted child of a white doctor, her return in midlife, and her lifelong struggle to cope with the trauma of the departure and of her efforts to reconcile the two cultures, of dances, mukluks, drums, traders, owls, dogs, migrants in hopfields, drunken Indians, and in particular her maternal ancestors. Here is an articulate, sometimes witty, often troubled voice. The book itself, with its fluid, black-and-white line drawings and cover painting entitled "Three Generations," by an Alaskan artist, is distinctively designed and very attractive. A glossary and an introduction by Paula Gunn Allen are included. For TallMountain's poems in this book, see no. 565.

464 Tapahonso, Luci, *Saanii Dahataal: The Women Are Singing*, University of Arizona Press, 1993 (hardcover), ISBN 0-8165-1351-1, $19.95, 94 pp.; (paper), ISBN 0-8165-1361-9, $9.95, 94 pp. Ages 11 up, grades 6 up.

Poems and stories by a Navajo woman originally from Shiprock, New Mexico, many of them celebrating the beauty of the arid region and the closeness of the traditional Native-American family. Among the recurring images in both poems and stories are horses, pickup trucks, cowboys, wind, stars, and old people who pass on songs and stories to the youngsters. The stories have an artless simplicity, almost as if they are orally transmitted, and they deal with such subjects as dogs which have been lost or stolen, the death of an uncle, and life in the dormitory at the children's boarding school. Together with the poems, they give a warm and loving picture of Navajo life. For Tapahonso's poems in this book, see no. 566.

465 Thomasma, Kenneth, *Pathki Nana: Kootenai Girl Solves a Mystery*, illus. Jack Brouwer, Grandview Publishing, 1991 (hardcover), ISBN 1-880114-10-0, $9.95, 163 pp.; (paper), ISBN 1-880114-09-7, $6.95. Ages 8–11, grades 3–6.

Historical novel of a Kootenai girl who lives in the Flathead Lake country of western Montana, set in the period when horses were new to the area and rare. Awkward and shy, nine-year-old Pathki Nana always seems at odds with her mother, and she turns to her maternal grandmother, Quiet One, who tells her that her own mother died at her birth and the woman who has raised her is really her aunt. The old woman advises her to go alone into the mountains to seek her guardian spirit. She comes upon Cut Ears, a man from another tribe who lives with her people, trading one of the prized horses to a stranger, and she realizes that this is the explanation for a number of horses that have disappeared in the past months. Unfortunately, Cut Ears sees her, and the rest of the book details her efforts to escape from him and to survive until she can safely return to her village and expose his treachery. While she is alone and watching otters in a stream, she discovers the way to make a fish trap, a skill she passes on to her people that brings her respect and honor. Although overwritten to enhance the excitement and provide cliffhangers at chapter ends ("The next few hours would decide her fate"), the actions are plausible, and the background seems to be well researched. A preface about the Kootenai people and a map are provided. Other books for the same age group by Thomasma include *Kunu: Winnebago Boy Escapes* (1989), *Om-kas-toe: Blackfeet Twin Captures an Elkdog* (1986), *Soun Tetoken: Nez Perce Boy Tames a Stallion* (1984), and *Naya Nuki: Shoshoni Girl Who Ran* (1983).

466 Trimble, Stephen, *The Village of Blue Stone*, illus. Jennifer Owings Dewey and Deborah Reade, Macmillan, 1990 (hardcover), ISBN 0-02-7899501-7, $13.95, 58 pp. Ages 8–12, grades 3–7.

Short historical novel set about 1100 A.D., when the Anasazi culture was at its height, in the imaginary Village of Blue Stone, a small pueblo just north of the San Juan River in what is now New Mexico. More sociology than literature, the linear, tension-less, undramatized narrative focuses on the major events of a year in the life of the pueblo, beginning with the winter solstice. The few named, faceless, unfleshed characters serve to personalize somewhat such activities as pottery making, corn planting, ceremonial dancing, a wedding, and a birth. The details of community and family life are drawn from "technical books about Southwest archaeology" and from "the daily life of modern pueblos," whose people are believed to be the direct descendants of the Anasazi. Maps and skillfully executed pencil sketches add some drama.

Notes, bibliographies, a glossary of terms, a brief history of the discovery of the Anasazi ruins in 1888, and an index are included.

467 VanEtten, Teresa, *Dead Kachina Man*, Sunstone, 1986 (hardcover), ISBN 0-86534-072-2, $10.95, 131 pp. Ages 12 up, grades 7 up.

Realistic mystery-detective novel set in New Mexico in the late twentieth century. Investigating the mysterious death of famous kachina carver Ray Hava of the San Jaime Pueblo plunges Mexican-American police captain Dominique Rios into a frightening and amazing series of events, including conflict with tribal policeman Ed Cruz, Cruz's son, and other pueblo dwellers and threats against his own life, not to mention drugs, pornography, blackmail, closet skeletons, shady characters, colorful townspeople, long-lost relatives who reappear, a little romance, and a chain of murders—conventional elements skillfully concocted and woven together to keep the plot boiling. The emphasis is on thrills, but some sense of the natural terrain, the social problems caused by the intrusion of white culture, and the Native cultural ambience comes through. See also Teresa Pijoan de Van Etten, *Spanish-American Folktales* (no. 397), and Teresa VanEtten, *Ways of Indian Magic: Stories Retold* (no. 468).

468 VanEtten, Teresa, *Ways of Indian Magic: Stories Retold*, illus. Fred A. Cisneros, Sunstone, 1985 (paper), ISBN 0-86534-061-7, $8.95, 91 pp. Ages 12 up, grades 7 up.

Six short stories of fantasy. According to the book cover, the stories are fictionalized accounts "based on Pueblo Indian legends collected by the author over a ten-year period. The majority of the stories were told to her in Tewa, the Pueblo language she learned while working in her family-owned trading post, the San Juan Mercantile at the San Juan Pueblo." Although they obviously utilize the story material of old Pueblo tales, being stories of magic, transformation, gods, spirits, talking animals and the interactions between supernaturals and humans, the accounts have more details of plot and description of people and setting and more emotion than old oral stories normally do. The selections, presented in the frame of an old Indian woman storyteller, tell of an Indian Cinderella who is aided by a magical cornstalk; trouble when a medicine woman becomes jealous of her medicine-man husband's powers; an abused youth who runs away to the mountains where he is cared for by birds and from where he returns when grown to become a powerful medicine man; Montezuma and the first people, his departure from them by eagle, and his promise to return some day; a brave basket maker whose enduring love disenchants his snake-wife; and a girl born of Mother Earth and Father Sky who mates with an Eagle Man. Except for the last one, which drags, the stories are consistently interesting but more careful editing would have eliminated awkward phrasing and punctuation errors. Nevertheless, they project a good sense of the southwestern setting and ethic. Uncomplicated black-and-white line drawings head chapters and add to the setting. *Ways of Indian Wisdom: Stories Retold* (1987) supplements this collection with twenty more stories. See also Teresa Pijoan de Van Etten, *Spanish-American Folktales* (no. 397), and Teresa Pijoan, *White Wolf Woman: Native American Transformation Myths* (no. 527) collected and retold by this well-known southwestern storyteller.

469 Vizenor, Gerald, *The Heirs of Columbus*, Wesleyan, 1991 (hardcover), ISBN 0-8195-5241-0, $18.95, 189 pp.; (paper), ISBN 9-8195-6249-1, $12.95, 189 pp. Ages 15 up, grades 10 up.

Complicated, *avant-garde* novel of contemporary Ojibwa (Chippewa). Appealing to sophisticated readers with a liking for satire and revisionist history, the book includes such sources as journals and anthropological reports in the epilogue. Five centuries after the landing of Columbus, himself half–Native American through his mother who was a Maya of a group that explored Europe, Columbus's "cross-blood descendants" . . . "declared a new tribal nation." Led by trickster-gambler Stone Columbus and his family of motley figures, they accumulate a fortune operating a bingo ship, the *Santa Maria Casino*, on the international line in the Lake of the Woods between Minnesota and Canada. After a storm wrecks the casino, the Heirs declare another sovereign nation at Point Assinika in the Strait of Georgia between Washington and Vancouver Island, where Stone becomes a late-night radio celebrity, and, at the foot of the statue of the Trickster of Liberty, they bury the remains of Columbus and Pocahontas, which with considerable pains they have recovered. Plays on words, double meanings, commentary on the mass media, chemical poisoning, genetic engineering, taxation, cross dressing, governmental agencies, feminism, dreaming, the nature of reality, survival, language, and myth—these and more combine for a complex, disturbing, often frustrating, occasionally too clever, highly entertaining, intellectual tease of a story. Compare with *The Crown of Columbus* (no. 424) by Michael Dorris and Louise Erdrich, published in 1990. Similarly seriocomic is Vizenor's later novel, *Dead Voices: Natural Agonies in the New World* (1992).

470 Vizenor, Gerald, *Landfill Meditation: Crossblood Stories*, Wesleyan, 1991 (hardcover), ISBN 0-8195-5243-7, $35.00, 201 pp.; (paper), ISBN 0-8195-6253-X, $14.95, 201 pp. Ages 15 up, grades 10 up.

Fourteen seriocomic, bitter-funny short stories about Native-American Indian-white cross-bloods that are on the edge between realism and surrealism and satirize present-day Indian life on and off the reservation and historical and current Anglo-Indian relations. The stories are set mostly on the Ojibwa (Chippewa) White Earth and Leech Lake reservations in Minnesota or in nearby urban areas. They involve the trickster-shaman descendants of the trickster Luster Browne of *The Trickster of Liberty: Tribal Heirs to a Wild Baronage* (1988), an earlier collection of short stories by Vizenor. In the later book, among other stories, Almost Browne, called so because he was almost born on the reservation, operates a "sovereign tribal blank book [sales] business in an abandoned car"; he masters the laser for light shows, is thus thought to be a shaman, and is ordered off the reservation, "the first tribal member to be removed to the cities, a wild reversal of colonial histories"; Bunnie La Pointe finds men on the reservation unbearable and leaves for the city where clocks drive her to take refuge in a cave; Father Father Mother Browne [*sic*], a priest, reopens a church on the reservation that has been closed for fifty years and is thought to precipitate thereby a storm that knocks houses off their foundations; Newcrows, a psychotaxidermist, is arrested for "animule" killing, but the charges are dropped when the judge and prosecutor suffer from bear ticks; and Rattling Hail, plastic-legged veteran of a recent Anglo war, ironically visits a Minneapolis urban Indian help center. Vizenor sports with words as well as ideas and history, and the characters' names in themselves are hilariously telling: Griever de Hocus, Fast Food, Touch Tone, Injun Time, and Token White, to name some. The stories are so precisely dictioned that the reader must attend carefully, and, as with Lewis Carroll's Alice books, must surrender to the writer to grasp the intention as well as the humor, which is at times raucous and bawdy, slapstick, rueful, and sophisticated. The stories in *The Trickster of Liberty: Tribal Heirs to a Wild Baronage* operate similarly. Intellectual teases, both books are for mature, sophisticated readers.

471   Vizenor, Gerald, ed., *Touchwood: A Collection of Ojibway Prose*, New Rivers, 1987 (paper), ISBN 0-89823-091-8, $9.95, 180 pp. Ages 14 up, grades 9 up.

History, personal experience narratives, and short stories about Native American Chippewa (Ojibwa) of northern Wisconsin and Minnesota. The first half of the book consists of selections from Indian writers born in the nineteenth century: William Whipple Warren, who wrote a history of the Ojibwa nation from which a selection is reproduced, George Copway, and John Rogers, who wrote memoirs. The rest of the pieces are by late twentieth-century writers. Gerald Vizenor fictionalizes other memoirs into revisionist history, and Louise Erdrich, Jim Northrup, and B. Wallace are represented by fiction— Erdrich by a portion of her novel *Love Medicine*, Northrup by fourteen ironically funny short stories, and Wallace by a short satire on academe. The Northrup stories featuring Luke Warmwater are gems and alone make the volume worthwhile, being hilarious and incisive looks at present-day reservation Indians trying to reconcile what is left of their culture with that of the dominant one, and simply survive at the same time. For another short story by Vizenor, see Joyce Carol Thomas's *A Gathering of Flowers* (no. 146).

472 Walters, Anna Lee, *Ghost Singer: A Novel*, Northland, 1988 (hardcover), ISBN 0-87358-472-4, $15.95, 220 pp. Ages 14 up, grades 9 up.

Realistic novel mainly of contemporary Navajos on the reservation and in Washington, D.C. After a gripping preface in which in 1830 slavers enter Navajo country, kidnap Red Lady and one of her baby twin daughters, and scalp and cut the ears from her father, the story skips 130 years ahead and focuses on two intertwined concerns: the reason for a series of mysterious deaths—attributed to suicide after "ghostly" sightings—of government employees who work with Indian artifacts, and the efforts of Red Lady's descendant, elderly Jonnie Navajo, a singer, and his teenaged granddaughter, Nasbah, to learn the fate of Red Lady's daughter and to cure Nasbah's cousin-brother, Willie Begay, of a curious mental malady picked up in Washington. Neither problem is completely solved. Although the reader meets the modern descendant of Red Lady's child, because of a fluke, Jonnie never does. Various Indians attempt to help the workers with curing or protective ceremonies, but unsuccessfully it appears, since the spirits remain angry over the disappearance of sacred objects and various atrocities committed against Indians. At the end, the whites seem no wiser, and the Indians hope that the looting will stop. The large cast is sufficiently developed for identification, and in spite of the discursiveness that comes from the many shifts in scene, the awkwardness that arises from information about Indian history, ceremony, and outlook ineptly worked into the narrative, and poor proofreading, the novel grips from beginning to end with remarkable plot suspense and high emotional appeal.

473 Walters, Anna Lee, ed., *Neon Pow-Wow: New Native American Voices of the Southwest*, Coffee House, 1993 (paper), ISBN 0-87358-562-3, $12.95, 131 pp. Ages 13 up, grades 8 up.

Anthology of thirty-five selections from twenty-three writers of different tribal groups, all originating in or residing in the American Southwest. These are "fairly new writers . . . .For about half, this is the first time they have been published . . . these selections were . . . carefully chosen to show a fuller range of contemporary Native American literature." About half the inclusions are poems; two are plays, one, "The Turkey Tender," a version of the Cinderella story; the remainder are short stories and several essays. Most deplore cultural erosion and long for self-validation and the integrity and respectability of the old ways; for example, "Carnival Lights," by Stacey Velarde, in which Kellie, who had yearned for the fun making that came after rodeos and carnivals when she was a child, as an adult away from her family sees how raw and unglamorous the scene really is; or "Neon Powwow," by Dan L. Crank, which tells of a present-day gathering under garish bar lights and heavy drinking among the young people; or the depressing "Squatters," by Irvin Morris, about dying street people on the edge of the desert left to their own devices and despised. One of the few light stories is "San Lorenzo Day in Laguna," which tells of the exuberant festivities celebrating the saint's day in the pueblo. On the whole, these are bleak stories, not difficult to read but sad, yearning, sometimes cynical, always enlightening about the present-day attitudes of young Indians, for the most part downbeat. Biographical information is included. For the poems in this book, see no. 568.

474 Walters, Anna Lee, *The Sun Is Not Merciful*, Firebrand, 1985 (hardcover), ISBN 0-932379-11-7, $16.95, 136 pp.; (paper) ISBN 0-932379-10-9, $7.95, 136 pp. Ages 14 up, grades 9 up.

Eight short stories about Plains Native Americans by a Pawnee-Otoe author. Marked by careful characterizations and skillful buildup of tension, the stories, among others, tell of Uncle Ralphie's attempts to cling to and perpetuate old Pawnee ways; old (historical) John Stink, who is buried while unconscious from a seizure and saved from the grave by his dogs; tribal elders who marshal the group to discipline by whipping increasingly recalcitrant, defiant Sonny; little Wanda, who is sexually molested by an arrogant, rude, Indian-disliking salesman while he fits her for shoes; and two septegenarian women who continue to fish without a license in the dammed-up lake that flooded their father's farm. A strong sense of the differences between Indian and white ways of looking at life, the importance of old, long-held beliefs, the continuing indignities inflicted on Indians, and their stubborn will to survive underscore these well-written, finely paced stories.

475 Welch, James, *Fools Crow*, Viking, 1986 (hardcover), ISBN 0-670-81121-1, $18.95, 391 pp. Ages 14 up, grades 9 up.

Historical novel of the Blackfeet people in northern Montana in the period after the Civil War, when the encroachment of whites, depletion of buffalo herds, and disease spell an end to their traditional way of life. White Man's Dog, a young man of the Lone Eaters group of the Siksikas Pikuni (Blackfeet) Indians, lacks confidence and the respect of his contemporaries until he acquits himself well in a horse raid on the Crows, where he earns himself a new name, Fools Crow. He marries Red Paint, daughter of Yellow Kidney, who has been captured and mutilated by the Crows; studies under the healer, Mik-api, the old "many faces" man of the Lone Eaters; and experiences visions brought on by his power animal, the wolverine. Although he grows in stature, he cannot avert the fate of his people, which is finally sealed by a smallpox epidemic and massacres of whole villages by the seizers, the cavalry soldiers. While the worst atrocities are committed by the whites, some of the Indians are also pictured as unreasonably vicious, like the renegade Owl Child, whom Fools Crow's friend Fast Horse joins. Most of the action is seen through the eyes of Fools Crow, but the point of view also shifts to his father, other members of the tribe, and occasionally to one of the soldiers or settlers. The length of the book and its rather slow pace may make it hard for many high schoolers, but the picture of life among the Indians at this crucial period in the history of the West will be worth the effort for better readers.

476 Welch, James, *Indian Lawyer*, Norton, 1990 (hardcover), ISBN 0-393-02896-8, $19.95, 349 pp. Ages 14 up, grades 9 up.

Novel of a modern, educated Indian, Sylvester Yellow Calf, raised by grand-parents on the Blackfeet reservation in northern Montana, now a rising attor-ney in a prestigious law firm in Helena. Since he serves on the parole board at the state prison in Deerlodge, he is targeted in a blackmail scheme by an inmate who wants his beautiful, decent wife to seduce the lawyer and involves two recent parolees in the extortion plan. Because the lonely wife is genuinely attracted to Yellow Calf, the affair is one of mutual consent, and because he has just been asked to run for the House of Representatives, the threat to demolish his reputation is critical. He is forced to drop out of the race, but he saves the girl from possible violence and retains some of his own self-respect. Although only a few of the scenes occur among the Native-American people, the novel deals with questions of the exploitation of a minority person by the white culture, of how much he owes himself and how much he owes his people, and of whether his seeming acceptance by the whites can ever be genuine. At first slow paced, the novel picks up tension at about midpoint but might be hard going for all but the best high school readers. Welch is best known for his first novel, *Winter in the Blood* (1974), also about Native Amer-icans in the late twentieth century, a much more readable book.

477 White Deer of Autumn (Gabriel Horn), *The Great Change*, illus. Carol Grigg, Beyond Words, 1992 (hardcover), ISBN 0-941831-79-5, $13.94, unp. Ages 5–10, grades K–5.

Realistic picture-story book of a Native-American Indian (group not speci-fied) grandmother who explains the meaning of death to her granddaughter.

While she and Grandma are going about their daily tasks of fishing and plant-ing, nine-year-old Wanba wonders why Grandpa had to die and why the fish must die. Grandma explains that death, the Great Change, is part of the Circle of Life, which must remain unbroken. Death is not the cessation of life, but "all dying means, Wanba, is *change*." Although Wanba seems a little old to be posing the questions she does in the way she does, the story's basic ob-jective has value. The text has unintentional errors in grammar, seems un-necessarily stretched out, and self-consciously blends realism and mysticism. The delicate watercolors, free on the page, contribute to the mystical atmos-phere. Also predominately instructive, ponderous in style, and disturbingly mystical is an earlier picture-story book, *Ceremony—In the Circle of Life* (1983), illustrated by Daniel San Souci, in which a spirit being calling himself Star Spirit appears and teaches a Native-American Indian boy, who has been ignorant of his heritage. Although they belabor their points, both books do introduce certain Native-American beliefs.

478 Wosmek, Frances, *A Brown Bird Singing*, illus. Ted Lewin, Lothrop, 1986 (hardcover), ISBN 0-688-06251-2, $10.25, 120 pp. Ages 9–12, grades 4–7.

Girl's growing-up novel. Anego, about nine, has lived with the Veselka fam-ily since infancy, when her mother died and her Indian father left her with warm-hearted, outgoing Ma; sensitive, kindly Pa; and Sheila, now a seventh grader. Despite occasional rebuffs because of her Native-American heritage, she is happy and dreads the possibility of Hamigeesek, her real father, coming to claim her. After various domestic adventures—she raises an orphaned fawn, Pa buys the first car in the neighborhood, and Ma has a baby boy, little Mike, whom Anego helps save from severe croup—she learns that Hamigeesek is on his way, having gone to school and qualified to become the reservation teacher. In a panic, Anego runs away and gets lost, but she is found by tall, handsome Hamigeesek, who wins her confidence by attracting a small brown bird which she holds, evoking memories of her mother, and then allows to fly free and sing. Life in rural Minnesota in the early twentieth century is well drawn, and the story is sympathetic to Native Americans, but the difficult questions of how this child, raised in a German and Irish-American family, will adjust to reservation life and Chippewa culture are not tackled.

479 Yolen, Jane, *Sky Dogs*, illus. Barry Moser, Harcourt, 1990 (hardcover), ISBN 0-15-275480-6, $15.95, unp. Ages 5–10, grades K–5.

Fantasy picture-story book based on several legends about how horses first came to the Blackfeet people, as related by an old man, He-who-loves-horses, about an incident in his childhood. Two Kutani approach a Piegan Blackfeet village clinging to the backs of strange creatures big as elk, with a third creature pulling a travois, on which lies a sick woman. The two men die that night, but the woman lives and becomes stepmother to the little boy, who is the first to approach the strange beasts and see that they are friendly. The oversized book is illustrated handsomely, mostly in shades of yellow and red-browns. The text is perhaps too conventionally formal in the "noble savage" mode, but for legend it is not inappropriate. An author's note tells something of the mythic and historical background.

11
Native-American Indians: Books of Oral Tradition

480 Allen, Paula Gunn, ed., *Spider Woman's Granddaughters: Traditional Tales and Contemporary Writing by Native American Women*, Beacon, 1989 (hardcover), ISBN 0–8070–8100–0, $19.95, 242 pp.; Fawcett, 1990 (paper), ISBN 0-449-90508-X, $12.00, 256 pp. Ages 14 up, grades 9 up.

Twenty-four short stories by and about women and women's concerns, seven from the oral tradition of the Oneida, Mohawk, Okanogan, and Pueblo peoples. The remaining are short stories or biographical accounts by authors of the nineteenth and twentieth centuries. Two of the traditional stories are creation myths, "The Woman Who Fell from the Sky," from the Mohawk, and "The Beginning and End of the World," from the Okanogan. Another Okanogan tale, "Coyote Kills Owl Woman," tells how the wily trickster outwits a terrible old woman who steals children. In "The Warrior Maiden," an Oneida story, a brave young woman saves her people from their traditional enemies, the Mingoes; in the remaining three tales, all Pueblo, Yellow Woman, who represents corn, is stolen by evil beings. Adventure and conflict pervades these old stories, which offer interesting and valuable contrasts to the short stories among which they are arranged. An introduction, notes on the stories, a glossary, and a short bibliography are included. For the short stories in this book, see no. 413.

481 Ata, Te, ret., *Baby Rattlesnake*, ad. Lynn Moroney, illus. Mira Reisberg, Children's Book, 1989 (hardcover), ISBN 0-89239-049-2, $13.95, 32 pp.; (paper), ISBN 0-89239-111-1, $5.95, 32 pp. Ages 5–8, grades K–3.

Chickasaw folktale of a baby snake who cries and fusses for a rattle before he is old enough to grow his own and then, when given one, misuses it until the beautiful daughter of the chief crushes it under her foot. The didacticism of this tale is tempered by cartoonlike illustrations in bright colors—predominantly oranges, reds, deep greens, and blues—surrounded by frames of Native-American motifs that give a feel of the Southwest. The amusing snakes even have distinctive expressions.

482 Begay, Shonto, ret., *Ma'ii and Cousin Horned Toad: A Traditional Navajo Story*, illus. Shonto Begay, Scholastic, 1992 (hardcover), ISBN 0-590-45391-2, $14.95, unp. Ages 5–10, grades K–6.

Retelling of a Navajo trickster tale explaining why coyotes avoid horned toads. Always hungry, lazy Ma'ii the coyote persuades generous Horned Toad to share his corn, and, when asked to help work the cornfields, gobbles the toad up. Ma'ii's trickery backfires when the toad inside causes him extreme discomfort. Several amusing misfortunes later, Ma'ii faints when Horned Toad tugs at his heart, and the toad emerges at his convenience. Shonto's retelling of a tale he learned in childhood captures the mischief and whimsey of traditional trickster stories and allows several morals to come out implicitly. It reads smoothly for the most part and incorporates some songs. The full-color, mixed-media, sometimes double-page, off-the-page illustrations depict incidents, reveal the nature of the characters, and portray the beauty and majesty of the desert mesa country. They invite careful examination to appreciate small details that enhance the setting and tables-turned humor. Notes and a glossary of Navajo words are included.

483 Bernard, Emery, ret., *Spotted Eagle & Black Crow: A Lakota Legend*, illus. Durga Bernhard, Holiday, 1993 (hardcover), ISBN 0-8234-1007-2, $15.95, unp. Ages 5–10, grades K–5.

Retelling of a Lakota legend, which, according to the reteller's note, was related more than a century ago by Chief Red Cloud. The action-filled story concerns two young men—good-hearted, brave Spotted Eagle and his evil-minded brother, Black Crow—who are in love with the same girl. Left behind to die in an eagle's nest by his brother, Spotted Eagle prays to Wakan Tanka, is nourished by an eagle, eventually returns and forgives his brother for his betrayal, gives thanks in sacred manner to the eagles, survives a battle with the Pawnees, during which his brother is slain, and marries the girl. Although the pictures accompanying this account of the triumph of virtue and the importance of spirituality appear to reinforce the stereotypes of all Indians being stoic and looking alike and the pinky tones strike a false note, many cultural motifs individualize the book, among them circles, thunderbird lines, and the use of two's. The two-page spread of the Pawnee battle appears to take its origin from Plains Indians' buffalo hide paintings. The story is better than the pictures.

484 Bierhorst, John, sel. and ret., *The Mythology of North America*, Morrow, 1985 (hardcover), ISBN 0-688-04145-0, $14.95, 259 pp.; (paper), ISBN 0-688-06666-6, $10.00, 259 pp. Ages 14 up, grades 9 up.

Retellings of and detailed comments on myths of the Native Americans of the North American continent north of Mexico, pointing out their peculiar characteristics and likenesses to stories of other cultures. After an authoritative introduction on the nature of Native-American myths, Bierhorst, a noted expert on traditional literatures, presents stories by major geographical regions. For example, for the Midwest he concentrates on significant aspects of the Manabozho and Wisakedjak trickster cycles and the epic Walam Olum of the displaced Delaware. Typically stories are summarized with comments intermingled with the narratives, all in lucid, easily followed terms. Maps, a list of sources, endnotes on stories, an index, photos of both pictorial and concrete art, and notes on pronunciation are included. Other volumes are *The Mythology of South America (1988)* and *The Mythology of Mexico and Central America* (1990). As with Bierhorst's earlier publications, these books are outstanding not only for the good narratives they make available but also for Bierhorst's ability to render complex concepts accessible to the reader while remaining respectful to substance, cultures, and readers.

485 Bierhorst, John, sel. and ed., *The Naked Bear: Folktales of the Iroquois*, illus. Dirk Zimmer, Morrow, 1987 (hardcover), ISBN 0-688-06422-1, $14.95, 123 pp. Ages 8–12, grades 3–7.

Carefully prepared selection of sixteen stories collected by Jeremiah Curtin and J.N.B. Hewitt from the League of Five Nations, known together as the Iroquois, of the late 1800s and early 1900s. These folktales, a term referring to "stories of romance or adventure" rather than "sacred lore," are original texts edited, not retellings, and hence are closer to the spirit and worldview of the tellers. Concerning talking animals, magic, ordinary people, and supernatural beings, they are filled with action and humor. Here are escapades of the wily trickster Turtle, whose life is twice saved in a Brer Rabbit briar patch–like episode, and an Orpheus-type tale of a woman's successful search to bring her husband back from the dead, among other fast-moving narratives. Cartoonish, black-and-white sketches contribute to the liveliness and humor. Notes, an introduction with background about the stories and the cultures, and a fine list of references are included. Other entertaining collections by this much-honored writer on American Indian lore are *The Monkey's Haircut and Other Stories Told by the Maya* (1986; illus. Robert Andrew Parker), twenty stories from different Maya groups, and *Doctor Coyote: A Native American Aesop's Fables* (1987; illus. Wendy Watson), twenty short fables with morals starring the trickster Coyote adapted by the Aztecs in the 1500s from Spanish versions of Aesop. Both books have humorous illustrations that add to the fun and authoritative notes about sources and tale types.

486   Bierhorst, John, ret., *The Woman Who Fell from the Sky: The Iroquois Story of Creation*, illus. Robert Andrew Parker, Morrow, 1993 (hardcover), ISBN 0-688-10680-3, $15.00, unp. Ages 5 up, grades K up.

Retelling of an Iroquois myth, whose sources in the Iroquois confederacy of nations are given in the writer's note at the end. The myth combines Native-American Indian sky-faller, earth-diver, and war-twins motifs in describing how the earth begins. A woman falls from the country in the sky through a hole in its floor, lands on a turtle's back, and spreads mud secured by a musk-rat to form earth, to which then her sons, Flint and Sapling, give physical features like rivers and trees. The tone supports the importance of the story as do the watercolors that picture the incidents, add details of action, and utilize traditional motifs or ways of portraying certain story aspects, as for example, the impressive full-page illustration of the woman as she calls up and welcomes the sun with out-stretched arms.

487   Big Crow, Moses Nelson (Eyo Hiktepi), ret., *A Legend from Crazy Horse Clan*, ad. by Renee Sansom-Flood, illus. Daniel Long Soldier, Tipi, 1987 (paper), ISBN 1-877976-03-2, $4.95, unp. Ages 7–13, grades 2–8.

Retelling of a Native-American Indian Sioux (Lakota) family legend. When she is perhaps five years old, little Sioux girl Tashia and her pet raccoon, Mesu, are separated from her people in a midnight buffalo stampede. She is found by an errant buffalo bull-calf, who attaches himself to her. She lives with his herd for many years, calling him her husband. Eventually the herd wanders into the girl's people's area, where she is found by warriors, one of whom shoots the buffalo. She is taken back to her people, along with the now aged raccoon, and later marries and has a family, one of whom becomes known as the mighty leader Crazy Horse, ancestor of Big Crow. Although edited, the text has the feel of oral story and in a natural way also incorporates cultural information. The black-and-white line drawings with touches of tan for the girl's dress and the shoulders of the buffalo have a strength that comes from actual experience of the terrain and intimate knowledge of the culture. Disconcertingly, the pictures do not always correspond to the accompanying text, and the girl does not grow older while she is with the animals, though the text clearly says that many years pass and the raccoon ages. The generous use of Sioux words, which are explained in a glossary, contributes authenticity. Altogether text and pictures have a simple dignity that inspires liking and respect. A teller's note is included. Also by Big Crow is *Hoksila and the Red Buffalo* (1991), which is called a sequel but has no narrative connection to *A Legend from Crazy Horse Clan*. Somewhat longer and more complicated with incidents, it tells of the journey of a young warrior to kill the ugly red buffalo that has captured his bride-to-be and other maidens. Five full-page, brown-toned sketches by Sioux artist Bernard W. Provencial, a glossary, and a note about the source are included.

488 Bright, William, sel. and ed., *A Coyote Reader*, University of California Press, 1993 (hardcover), ISBN 0-520-08061-0, $30.00, 202 pp.; (paper), ISBN 0-520-08062-9, $13.00, 202 pp. Ages 15 up, grades 10 up.

A large collection of originally oral stories about the trickster Coyote, with emphasis on those from the Karok people of northern California. Since the book is intended as a scholarly examination of the figure, the introductory material is often anthropologically and linguistically technical but at the same time has much of value for the persistent lay reader. The book divides the stories into categories intended to give a feel not only for the many phases of the character but also for the different ways, from Indian to white, from old times to the present, of looking at the figure. Hence there are such sections as "Coyote in English Literature" (with a passage from Mark Twain), "Coyote the Wanderer," "Coyote the Lecher," "Coyote the Clown," and "Coyote the Survivor," along with twelve other similar groupings of stories. Many stories are quite bawdy, even pornographic in content, and most follow the ethnopoetic approach of being cast into a kind of poetry, a form which, while perhaps true to the original genre, can be disconcerting to read because as given the stories do not read well and might perhaps have been better for the sake of sense if cast into prose. Some very good reading appears, however, for the persistent person, but best are the selections composed about Coyote by such modern writers as Gary Snyder and Peter Blue Cloud. An excellent bibliography is included.

489 Bruchac, Joseph, *The First Strawberries: A Cherokee Story*, illus. Anna Vojtech, Dial, 1993 (hardcover), ISBN 0-8037-1331-2, $13.99, unp. Ages 4–8, grades PS–3.

Native-American folktale of the first man and woman, who quarrel when he discovers her picking flowers instead of fixing his dinner and speaks harshly to her. The woman leaves, and although the man follows, contrite, he cannot catch her until the sun takes pity on him and tries to slow her by shining brightly and ripening first raspberries, then blueberries to no avail. When the sun ripens the strawberries, which the woman has never seen before, she cannot resist trying one, then one more, until the man reaches her, apologizes, and shares the berries she gives him as a peace offering. With minimal text, the illustrations done in watercolors and colored pencils dominate, filling each page and in several places flowing over a two-page spread with no words. This is an interesting example of how male-female disputes and reconciliations are not limited to modern times.

490 Bruchac, Joseph, ret., *Flying with the Eagle, Racing the Great Bear: Stories from Native North America*, illus. Murv Jacob, BridgeWater, 1993 (hardcover), ISBN 0-8167-3026-1, $13.95, 128 pp. Ages 10 up, grades 5 up.

Sixteen Native-American coming-of-age folktales from four sections of the country. From the Northeast, among others, are "The Dream Fast," an Anishinabe story of a vision quest, and "Racing the Great Bear," an Iroquois story of a poor boy who chases Nyagwahe, the monstrous bear, until he gets the creature's great teeth which contain its power and restores life to the bones of his people, thereby protecting the peace of the Five Nations. From the Southeast comes the Muskogee (Creek) tale, "The Underwater Lodge," about the boy who braves the world of the tie-snakes to carry out his father's mission; from the Southwest comes the Dine (Navajo) story, "How the Hero Twins Found Their Father," a quest story of two boys who seek their father, the sun, prove their relationship to him through a series of tests, and are given weapons to destroy the monsters that plague their people; from the Pacific Northwest Tlingit people comes "Salmon Boy," about the thoughtless boy who throws away half-moldy fish and is transformed into a salmon, lives with the fish people, and learns to respect them. From the Inupiaq comes "Tommy's Whale," a story of an actual hunt in which the lessons learned from several folktales that teach honor for the whale make success possible for a boy of thirteen. The tales are direct and unadorned, related in a serious storytelling manner, and illustrated with handsome black-and-white illustrations that seem to be woodcuts. A general introduction opens the book, and specialized introductions precede each section. Other collections by Bruchac include *The Wind Eagle and Other Abenaki Stories* (1985), *Iroquois Stories: Heroes and Heroines, Monsters and Magic* (1985), *Return of the Sun: Native American Tales from the Northeast Woodland* (1989), *Native American Stories* (1991), and *Native American Animal Stories* (1992).

491   Bruchac, Joseph, and Jonathan London, *Thirteen Moons on Turtle's Back: A Native American Year of Moons*, illus. Thomas Locker, Philomel, 1992 (hardcover), ISBN 0-399-22141-7, $15.95, unp. Ages 5–12, grades K–7.

In a frame story of an old Indian woodcarver explaining to his grandson that, on the back of the turtle he has fashioned, are thirteen scales, one for each moon of the year, the book relates thirteen Native-American legends of the different times of the year, each from a group in a different part of the country. Midwinter is represented by a Northern Cheyenne story of the Moon of Popping Trees; early spring by an Anishinabe story of the Maple Sugar Moon; summer by a Menominee tale of the Moon of Wild Rice; autumn by legends of the Micmac ("Moose-Calling Moon"), the Cherokee ("Moon of Falling Leaves"), and the Winnebago ("Moon When Deer Drop Their Horns"). All are told in serious, rhythmical prose, with respect for the meaning and the original tellers. Illustrations are lavish oil paintings, taking up three-quarters of each oversized, double-page spread. This is a book for a wide range of ages.

492   Carey, Valerie Scho, *Quail Song*, illus. Ivan Barnett, Putnam, 1990 (hardcover), ISBN 0-399-21936-6, $14.95, unp. Ages 4–8, grades PS–3.

Retelling of a Pueblo story about Coyote, here in his buffoon mode. Coyote is so struck by what he thinks is a beautiful song, but is really Quail's cry of pain, that he persuades her to teach it to him. Three times he forgets the song, and, frustrated with his silliness, she tricks him into biting a stone. When Lizard calls Coyote's cries of pain beautiful, toothless Coyote flies off the handle but is unable to bite Lizard. Language that imitates the animals' sounds adds interest to this amusing, lively, ironic story. Two-dimensional, posterlike, earth-toned, stylized collages on white grounds show incidents, add humor, and make this a very beautiful book.

493   Cohen, Caron Lee, ret., *The Mud Pony*, illus. Shonto Begay, Scholastic, 1988 (hardcover), ISBN 0-590-41525-5, $12.95, unp.; 1989 (paper), ISBN 0-590-41526-3, $3.95, unp. Ages 5–10, grades K–6.

Oral tradition hero-story of the Skidi Pawnee. A poor boy yearns for a pony of his own and fashions one with a white face from clay, which then Mother Earth brings to life. Mounted on the white-faced mare, the boy leads his people to victory in battle and then to great success on a buffalo hunt. Years later, when the boy is grown and is a noted chief, the horse returns to Mother Earth, from whom she had come and who assures the man that she (Mother Earth) remains with him. The text is powerful because it is spare and unadorned. It is extended well by the softly toned, full-color, impressionistic pictures. The sense of the culture appears in such numerous small details as leggings, travois, and knife cases. The people look like real people and not the cliche Plains Indian.

494   Cohlene, Terri, ad., *Turquoise Boy: A Navajo Legend*, illus. Charles Reasoner, Rourke, 1990 (hardcover), ISBN 0-86593-003-1, $19.95, 47 pp.; Troll (paper), ISBN 0-8167-2360-5, $3.95, 47 pp. Ages 4–11, grades PS–6.

Retelling of the myth of how the Navajos got horses. Turquoise Boy journeys without success to the east, south, west, and north and to his father, Sun Bearer, seeking something that will make the people's lives easier. On his way home, he encounters Mirage Man, who teaches him a holy song that enables him to bring horses to the people. Two-dimensional, abstract, full-page paintings in deep red, purple, and turquoise tones make use of Southwestern desert features and Navajo motifs to establish setting. They depict the characters, show episodes, and make the book attractive. The narrative moves fast with just the right amount of detail, in a respectful tone, and with some brief chants, but a note about sources would be helpful. The last twenty pages of the book contain a history of the Navajo people and a discussion of their customs and beliefs, supplemented by photographs. One in a series by Cohlene called Native-American Legends that includes *Clamshell Boy: A Makah Legend* (1990), a cautionary tale about the origin of the potlach, which has stunning illustrations of totem poles and masks; *Quillworker: A Cheyenne Legend* (1990), a story in which buffalo are important and explains how the Big Dipper and the North Star came to be; *Dancing Drum: A Cherokee Legend* (1990), an Orpheus-type story involving the Sun and explaining the origin of death and the cardinal bird; and *Little Firefly: An Algonquian Legend* (1990), a Cinderella-type story, the least successful of these for pictorial and cultural reasons. All are handsomely illustrated by Reasoner with appropriate iconography and have cultural information at the end. Although it is unfortunate that information about the sources of the tales has not been included, on the whole, this is an attractive, well-done set.

495   Connolly, James E., ret., *Why the Possum's Tail Is Bare and Other North American Indian Nature Tales*, illus. Andrea Adams, Stemmer House, 1985 (hardcover), ISBN 0-88045-069-X, $12.95, 64 pp. Ages 8 up, grades 3 up.

Thirteen short folktales retold from eight Native-American Indian groups of the Eastern Woodlands and Western Plains and West Coast. They tell why, among others, the bear, the rabbit, and the bobcat have short tails, the owl hunts at night, the mallard's tail feathers curl, the possum plays dead and has a bare tail, and the thrush has a beautiful song and is shy—all stories of how animals originated or came to look or behave as they do. Most are enlivened by dialogue, employ such familiar motifs as the bungling host and running a race against a series of identical opponents—and convey morals, cautioning against misplaced confidence, boastfulness, arrogance, and vain imitation. The lessons are made less pointed by abundant humor and action. A brief, generalized essay about the life and customs of these groups opens the book, but the italicized introductions before each tale that provide factual information about the animals, some as long as two dozen lines, add an unfortunate teaching element. The black-and-white line drawings of animals in various situations add visual beauty to the book. Specific sources are included.

496 Crespo, George, ret., *How the Sea Began,* illus. George Crespo, Clarion, 1993 (hardcover), ISBN 0-395-63033-9, $14.95, unp. Ages 4–10, grades PS–6.

Retelling of a Taino Indian myth about the origin of Puerto Rico. When Guabancex, the dread goddess of hurricanes, sends a storm that kills Yayael, the village's most skillful hunter, his parents place his magic bow and arrows in a gourd suspended from the ceiling of their hut. Told to guard the gourd, four disobedient boys accidentally break it. Water gushes out, sweeping the boys away and creating a salt ocean filled with sea life and isolating the mountains that became Caribbean islands including Boriquen, or Puerto Rico. The narrative, based on a story collected in Columbus's time, according to an endnote, has a strong storytelling flavor. The colorful oil paintings have amusing touches but remain respectful, extend the narrative with details of setting and action, and skillfully augment the rhythm and pace of the story.

497 Curry, Jane Louise, ad., *Back in the Beforetime: Tales of the California Indians,* illus. James Watts, McElderry, 1987 (hardcover), ISBN 0-689-50410-1, $13.95, 134 pp. Ages 8–11, grades 3–7.

Twenty-two retold myths and folktales from "a number of California tribes, from the Klamath River Region in the north to the inland desert mountains and the southern coastlands." The stories start with Old Man's creation of the world, proceed through the times when animals were the only people, through the coming of such essentials as fire and light, and end with the creation of humans. A lot of good story material appears here, exciting, action-filled, often humorous versions mostly about the deeds and antics of Coyote the trickster.

The group from which a specific tale comes is never given, however, and in an afternote the reteller indicates that sometimes tales have been pieced together from more than one tribe, a dubious practice. Moreover, she says that her intent was to "tell the larger tale of Creation from the making of the world to man's rise to lordship over the animals." The idea of human dominion over animals is a Judeo-Christian one, quite different from the basic Indian belief in the symbiotic relationship among all living things. Black-and-white drawings add interest.

498   dePaola, Tomie, ret., *The Legend of the Indian Paintbrush*, illus. Tomie dePaola, Putnam, 1988 (hardcover), ISBN 0-399-21534-4, $13.95, unp.; 1991 (paper), ISBN 0-399-21777-0, $5.95, unp. Ages 4–8, grades PS–3.

Retelling of a Native-American Indian folktale from Texas, although the group is not specified in the writer's note about sources at the end of the book. Little Gopher, too small to keep up with the other boys but good at making artistic things, is told by the shaman that he will earn a place among his people for a different reason than most boys. On his vision quest, he has a Dream-Vision in which a maiden and a grandfather provide him with implements for painting and predict that he "will paint a picture that is as pure as the colors in the evening sky." Over the years his skill develops, but he is unable to paint as tellingly as he wishes, especially the sunset, until one evening brushes appear magically on a hillside, with which he catches its wonder and beauty. The brushes turn into the red-orange wildflower called Indian Paintbrush, and Little Gopher becomes known as He-Who-Brought-the-Sunset-to-the-Earth. DePaola captures the essence of this story of perseverance rewarded in paintings that are typical of his work: two-dimensional, full-color primitives that here are generic for people and utilize such cultural motifs as shields and hide paintings. The somewhat abstract style universalizes the theme and the frequent orangy-red hues correlate with the wildflower and give the story warmth. Earlier, dePaola published *The Legend of the Blue-bonnet: An Old Tale of Texas* (1983), a Comanche story in a similar vein.

499   Dixon, Ann, ret., *How Raven Brought Light to People*, illus. James Watts, McElderry, 1992 (hardcover), ISBN 0-689-50536-1, $13.95, unp. Ages 4–10, grades PS–5.

Retelling of a Tlingit Native-American Indian tale, one in the cycle about Raven. "Long ago when the earth is new" and everything is dark, Raven, who causes himself to be born as a human boy, tricks the chief who keeps the sun, moon, and stars in three beautiful wooden boxes and thus brings light. The pictures of the masks and canoe prows show the influence of Pacific Northwest indigenous artwork, and those of interiors seem based on drawings done by people who traveled among the coastal Indians. The chief is shown as a husky, dignified, warm person, and Raven-the-boy is aptly charming and mischievous. Some of the full-color, often double-page spreads are dark and brooding, while those inside the chief's house are striking contrasts, being suffused with yellows and oranges, the colors of light. Although sometimes the language jars, as for example when the word "madder" is used for "angrier," on the whole the spare retelling is appropriate and moves along at a good pace. The conclusion is felicitous, with "the sun vaulted into the heavens," a phrase accompanied by a scene of a brilliant red and yellow orb bursting upward from its box with such force that Raven loses his balance and falls backward. Compare the versions by Gerald McDermott (no. 521) and Susan Hand Shetterly (no. 536.)

500 Dupre, Judith, ret., *The Mouse Bride*, illus. Fabricio Vanden Broeck, Knopf, 1993 (hardcover), ISBN 0-679-83273-4, $8.99, unp. Ages 4–10, grades PS–5.

Retelling of a Chol (Maya) folktale. A mouse couple, seeking "the perfect husband" for their lovely daughter, one who is the "most powerful in the universe," approach in turn the Moon, the Sun, the Cloud, the Wind, and the Wall, only to be told each time that the next one is the more powerful. When the Wall points out that he crumbles when mice burrow, the couple return home and find a mouse groom for her. The highly detailed, delicate, double-spread watercolors are appropriately romantic and give viewers a mouse's-eye view of the world. The Wall is part of a Maya (actual Palenque) ruin on which appear Maya picture-writing symbols. Maya symbols also decorate the endpapers. Strong and interesting diction distinguishes the text ("marvel at her perfection," "protect her from the dark corners of the world"), keep it from becoming sentimental, and alleviate the occasional cuteness of the mice in the pictures. A reteller's note gives the source, tells about the Chol Indians of the Mexican rain forest, and concludes, "This myth is told and retold to each generation of children so that they might understand the circular ways of Nature and make peace with the harsh sun and torrential rains of their home." For Oriental variants of the tale, see *The Greatest of All* (no. 306), *The Wedding of the Rat Family* (no. 305), and *The Moles and the Mireuk* (no. 307), and for a Hopi version, see *The Mouse Couple* (no. 515).

501 Esbensen, Barbara Juster, ret., *The Star Maiden: An Ojibway Tale*, illus. Helen K. Davie, Little, Brown, 1988 (hardcover), ISBN 0-316-24951-3, $14.95, unp.; (paper), $4.95, unp. Ages 4–8, grades PS–3.

Retelling of an Ojibwa (Chippewa) folktale about the origin of the water lily. The story comes from the collection of Ojibwa Chief Kah-ge-ga-gah-bowh, or George Copway. A brilliant, glowing star, tired of wandering in the sky, descends to earth at the invitation of the Ojibwa, and, after trying unsuccessfully to live as a rose and as a small blue prairie flower, she, along with her sisters, find a home on a lake, where their points of light change into shining water lilies. The softly hued paintings incorporate woodland scenes (often two on the same page, one large with close-ups, the other a landscape or faraway shot). Patterns from Ojibwa art appear in frames around the other scenes. The pictures' romanticism emphasizes the story's poetic tone. *Ladder to the Sky: How the Gift of Healing Came to the Ojibway Nation* (1989), another story from Copway, tells how the important Grand Medicine Society, or the Mi-di-wi-win, originated. The romanticized paintings by Helen Davie do not work well with the dramatic story. Both stories have notes about sources. *Ladder* also has a note about pronunciation.

502   Espinosa, Carmen Gertrudis, col., *The Freeing of the Deer and Other New Mexico Indian Myths*, illus. Jorge Ambrosoni, University of New Mexico Press, 1985 (hardcover), ISBN 0-8263-0840-6, $10.95, 83 pp. Ages 7–12, grades 2–7.

Eleven folktales and myths from the Native-American Zuni and Jemez groups in New Mexico. The stories are not differentiated by group because they were collected many years prior to publication on an archeological dig and the informants' names were forgotten. After transcription an aged Indian, group unspecified, verified and approved them. The stories tell of the emergence from the underworld of the first people; of the securing of corn, watermelons, and pumpkins; of gods, monsters, talking animals, hoarded deer freed; of why crows have a propensity for corn and how the Warrior God defeated a people-eating giant and a water-hoarding one; of magic and medicine men; and of other matters of varying importance in making the world as it is today and habitable for humans. The stories are simply and directly told in both English and Spanish without flourishes and extraneous dialogue. Several black-and-white line drawings of scenes, objects, and beings that appear in the tales add interest. A note about collection is included.

503   Goble, Paul, ret., *Iktomi and the Buffalo Skull*, illus. Paul Goble. Orchard, 1991 (hardcover), ISBN 0-531-05911-1, $14.95, unp. Ages 4–8, grades PS–3.

One of a series of Iktomi tales, each published as an oversized picture book starring the Plains Indian trickster-buffoon figure who is self-important, impulsive, and often foolish. Iktomi, dressed in his best to impress the girls in the next village, sticks his head in a buffalo skull where mice are having a powwow, and he becomes stuck. Only after the mice have eaten off much of his hair, he has fallen in the river and floated home, and his angry wife has bashed him with her heavy stone hammer, is he freed. Also in the series are *Iktomi and the Boulder* (1988), *Iktomi and the Berries* (1989), and *Iktomi and the Ducks* (1990). All are highly illustrated in oversized format, with the story in ordinary large type, suggested questions or comments for the storyteller in gray italics, and the words or thoughts of Iktomi in small black type. The language and references are often modern, since, a note from the reteller points out, the stories are still being told and are often changed to fit a contemporary situation. All are amusing but have strong moral lessons. Each book has a list of references and a discussion of the Iktomi figure as an introduction to adult readers.

504 Goble, Paul, ret., *The Lost Children*, illus. Paul Goble, Bradbury, 1993 (hardcover), ISBN 0-02-736555-7, $14.95, unp. Ages 5–8, grades K–3.

Blackfeet Indian legend of the origin of the Pleiades, versions of which come from all the Plains Indians. Six orphan brothers who are neglected and mistreated by the people of their village decide to leave and become stars. In the sky, Sun Man is so angry at the people that he produces a terrible drought. The camp dogs, which have loved the children, howl to the sky and beg for water until Sun Man relents and sends rain. The beautifully illustrated story is preceded by a list of references and an author's note about the myth and followed by a note about the paintings on tipis from the Blackfeet nation, most of which are decorated on the south smoke flap by discs symbolizing the Lost Children. Similar picture-book retellings of Native-American legends by Goble are *The Great Race of the Birds and Animals* (1985), telling about how, through the cleverness of Magpie, humans became dominant over animals; *Her Seven Brothers* (1988), about the origin of the Big Dipper; *Beyond the Ridge* (1989), about the Plains Indian ideas of death; *Crow Chief* (1992), about hunting buffalo before the adoption of the horse; and *Love Flute* (1992), about the origin of the courting flute. Unlike some of Goble's earlier books, these all include references and notes about where the stories were collected and often what parallel tales are found among other groups. All are handsomely illustrated with brilliant colors in large format.

505 Greene, Ellin, *The Legend of the Cranberry: A Paleo-Indian Tale*, illus. Brad Sneed, Simon & Schuster, 1993 (hardcover), ISBN 0-671-75975-2, $15.00, unp. Ages 4–8, grades PS–3.

Retelling of an ancient Native-American Delaware *pourquoi* tale. When Yah-qua-whee (mammoths and mastodons) go on rampages and attack the people and small animals they have previously befriended, the Great Spirit gets angry and tells the people and animals to band together against them. After many Yah-qua-whee are trapped in pits and killed, the rest attack, and in a tremendous battle, the Great Spirit uses his thunderbolts to ensure victory. Then he gives cranberries to the people as a symbol of peace and his "abiding love." The smooth, flowing quality of the text and the conflict of the story are enhanced by the full-page watercolors with their panoramic views of the landscape and close-ups of people and animals. Such shots as that of a charging Yah-qua-whee, shown head on, and another of the combatants from the elevated perspective of the Great Spirit contribute to the drama. A reteller's note about sources is included.

506 Guard, Jean Monroe, and Ray A. Williamson, *They Dance in the Sky: Native American Star Myths*, illus. Edgar Stewart, Houghton, 1987 (hardcover), ISBN 0-395-39970-X, $12.95, 130 pp. Ages 10 up, grades 5 up.

Substantial collection of Native-American myths concerning stars seen in the Northern Hemisphere. The first section tells legends of the Pleiades, the second of the Great Bear or Big Dipper. The next six sections tell myths of separate regions. Each story is preceded by a commentary discussing the background of the myth, the star patterns as they appear to the people of the particular area, and sometimes briefly the comparable myth in the European and Near Eastern traditions. A preface explains the importance of the stories to the Native-American cultures. The book includes an extensive glossary, a bibliography, and a list of suggested further readings. The stories, most of which have not appeared previously outside of scholarly collections, are retold clearly, with occasional humor, and without pretentious language.

507 Helbig, Alethea K., ed., *Nanabozhoo, Giver of Life*, Green Oak, 1987 (hardcover), ISBN 0-931600-06-5, $15.95, 269 pp. Ages 11 up, grades 6 up.

Selection of more than sixty stories about the god-hero-trickster figure of the Anishinabeg (or Algonquin) Indians, variously known as Nanabozhoo, Manabus, Manabozho, and other names. These particular tales almost all come from out-of-print or unpublished sources collected from the southeastern Ojibwa who occupied what is now Michigan and a portion of Ontario. The stories are divided into eight chapters following the life and functions of Nanabozhoo, each section starting with a general introduction describing the group of tales and their meaning and each story by a discussion of where and by whom it was told or written and its special significance, often with mention of other versions and important stylistic elements. Some of the retellings are literary, including those of Henry Rowe Schoolcraft in the nineteenth century; others, often directly from storytellers, are informal in the style of the oral tradition. Many are humorous. Extensive notes and an index support this as a scholarly work, but the presentation, variety, and liveliness of the stories themselves make it a book attractive to young people with an interest in Native-American culture or just looking for interesting tales to read.

508 Hinton, Leanne, tr. and ret., *Ishi's Tale of Lizard*, illus. Susan L. Roth, Farrar, 1992 (hardcover), ISBN 0-374-33643-1, $14.00, unp. Ages 4 up, grades PS up.

Retelling of a story told in 1915 by Ishi, the last member of the Native-American Yahi of California. After Lizard sends Long-Tailed Lizard for wood for arrow shafts and Grizzly Bear gobbles him up, Lizard lassos Grizzly Bear, strangles her, and releases his friend from her stomach. The next night, Lizard dances with the Dwar People, and the following day he continues his arrow making. Later, while gathering pine nuts, he encounters enemy Yawi, who he repels with his arrows. The story moves without buildup or climax, like many Indian tales comprised of a series of almost unrelated incidents complete in themselves. The style makes effective use of listing and repetition, Native-American story attributes that give the account a simple poetic quality. The colorful collages constructed of various textured materials depict scenes in a variety of illustrative modes and contribute humor. They have a rough-hewn yet sophisticated entity. An unusual book that will have different appeal to different ages. Reteller's notes about the translation and adaptation and about Ishi are included.

509 Kimmel, Eric A., ad., *The Witch's Face: A Mexican Tale*, illus. Fabricio Vanden Broeck, Holiday, 1993 (hardcover), ISBN 0-8234-1038-2, $15.95, unp. Ages 5–11, grades K–6.

Retelling of a folktale from both the Hispanic-Mexican and central Mexican–Mazahua Indian traditions. Young gentleman Don Aurelio stops for the night at a large, isolated homestead, where he falls in love with a beautiful young witch who saves his life. She accompanies him home, and they plan to marry, but when he fails to obey her and destroy her human face, he loses her forever. Although an introductory note clearly identifies the tale as Indian, the characters, details, illustrations, and overall tone emphasize the Hispanic tradition. Amplifying the detailed, engrossingly told story of the importance of trust in love are full-color, mostly double-spread, very handsome, impressionistic paintings. Sources are given.

510 Lacapa, Michael, ret., *Antelope Woman: An Apache Folktale*, illus. Michael Lacapa, Northland, 1992 (hardcover), ISBN 0-87358-543-7, $14.95, 44 pp. Ages 4–10, grades PS–5.

Retelling of an Apache folktale. A handsome young stranger visits a village, repeating his message "to honor all things great and small" to everyone he meets. A beautiful young village woman observes him change into an antelope, follows him, and also turns into an antelope. Later the two return to her family to share the secrets he has taught her about the interrelationship of living things. They are married but rejected by the village after she gives birth to twins. The husband decides they must return to his antelope people because her people do not respect all living beings as they should. Awkward phraseology mars the narrative occasionally, impeding flow and sense. The full-color, off-the-page, glowing illustrations also have some awkward aspects but capture well the Southwestern setting, depict figures and animals with strength and dignity, support the story's rhythm with action or stasis as required, and enlarge the narrative with many cultural motifs. The pictures make this a strikingly beautiful book. Lacapa has also retold and illustrated *The Flute Player: An Apache Folktale* (1990), a romantic tale about two ill-fated young people who meet at a dance and fall in love. She admires his sensitive flute playing and places a leaf in the stream that flows by him each time she hears him play as a sign of her appreciation. When he goes on a hunt as instructed by his uncle without leaving word for her, she dies of heartbreak. After he discovers she is dead, he leaves the area and is never seen again, but the sound of his flute can still be heard in the canyon winds. The diction and sentence structure are awkward and commonplace, especially at the beginning, and in general the text lacks narrative flow. The bold, two-dimensional, geometrical, stylized, full-color paintings are magnificent. A continuing pleasure, their strong composition keeps the tale from becoming saccharine. A note about the story is included.

511 Lattimore, Deborah Nourse, ret., *Why There Is No Arguing in Heaven*, illus. Deborah Nourse Lattimore, Harper, 1989 (hardcover), ISBN 0-06023-717-1, $13.95, unp. Ages 5–10, grades K–5.

Retelling of the Maya myth of the creation of the earth and of men. In order to stop the arguing among the lesser gods as to who is the most important among them, the first Creator God, Hunab Ku, having created the earth, challenges the disputants, Lizard House and Moon Goddess, to create "a being worthy of worshipping him." After each fails with mud and wood people, the Maize God succeeds, using his substance. Although the text does not always move logically, as it should in a retelling, the humor and drama that arise from the bickering among the anthropomorphically depicted gods and the unsuccessful attempts at creation hold the interest well. The illustrations dominate the book and give it distinction. Blue-green toned, framed paintings wrap around the text and show the gods in their various deliberations, while full-color, full-page paintings face the text and elaborate on the story by showing, for example, the unsuccessful attempts at creation. All the illustrations exhibit the influence of Maya painted art and stonework reliefs and sculptures, in particular, the blue-green toned ones. The endpapers are fascinating representations of glyphs from codices with the English translations. A reteller's note is included at the end. By the same writer is the picture-story book *The Flame of Peace: A Tale of the Aztecs* (1987), an action-filled account about how a prehistoric Aztec youth brings peace to the warring tribes in the Mexico Valley. It makes use of such old-story motifs as surmounting a series of impossible tasks. As in the Maya tale, the illustrations are based upon tribal art.

512 Levitt, Paul M., and Elissa S. Guralnick, rets., *The Stolen Appaloosa and Other Indian Stories*, illus. Carolynn Roche, Bookmakers Guild, 1988 (paper), ISBN 0-917665-19-8, $12.95, 76 pp. Ages 8–12, grades 3–7.

Five originally oral stories from the Pacific Northwest Native-American Indian groups. According to the book cover, these are taken from the "notes" of anthropologist Franz Boas and "as authors do, [the retellers have] embellished them, using the bright colors of Indian life." Although Boas worked in the British Columbia area, the related Native groups to the south shared similar stories. The stories have the flavor and movement of fiction rather than old story in relating how thief Bush-Tailed Rat Man is undone by the combined efforts of crippled Wayfarer and the village elder; Young Heat-Man overcomes trials to win Snow-Bird, daughter of the Cold in a seasonal story; a woman shaman makes a lake freeze over so the people can escape from the whites; a beautiful princess refuses all suitors, unwittingly marries a dog-man, and gives birth to puppy-boys who save her village from starvation; and a young man employs magic and endurance to win back his stolen magic Appaloosa from an evil medicine man. Often exciting, the stories employ narrative elements and structure of old stories and are classified as legends by the Library of Congress, but they have dubious value as legends. Moreover, the writers should have specified the groups from which the stories came. The full-color, softly realistic paintings depict such cultural details as totem poles and masks, but the definitive black-and-white drawings are more delicately expressive. Together they make the book attractive.

513 Lewis, Richard, ret., *All of You Was Singing*, illus. Ed Young, Atheneum, 1991 (hardcover), ISBN 0-689-31596-1, $13.95, unp. Ages 5 up, grades K up.

Retelling of an Aztec myth of the creation of the world and the securing of music. After the earth and sky come into existence from the pieces of a slain water monster, the sky sends the wind god to the house of the sun from which he brings back heavenly musicians to relieve the silence of the earth. The understated, reverent, poetic text departs from the usual source occasionally, for example, in not naming the gods and in having the earth and not the trickster god Tezcatlipoca suggest that Quetzalcoatl (wind god) get music. Young's expressive paintings underscore the most significant moments from the story and make this unusual book very attractive. Notes about sources are included. The title seems grammatically incorrect but in context occurs as part of a concluding statement sky makes to earth.

514 London, Jonathan, with Lanny Pinola, *Fire Race: A Karuk Coyote Tale*, illus. Sylvia Long, Chronicle, 1993 (hardcover), ISBN 0-8118-0241-8, $13.95, unp. Ages 5–12, grades K–7.

Legend of the Karuk Indians of the Klamath River region of northwest California. The story tells how Coyote, in his role as culture hero, steals fire from the Yellow Jackets and, with the help of other animals, makes it available to people. Having decorated the Yellow Jackets, who alone have fire, with black charcoal stripes, Coyote persuades them that he can make them even more beautiful if they will close their eyes, whereupon he grabs a burning brand in his teeth and races away. As he trips and rolls downhill in the snow, Eagle snatches the glowing coal and flies off, and so it passes to Mountain Lion, Fox, Bear, Measuring Worm, Turtle, and Frog, with the furious Yellow Jackets swarming after each in turn. Frog leaps into the river and hides the fire in his mouth until the Yellow Jackets give up. Then he bursts from the water and spits the hot coal into the roots of the willow tree, which swallows it. The baffled animals again turn to Coyote, who shows them how to coax fire from the willow again by rubbing two sticks together over dry moss. The rich, detailed illustrations cover the large pages, with text imprinted in boxes or on wide margins. Except for Coyote, who wears a leather robe and a skull cap, and for necklaces on Eagle, Mountain Lion, and Bear, the animals are depicted realistically in settings of wintry mountainous scenery. This is a beautiful, well-documented book.

515 Malotki, Ekkehart, ret., *The Mouse Couple: A Hopi Folktale*, illus. Michael Lacapa, Northland, 1988 (hardcover), ISBN 0-87358-473-2, $14.95, 56 pp. Ages 5 up, grades K up.

Retelling of a Hopi folktale collected by Malotki, according to an endnote, in which several motifs familiar to old stories appear. An aging mouse husband and wife long for a girl-child to care for them in their senior years, find a female mouse baby just outside their hole, and raise her to become a virtuous, hardworking, and obedient young woman. Desiring the best husband possible for her, the father journeys to the Sun, the Clouds, the North Winds, and the Butte, all of whom refuse the honor, each mentioning the next as being greater. The Butte suggests that, since mice are the most powerful creatures, the father should choose one of them for his daughter. Accordingly, a marriage is arranged with a youth from a nearby village, one who is equally as virtuous as the girl. Although sometimes awkwardly expressed, the text as adequate. It is longer and more complex than most retellings, and such added details as the names of actual places in northern Arizona ground the story and make it seem more real, but at other times slow it down. The beautifully executed, sophisticated, abstract, two-dimensional paintings extensively employ such Southwestern Indian cultural motifs and features as kivas and pueblo dwellings to create setting. Their abstractness avoids cultural stereotyping. Some have borders with patterns drawn from the culture located horizontally at the bottom of the page which also help to move the story. The colors build up in intensity as the story proceeds, and although most pictures are serious, some employ humor, for example, the "touseled" Winds in their kiva are appropriately so. This is an unusual book. A note about the cultural motifs in the pictures would be helpful. For a Maya version of this story, see *The Mouse Bride* (no. 500), and for Oriental variants, see *The Wedding of the Rat Family* (no. 305), *The Greatest of All* (no. 306), and *The Moles and the Mireuk* (no. 307).

516 Malotki, Ekkehart, and Michael Lomatuway'ma, colls., *Gullible Coyote/Una'ihu: A Bilingual Collection of Hopi Coyote Stories*, illus. Anne-Marie Malotki, University of Arizona Press, 1986 (hardcover), ISBN 0-8165-0908-5, $35.00, 181 pp. Ages 14 up, grades 9 up.

Twelve Hopi stories featuring the trickster Coyote, presented in both Hopi and English on each page, collected mostly from Third Mesa. After an introduction about the Coyote figure among the Hopi, the tales tell of anthropomorphized Coyote's interactions with mostly other humanized small animals, including birds, skunks, owls, and lizards. Gullible Coyote allows ants to tie him about the waist with yucca ropes so tightly he can barely breathe. He

insists that Little Turtle sing for him, threatens him with various dire conse-
quences if he does not, then throws him into the Little Colorado, where Little
Turtle wanted to go all along. He loses his eyes when he tries to imitate
Skeleton who can pop out his eyes and then retrieve them. Some tales involve
Coyote Woman, for example, when she eats Antelope and loses her children
as a result. Stories of greed, silliness, laziness—a variety of vices and short-
comings of character that reveal the Hopis' view "that the animal [coyote] is
a rather ordinary critter with no positive attributes whatsoever," except as a
reverse moral force and as fun. Unabridged, unexpurgated, the stories are fine
examples of folk materials, exuberant, lively, but also frequently very earthy.
While the tales themselves are ridiculous in the antics they describe and
satirize the figure and similar human behavior, the tone is consistently respectful and dignified. For a scholarly work, the stories read unusually well
and offer much entertainment. The angular, rusty-red and black designs that
occupy full pages and are scattered about are based on Southwestern Indian
motifs. They add to the sense of setting and make the book visually attractive.
References, a Hopi alphabet, and a glossary are included. The same two collectors have also published *Hopi Coyote Tales/Istutuwutsi* (1984).

517 Malotki, Ekkehart, and Michael Lomatuway'ma, colls. and trans.,
Stories of Maasaw, a Hopi God, illus. Petra Roeckerath, University of
Nebraska Press, 1987 (hardcover), ISBN 0-8032-3117-2, $30.00, 547
pp. Ages 15 up, grades 10 up.

Sixteen well-told myths about Maasaw, "probably the most intriguing and
multifaceted divine personage in Hopi mythology." The stories are collected,
translated, and edited by Malotki, a language scholar, and Lomatuway'ma,
whose family contributed some stories. The stories, which come mostly from
Third Mesa, are presented in both English and Hopi. They show Maasaw in
various phases, for example, in the opening story as a tall, handsome youth
(the form he usually assumes when associating with humans), who woos a
beautiful Hopi maiden. When he patrols the mesas and villages at night to
see where he might help his people, he usually wears a mask that is so grotesque it causes viewers to faint. Once it so frightens Skunk that Skunk uri-
nates on Maasaw, and as a result Skunk receives the putrid stench that skunks
have today. Sometimes Maasaw is a boy with parents and a grandmother who
plays games and yearns for friends, but mostly he is an anthropomorphized,
beneficent deity with trickster aspects. Although intended as a scholarly work
to preserve the stories and the language as well, the myths read more smoothly
than those in most such references. They are filled with names of real Hopi
villages and sites and details of everyday practices and cultural ideas that make
what happens seem very real. An extensive glossary and a Hopi alphabet are
included. The stiff, black-and-white, angular illustrations employ Hopi masks,

costumes, and motifs. The sequel is *Maasaw—Profile of a Hopi God* (1987). Malotki has also published *Hopi Ruin Legends* (1993), less readable stories about various Hopi villages, and *Earth Fire: A Hopi Legend of the Sunset Crater Eruption* (1987), a pleasingly retold and beautifully designed book by Northland Press about the volcanic event of from 700 to 900 years ago that produced the major tourist attraction northeast of Flagstaff, Arizona, known as Sunset Crater National Monument. The legend, a long kachina tale related in English and Hopi, is illustrated with stunning photographs by Stephen Trimble and is accompanied by essays about the geology of the area and a glossary.

518 Martin, Rafe, ret., *The Boy Who Lived with the Seals*, illus. David Shannon, Putnam, 1993 (hardcover), ISBN 0-399-22413-0, $14.95, unp. Ages 4–10, grades PS–5.

Retelling that elaborates on a Wasco (Chinook) folktale from Jarold Ramsey's collection of Oregon tales, *Coyote Was Going There* (1977). While on spring migration with his people along the Columbia River, a boy of five or six wanders away from his father, and although the tribe searches diligently, they cannot find him and continue on their journey. Time passes, and word comes of a boy living with seals on an offshore Pacific island. He is brought home, and his parents patiently help him relearn human speech and ways, but he is never again comfortable with his people. He becomes a talented carver, often working at the edge of the river, whose seals call to him, until he breaks away and rejoins them in their home beneath the sea. The dark, haunting paintings catch the story's intensity and poignancy and are particularly memorable for the beauty of the Northwest carvings and the arresting patterns in the bold compositions, for example, in the illustration of the search and those combining seals, waves, and boy. Some have a carefully controlled, understated eloquence that stretch the story, but some are so dark that it is hard to discern figures and determine what is intended. A reteller's note gives information about the story and the people.

519 Martin, Rafe, ret., *The Rough-Face Girl*, illus. David Shannon, Putnam, 1992 (hardcover), ISBN 0-399-21859-9, $14.95, unp. Ages 4–10, grades PS–5.

Retelling of an Algonquin folktale of the Cinderella variety. The text is adequate, but the illustrations fall far short. Two cruel sisters fail to win the presumably marvelous and handsome Invisible One who lives in the huge wigwam at the edge of the settlement, but their younger sister, the Rough-Face Girl, whose face is scarred from working by the fire, has the goodness of heart to see beauty in nature. She passes the tests to win him, and, after bathing in the lake as instructed, becomes as lovely on the outside as she is within. The dark, atmospheric paintings with bold figures overpower the story and are sometimes inaccurate. They depict tipis instead of wigwams and employ costumes and motifs of questionable validity. In places they are humorous to the point of absurdity. A brief reteller's note gives information about the story type but does not specify the source of the story other than by group. This is a valuable and interesting version of the tale type but less successful as a whole than *The Boy Who Lived with the Seals* (no. 518) by the same writer and illustrator.

520 Mayo, Gretchen Will, ret., *Star Tales: North American Indian Stories about the Stars*, illus. Gretchen Will Mayo, Walker, 1987 (hardcover), ISBN 0-8027-6672-2, $11.95, 96 pp. Ages 5–12, grades K–7.

Fourteen respectfully and entertainingly retold tales from different Native-American Indian groups, almost all in the continental United States, about the stars, moon, and sun, most of them of the *pourquoi* variety. A Salish story humorously sees the constellations of Auriga and Perseus as angry women trapping a hungry skunk attempting to raid their food. A Coeur d'Alene story explains the Swan as a tragically slain snow goose. Also included are Blackfeet stories about the angry moon, the Iroquois explanation of the Pleiades as disobedient, dancing youths, and an Ojibwa tale of the star marriage genre, among others. The black-and-white, atmospheric illustrations are based on museum artifacts. Sometimes too romantic, the human faces and bodies are usually superbly realized, and animals have muscles and textured hides and skins and are incredibly lifelike. Interestingly written, short notes precede each story, a list of sources and a glossary of terms appears at the end, and a helpful map at the beginning shows the location of the tribes. *Earthmaker's Tales: North American Indian Stories about Earth Happenings* (1989) contains sixteen stories from a wider continental range, about such matters as how the earth began for the Wyandot, why the Otos say earthquakes occur, and why the volcano erupts according to the Nisqually. Sequels are *More Star Tales* (1991) and *More Earthmaker's Tales* (1991).

521 McDermott, Gerald, ret., *Raven: A Trickster Tale from the Pacific Northwest*, illus. Gerald McDermott, Harcourt, 1993 (hardcover), ISBN 0-15-265661-8, $14.95, unp. Ages 4–10, grades PS–5.

Retelling of the Pacific Northwest Indian (specific group not indicated) story of how Raven the trickster puts the sun in the sky. Born as the grandson of the Sky Chief, Raven fusses until the old man gives him the shining ball of the sun. Raven then changes back into his bird form, flies off, and flings the sun into the sky, thus bringing light into a hitherto dark world. Typical of McDermott's work, the sophisticated illustrations are very dramatic, deeply colored, stylized paintings, tending toward the abstract and patterned after Northwest Indian visual art. They retell the very spare, almost poetic text, adding details of place, characterization, and action. The people in the Sky Chief's dwelling have facial characteristics and costumes that identify them as of different Indian groups. The depiction of Raven is based on the coastal raven masks. Although the flow of the narrative is interrupted by occasional questions addressed to the reader, this is a stunning book, with powerfully done exteriors, interiors, and close-ups appropriate for so magnificent an event. See, for comparison, the versions by Ann Dixon (no. 499) and Susan Hand Shetterly (no. 536).

522 Mike, Jan M., ad., *Opossum and the Great Firemaker: A Mexican Legend*, illus. Charles Reasoner, Rourke, 1993 (hardcover), ISBN 0-8167-3055-5, $11.95, 32 pp.; Troll, 1993 (paper), ISBN 0-8167-3056-3, $3.95, 32 pp. Ages 4–11, grades PS–6.

Retelling of a legend of the Cora Indians, Native Americans of the Aztecan group in Mexico. When Great Firemaker Iguana takes fire away from the village and carries it high up the cliff, the people persuade nondescript, little Opossum to try to recover it. She makes the precarious ascent, cleverly outwits Iguana by twisting her tail around a burning stick, and flings the stick like a torch over the cliff. When Iguana beats her with a stick, she feigns death, then rolls over the cliff to the people below who catch her in a blanket. Thus opossums today have gray bodies and black, hairless tails and "play possum." Iguana vents his anger by stamping the cliff with his foot, with each stamp growing smaller, and thus he is the size of a lizard today. Two-dimensional, boldly constructed pictures dramatically done in rich color with black lines filling in the angular figures retell the pleasingly phrased story and emphasize the action and trickery. A note about the Cora people and tricksters concludes the book, but unfortunately no source for the story is given. This is a Legends of the World book.

523 Norman, Howard, ret., *How Glooskap Outwits the Ice Giants and Other Tales of the Maritime Indians*, illus. Michael McCurdy, Little, Brown, 1989 (hardcover), ISBN 0-316-61181-6, $14.95, 60 pp. Ages 8–12, grades 3–7.

Six retold tales from the Abenaki of Maine and the Maritime Provinces of Canada. The stories show the giant Glooskap primarily in his creator and protector aspects, but occasionally his buffoon side appears. They tell of how, after he creates the earth, he makes humans and then by wit, strength, and magic he saves them from the cannibal Ice Giants and Panther-Witch and from a mischievous stormbird named Wuchowsen, among other beneficial acts, before retiring with his wolf helpers to a home beyond a mystical river. The stories move directly and simply with uncomplicated sentences and concrete diction. They have plenty of action and conflict and here and there touches of humor and tall tale. The beautifully rendered, stylized, black-and-white wood engravings reveal Glooskap's character and picture his deeds. *Who-Paddled-Backward-with-Trout* (1987; illus. Ed Young) is a single Cree folktale from northern Manitoba for younger readers, and *The Owl Scatterer* (1986) is a picture-story book of fiction about Native Americans also set in Canada and illustrated by Michael McCurdy.

524 Norman, Howard, sel. and ed., *Northern Tales: Traditional Stories of Eskimo and Indian Peoples*, Pantheon, 1991 (hardcover), ISBN 0-394-54060-3, $24.95, 343 pp. Ages 12 up, grades 7 up.

More than one hundred traditional tales, selected from sources and edited for readability. Almost all the stories in this fine collection are from the Inuit (Eskimo) and Native-American Indians of Canada, but a dozen of the Wenebojo myths of the Wisconsin Ojibwa (Chippewa) and a half-dozen about Kuloscap of the Micmac of the Maritimes, including Maine, appear, along with a short but good introduction about the trickster figure, and also a few Abenaki tales of Maine. Introductory essays, maps, and an excellent bibliography of sources are included. Compare with Howard Norman's *How Glooskap Outwits the Ice Giants* (no. 523), Alethea K. Helbig's *Nanabozhoo, Giver of Life* (no. 507), and several other stories about Coyote. Norman has also published novels about Cree in Canada, including *Northern Lights* (1987), which has a white protagonist, and picture books of folklore and fiction.

525 Oughton, Jerrie, ret., *How the Stars Fell into the Sky: A Navajo Legend*, illus. Lisa Desimini, Houghton, 1992 (hardcover), ISBN 0-395-58798-0, $14.95, unp. Ages 4–10, grades PS–5.

Adaptation of a creation myth told by Hosteen Klah, renowned Navajo medicine man of the very early 1900s. At the beginning of things, First Woman, the leading character, informs First Man that people need a way of finding out about the laws. After suggesting she write them in sand and on waves, both judged unsatisfactory, he suggests she write them in the night sky with her jewels, the stars. Coyote asks to help but soon grows impatient at the slow progress and flings the remaining stars into the sky. Hence "confusion . . .

would always dwell" among people because of the helter-skelter disarray among the constellations. For the most part, the narrative has a quiet, almost poetic movement and appropriate dignity, which are pleasingly supported by the dark-toned, sparsely detailed, organically patterned, highly dramatic paintings, although the Biblical Madonna-like presentation of First Woman in one picture is startling. The hogans shown are the early conical type, a touch that is welcome in its accuracy. This is a particularly beautiful book. For comparison, see Harriet Peck Taylor's *Coyote Places the Stars* (no. 539).

526 Palacios, Argentina, ad., The Hummingbird King: A Guatemalan Legend, illus. Felipe Davalos, Rourke, 1993 (hardcover), ISBN 0-8167-3051-1, $11.95, 32 pp.; Troll, 1993 (Paper), ISBN 0-8167-3052-0, $3.95, 32 pp. Ages 4–11, grades PS–6.

Retelling of a legend from the Maya of Guatemala. The appearance of an exceptionally beautiful hummingbird at his birth indicates that Kukul will be extraordinary, and at his naming the priest gives the baby a protective red feather found beneath the hummingbird's tree. Kukul grows to be unusually handsome and intelligent; he is chosen king and is invincible in battle. His jealous uncle steals the feather and kills Kukul for the throne. Kukul is metamorphosed into the brightly colored quetzal bird, an ancient symbol of authority and today a mark of freedom. The brilliant paintings capture the feel of the tropics in their colors, while the people and objects are patterned after Maya reliefs, sculptures, and pictures in codexes and are set against the background of the Mesoamerican pyramids. They are very decorative and dramatic. Although the terms used to refer to the people are incorrect and occasional overwriting mars the tone, this is an attractive book and an excellent sample of a Maya story. A page of information about the Maya concludes the book, but no source is given for the tale. This is a Legends of the World book.

527 Pijoan, Teresa, coll. and ret., *White Wolf Woman: Native American Transformation Myths*, August House, 1992 (hardcover), ISBN 0-87483-201-2, $17.95, 160 p.; (paper), ISBN 0-87483-200-4, $8.95, 160 pp. Ages 8 up, grades 3 up.

Three dozen retold stories from thirty Native-American Indian groups across the North American continent. They are divided into four sections, stories of snakes, wolves, bears, and miscellaneous animals, that reveal "the wonder of transformation" and the perpetual change of life and show that in Native thought "[t]here is no division between animals and people." The book opens with a helpful essay about Native-American story tradition and important beliefs and ends with notes about the sources of the tales and the tellers. The title story, for example, tells of a kidnapped Zuni maiden who survives with the help of a great white wolf and when aged becomes a wolf herself. Other stories tell of the youth who becomes the snake-man who guards the Mississippi River, of the wolf son of the great Wolf-Chief who helps out the starving people until they mistreat him, of animal-human marriages, magic, shape changing, broken taboos that bring trouble—a wide variety of subjects in mostly short and consistently interesting stories. The tales are sparse in detail of character and setting and are plot oriented, as is the nature of stories from oral tradition, but they are often awkwardly phrased and hence lack the smoothness that makes for fluent eye reading. Nevertheless, the book offers valuable insights and much good material for storytellers. See also other books by this well-known storyteller: under Teresa Pijoan de Van Etten, *Spanish-American Folktales* (no. 397), and under Teresa VanEtten, *Ways of Indian Magic: Stories Retold* (no. 468), stories of fantasy based on Tewa legends, and a novel, *Dead Kachina Man* (no. 467).

528 Rodanas, Kristina, ret., *Dragonfly's Tale*, illus. Kristina Rodanas, Clarion, 1992 (hardcover), ISBN 0-395-57003-4, $14.95, unp. Ages 4–10, grades PS–5.

Retelling of a Zuni folktale. Blessed by the two Corn Maidens with more corn than they need, the people of Hawikah stage a mock battle, their weapons being cornbread and dough. Disguised as beggars, the Corn Maidens visit the village and observe the sacrilegious battle with disgust. They withdraw their gift of good weather, and a famine results. The people flee the village in search of food, leaving behind two children, a boy and a girl. The boy fashions an insectlike creature of corn husks, who comes alive as a dragonfly and carries word of their plight to the Corn Maidens. Because the two children had extended hospitality to the Corn Maidens as beggars, the spirits send their messengers with ample corn, beans, and squash to enable the two children to survive and enjoy an ample harvest the next year as well. When the people return, they realize the error of their ways and honor the spirits. Done in tawny tones, the oversize, off-the-page, representational paintings recreate the Southwestern setting, with very lifelike, three-dimensional human figures, tiered houses atop mesas, vegetables, animals, and pots, which are decorated with appropriate motifs. The illustrations ground this story of miracle and respect for nature's gifts firmly in reality. According to a note, this tale, which is related with dignity in somewhat formal language, comes from the collection gathered by Frank Cushing. This is an exceptionally beautiful book.

529 Rohmer, Harriet, Octavio Chow, and Morris Vidaure, rets., *The Invisible Hunters/Los Cazadores Invisibles*, illus. Joe Sam, Children's Book, 1987 (hardcover), ISBN 0-89239-031-X, $10.95, 32 pp.; 1993 (paper), ISBN 0-59239-109-X, $5.95, 32 pp. Ages 5–10, grades K–5.

Retelling from various oral sources of a Miskito Indian legend from Nicaragua, that traces back to pre-Conquest times and is "a metaphor for what has happened to traditional cultures." The dramatic and ultimately instructive events are repeated in colorful, decorative, detailed pictures made of primitively stylized paper cut-collages and paintings in which the human figures are sticklike, nude, and masked. The illustrations give the feel of the jungle setting and intensify the horror of the characters' foolishness and subsequent punishment. Three hunters of wari (wild pig), brothers, receive from the sacred, magical Dar vine the gift of invisibility with the proviso that they must always share the meat with their people and never sell it or hunt with guns. When outsiders (Europeans) arrive and persuade them otherwise, the Dar makes them invisible permanently, after which they are outlawed by their tribe. The story is told first in English, then in Spanish on each page. A note about the story's source appears at the end. Equally impressive is Rohmer's retelling of another Miskito myth, decorated by Virginia Stearns's richly colored, strongly composed paintings, *Mother Scorpion Country/La Tierra de la Madre Escorpion* (1987). A loving, brave, young husband accompanies his beautiful, just-deceased wife to the land of the dead where welcoming Mother Scorpion rules, only to discover that he does not want to remain there. This compelling version of the widespread "harrowing of hell," or Orpheus, type of story is told in both English and Spanish. A note about how Rohmer discovered the tale is included. Earlier, Rohmer published *How We Came to the Fifth World/Como Vinimos al Quinto Mundo* (1976; reissued 1990), an adaptation of the Aztec "myth of the ages," in which each age, or world or sun (terms vary), was created and then destroyed until the current one, the fifth, came to be. Brilliantly colored, highly decorative, abstract collages by Graciela Carrillo emphasize the drama of the story. These are all fine books.

530 Roth, Susan L., ret., *Kanahena: A Cherokee Story*, illus. Susan L. Roth, St. Martin's Press, 1988 (hardcover), ISBN 0-312-01722-7, $9.95, unp. Ages 4–8, grades PS–3.

Retelling of a Cherokee trickster tale with a *pourquoi* ending. After Bad Wolf chokes on a persimmon, Terrapin uses Bad Wolf's ears as spoons to eat kanahena (cornmeal mush), angering Bad Wolf's companions who capture Terrapin. They threaten to kill him by boiling and roasting, but each time he laughs at them. When they threaten to drown him, he feigns fright, and thus through trickery he escapes. The scars where he broke his shell on a rock can still be seen on his back. The frame story of an old woman telling the tale to a little girl while making kanahena seems an unnecessary and condescending contrivance, but the story is otherwise smoothly told. Decorating it are full-color collages of "natural materials, including leaves, grasses, cotton, and real cornmeal, along with colored paper." Although sometimes too fussy and cutesy, they bring out the story's homespun, underdog humor. Best are the cut-paper ones, especially those of the angry wolves, done in black on white grounds, appropriately snarling, their eyes red with fury, their bodies angular and distorted, vividly memorable.

531   Roth, Susan L., ret., *The Story of Light*, illus. Susan L. Roth, Morrow, 1990 (hardcover), ISBN 0-688-08676-4, $12.95, unp. Ages 4–10, grades PS–5.

Retelling of a version of the Cherokee myth of how light was brought to earth. When both possum and buzzard fail to bring back a spark from the sun so that animals may see, the smallest of all, the denigrated spider, volunteers. She spins a web as she follows the sun's rays eastward, places the tiniest of sparks in a pot she molded for the purpose, and follows her thread home. Other elements explained by the story are the appearance of the buzzard's head and the possum's tail, both burned bare in their unsuccessful attempts. The text is brief and to the point; its spirit is elaborated by the very dramatic, stylized woodcuts in black and white with points of yellow for the light-reflected eyes and the yellow sun or its symbols. When the possum is at the sun's place, both pages are entirely yellow, a technique that gives a startling impression of intense brightness. The cuts flow around the text, integrated with it in placement, move the action along, and make the book a beautifully composite work of art.

532   Rucki, Ani, ret., *Turkey's Gift to the People*, illus. Ani Rucki, Northland, 1992 (hardcover), ISBN 0-87358-541-0, $14.95, unp. Ages 4–10, grades PS–5.

Retelling of a Navajo folktale. When Crow reports that a wall of water is approaching from the west, the People (animals) gather and at the suggestion of Mouse take refuge in a huge reed, the different animals contributing variously for the salvation of all. Last to enter before Wasp seals the entrance hole are a Turkey couple, who have been delayed by gathering seeds in order to ensure survival after the waters recede. This account of the importance of community effort and appreciation for everyone's contribution holds the attention even if marred occasionally by awkward and condescending phraseology. The dark, brooding, stylized illustrations, close up, boldly composed, and arresting, add to the drama and feeling of urgency and are clearly the best part of the book. While the spread of the flood engulfing the hills is confusing, some pictures, like the close-ups of the bear, eagle, and wolf and of spider weaving a web, are strong, involving, and textured. Although it does not indicate the specific source, an introductory note says that the narrative is "based upon a traditional Navajo folktale" and "is not meant to be an accurate retelling of the traditional folktale, but an adaptation and interpretation of it," a puzzlingly ambiguous statement. The title seems in error. Although the possessive is singular, both Mr. and Mrs. Turkey (as they are referred to in the book) collected the seeds.

533 Sexton, James D., trans. and ed., *Mayan Folktales*, Doubleday, 1992 (paper), ISBN 0-385-42253-9, $14.00, 265 pp. Ages 12 up, grades 7 up.

Thirty-five pleasingly retold folktales and myths from the Maya Indians of the Lake Atitlan area of Guatemala. Most were either told by or collected by the translator and reteller's Maya research assistant, Ignacio Bizarro Ujpan, who also collaborated on producing the book. A combination of indigenous and Spanish motifs, characters, and episodes, the stories range from the robustly humorous, including the one about the woman who unwittingly eats a portion of her lover's penis, through a trickster tale embodying a tar baby variant, to a serious version of the Adam and Eve story, which is part Christian and part pagan and ends with the death of God's son. Many of the tales are cautionary, warning against such behaviors as laziness and arrogance and stressing the importance of keeping one's word and using one's wits. Some stories describe ceremonial dances, for example, "Story of the Dance of the Deer" and "Dance of the Flying Monkey." A lot of very entertaining reading is presented with a highly informative introduction, detailed notes, a bibliography, and a glossary of Spanish and Indian terms that appear in the tales and increase their flavor.

534 Shetterly, Susan Hand, ret., *The Dwarf-Wizard of Uxmal*, illus. Robert Shetterly, Atheneum, 1990 (hardcover), ISBN 0-689-31455-8, $13.95, unp. Ages 5–10, grades K–5.

Retelling of a Maya folktale. This amusing, droll (numbskull) story explains the origin of the huge temple pyramid that dominates the ruins of the ancient Maya city of Uxmal in the Yucatan of Mexico. A little boy, who is magically hatched from an egg, is helped by a supernatural old woman and some animals to become the ruler of Uxmal, putting in place the pyramid she models from corn meal and causes to grow to its current size. The text of this account of how the least one triumphs with extraordinary luck and pluck is overwritten with many details of setting and action that clutter the story and make it more like a short story than the finely honed narratives of folklore. The detailed illustrations evoke the lush, dark jungles, catch the occasional humor and frequent instances of drama, and reveal the influence on the artist of ancient Maya drawings and sculptures.

535   Shetterly, Susan Hand, ret., *Muwin and the Magic Hare*, illus. Robert Shetterly, Atheneum, 1993 (hardcover), ISBN 0-689-31699-2, $14.95, unp. Ages 4–10, grades PS–5.

Retelling of a Passamaquoddy trickster tale about the Great Magic Hare. When hungry Muwin, the big black bear, decides to have rabbit for dinner before he retires to his den for the winter, he does not realize that the Passamaquoddy hunter, medicine woman, and chief whom he meets and who feed and entertain him are really the trickster and creator rabbit, the Great Hare, Mahtoqehs, transformed. Impressive, full-palette paintings capture the physical power and also the slow wit of Muwin, as well as the cleverness and resourcefulness of the rabbit. They support the story's rhythm by slowing down so the viewer can view landscapes or take in close-ups of the characters. Sometimes they speed up the action and add details to the story. The Indians are individualized and given strength of character, and the portrait pictures of all the figures are arresting. The book opens with a glossary of Passamaquoddy terms and a note about combined efforts being made by the Waponahki Nation, of which these people are one group, to preserve their culture.

536   Shetterly, Susan Hand, ret., *Raven's Light: A Myth from the People of the Northwest Coast*, illus. Robert Shetterly, Atheneum, 1991 (hardcover), ISBN 0-689-31629-1, $13.95, unp. Ages 4–10, grades PS–5.

Retelling of an old story, according to the book jacket, of the Tlingit, Haida, Kwaklutl [*sic*], and Tsimshian Native-American Indians of the Pacific Northwest. After creating the earth, vegetation, animals, and humans, Raven the trickster brings light to earth from the sky world by causing himself to be born as a baby boy to the daughter of the Great Chief, from whom he steals Day. Raven's trickster aspects are indicated by his sly characterization in the often dramatic, mostly dark-toned, handsome paintings. They utilize such details of the Northwest people as colorful masks and distinctively patterned blankets to establish setting. The pictures in which the different heavenly lights are put in place are striking, with the sudden, brilliant glows against the dark grounds, and the final scene shows Raven guffawing in glee as the glare of the rising sun turns his feathers fiery red. Although the faces of the Indians have a disturbing comic quality, the pictures' frequent witticisms support the trickster genre, and the reproductions of the masks at book's opening,

Raven hiding inside the beak of the raven one, strike the right introductory note. Two shorter versions of the same story are by Ann Dixon (no. 499) and Gerald McDermott (no. 521).

537   Stevens, Janet, ret., *Coyote Steals the Blanket: A Ute Tale*, illus. Janet Stevens, Holiday, 1993 (hardcover), ISBN-0-8234-0996-1, $15.95, unp. Ages 4–8, grades PS–3.

Retelling of a folktale of the Ute people. In spite of Hummingbird's warning, Coyote the trickster helps himself to a beautiful blanket he finds draped over a big stone. The stone rolls after him in angry pursuit through canyons and desert, finally, when Coyote is exhausted and can flee no further, landing on his tail and flattening it. Hummingbird attacks the stone very aggressively, forcing it to move and allowing Coyote to get away and his tail to return to normal. The hilarity plays down the didacticism and is perfectly caught in the large, colorful, almost cartoonish pictures that show the nature of the characters—lazy, unkempt, silly Coyote, determined fighter Hummingbird, and the stubborn, persistent stone—and exude a marvelous sense of movement and action. A hint that Coyote has not learned his lesson (typical of the trickster character) appears on the last page, which depicts him dashing madly away again, the blanket streaming out behind him and the stone again rolling in hot pursuit. A very funny story about taking what is not one's property, about helpfulness, and about the inability of certain people to learn lessons. A note about the source appears at the beginning of the book.

538   Strauss, Susan, ret., *Coyote Stories for Children: Tales from Native America*, illus. Gary Lund, Beyond Words, 1991 (hardcover), ISBN 0-941831-61-2, $10.95, unp.; (paper), ISBN 0-941831-62-0, $6.95, unp. Ages 6–12, grades 1–7.

Four retold stories about Coyote the trickster-culture hero-fool from the Okanogan, Wasco, Karok, and Assiniboin groups, and one very short fiction story contributed by a kindergarten student, plus two introductory notes about the figure and the genre. Coyote props his eyes open with sticks in order to stay awake all night but falls asleep anyway, gets rid of a monster woman by throwing her out to sea, gets in trouble by laughing at Spider Woman's "butt," and eats the grass people to try to show them he is stronger than they and then suffers from the gas they cause. The narrative voice is strong, intimate, and occasionally digressive in the manner of actual oral tellers. The slightly scurrilous nature of the last two tales is characteristic of Coyote tales, but usually when this kind of tale appears in children's collections, such words as "butt" and "fart," which are authentic and used here, are avoided. The pen-and-ink comic sketches are busy with patterning. The kindergartner's story, which has Coyote tricking squirrels, shows that the writer has caught Coyote's nature.

539 Taylor, Harriet Peck, ret., *Coyote Places the Stars*, illus. Harriet Peck Taylor, Bradbury, 1993 (hardcover), ISBN 0-02-78845-2, $14.95, unp. Ages 4–8, grades PS–3.

Retelling of a Wasco (Chinook) story about the trickster Coyote, here in his culture-hero aspect. One summer night, curious about the secrets of the heavens, Coyote makes an arrow ladder to the moon. From there, he shoots arrows to push the stars around into the shapes of his friends Bear, Mountain Lion, Fish, Goat, Eagle, and others. Returned to earth, he howls to call his friends together to admire his handiwork. He howls yet today to remind people to admire the beauty of the night sky. This pleasantly told story explaining the constellations and the coyote's howl is extended by full-color, off-the-page, posterlike illustrations made of dye on cloth, their details done with wax resist. Their bold patterns complement Coyote's brashness and emphasize the magnitude of his creation, while at the same time their slightly comic attitude catches that aspect of his character also, as well as his arrogance and conceit. The picture showing the animals gathered together and gazing up at their pictures done in stars captures the beauty of the night heavens. See also Jerrie Oughton's *How the Stars Fell into the Sky* (no. 525).

540 Van Laan, Nancy, ret., *Buffalo Dance: A Blackfoot Legend*, illus. Beatriz Vidal, Joy Street, 1993 (hardcover), ISBN 0-316-79728-0, $15.95, unp. Ages 4–10, grades PS–5.

Retelling of an explanatory folktale about a Blackfeet girl who rashly promises to marry one of the herd if the buffalo willingly jump into her starving people's trap, is held to her bargain by the bull-chief, and is eventually taught the ritual buffalo dance, which she takes back to her people. Reducing the impact of this attractively illustrated version of a traditional *pourquoi* legend from George Bird Grinnell's important collection, entitled *Blackfoot Lodge Tales* (1892), are inept pacing, unclear motivations, and poor choice of language in the narrative; in the pictures, the costumes are of dubious authenticity and the protagonist is depicted as the stereotypical Indian princess and the bull-chief like the fairy-tale beast in "Beauty and the Beast." He even stands upright while the rest of the herd remain on all fours. A glossary and an introductory note are included.

541   Van Laan, Nancy, ret., *Rainbow Crow: A Lenape Tale,* illus. Beatriz Vidal, Knopf, 1989 (hardcover), ISBN 0-394-89577-0, $12.95, unp.; 1991 (paper), ISBN 0-679-81942-8, $5.99, unp. Ages 4–10, grades PS–5.

Retelling of an explanatory folktale of the Lenape people. When, in the "long, long ago," so much snow falls that the animals fear they will be buried, Crow, who at that time had rainbow-colored feathers and a sweet voice, volunteers to fly to the Great Sky Spirit for help. The Spirit gives him fire with which to melt the snow, but before Crow gets back the soot turns his feathers black and the ashes make his throat hoarse. The Great Spirit rewards his bravery and unselfishness with the gift of freedom. The text is stronger than the pictures, although the occasional little verses seem incongruously "cute." Many of the full-color, stylized, abstract illustrations resemble greeting-card art, with cuddly animals on antiseptic snowscapes, but the pictures of rainbow-hued Crow going to and returning from the Great Spirit are more strongly composed as is that of the blackened Crow. A note about the story is included.

542   Walters, Anna Lee, ret., *The Two-Legged Creature: An Otoe Story,* illus. Carol Bowles, Northland, 1993 (hardcover), ISBN 0-87358-553-4, $14.95, unp. Ages 4–10, grades PS–5.

Retelling by a Pawnee-Otoe writer of an Otoe (Plains) explanatory tale. Man and animals live together in peace and harmony. They help one another and call one another Brother. But Man turns mean for some reason, speaks rudely to the creatures, and whines and pouts for his own way. Concerned for his well-being, the animals deliberate to no conclusion about what to do with this unruly person. Finally, Dog and Horse volunteer to "go with Man. We will keep him company and be his friend." Thus "dogs and horses are so close to people today." This amusing, straightforwardly told story is handsomely complemented by bright, full-color, off-the-page, expressionistic paintings. In their diagonal, wavy lines, patchily constructed forms, and such varied motifs as small tracks, floating stars, rainbows, and leaning trees, they show the action and the characters and convey a strong sense of an early, undifferentiated time when the world was very young.

12
Native-American Indians: Books of Poetry

543 Alexie, Sherman, *The Business of Fancydancing: Stories and Poems,* Hanging Loose, 1992 (hardcover), ISBN 0-914610-24-4, $18.00, 84 pp.; (paper), ISBN 0-914610-00-7, $10.00, 84 pp. Ages 14 up, grades 9 up.

A collection of forty patterned and prose poems and five short stories about contemporary Spokane Indian reservation life in eastern Washington State. Some poems express the hopelessness of deep poverty, lost cultural identity, and deeply wounded ethnic pride, what Alexie calls "Crazy Horse dreams," that is, "the kind that don't [ever] come true," and exploitation by whites, but most are portraits of enduring, hopeful people trying to make the best of bad situations and sometimes having fun together doing it. The wryly humorous "Evolution" tells how "Buffalo Bill opens a pawn shop on the reservation" opposite the liquor store, and "Futures" ironically describes when "We lived in the HUD house" and ate welfare cheese and meat. Most poems are free and lacking in music, but some are metered with varied rhythms, and some are tightly structured, among them clever sestinas, like the title poem. Although the poems exude sadness and speak of deplorable conditions, the overall tone is upbeat, and there is some humor, usually ironic. The thought-provoking pieces have levels of meaning, but they present no problems with accessibility and have a strong oral flavor. For the short stories in this book, see no. 411.

544 Alexie, Sherman, *Old Shirts & New Skins,* illus. Elizabeth Woody, University of California Press, 1993 (paper), ISBN 0-935626-36-0, $12.00, 94 pp. Ages 14 up, grades 9 up.

Fifty poems, among them a few prose-poems, by one of the most highly regarded of today's young, Native-American Indian poets, a Spokane–Coeur d'Alene from the state of Washington. Some pieces are tightly structured couplets or quatrains, but most are loosely free and move fluently if prosily to punchy, ironic endings. Informed by the poet's growing up and life on the reservation and among urban Indians, they paint vivid pictures of mothers in poverty and on welfare, drunks in bars, commodity foods, HUD housing, fathers disappearing, Indians in hospitals, playing basketball, an Indian girl lying dead in a field—a wide variety of subjects. The poems are in fluenced also by historical events, for example, the capture and slaying of 1,000 Spokane ponies by the U.S. Cavalry. In one piece, Custer attempts to justify himself, and others feature Crazy Horse. The poet assumes his own and other personas to speak of cynicism, anger, depression, and degradation. He speaks also of joys and of family and individual closeness, and, finally, of an underlying hope for the survival of Native peoples. In this varied, engaging collection, the best poems are the shorter ones. The book is beautifully illustrated with lithographs. Other collections of poems by Alexie are *I Would Steal Horses* (1993) and *First Indian on the Moon* (1993).

545 Allen, Paula Gunn, *Skins and Bones: Poems 1979–87,* West End, 1988 (paper), ISBN 0-931122-50-3, $6.95, 69 pp. Ages 15 up, grades 10 up.

Two dozen original poems by a Laguna-Sioux-Lebanese-American poet "in celebration of our lives and our deaths," with a strongly feminine and feminist bent about matters both Native American and general. Free-verse poems from the points of view of Eve, Malinche (Maya companion of Cortes), Pocahontas, and Sacagawea intermingle, among others, with pieces about lost dreams, a son who fails to call, callous anti-ecologists, teaching poetry to uninterested students, a dying grandmother, deer woman, and the amazing joy of a new morning. The shorter poems have punch; their pithiness and skillful craft achieve power. In *Wyrds* (1987), forty cleanly crafted poems speak reflectively and introspectively about mostly general topics, although the Southwestern setting dominates. Particularly notable are a set of school poems that rose from Allen's experience teaching in an alternative school in Santa Fe, New Mexico, and the character sketch of the real, and symbolic, Indian uncle, who will "Never Cry Uncle." The book's central set of thirty short poems, collectively called "Runes," though monochromatic and overly imagistic, will appeal to teen readers. As in *Skins*, the shorter poems, though lacking in music, rise above the others.

546 Carlstrom, Nancy White, *Northern Lullaby,* illus. Leo Dillon and Diane Dillon, Philomel, 1992 (hardcover), ISBN 0-399-21806-8, $15.95, unp. Ages 1 up, grades PS up.

Lullaby wishing good night to Papa Star, Mama Moon, Grandpa Mountain, and other figures of nature, including Cousins Beaver, Deer Mouse, and Red

Fox. The simple poem is printed beside handsome, oversized, page-and-a-half illustrations personifying the animals and natural elements. The last page shows a black-haired Native-American baby asleep, with snowshoes beside him. Although no specific group is mentioned and the language is generic, decorative motifs seem to come mostly from the Indians of the Northwestern Coast and Alaska.

547 Dodge, Robert K., and Joseph B. McCullough, eds., *New and Old Voices of Wah'Kon-Tah: Contemporary Native American Poetry*, International, 1985 (hardcover), ISBN 0-7178-0630-8, $9.50, 139 pp.; 1985 (paper), ISBN 0-7178-0629-4, $4.95, 139 pp. Ages 14 up, grades 9 up.

Anthology of more than one hundred poems by forty-six Native-American Indian poets from various groups, arranged in alphabetical order by poets, a reissue with additions of the same editors' *Voices from Wah'Kon-Tah* (1974), which was "the first anthology of Native American poetry that attempts to be comprehensive." Most poems speak of Native conditions, concerns, or interests, rely heavily on Native allusions or images, but use modern modes of poetic expression. Some vary traditional forms. A few selections are well known, like N. Scott Momaday's "Buteo Regalis" and James Welch's "The Man from Washington," but newer voices and selections are evident, for example, Wendy Rose, Joy Harjo, Louise Erdrich, Duane Niatum, and Harold Littlebird. Although the poems do not all succeed in the technical sense, they speak in a variety of voices, forms, and tones; retain their intellectual and emotional interest; and have the added advantage of appealing to high school–aged readers of poetry. A foreword by Vine Deloria, Jr., an introduction about Indian poetry, and biographical sketches of the poets are included.

548 Erdrich, Louise, *Baptism of Desire: Poems*, Harper, 1989 (hardcover), ISBN 0-06-016213-9, $16.95, 78 pp.; HarperCollins, 1991 (paper), ISBN 0-06-092044-0, $9.95, 96 pp. Ages 15 up, grades 10 up.

Twenty-nine poems of varying length, but mostly one or two pages. Some of these poems reveal the writer's Native-American Ojibwa (Chippewa) background while others are not culture specific; seven humorous, short, related prose pieces concern a trickster figure called Potchikoo. Poems deal with such matters as religious faith, giving birth, love, and everyday life. Most are serious; all have an underlying seriousness. The diction is tightly controlled, and the surrealism that drives most of them and gives them impact will appeal to more mature readers or those particularly interested in contemporary poetry, but some others and the Potchikoo stories will have a wider audience. Widely anthologized, Erdrich earlier published the much-praised *Jacklight: Poems*

(1984), in which the forty poems are similarly constructed but less religiously oriented, less intellectualized and surrealistic in the use of imagery, more varied in subject matter, and more accessible to high school–aged readers. In this collection especially, Erdrich reveals a remarkable capacity for capturing ordinary life and people. Potchikoo is introduced in this book.

549 Evers, Larry, and Felipe Molina, *Yaqui Deer Songs*, University of Arizona Press, 1986 (paper), 0-8165-0991-3, $15.95, 239 pp. Ages 14 up, grades 9 up.

Anthropological study of the ceremonial songs of the people of the Yaqui communities in Arizona and northern Mexico, including the words of many of the songs in the native language and in English translation. The work is a combined effort of Evers, a native English speaker, and Molina, whose first language is Yaqui, and it includes commentaries about and transcriptions of songs from a number of deer singers, most notably Don Jesus Yoilo'i, a master of the art form who died in 1982. A scholarly work, the book records what is known about the origin and cultural meanings of the songs and speculates about what is not known, holding that, contrary to some studies, the songs were never closely associated with hunting and that, although often included in church festivals, they long predate the coming of Christianity. The songs, which depend heavily on repetition, typically consist of three to five stanzas of which all but the last are nearly identical, with the final one adding to or varying the idea, often resolving or bringing to a culmination the action expressed. Within the stanzas, also, lines are repeated, sometimes with a word or two changed. Only students with a strong interest in the culture will wade through all the commentary, which is heavily footnoted and documented with bibliography, glossary, and maps, and without the accompanying dance and ethnic background, the poems must be considered incomplete, but taken by themselves they give some idea of the poetic elements in the still current rituals.

550 Francisco, Nia, *Blue Horses for Navajo Women*, illus. Wallace Begay, Greenfield Review, 1988 (paper), ISBN 0-192678-72-0, $9.95, 78 pp. Ages 12 up, grades 7 up.

Forty short, free verse poems by a Navajo poet that are greatly influenced by the culture and by the poet's experience and viewpoint as a woman Navajo of intelligence, pride, and perception. Pride in self and race are notes struck at the very beginning with "Brown Children," while the history of remembered terror and death informs the woman storyteller in the poem about the 1864 Long Walk. The poems speak seriously of such serious matters as poverty, hunger, and drunkenness on the reservation, the rape of the earth by strip-mining, and the debilitating inroads of popular American culture. She draws a sharp parallel, for example, between the Navajo girls' vain face-painting of today and the ritual face-painting of the old days. Many poems have a chantlike quality, and most project a strong sense of the landscape, speaking of such actual places as Kayenta and Canyon de Chelly, of the mountains, rocks, horizon, blue butterflies, horses, hogans, eagles, and many times of sheep and goats. Grandparents play a large role, and the woman's view is predominant. She describes a Navajo (Naabeeho) woman eating mutton stew and fire bread at breakfast, and for the poet, "A Navajo woman's moment is eternity." The collection is tastefully decorated by several expressive black-and-white line drawings and is easily within the range of teens and of advanced middle-graders.

551 Glancy, Diane, *Claiming Breath*, University of Nebraska Press, 1992 (hardcover), ISBN 0-8032-2140-1, $15.95, 115 pp. Ages 15 up, grades 10 up.

Sixty-three prose-poems, some very close to essay, others more conventionally metered, some only a few lines, others several pages long, of personal experience and observation, by a Cherokee-Irish-American poet. Glancy ranges widely as she speaks of the satisfaction of writing, her thoughts as she drives across Kansas and Oklahoma as part of the writer-in-schools program, her dying mother, her broken marriage, what being Anglo-Indian means to her, assimilation, culture retention—of matters that are part of universal human experience and of some more specifically Indian. Her voice is mostly ruminative and serious, occasionally light and sometimes playful. Some poems are sharply feminist "shedonism"; she looks at the Anglo invasion philosophically, insisting that every ethnic group endures fracturing experiences; and she can be epigrammatic, as when she maintains that art can "hold disaster in artistic control." Some poems overextend themselves, but the book offers much simply good reading. The same can be said of *Offering: Poetry & Prose* (1988), which contains forty poems, among them a handful of prose-poems, and which is also eclectic substantively. There are some fine poems about animals and wry ones about white versus Indian use of language. *Lone Dog's Winter Count* (1991) is a mixture of forty-four poems and prose-poems in a variety of tones and approaches that are on the whole more demanding and self-conscious in technique but otherwise much like those in *Claiming Breath* and *Offering*.

552 Glancy, Diane, *Iron Woman: Poems*, New Rivers, 1990 (paper), ISBN 0-89823-128-0, $7.00, 63 pp. Ages 13 up, grades 8 up.

Sixty-two free but rhythmical, short poems with a strong narrative quality by a Cherokee-Irish-American poet, among them a handful of prose poems.

Historical events inform many, including the Cherokee removal in "Red Moonwalking Woman," presented as the remembrance of the poet's grandmother of *her* grandmother; grim encounters between Indians and white soldiers; the medicine man Wovoka and the buffalo slayer, Buffalo Bill; the land run; and homesteading. The Oklahoma that she sees touches her, the oil fields, and the West Texas of her travels, and she imagines ghost herds of buffalo on the plains. She speaks in a particularly musical piece of a young woman dressed in her finest and dancing at a powwow, and in an eloquently poignant one of an old woman in a home for the aged, sitting "flightless" in her chair, "her knees like two eggs" under the quilted covering. Glancy's double heritage, which causes her to feel herself somewhere between two conflicting cultures and sometimes renders her inarticulate, finds expression in the title poem, where she acknowledges, "It takes a while to speak with these two voices." Deliberately baroque images rivet the attention, although they sometimes compel more shock reaction than sense: "a squaw with a fetus" lashed to her body like a vegetable, and "His heart a kiva," where seeds can be kept warm. This is an always interesting collection, with much to appeal to mature, late middle-schoolers and teen readers. An earlier collection of sixty-eight poems similar in content and structure is *One Age in a Dream* (1986). *Brown Wolf Leaves the Res & Other Poems* (1984) is a very short set of only ten poems that late preteens and teens should like and relate to easily.

553 Harjo, Joy, *Secrets from the Center of the World*, with photographs by Stephen Strom, University of Arizona Press, 1989 (paper), ISBN 0-8165-1113-6, $11.75, 67 pp. Ages 11 up, grades 6 up.

Thirty brief prose-poems by a leading Native-American poet of Creek ancestry celebrating and honoring the land of the Navajo reservation, accompanied by an equal number of colored photographs of the areas described taken at different times of the day. The poems are arranged paragraph style, one poem per page with the framed picture opposite, as, for example, the opening poem, which begins "My house is the red earth," and the illustration depicts the flat, broad, red expanse of landscape at Chinle Wash, with reddish sagebrush, rust mesa rising rear stage, a small flat-roofed, brick-red house, red-tinged corral, and shiny red car, all blending almost indistinguishably into one another. Carrying the conviction of lived observation, other poems talk about crows at Shiprock, which appear to be "at the edge of the world, laughing"; dinosaur footprints that seem to be "climbing toward the next century" near Moencopi Rise; horses that appear perplexed at the ways of humans who have produced "the smoking destruction" of the Four Corners power plant; the "tamaracks [that, humorously,] pretend to be tamaracks," they are so typical of their species; and "smoky bluffs [that] are old traveling companions," plodding through the ages. More like poetic essays than poetry, this is a small, quietly beautiful book. Also by Harjo is *In Mad Love and War* (1990), which contains some forty poems, mostly free, some of them prose, about a range of topics. Employing striking images and telling emotion, these will probably appeal most to sophisticated and mature teens able with poetry. Mature in content but shorter and less demanding in structure and diction are the fifty-seven poems in *What Moon Drove Me to This?* (1979), while those in *She Had Some Horses* (1983) lie somewhere in between. Among the forty-two poems in *She Had Some Horses* are the autobiographical title poem, probably Harjo's best-known piece, a cycle about horses, and her also well-known "I Give You Back," about conquering fear.

554   Hirschfelder, Arlene B., and Beverly R. Singer, sels., *Rising Voices: Writings of Young Native Americans*, Scribner's, 1992 (hardcover), ISBN 0-684-19207-1, $12.95, 115 pp.; Ivy, 1992 (paper), ISBN 0-8041-1167-7, 115 pp. Ages 12 up, grades 7 up.

Sixty-two poems and essays by school-aged Native Americans of different tribes, most written within the last twenty years and almost all unpublished previously except in small, local outlets. Included are a few letters by school-children in Indian boarding schools in the late nineteenth and early twentieth centuries. The selections are divided into six sections, the names for which indicate the nature of the writers' concerns: Identity, Family, Homelands, Ritual and Ceremony, Education, and Harsh Realities. These represent issues to which, say the collectors, the young people speak "with intelligence, dignity, wit, and remarkable insight." The essays are the best technically, being simple, direct, well-organized, short pieces. Although the poems lack skill with form and image, like the essays they seem sincere and honest and bear testimony on a literal level to the sentiments of youth who in large part feel different, unwanted, and looked down upon in a world dominated by an alien culture. Information about the authors, a helpful introduction to each section, and an author and title index are included.

555   Hogan, Linda, *Savings: Poems*, Coffee House, 1988 (paper), ISBN 0-918273-41-2, 74 pp. Ages 12 up, grades 6 up.

Forty-five, mostly one-page, freely formed, delicately rhythmical poems by a Chickasaw poet. Occasionally directed at such Native-American matters as "crooked chiefs" who "make federal deals," most poems tackle universal human or humanitarian concerns, some peculiar to women. Hogan reflects, ruminates, observes, considers, moving from the specific and concrete smoothly to the general as she makes her points, infrequently employing humor. Potholes in the streets, going fishing, small animals and birds, growing up, earth, air, wind, fire, everyday work, riding the bus, hands, knives, geraniums, urban shootings—these are some of the subjects that arouse the muse of this accomplished poet, who at her best speaks incisively and elegantly. Although layered in meaning, most poems have surface meanings that are easily grasped. Among other books of poems, Hogan has published *Seeing through the Sun* (1985) and *Book of Medicines* (1993), both of which contain some particularly telling moments, for example, from the latter, "The Grandmother Songs" in which she says, "The grandmothers were my tribal gods," embracing her with their blood relationship. Her other books include *Red Clay: Poems and Stories* (no. 436) and a novel, *Mean Spirit* (no. 435).

556 Louis, Adrian C., *Among the Dog Eaters*, West End, 1992 (paper), ISBN 0-931122-69-4, $9.95, 90 pp. Ages 14 up, grades 9 up.

Fifty-five poems by an enrolled Native-American Nevada Paiute who teaches on the Lakota (Sioux) Pine Ridge Reservation and whose poems are influenced by both areas, though mostly by the latter region. Louis speaks in pensive, ruminative, self-pitying, rallying, often angry tones mostly about the conditions he sees and his experiences in South Dakota, welfare, alcoholism, degradation, unemployment, and rejection, but also about such historical atrocities as the torture of Mangas Colorado and the massacre at Wounded Knee, as well as about such contemporary events as the bombing of Iraq in the Gulf War. He speaks about the hypocrisy of Christians, historical and present day, of do-gooder whites and Indians in protest marches across the "Pampers-strewn reservation," his anger erupting toward whites but also toward his own people as he tells them to "Wake up, you damn *people*, wake up!" and concentrate on making a better future for themselves. He speaks of his troubles with liquor and of driving across the area in his T-bird. Most poems are loose and free, tending to be prosy, much of the imagery is sexual or drawn from nature, and twists of ideas and of words provide surprises, some of them somewhat too clever, like "imperfect prefecture" at the conjunction of landscape and sky. The short poems are the keenest technically, except for a few very brief ones that do not come to enough, but the longer ones, though they tend to lose the reader, are more revealing of what the reservation looks like physically and must be like emotionally for those who live there—dreary, foreboding, trashy, and bleak, as seen from the vantage of a forty-year-old, educated Indian. Explanatory notes, a foreword, an afterword, and information about the author are included. An earlier collection, *Fire Water World* (1989), has many of the same characteristics. Of sixty-eight mostly short poems, only one is in rhymed regular meter. Most are set in South Dakota, though others reflect life in various cities and in the Southwest.

The predominant subject is, as the title implies, alcoholism and the love-hate relationship with liquor that has given the Indian both "courage and death."

557 Minty, Judith, *Dancing the Fault,* University of Central Florida Press, 1991 (hardcover), ISBN 0-8130-1079-9, $16.95, 76 pp.; (paper), ISBN 0-8130-1080-2, $9.95, 76 pp. Ages 13 up, grades 8 up.

Forty-eight poems, a few of them prose-poems, on various subjects by a part Mohawk poet. Many celebrate family, particularly female relatives, nature, and such outdoor activities as fishing and skiing. Lengths vary, but most are short, and they are only occasionally influenced by her Nordic-American Indian heritage. Seventeen are mellow, warm, sonnet-like pieces addressed to her daughters, which first appeared in her short collection, *Letters to My Daughters* (1980). Others talk about growing up in Detroit in the 1940s, or describe other places in Michigan, for example, the beach of Lake Michigan. Sets also take place in California and feature birds. Most poems are metered, but rhythms are gentle and flowing, tones vary but avoid pretension, rhyming occurs occasionally, mostly internal—in general, the poems are relaxed, and the imagery is natural and sensitive with the result that this is a pleasing, memorable collection marked by the woman's point of view. Minty's other collections include *Lake Songs and Other Fears* (1974) and *In the Presence of Mothers* (1981), in a similar vein. *Counting the Losses* (1986), an eighteen-page poem with prose-poem and feminist-statement portions, is best in its nature and growing-up parts.

558 Naranjo-Morse, Nora, *Mud Woman: Poems from the Clay,* University of Arizona Press, 1992 (hardcover), ISBN 0-8165-1248-5, $35.00, 127 pp.; (paper), ISBN 0-8165-1281-7, $15.95, 127 pp. Ages 12 up, grades 7 up.

Twenty-nine poems by a Pueblo ceramic artist, in four sections: Mud Woman, about making pots and clay figures; Wandering Pueblo Woman, about the problems of living in two cultures; Pearlene and Friends, about a modern Pueblo woman, the subject of some of the figures; and Home, autobiographical pieces about parents, sisters, and children. The unmetered, unrhymed poems are inclined to be prosy, with few images and no strong musical qualities, but the ideas expressed are often interesting. The strongest are about the artistic experience in working with clay, as in "There Is Nothing Like an Idea" and "Pit Firing a Milestone," and in two about her father, "My Father's Hands" and "My Father's Feet." Taken as a whole, they make a statement about modern Pueblo culture and the relation of the Native American to the earth.

The book is illustrated with fine photographs of samples of the artist's work in clay, a wide variety of pots and figures.

559 Niatum, Duane, *Drawings of the Song Animals: New and Selected Poems*, Holy Cow, 1991 (hardcover), ISBN 0-930100-43-3, $18.95, 148 pp.; (paper), ISBN 0-930100-44-1, $10.95, 148 pp. Ages 13 up, grades 8 up.

Omnibus collection of eighteen new poems and fifteen poems from each of four previously published books of this Klallam poet: *After the Death of an Elder Klallam* (1970), about his Indian heritage; *Ascending the Red Cedar Moon* (1974), about special women in his life and the elder poets who were his mentors; *Digging Out the Roots* (1977), about friends; and *Songs for the Harvester of Dreams* (1981), dedicated to his son and "the Children of the First Americans." In these tightly crafted, controlled, precisely dictioned, unpretentious, richly suggestive, metered but seldom end-rhymed poems, the poet speaks sometimes as an observer, occasionally in other personas, usually as the poet himself, about his childhood, family, and other personal matters, love, places he has visited or lived, and various people, including Marc Chagall, Louise Bogan, and Theodore Roethke (one of his poetry teachers). Moving from the historical standpoint are his elegy for Chief Sealth (Seattle) and his tribute to Chief Joseph, whom he graphically calls "a featherless hawk in exile." Nature plays a strong role: the coastal terrain, the birds, and animals of the Northwest. The next to last poem, "Round Dance," has a delightfully musical swing and evokes the sense of a social gathering; and the opening poem, "Portrait," is an expressive character sketch of a young Klallam man, his appearance and personality, "a Klallam with reservations." These are Niatum at his best, eloquent yet restrained, delicate with words, playful yet pointed. A glossary of Klallam terms and biographical information are included. Niatum's *Stories of the Moons* (1987) contains a dozen short, expressive poems about the moon that appeared earlier in *Ascending the Red Cedar Moon* but have been revised.

560 Niatum, Duane, ed., *Harper's Anthology of 20th Century Native American Poetry*, Harper, 1988 (hardcover), ISBN 0-06-250665-A, $24.95, 396 pp.; (paper), ISBN 0-06-250666-8, $15.95, 396 pp. Ages 15 up, grades 10 up.

Anthology of 240 poems by thirty-six Native American poets from various groups, sequel to the Klallam editor's earlier anthology of sixteen poets, *Car-*

riers of the Dream Wheel (1975). The jacket accurately describes this book as including the "Most Respected Poets of Native American Ancestry [*sic*]" of the century. Represented are N. Scott Momaday, Louise Erdrich, Paula Gunn Allen, Joy Harjo, Steve Crow, Ray Young Bear, Mary TallMountain, and A. Sadongei, among others, arranged roughly chronologically by poet. Although a wide variety of Native-American experience informs the writing, some poems are on general subjects, and most are free, though some are more strictly metered. Brian Swann's introduction discusses the nature of Native-American poetry, and biographies of the poets appear, along with indexes of titles and first lines. This is a wide-ranging collection, of varying technical quality and appeal to high school readers.

561 Ortiz, Simon, *Woven Stone*, University of Arizona Press, 1992 (hardcover), ISBN 0-8165-1294-9, 1992, 365 pp.; (paper), ISBN 0-8165-1330-9, 365 pp. Ages 15 up, grades 10 up.

Collection that brings together in one volume three previously published books of poems by an Acoma Pueblo who is considered a leading Native-American poet: *Going for the Rain* (1976), *A Good Journey* (1977), and *Fight Back* (1980), for a total of almost 200 poems and one prose-poem selection. New is a lengthy introduction by Ortiz about the significance of language, growing up as an Acoma in the 1940s and 1950s, and his development as a writer. In the first two books of poems, he attests he was "very aware of trying to instill that sense of continuity essential to . . . Native American life [and literary heritage] . . . and making it as strongly apparent as possible," while *Fight Back* "was set within the context of the uranium industry in the early 1960s . . . although not written until twenty years later . . . [and was] to be a political statement . . . [about] the Acoma-Grants-Laguna region." Some poems are about general relationships and home life, like "Pout," about his young daughter sitting "straddle-legged," frustrated because catalog pages stick together; however, almost all are informed by Native experience, philosophy, nature, the desert, or old stories and figures like Coyote. Some poems use Native poetic devices like repetition and listing, most are short and free, some are deliberate prose-poems, many are simply prosy, most are statements or reflections easy to apprehend in the literal or surface sense but are not without deeper nuances of meaning. Most are quite visual but without the extensive surrealism that pervades much modern poetry, and hence they are within the reach of teen readers. Tones vary from pensive to poignant to polemical. There is a lot of interesting reading here. Earlier, Ortiz published a fine anthology of short stories, *Earth Power Coming* (1983), with representative selections from leading Native-American authors.

562 Rose, Wendy, *The Halfbreed Chronicles and Other Poems*, illus. Wendy Rose, West End, 1985 (paper), ISBN 0-931122-39-2, $4.95, 71 pp. Ages 14 up, grades 9 up.

Thirty-one poems, mostly concerned with the Native-American experience, divided into four sections: Sipapu (the Hopi Place of Emergence), Haliksa'ii! (listen!), If I Am Too Brown or Too White for You (male-female relationships), and The Halfbreed Chronicles. In the last section, all the poems are prefaced by quotations or news items about such diverse subjects as the last of the Tasmanians, Koko the gorilla, Robert Oppenheimer, and a woman born retarded after her mother was exposed to radiation at Hiroshima. These are the most easily approachable poems in the collection, possibly because of clues in the prefaces. In the other sections, occasional poems work well: "Loo-Wit," which personifies Mount St. Helens as an old woman; "Naayawva Taawi," comparing the survival powers of the Hopi to the sparrows that nest in discarded bales of fence wire; "The Building of the Trophy," tracing the tempestuous life story of a woman from infancy to age thirty-four. Others are made difficult by obscure lines or extravagant images that may have emotive power but fail to convey literal meaning. All the poems are in free verse. Line drawings by the author precede each section.

563 Smith, Patricia Clark, *Changing Your Story*, West End, 1992 (paper), ISBN 0-931122-61-9, $6.95, 61 pp. Ages 15 up, grades 10 up.

Twenty-eight free verse poems, mostly a page-and-a-half long, by a Native-American mixed-blood Indian poet from New England who lives in New Mexico. Only a few of the poems are tied to being Native American, for example, the piece about her Sioux uncle, "My Uncle's Name Is Jim Crow," and another addressed to Paula Gunn Allen, "Survival Letter to Paula," which is also a feminist poem. Some poems reveal the New Mexican setting, like that about funland in Albuquerque at sundown, the one about visiting Jemez Pueblo, and another about driving through the desert. Others, like "The Cranberry Poem," trace back to her New England origins. Some are addressed to her sons about them as small boys, and some come from her professional experience, as when she talks about her Navajo students or about teaching poetry. The collection is varied in subject matter, and although most poems are overlong, Smith's voice is often compelling and usually interesting. Earlier she published *Talking to the Land* (1979).

564 Sneve, Virginia Driving Hawk, sel., *Dancing Teepees: Poems of American Indian Youth*, illus. Stephen Gammell, Holiday, 1989 (hardcover), ISBN 0–8234–0724–1, $14.95, unp.; 1991 (paper), ISBN 0-8234-0879-5, $5.95, unp. Ages 4–11, grades PS–6.

Anthology of twenty short poems and prose pieces by Native-American Indians. The selector, who grew up on the Rosebud Sioux Reservation in South Dakota, chose these pieces from several tribal sources to demonstrate the importance of the power of the word among Native Americans. Most selections come from the oral tradition or are anonymous, for example, the Hopi lullaby, the Zuni corn song, and the Dakota elk song, but others have known authors, including Black Elk, Plenty-Coups, and Sneve herself. Some are actually prose pieces, and all tend to be prosy in tone albeit expressive, but the sentiments presented have force, and the quietly colorful pictures, which draw motifs and scenes from various tribes, undergird the selections and make this slender book attractive.

565 TallMountain, Mary, *The Light on the Tent Wall: A Bridging*, illus. Claire Fejes, University of California Press, 1990 (paper), ISBN 0-935626-34-4, $12.00, 95 pp. Ages 12 up, grades 7 up.

Fifty-five poems, nineteen previously collected in *There Is No Word for Goodbye* (1981), and eight short essays and stories, by an Athapascan–Irish-American poet. TallMountain's writing is mainly informed by her life's experience—vividly visual, emotionally charged, and carefully controlled. She speaks of her Alaskan childhood, her uprooting to the continental United States as the adopted child of a white doctor, her return in midlife, and her lifelong struggle to cope with the trauma of the departure and of her efforts to reconcile the two cultures, of dances, mukluks, drums, traders, owls, dogs, drunken Indians, and in particular her maternal ancestors. An articulate, sometimes witty, often troubled voice, at her best she combines rhythm, images, and sense unpretentiously and very effectively, as in "*Ggaal* Comes Upriver," about a spawning she-salmon captured in migration who fights tenaciously for freedom. Most poems are short, and, since the language is not difficult, many are within the capacity of middle-schoolers. The book itself, with its fluid, black-and-white line drawings and cover painting entitled "Three Generations," by an Alaskan artist, is distinctively designed and very attractive. A glossary and an introduction by Paula Gunn Allen are included. For Tall-Mountain's stories in this book, see no. 463.

566 Tapahonso, Luci, *Saanii Dahataal: The Women Are Singing*, University of Arizona Press, 1993 (hardcover), ISBN 0-8165-1351-1, $19.95, 94 pp.; (paper), ISBN 0-8165-1361-9, $9.95, 94 pp. Ages 11 up, grades 6 up.

Poems and stories by a Navajo woman originally from Shiprock, New Mexico, many of them celebrating the beauty of the arid region and the closeness of the traditional Native-American family. Among the recurring images are horses, pickup trucks, cowboys, wind, stars, and old people who pass on songs and stories to the youngsters. All the poems are in free verse, rhythmical but unmetered and unrhymed; some of them were previously published in Tapahonso's earlier collections, *A Breeze Swept Through* (1987), *Seasonal Woman* (1982), and *One More Shiprock Night* (1981). The stories have an artless simplicity, almost as if they are orally transmitted, and deal with such subjects as dogs that have been lost or stolen, the death of an uncle, and life in the dormitory at the children's boarding school. Together with the poems, they give a warm and loving picture of Navajo life. For Tapahonso's stories, see no. 464.

567 Tremblay, Gail, *Indian Singing in 20th Century America*, Calyx, 1990 (hardcover), ISBN 0-934971-14-5; $16.95; 1992 (paper), ISBN 0-934971-13-7, $8.95, 71 pp. Ages 15 up, grades 10 up.

Forty-seven, mostly one-page poems, mainly in pentameters but some free, that contemplate both the Native-American Indian experience and situations that occur generally, by an Onondaga (Iroquois)–Mic Mac and French-Canadian poet. They speak of the beauty of the earth and the sun, traveling abroad and in the United States by plane and bus, deplore relocation and the urban Indian life, explore gender conflicts, and celebrate basket-grass gathering and the drum. References occur to Coyote and Raven and to Iroquois ceremonies, as well as to Indian artifacts in museums. The poems are strongly alliterative, often internally rhymed and chimed, and highly imagistic, much of which comes from nature. The atmosphere often seems static, particularly if the poems are read in sequence, but many poems are melodious, and a few are quite succinctly memorable. All show control of technique and substance. Her earlier publications include *Night Gives Women the Wind* (1979), also poems.

568 Walters, Anna Lee, ed., *Neon Pow-Wow: New Native American Voices of the Southwest*, Coffee House, 1993 (paper), ISBN 0-87358-562-3, $12.95, 131 pp. Ages 13 up, grades 8 up.

Anthology of thirty-five selections from twenty-three authors of different tribal groups, all originating in or residing in the American Southwest. These are "fairly new writers. . . . For about half, this is the first time they have been published. . . . These selections were . . . carefully chosen to show a fuller range of contemporary Native American literature." About half of the inclusions are poems, which range from the rhythmical, concrete "Ten Rounds" by Lorenzo Baca through the humorous "Blues-ing on the Brown Vibe" by Esther G. Belin, about Coyote the trickster, to "Bueno-Bye" by A. A. Hodge Coke, a short description of Santa Fe, where at dusk the "Mountain View transforms to street scene," and in spite of cars, concrete, and noisy children, hints of the adobe era linger. Some prose-poems, some metered, they vary in technical quality and in tone from light to pensive to intensely longing. The remainder of the pieces are stories, essays, and plays. Biographical information is included. For the stories in this book, see no. 473.

569 Woody, Elizabeth, *Hand into Stone*, illus. Juane Quick-To-See Smith, Contact II, 1988 (paper), ISBN 0-936556-18-8, $5.00, 47 pp. Ages 15 up, grades 10 up.

Twenty-five free verse poems of varying lengths and degrees of difficulty that reflect the Wasco (Chinook)-Navajo poet's heritage and interests, in particular, the Pacific Northwest. The static poems appeal more to the eye than to the ear, being strongly visual in their imagery. A serious tone marks their comments about such happenings as the loss of the traditional Columbia River salmon grounds to dams and the effect on the Native fishermen. Other matters touched on are Vietnam, the feelings and lot of women, birds, the forest, Custer, love, and sex. The short poems are the best. Some lines are exquisitely phrased, for example, where a grandmother's long fingers are described as "with the mobility of spiders," and aptly put across such an emotion as wonder in marveling how "birds can fly with a few scales" that have adapted, or anger and outrage over night drownings, hangings, and suicides. These are better for sophisticated and accomplished, or determined, readers.

570 Young Bear, Ray, *The Invisible Musician*, Holy Cow, 1990 (hardcover), ISBN 0-930100-32-8, $15.00, 101 pp.; (paper), ISBN 0-930100-33-6, $8.95, 101 pp. Ages 15 up, grades 10 up.

Forty-two poems by a Mesquaki (Sauk and Fox) writer, some on a single page, others several pages long, free but subtly rhythmed. Mesquaki history and culture and the poet's life as an Indian inform the poems, for example, the Mesquaki creation story and beliefs about spirits and the interrelatedness of living beings; the importance of family and of nature, both in land and animals; Indian history in losing and reclaiming lands; and experiences that he has had traveling and giving public readings of his works. While the poems employ vivid images and show careful crafting, a distance between the poet's personas and the audience renders the poems more difficult than those in his earlier *Winter of the Salamander* (1980). Here the eighty-some poems, which are in the main shorter, also build on his experiences as a Mesquaki as well as happenings in the general society, and often speak of family, earth, and animals.

Index of Titles

Index of Writers

(Numerals refer to entry numbers)

Index of Illustrators

(Numerals refer to entry numbers)

Index of Titles
by Grade Level

(Numerals refer to entry numbers. Symbols refer to ethnic groups: Af = African Americans; As = Asian Americans; H = Hispanic Americans; N = Native-American Indians.)

Index of Subjects

(Numerals refer to entry numbers. Where the ethnic group is not indicated in the subject heading, the following symbols are used: Af = African American; As = Asian American; H = Hispanic American; and N = Native-American Indian.)

About the Authors

ALETHEA K. HELBIG is Professor of English Language and Literature at Eastern Michigan University. She has been teaching Native-American literature for 20 years. A former president of the Children's Literature Association, she has received the State of Michigan Award for Outstanding Teaching and Publication. She has published over 100 articles in professional journals such as *Children's Literature* and *The Children's Literature Association Quarterly* and reference books such as *American Women Writers, Writers for Children,* and *Masterplots.*

AGNES REGAN PERKINS is Professor Emeritus of English Language and Literature at Easern Michigan University. She has published numerous articles in journals and reference books including *A Tolkien Compass, Unicorn, Children's Literature, Children's Literature Association Quarterly, Writers for Children,* and *Masterplots.* She is co-compiler of the poetry anthologies *New Coast and Strange Harbors* (with Helen Hill) and *Straight on till Morning* and *Dusk to Dawn* (both with Hill and Alethea Helbig).